TWIN SPICA

4

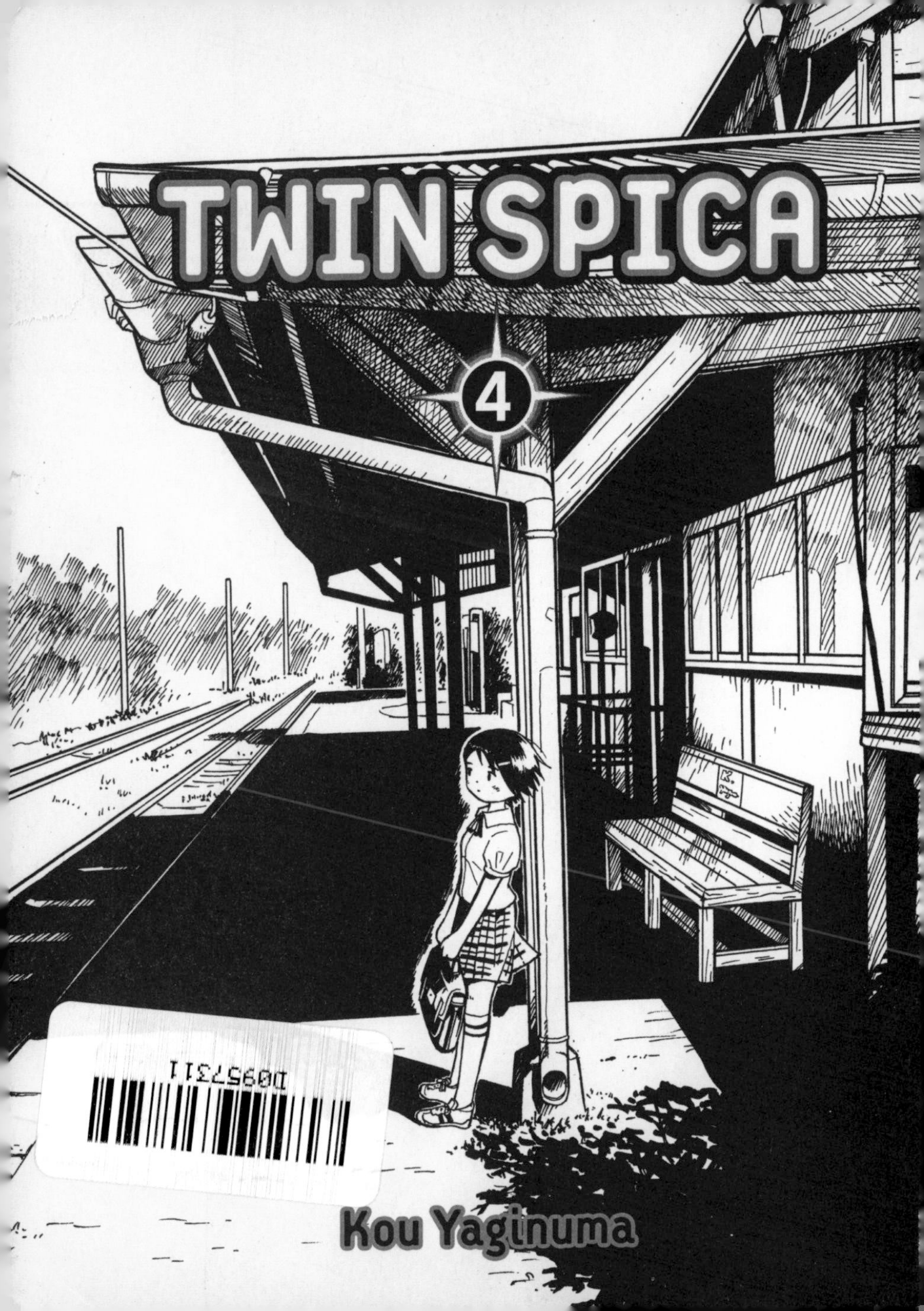

Kou Yaginuma

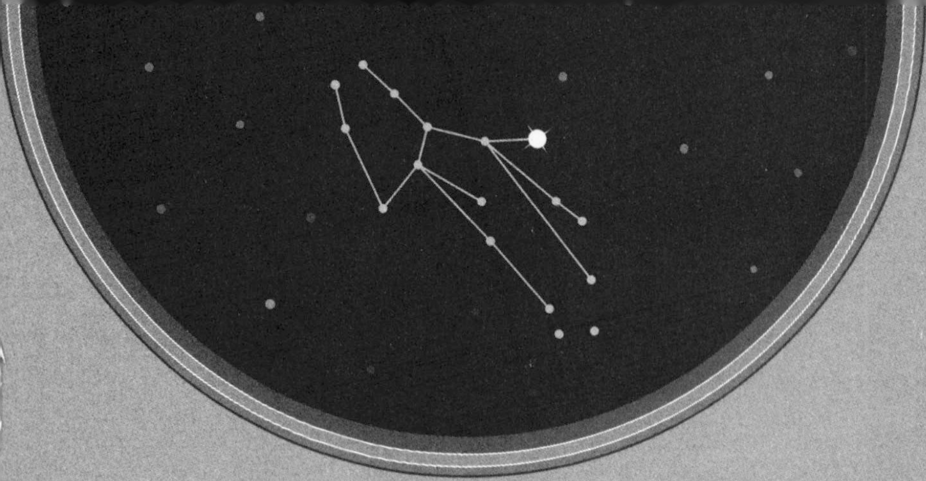

CONTENTS

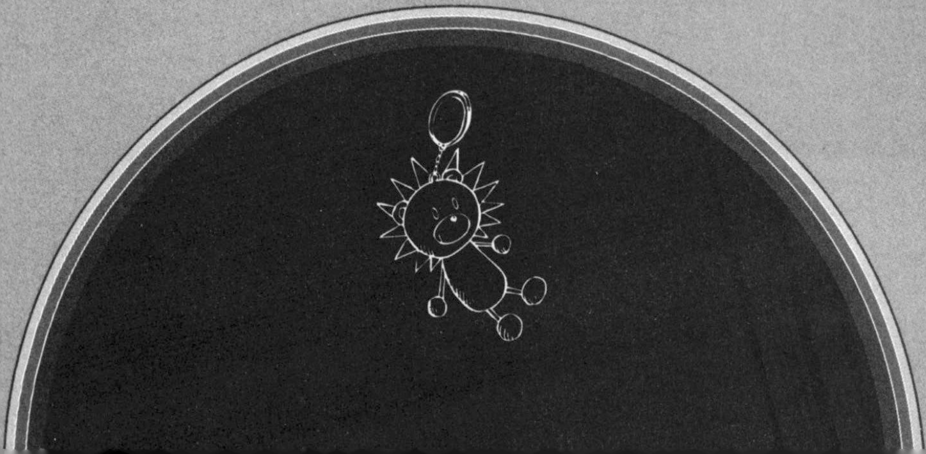

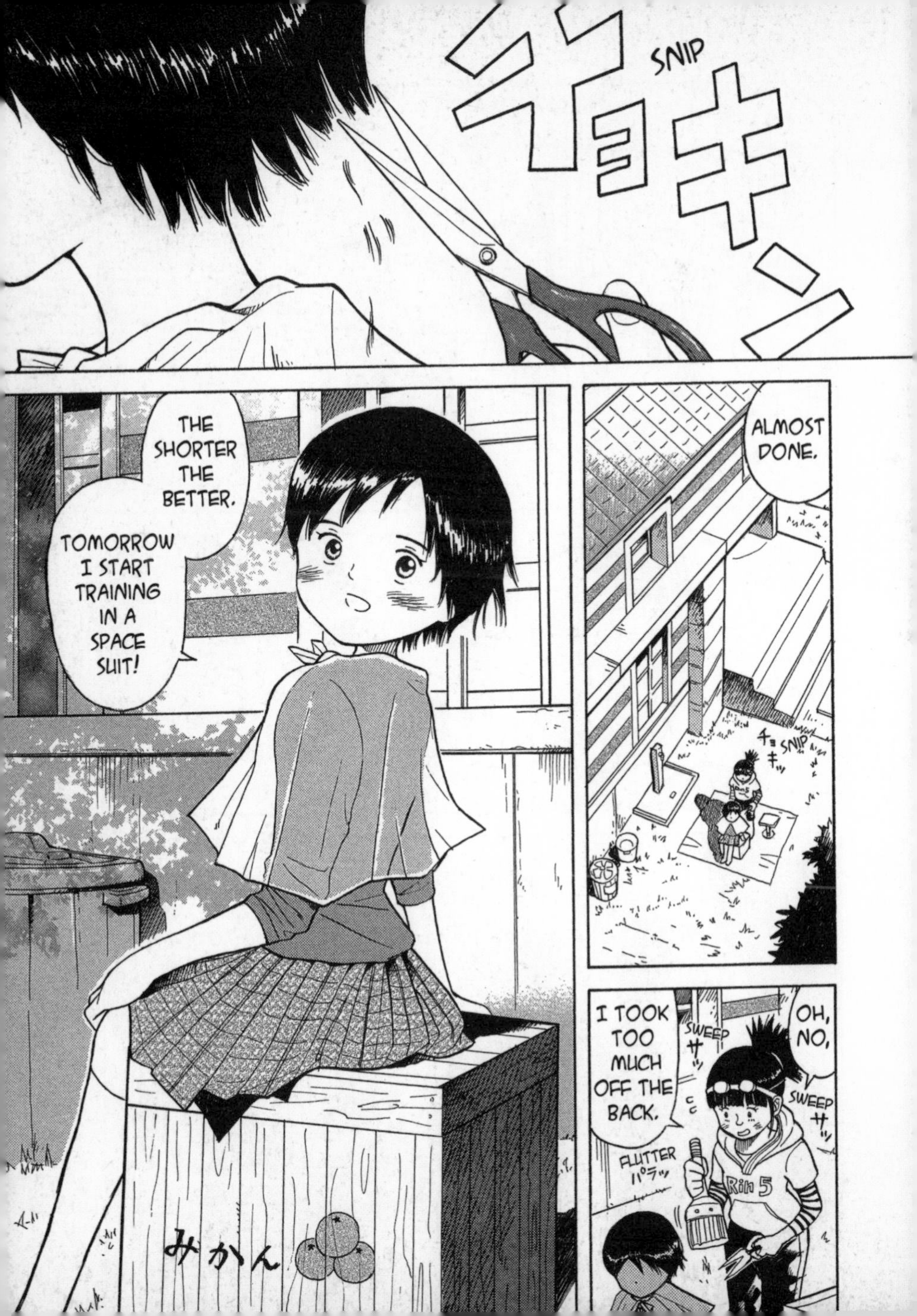
チョキン
SNIP
ALMOST DONE.
チョキッ
SNIP
OH, NO,
I TOOK TOO MUCH OFF THE BACK.
SWEEP
サッ
SWEEP
サッ
FLUTTER
パラッ
Rin 5
THE SHORTER THE BETTER.
TOMORROW I START TRAINING IN A SPACE SUIT!
みかん

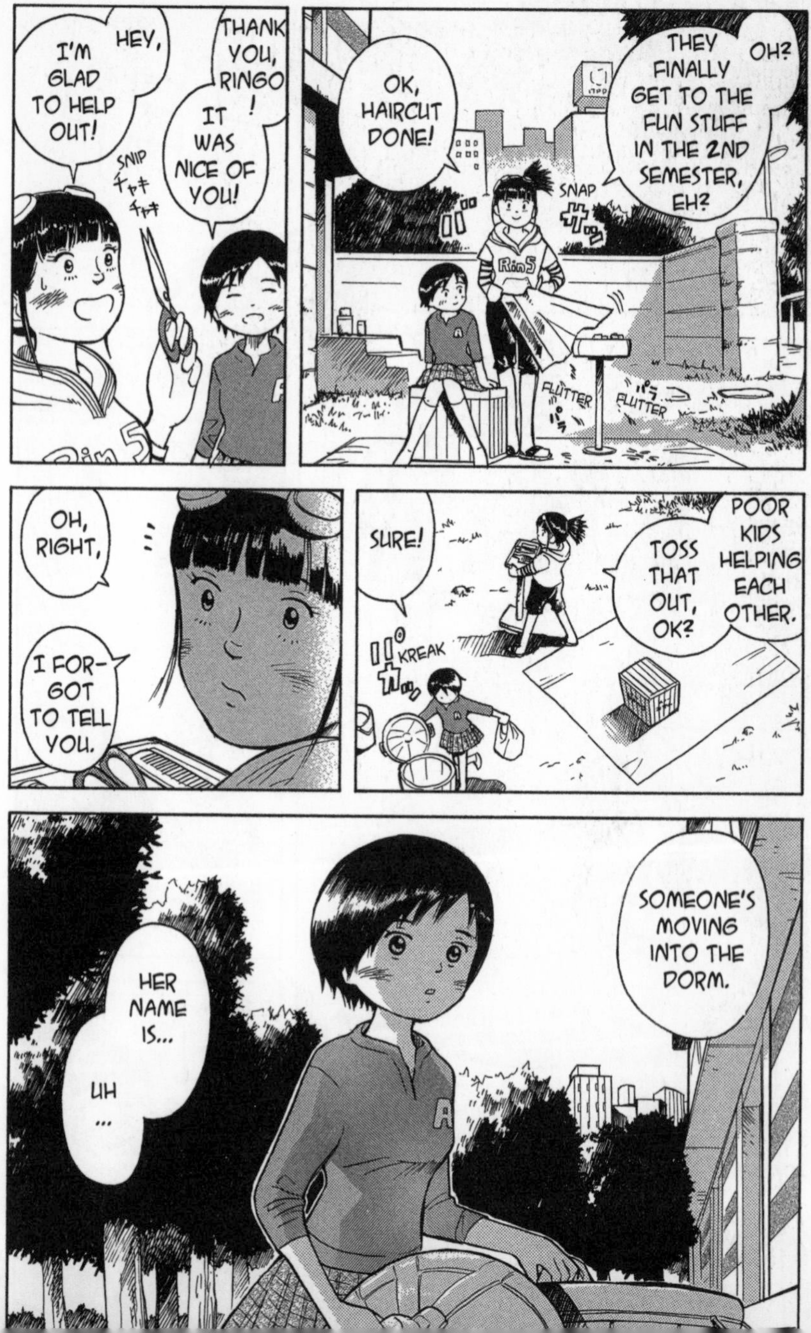
THEY FINALLY GET TO THE FUN STUFF IN THE 2ND SEMESTER, EH?
OH?
OK, HAIRCUT DONE!
SNAP
FLUTTER
FLUTTER
THANK YOU, RINGO!
IT WAS NICE OF YOU!
HEY,
I'M GLAD TO HELP OUT!
SNIP
POOR KIDS HELPING EACH OTHER.
TOSS THAT OUT, OK?
SURE!
KREAK
OH, RIGHT,
I FOR-GOT TO TELL YOU.
SOMEONE'S MOVING INTO THE DORM.
HER NAME IS...
UH ...

MISSION:14

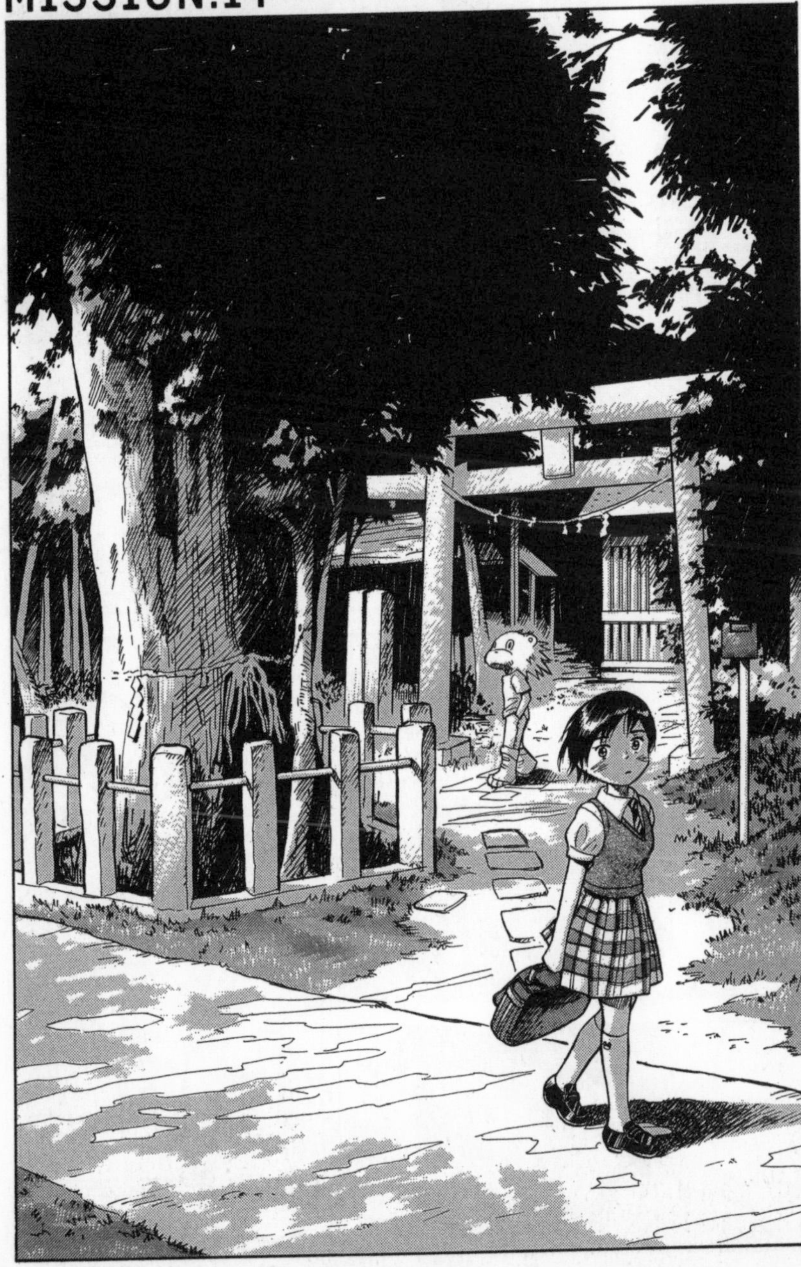

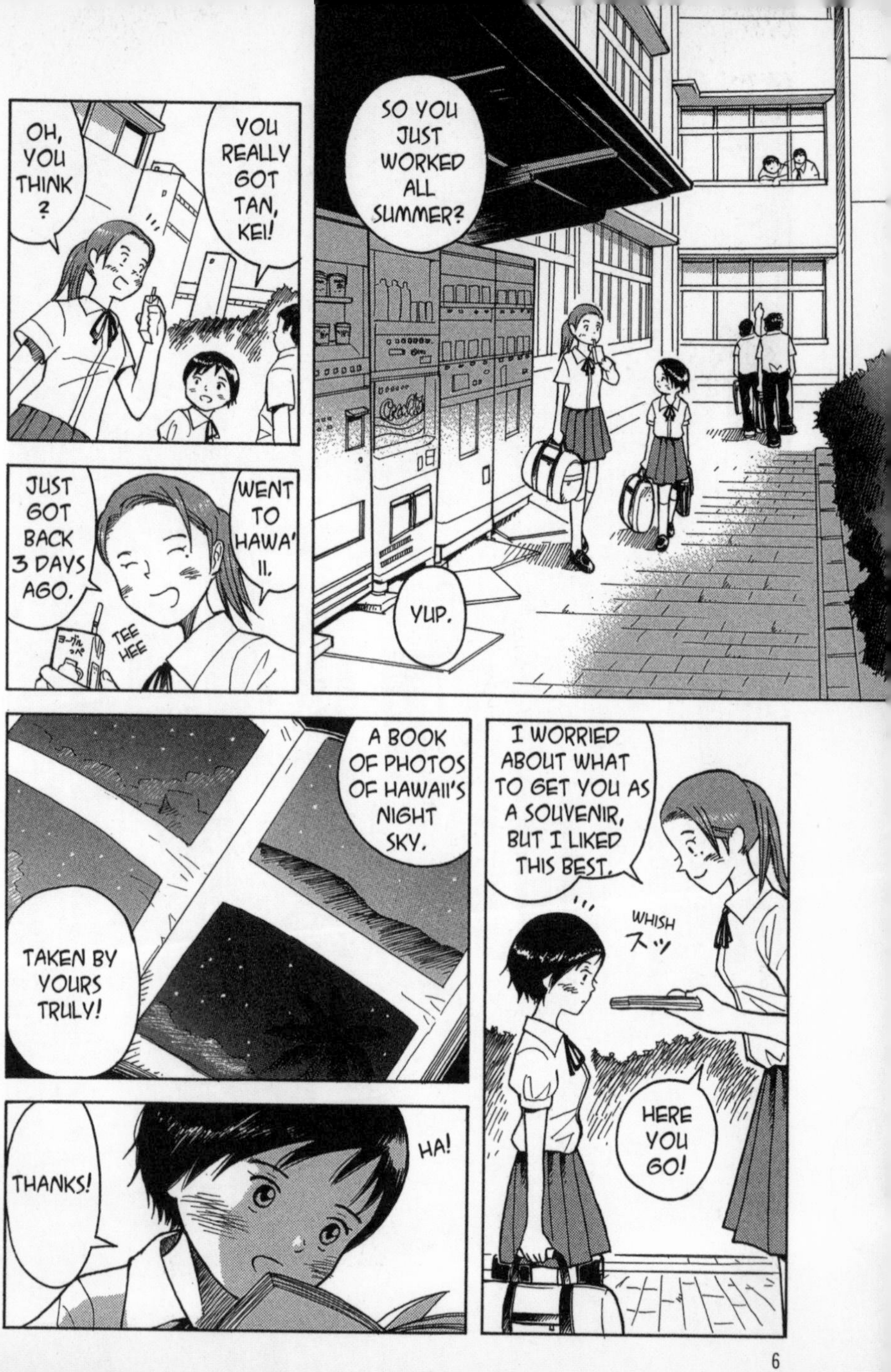
SO YOU JUST WORKED ALL SUMMER?
YUP.
YOU REALLY GOT TAN, KEI!
OH, YOU THINK?
WENT TO HAWA'II.
JUST GOT BACK 3 DAYS AGO.
TEE HEE
I WORRIED ABOUT WHAT TO GET YOU AS A SOUVENIR, BUT I LIKED THIS BEST.
WHISH
スッ
HERE YOU GO!
A BOOK OF PHOTOS OF HAWAII'S NIGHT SKY.
TAKEN BY YOURS TRULY!
HA!
THANKS!

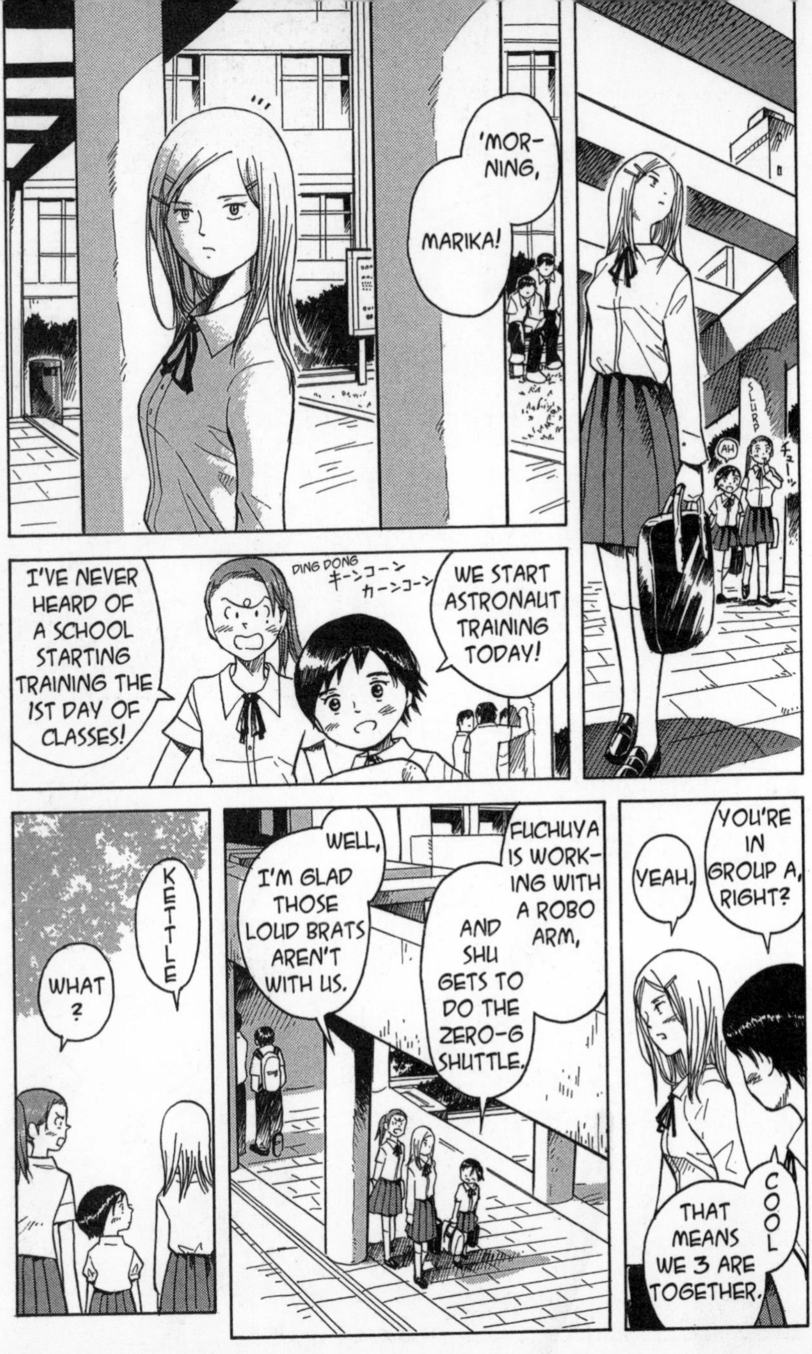
SLURP
AH
チューッ
'MORNING, MARIKA!
WE START ASTRONAUT TRAINING TODAY!
DING DONG キーンコーン カーンコーン
I'VE NEVER HEARD OF A SCHOOL STARTING TRAINING THE 1ST DAY OF CLASSES!
YOU'RE IN GROUP A, RIGHT?
YEAH.
COOL
THAT MEANS WE 3 ARE TOGETHER.
FUCHUYA IS WORKING WITH A ROBO ARM,
AND SHU GETS TO DO THE ZERO-G SHUTTLE.
WELL, I'M GLAD THOSE LOUD BRATS AREN'T WITH US.
KETTLE
WHAT?

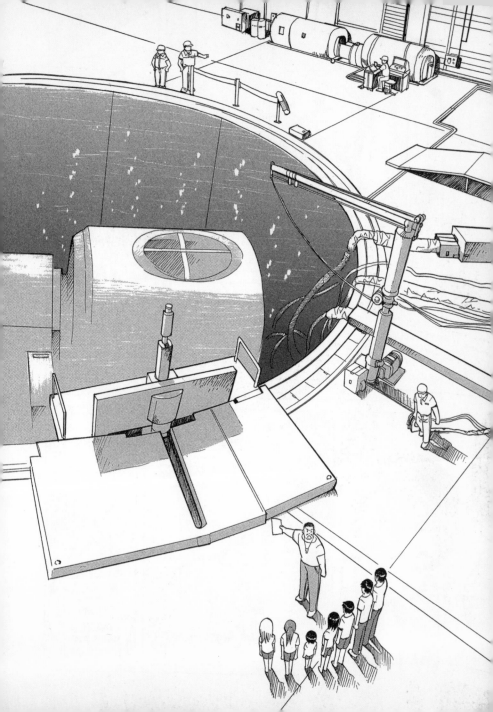

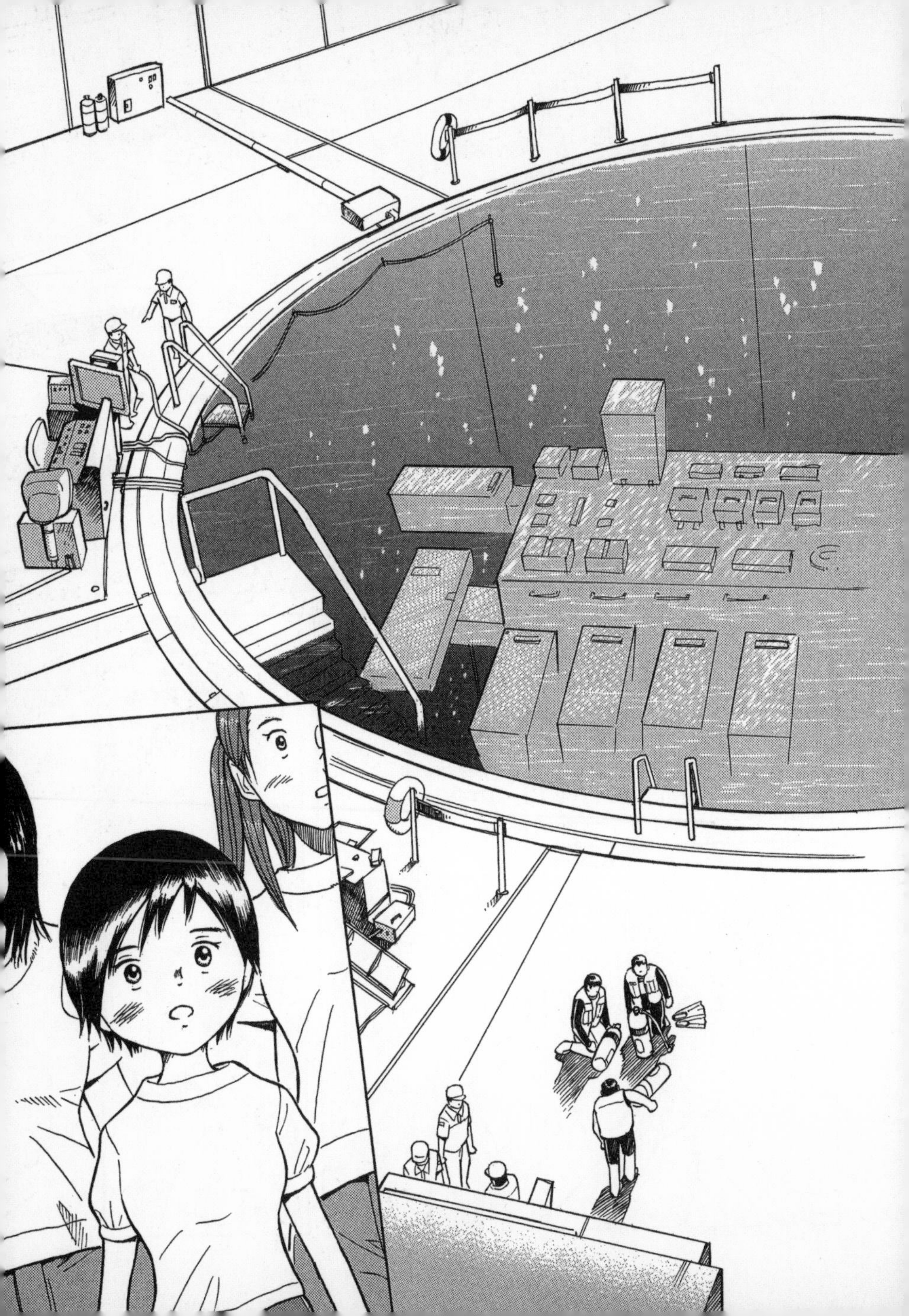

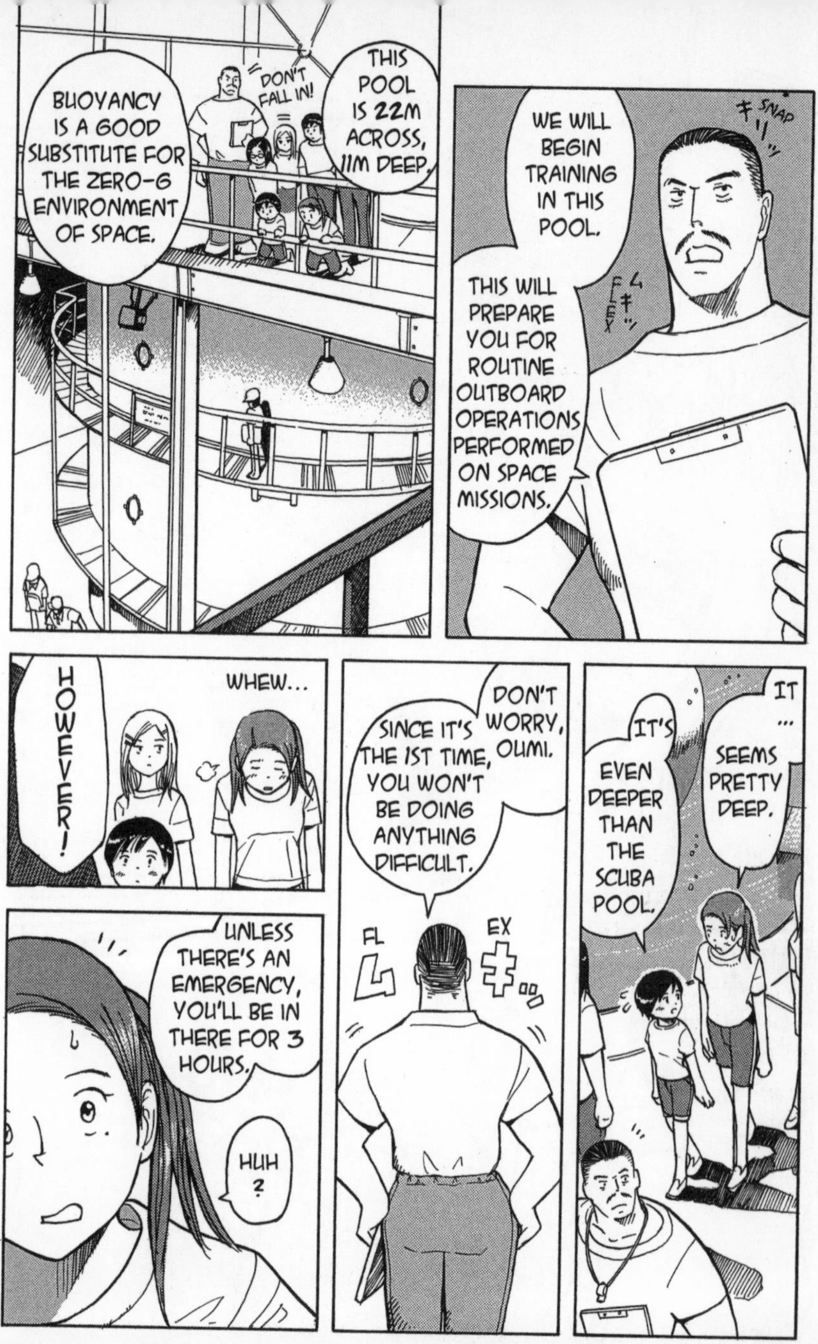
SNAP
WE WILL BEGIN TRAINING IN THIS POOL.
FLEX
THIS WILL PREPARE YOU FOR ROUTINE OUTBOARD OPERATIONS PERFORMED ON SPACE MISSIONS.
THIS POOL IS 22M ACROSS, 11M DEEP.
DON'T FALL IN!
BUOYANCY IS A GOOD SUBSTITUTE FOR THE ZERO-G ENVIRONMENT OF SPACE.
IT ... SEEMS PRETTY DEEP.
IT'S EVEN DEEPER THAN THE SCUBA POOL.
DON'T WORRY, OUMI.
SINCE IT'S THE 1ST TIME, YOU WON'T BE DOING ANYTHING DIFFICULT.
FL EX
HOWEVER!
WHEW...
UNLESS THERE'S AN EMERGENCY, YOU'LL BE IN THERE FOR 3 HOURS.
HUH ?

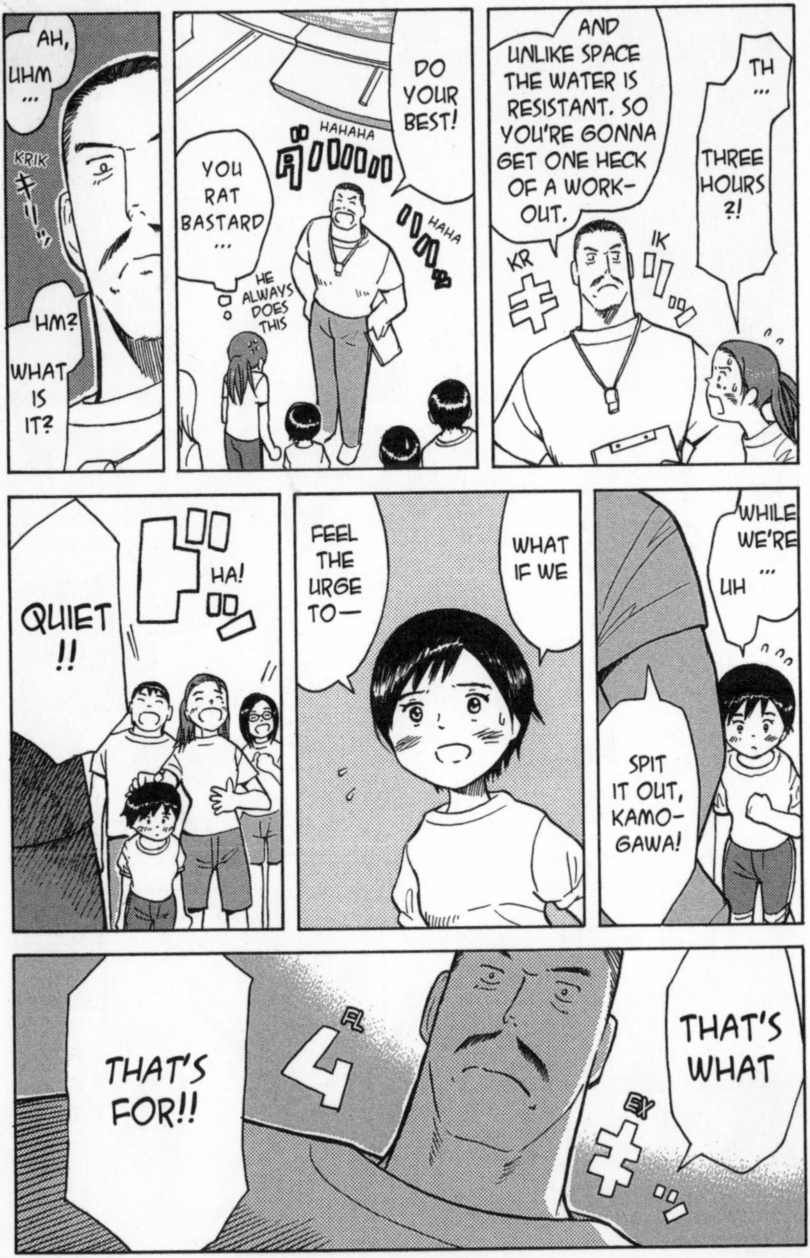
AND UNLIKE SPACE THE WATER IS RESISTANT. SO YOU'RE GONNA GET ONE HECK OF A WORK-OUT.
KR IK
TH ... THREE HOURS ?!
DO YOUR BEST!
HAHAHA
HAHA
YOU RAT BASTARD ...
HE ALWAYS DOES THIS
AH, UHM ...
KRIK
HM? WHAT IS IT?
WHILE WE'RE ... UH
SPIT IT OUT, KAMOGAWA!
WHAT IF WE
FEEL THE URGE TO—
HA!
QUIET !!
THAT'S WHAT
THAT'S FOR!!

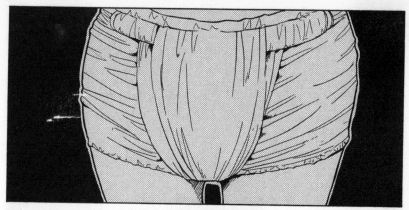

...

NEVER THOUGHT I'D WEAR A DIAPER AT SUCH AN AGE.

AH ...

SNEAK そっ...?

''' AH, RIGHT!

BUT IT DOESN'T LOOK WEIRD ON YOU.

HEE HEE

WHY NOT?

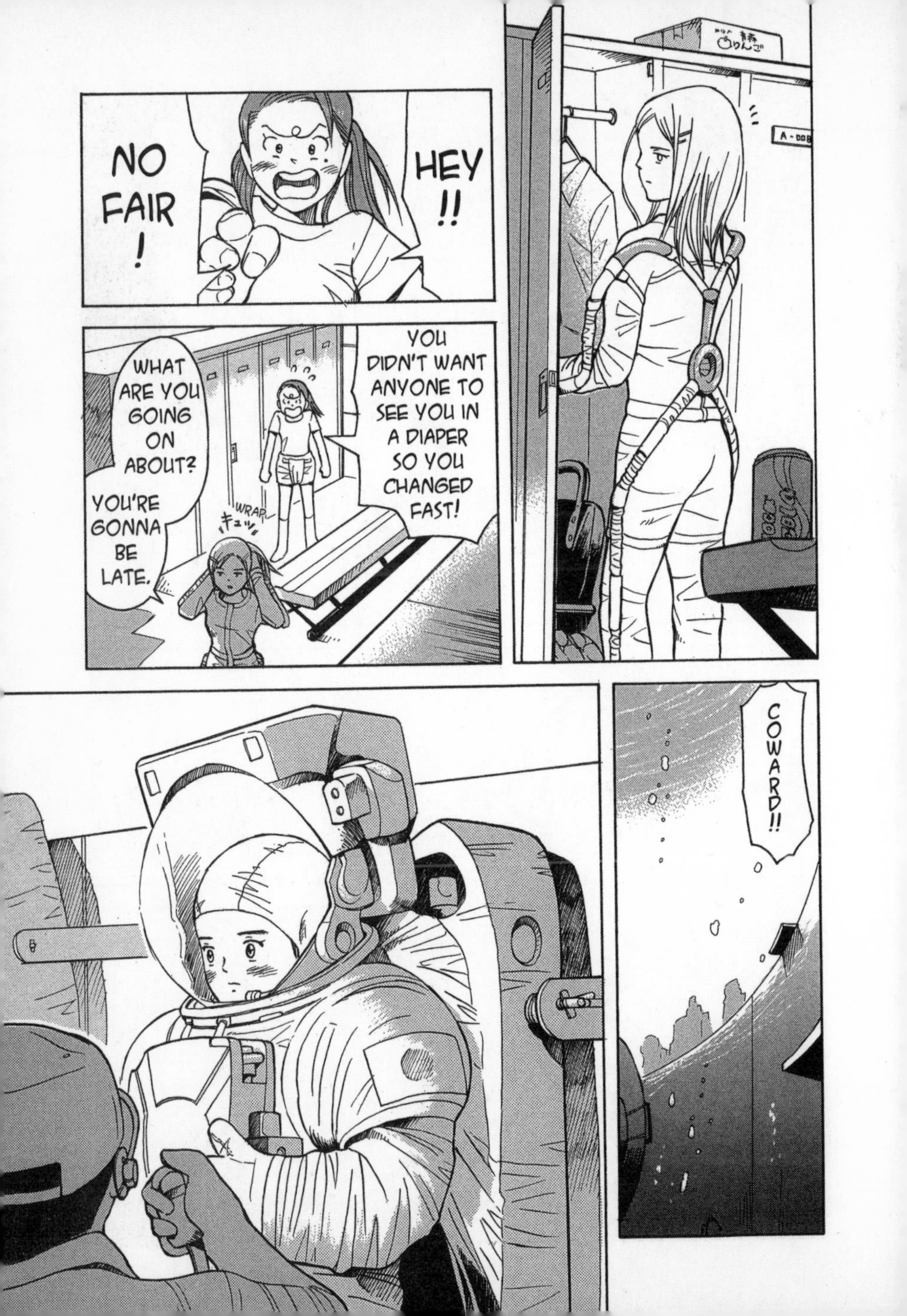
HEY!!
NO FAIR!
YOU DIDN'T WANT ANYONE TO SEE YOU IN A DIAPER SO YOU CHANGED FAST!
WHAT ARE YOU GOING ON ABOUT?
YOU'RE GONNA BE LATE.
キュッ WRAP
COWARD!!

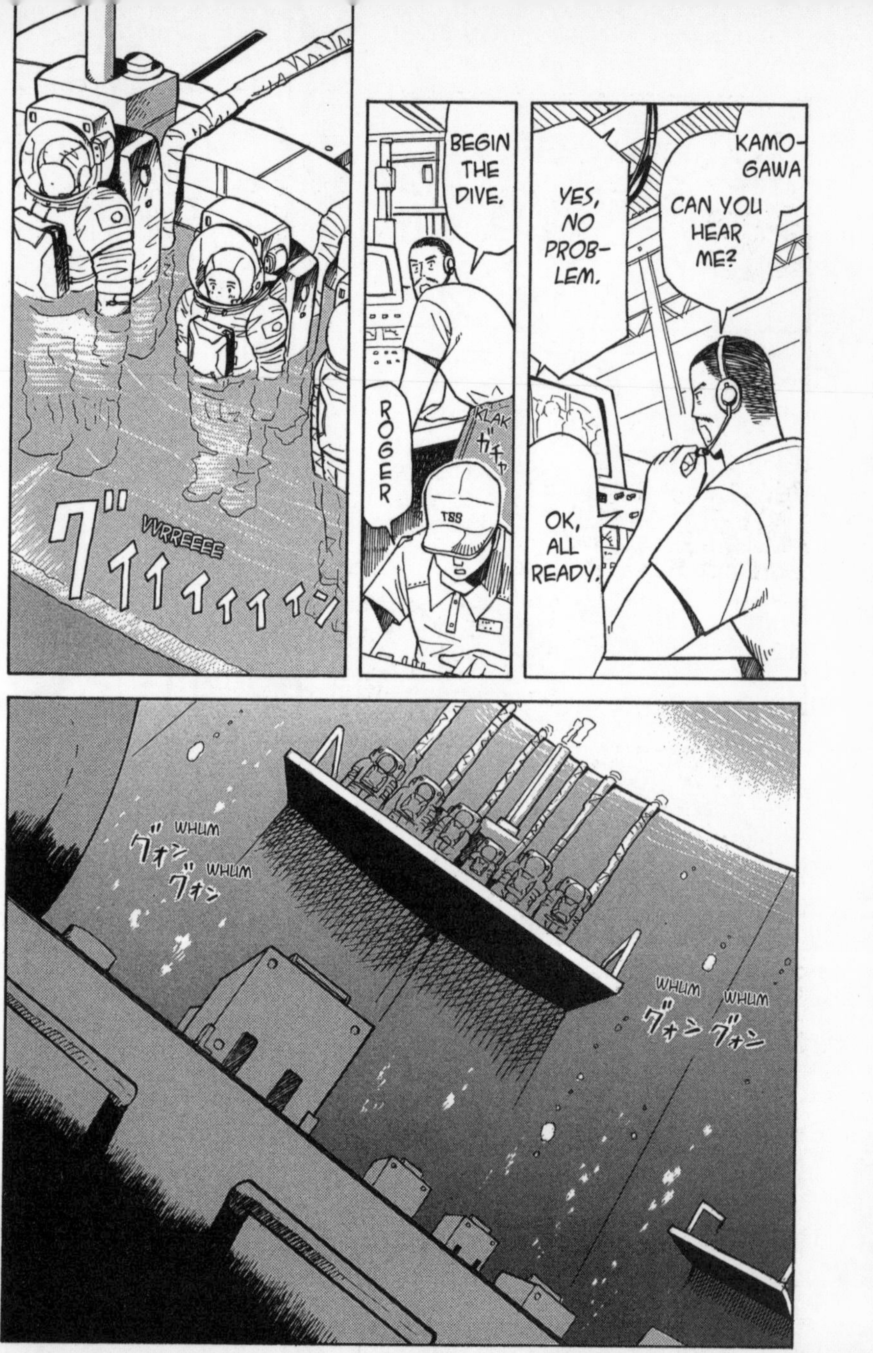
KAMO-GAWA
CAN YOU HEAR ME?
YES, NO PROB-LEM.
OK, ALL READY.
BEGIN THE DIVE.
ROGER
KLAK
ガチャ
グイイイイイイン
VVRREEEE
WHUM
グォン
WHUM
グォン
WHUM
WHUM
グォン グォン

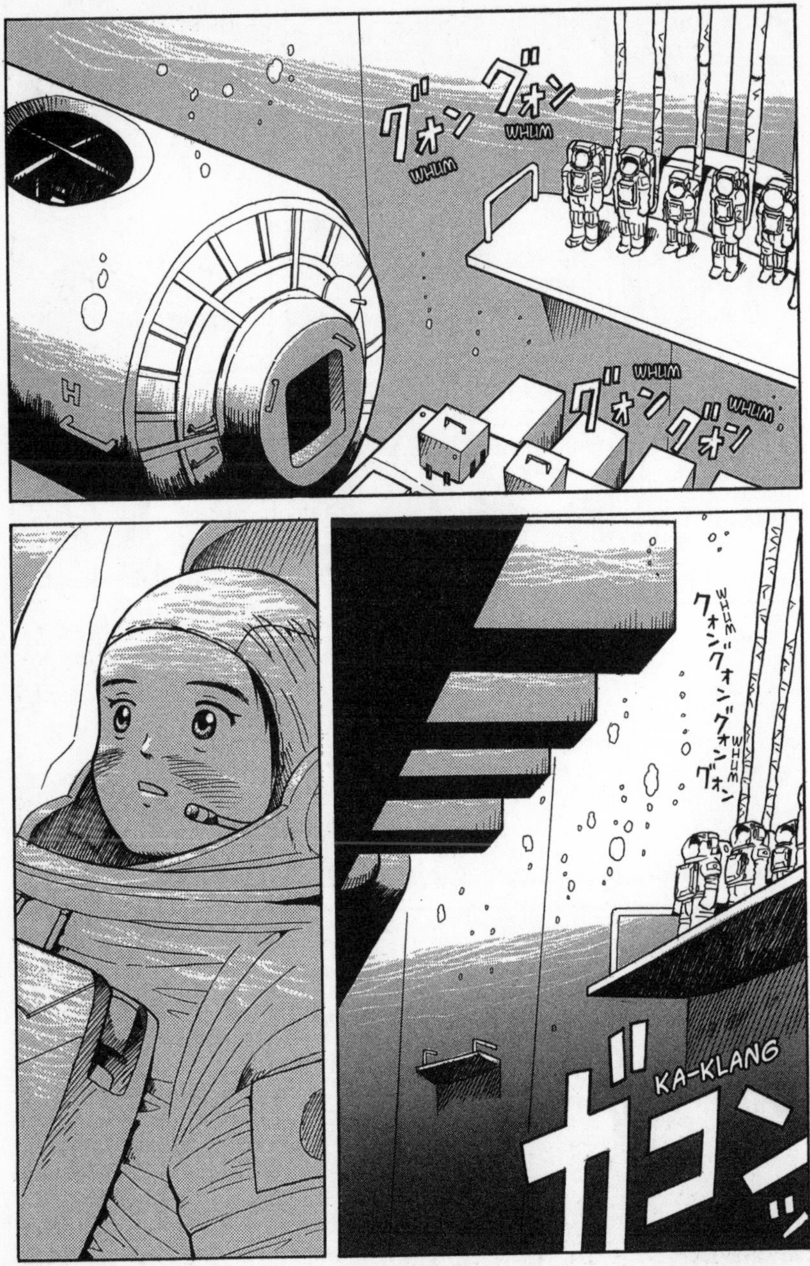
グォン
WHUM
グォン
WHUM
グォン
WHUM
グォン
WHUM
クォングォン
WHUM
グォングォン
WHUM
KA-KLANG
ガコンッ

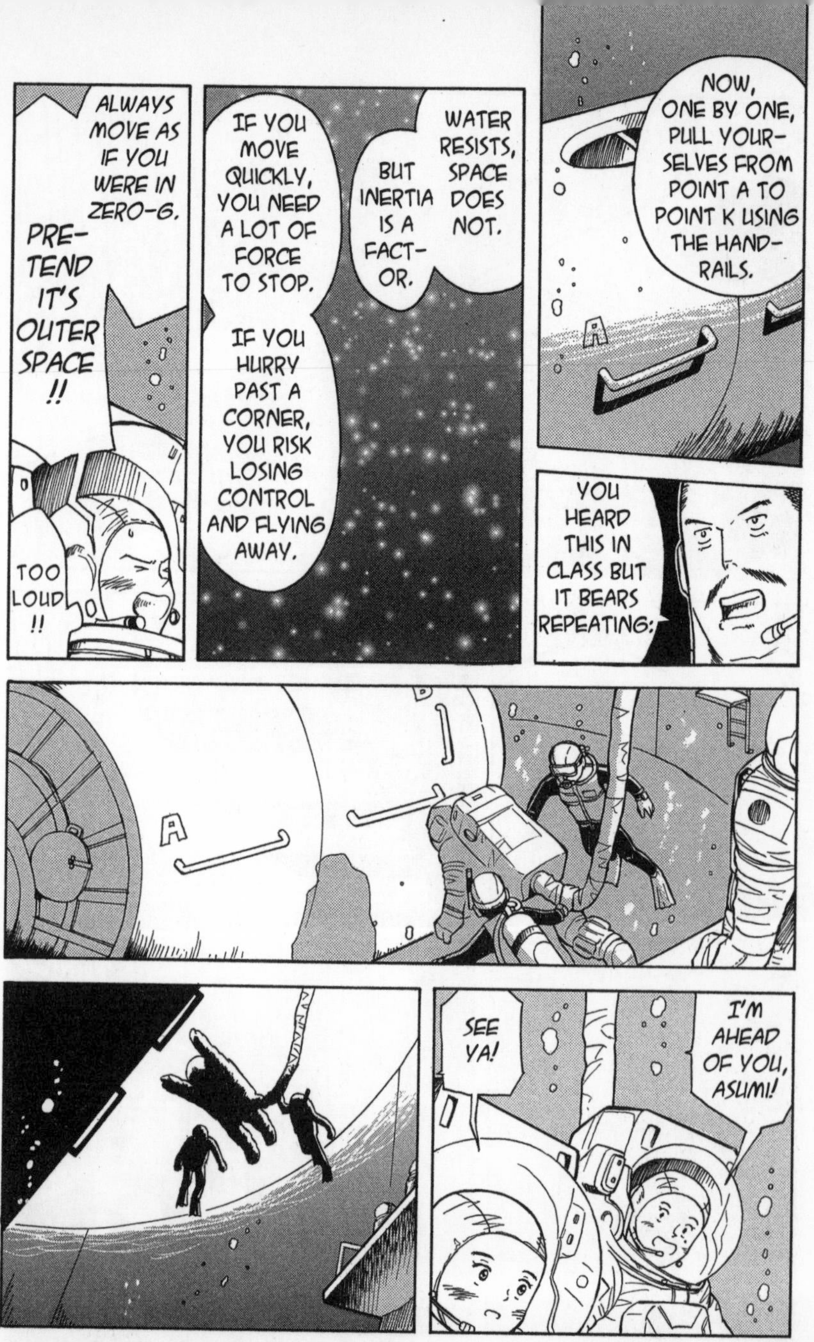
NOW, ONE BY ONE, PULL YOURSELVES FROM POINT A TO POINT K USING THE HANDRAILS.
A
YOU HEARD THIS IN CLASS BUT IT BEARS REPEATING:
WATER RESISTS, SPACE DOES NOT.
BUT INERTIA IS A FACTOR.
IF YOU MOVE QUICKLY, YOU NEED A LOT OF FORCE TO STOP.
IF YOU HURRY PAST A CORNER, YOU RISK LOSING CONTROL AND FLYING AWAY.
ALWAYS MOVE AS IF YOU WERE IN ZERO-G.
PRETEND IT'S OUTER SPACE!!
TOO LOUD!!
A
I'M AHEAD OF YOU, ASUMI!
SEE YA!

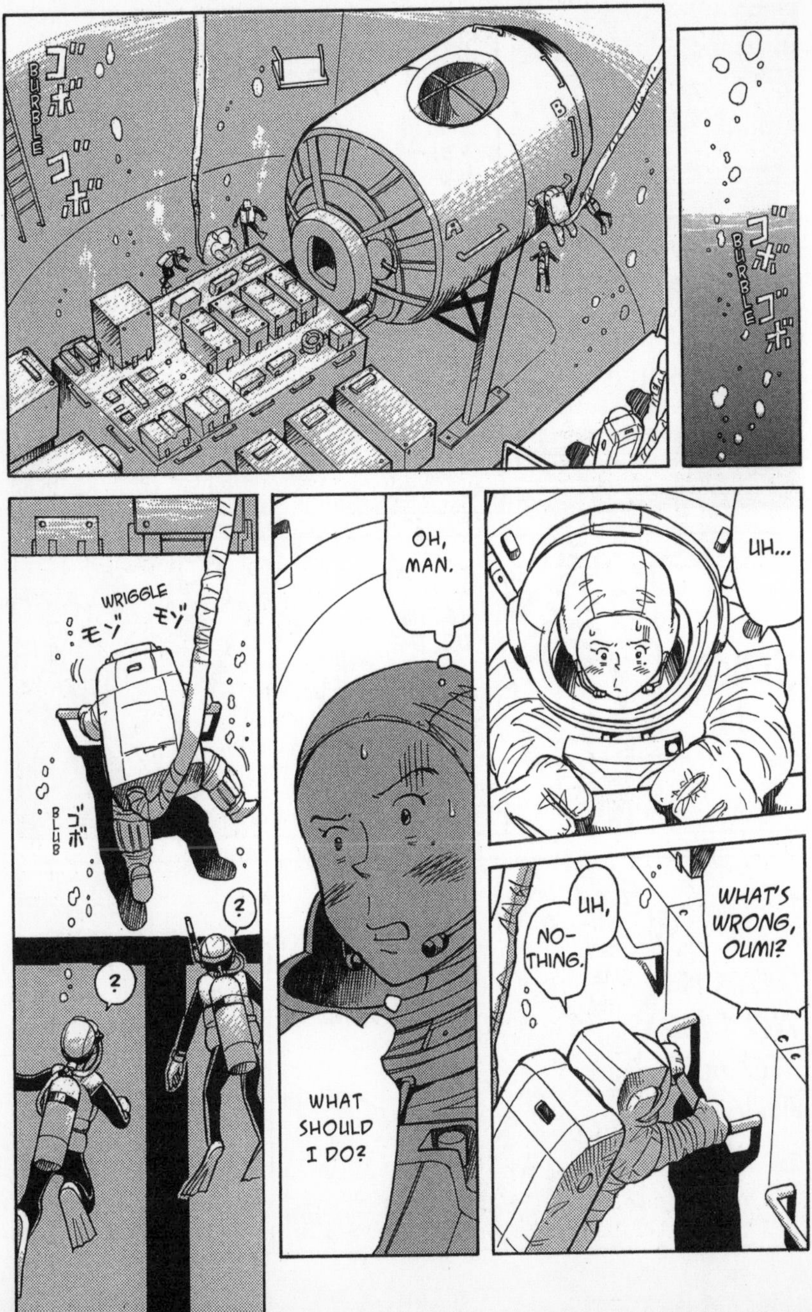
ゴボ BURBLE ゴボ
ゴボ BURBLE ゴボ
UH...
WHAT'S WRONG, OUMI?
UH, NO-THING.
OH, MAN.
WHAT SHOULD I DO?
WRIGGLE モゾ モゾ
BLUB ゴボ
?
?

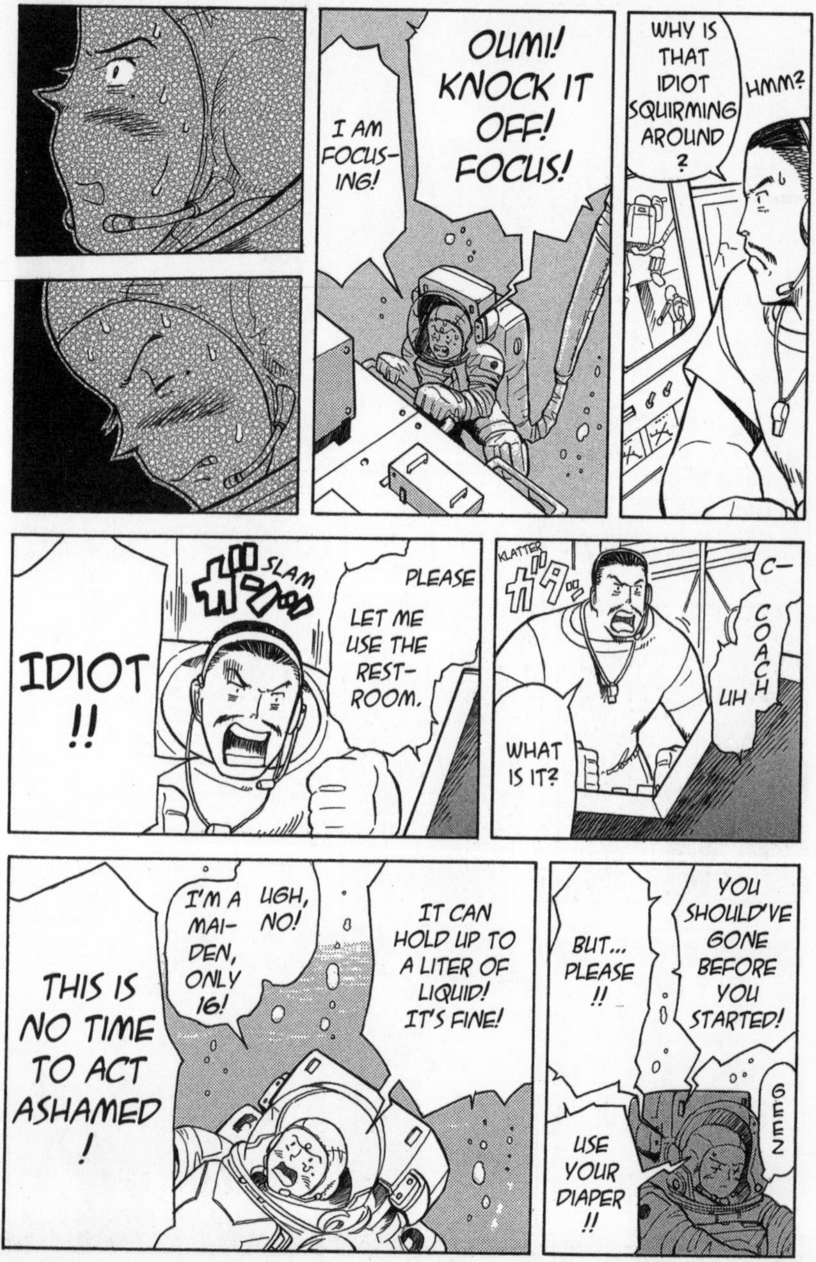
HMM?
WHY IS THAT IDIOT SQUIRMING AROUND?
OUMI! KNOCK IT OFF! FOCUS!
I AM FOCUSING!
C— COACH
UH
KLATTER
WHAT IS IT?
PLEASE
LET ME USE THE REST-ROOM.
SLAM
IDIOT !!
YOU SHOULD'VE GONE BEFORE YOU STARTED!
BUT... PLEASE !!
GEEZ
USE YOUR DIAPER !!
IT CAN HOLD UP TO A LITER OF LIQUID! IT'S FINE!
UGH, NO!
I'M A MAI-DEN, ONLY 16!
THIS IS NO TIME TO ACT ASHAMED !

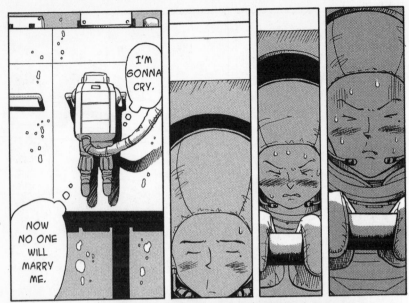

I'M GONNA CRY.

NOW NO ONE WILL MARRY ME.

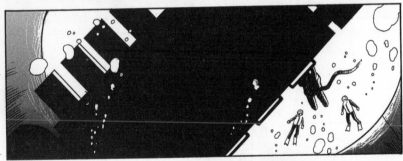

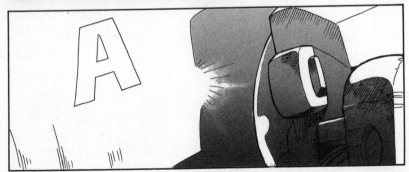

A

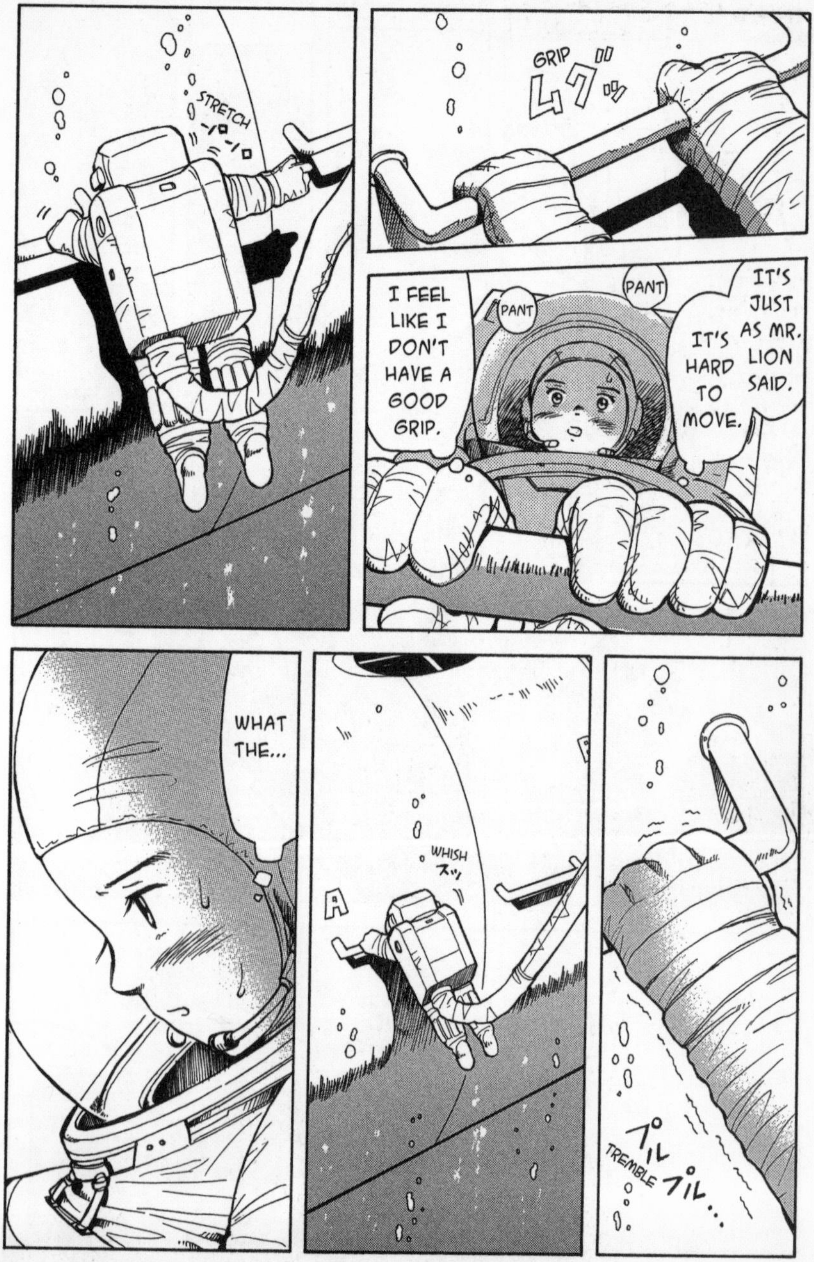
GRIP
IT'S JUST AS MR. LION SAID.
PANT
IT'S HARD TO MOVE.
PANT
I FEEL LIKE I DON'T HAVE A GOOD GRIP.
STRETCH
TREMBLE
WHISH
スッ
WHAT THE...

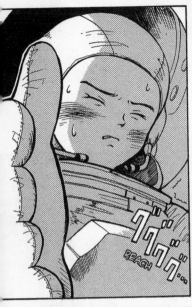

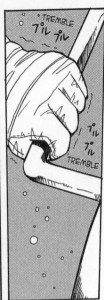

グググググ
REACH
TREMBLE
プルプル
プルプル
TREMBLE
ググググ...
REACH
WHISH
スッ
...
KAMOGAWA, NOW YOU'VE GOT A PROBLEM?
WHY AREN'T YOU MOVING AHEAD?
WHAT'S WRONG WITH YOU KIDS?
YOU'RE NOT EVEN TRYING!!
WHAT SHOULD I DO?
...

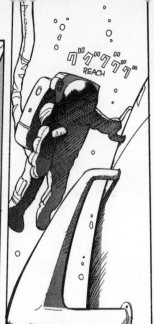

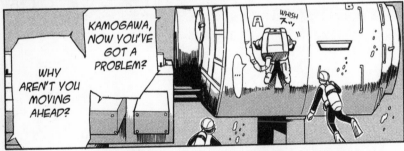

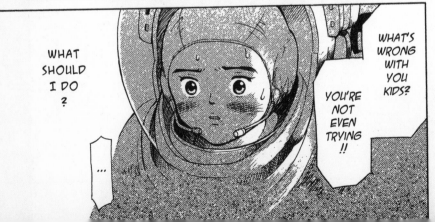

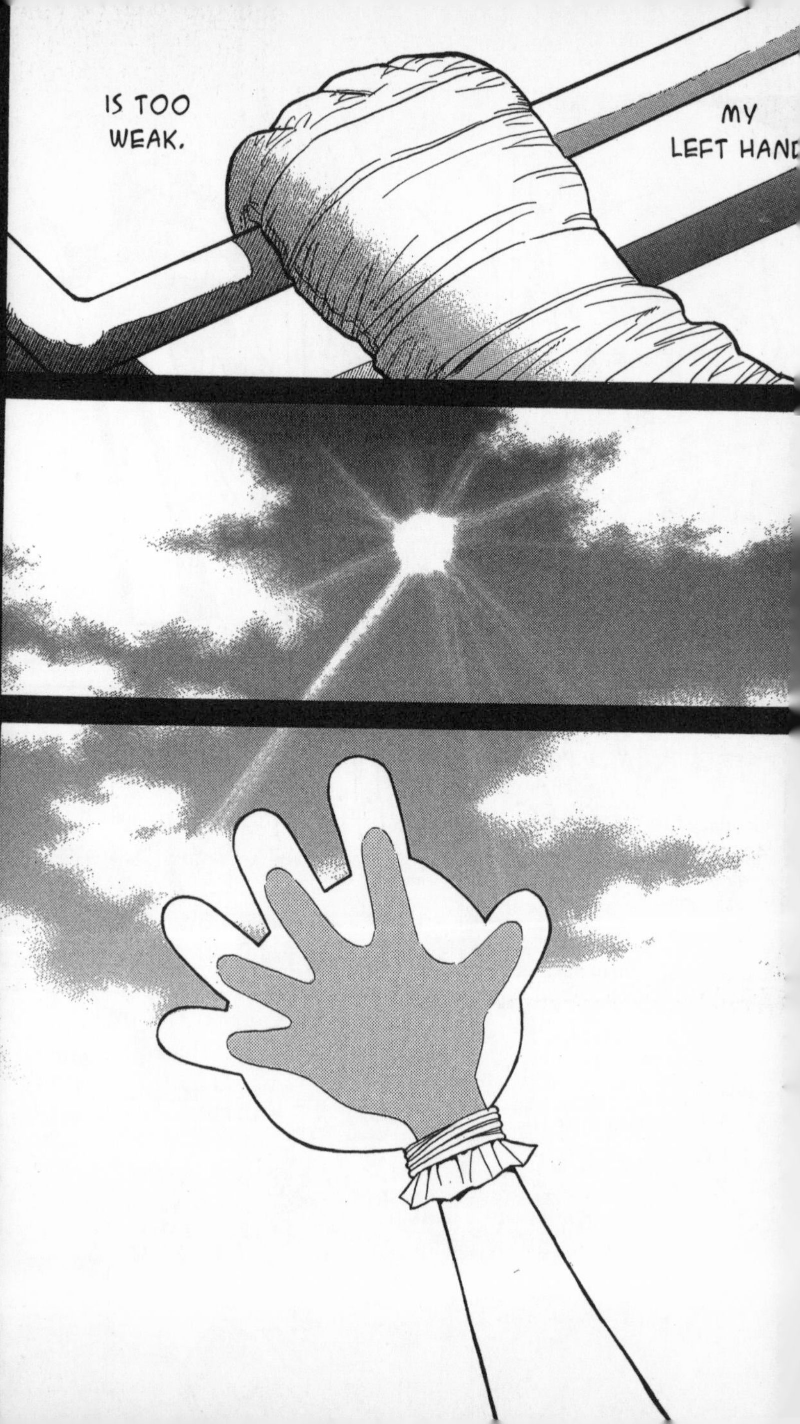
MY
LEFT HAND
IS TOO
WEAK.

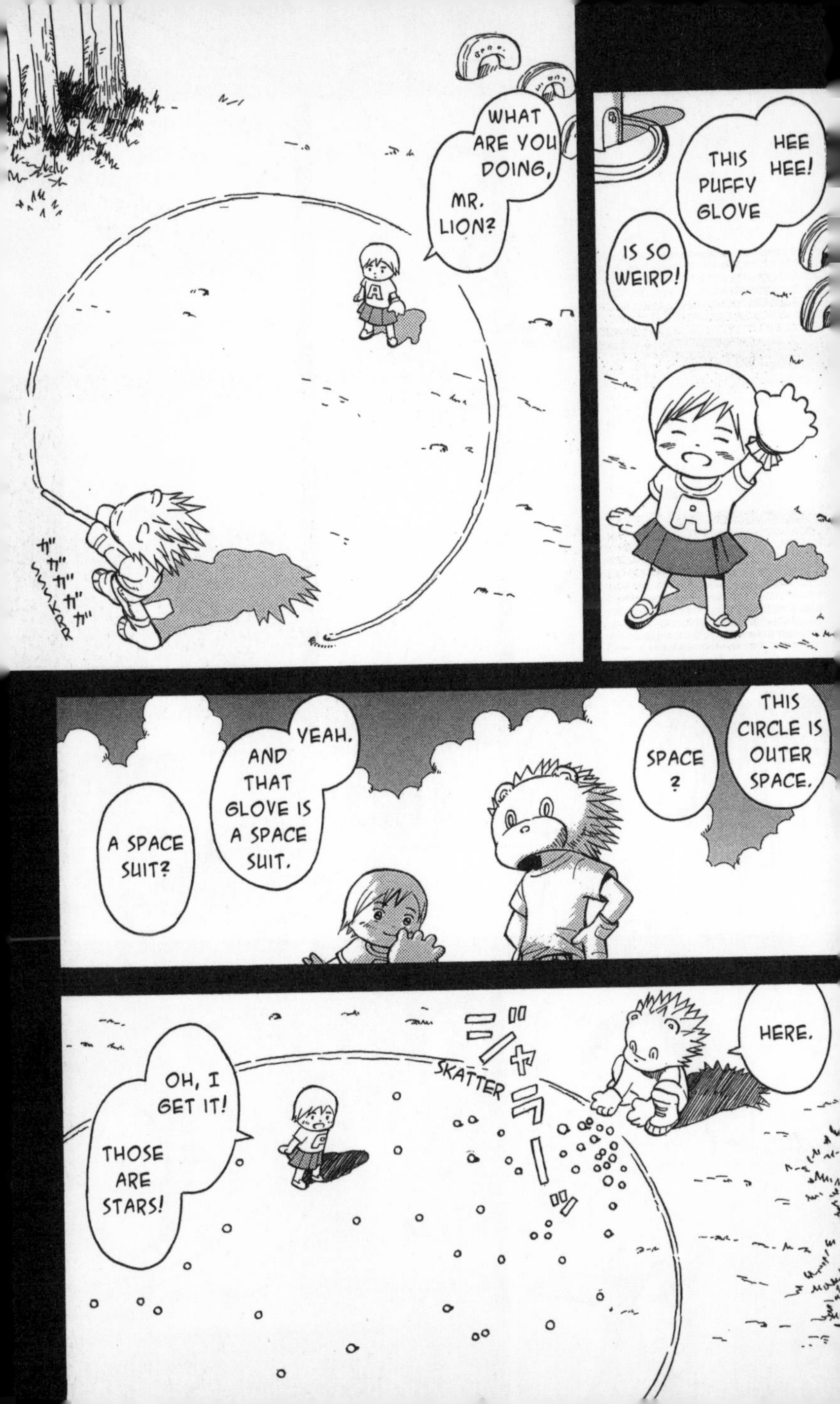
HEE HEE!
THIS PUFFY GLOVE
IS SO WEIRD!
WHAT ARE YOU DOING, MR. LION?
ガガガガガ
SSSKRR
THIS CIRCLE IS OUTER SPACE.
SPACE?
YEAH.
AND THAT GLOVE IS A SPACE SUIT.
A SPACE SUIT?
HERE.
ジャラーッ
SKATTER
OH, I GET IT!
THOSE ARE STARS!

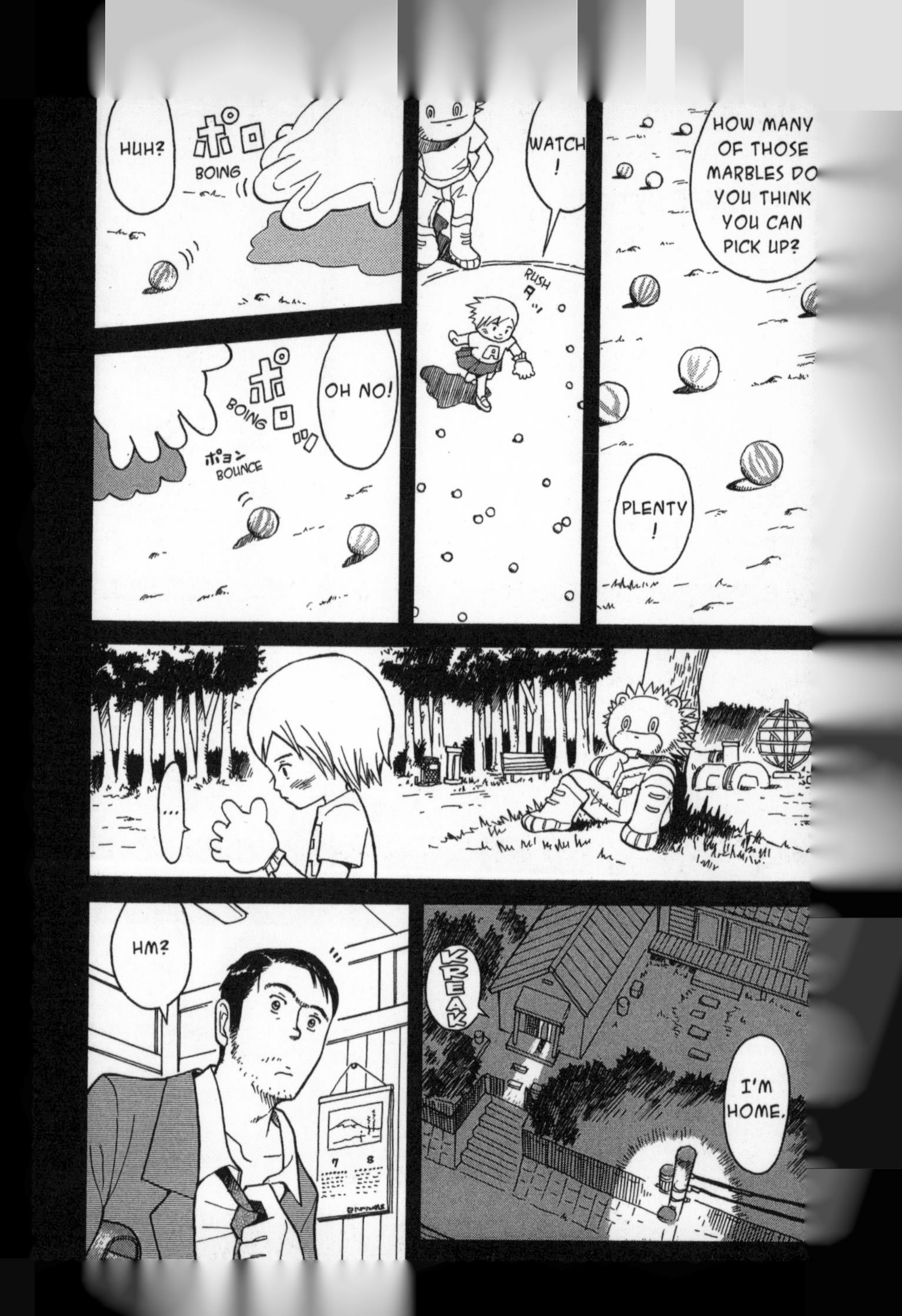
HOW MANY OF THOSE MARBLES DO YOU THINK YOU CAN PICK UP?
PLENTY!
WATCH!
タッ
RUSH
HUH?
ポロ
BOING
OH NO!
ポロ
BOING
ポヨン
BOUNCE
...
I'M HOME.
KREAK
HM?

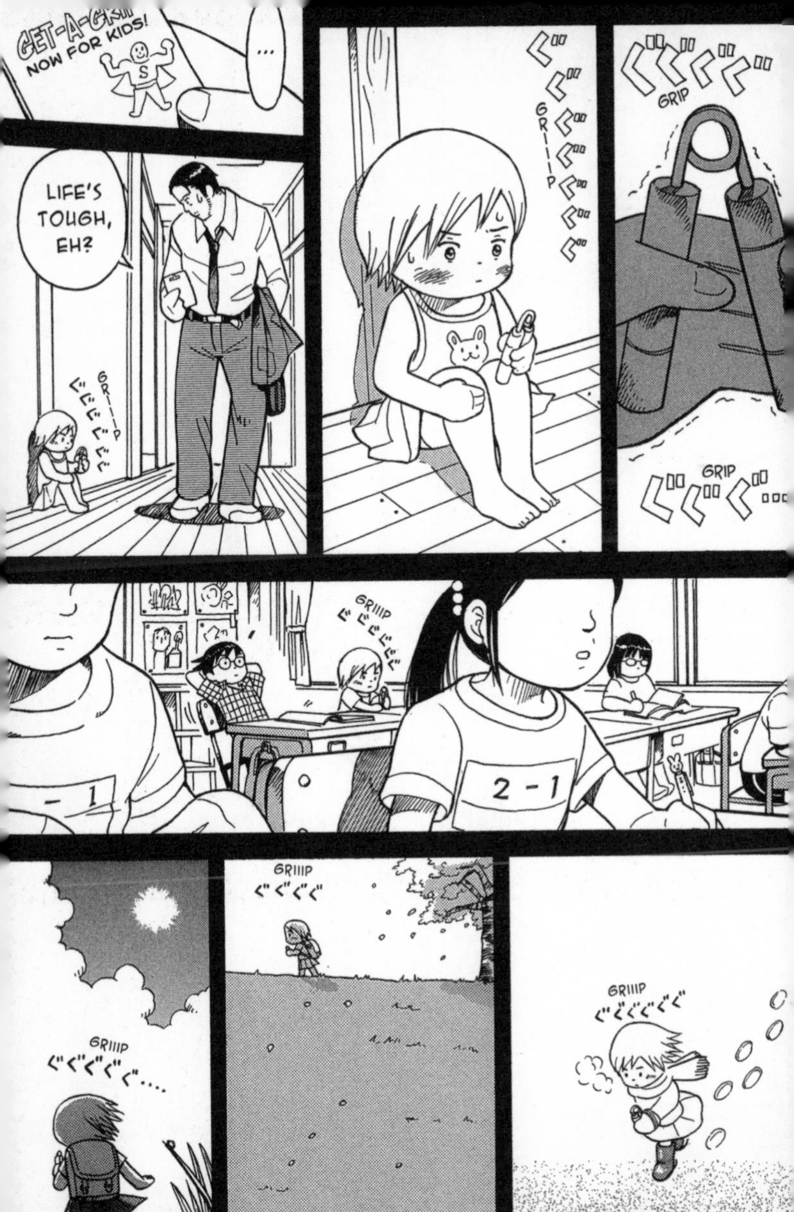
GRIP
GRIP
GRI-I-P
GET-A-GR
NOW FOR KIDS!
...
LIFE'S TOUGH, EH?
GRI-I-P
GRIIIP
GRIIIP
GRIIIP
GRIIIP

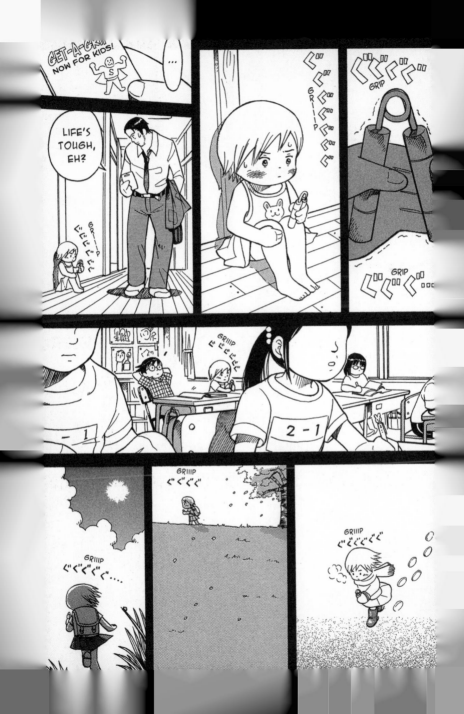

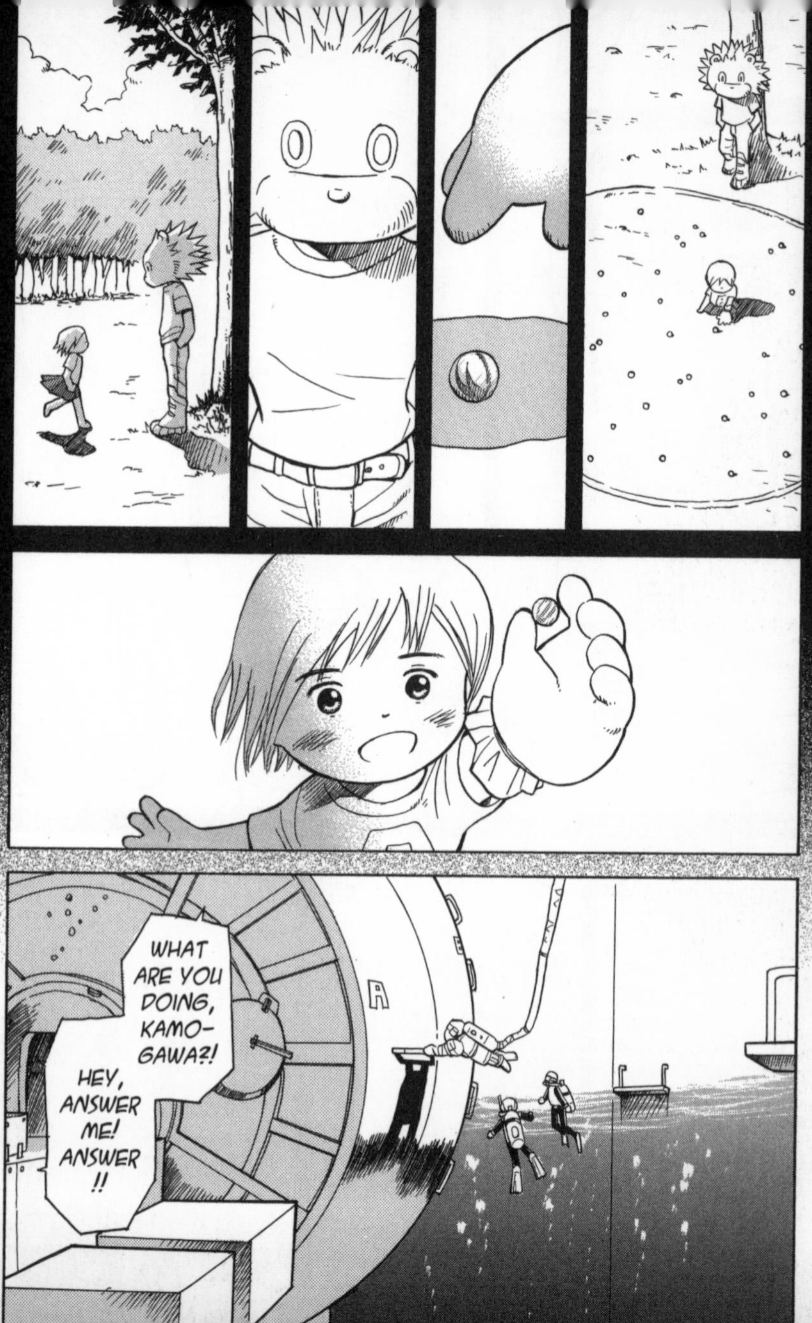
WHAT ARE YOU DOING, KAMO-GAWA?!
HEY, ANSWER ME! ANSWER !!

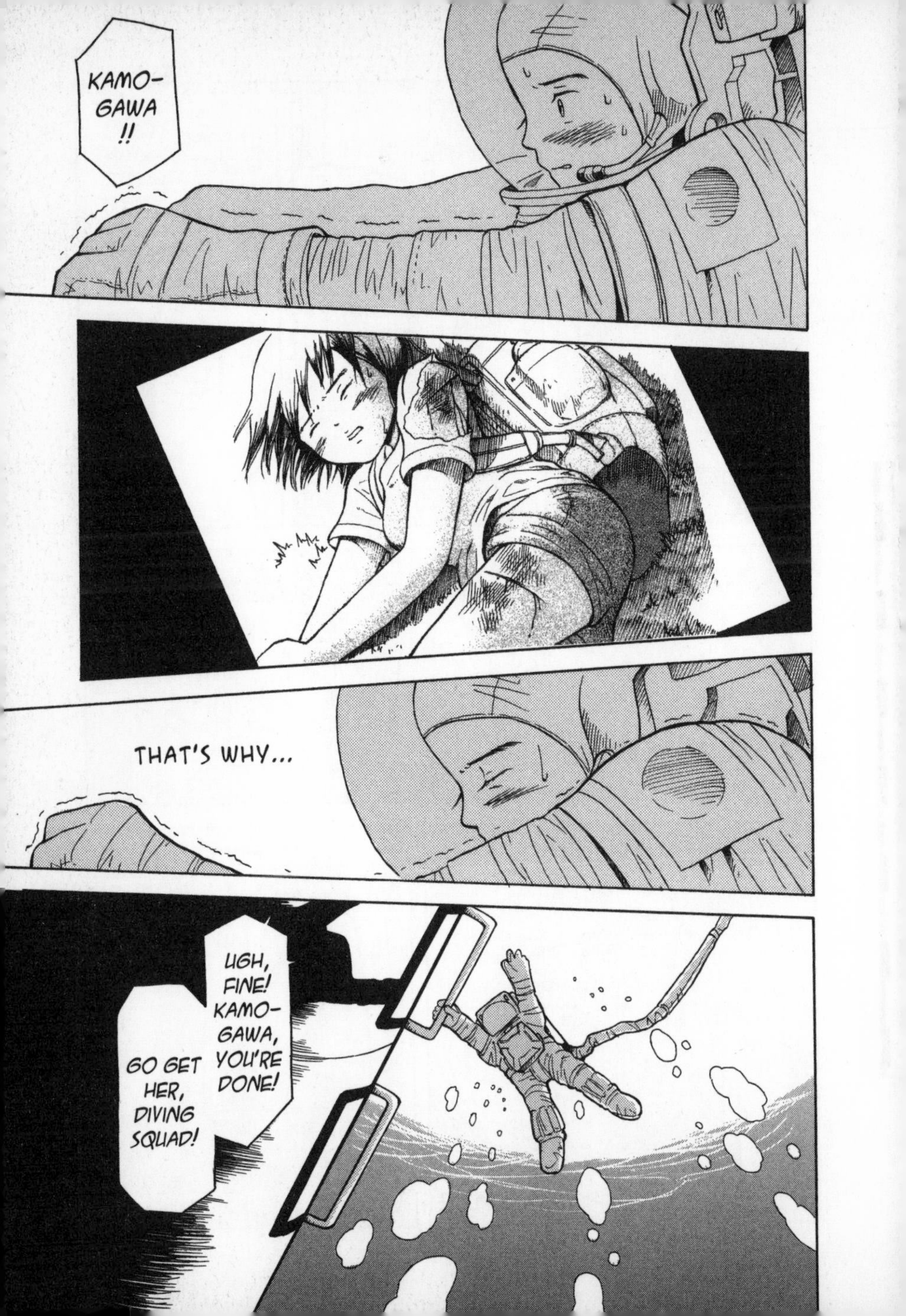
KAMO-GAWA !!
THAT'S WHY...
UGH, FINE! KAMO-GAWA, YOU'RE DONE!
GO GET HER, DIVING SQUAD!

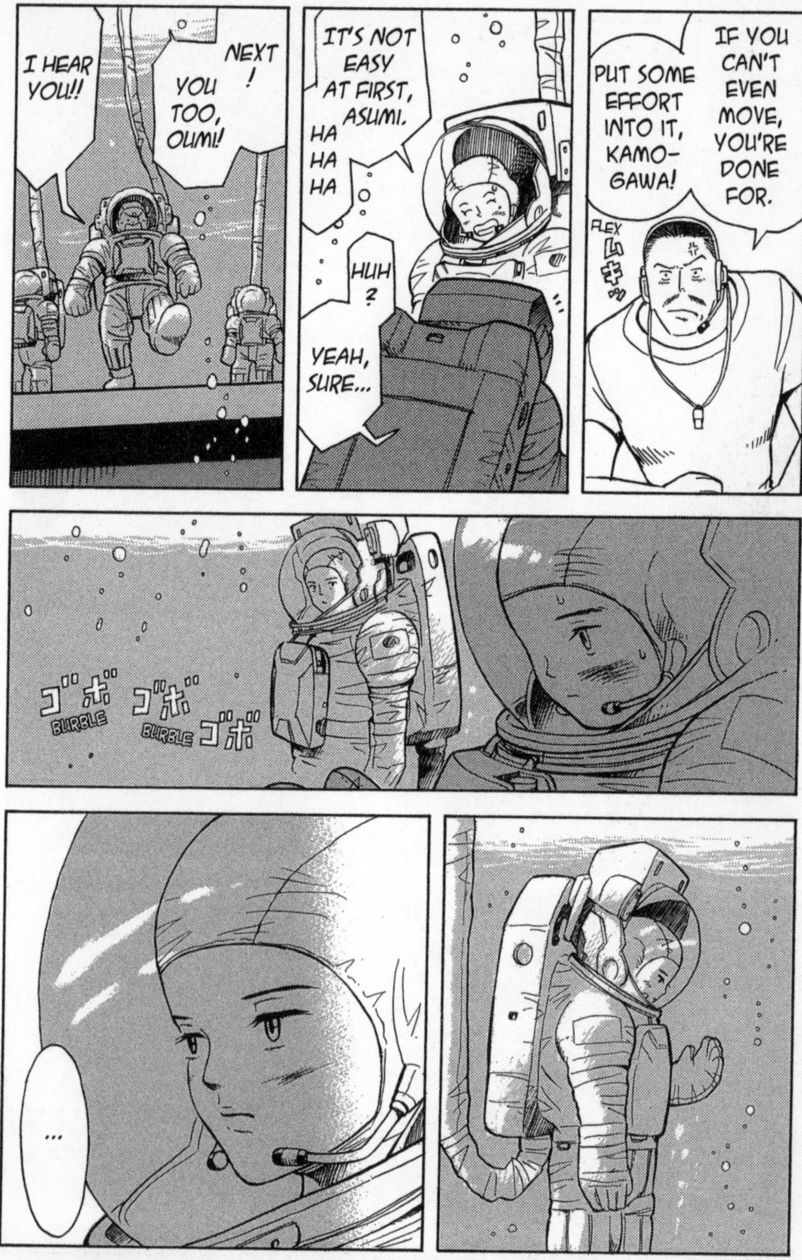
IF YOU CAN'T EVEN MOVE, YOU'RE DONE FOR.
PUT SOME EFFORT INTO IT, KAMO-GAWA!
FLEX ムキッ
IT'S NOT EASY AT FIRST, ASUMI.
HA HA HA
HUH?
YEAH, SURE...
NEXT!
YOU TOO, OUMI!
I HEAR YOU!!
ゴボ BURBLE ゴボ BURBLE ゴボ
...

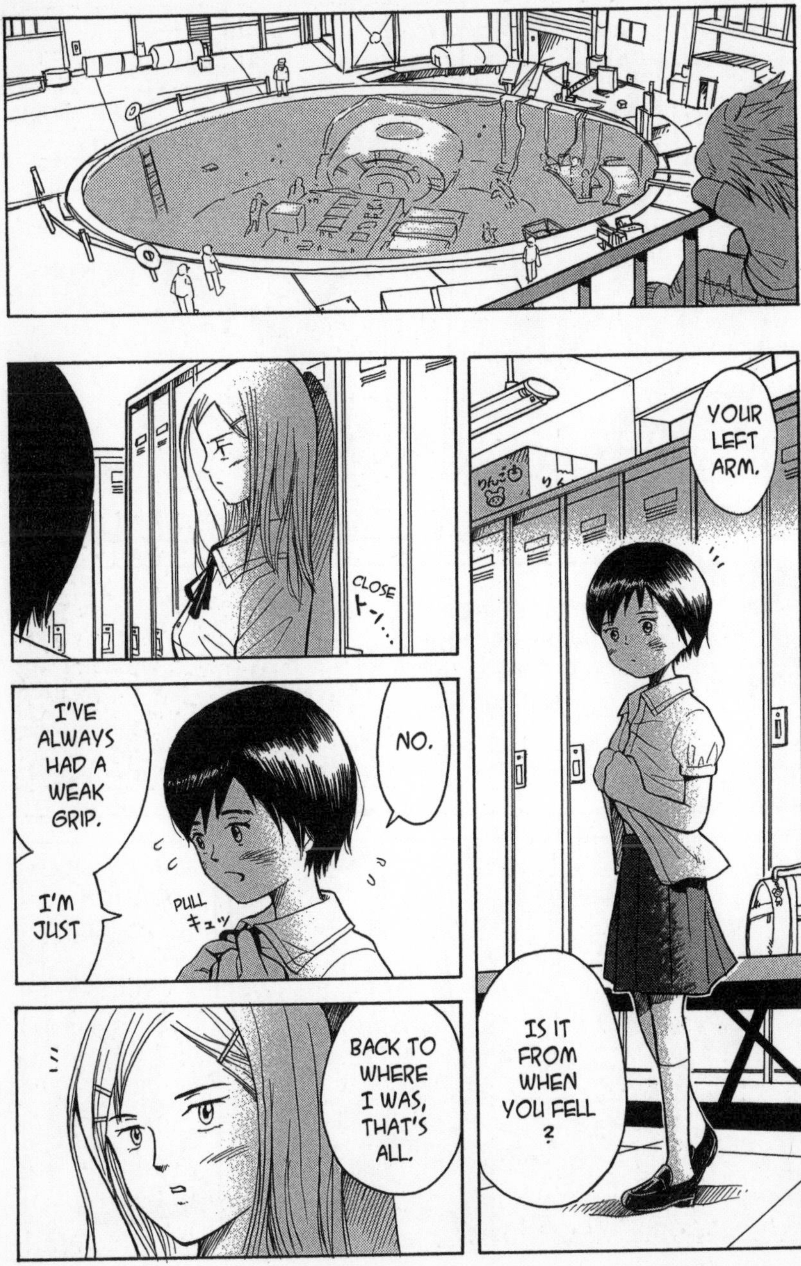
YOUR LEFT ARM.
IS IT FROM WHEN YOU FELL?
CLOSE
NO.
I'VE ALWAYS HAD A WEAK GRIP.
PULL
キュッ
I'M JUST
BACK TO WHERE I WAS, THAT'S ALL.

I'M NOT WORSE.

MY LEFT ARM IS WEAK BECAUSE OF "THE LION" ACCIDENT.

GRIP
ᒡᒡᒡ...

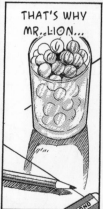

THAT'S WHY MR. LION...

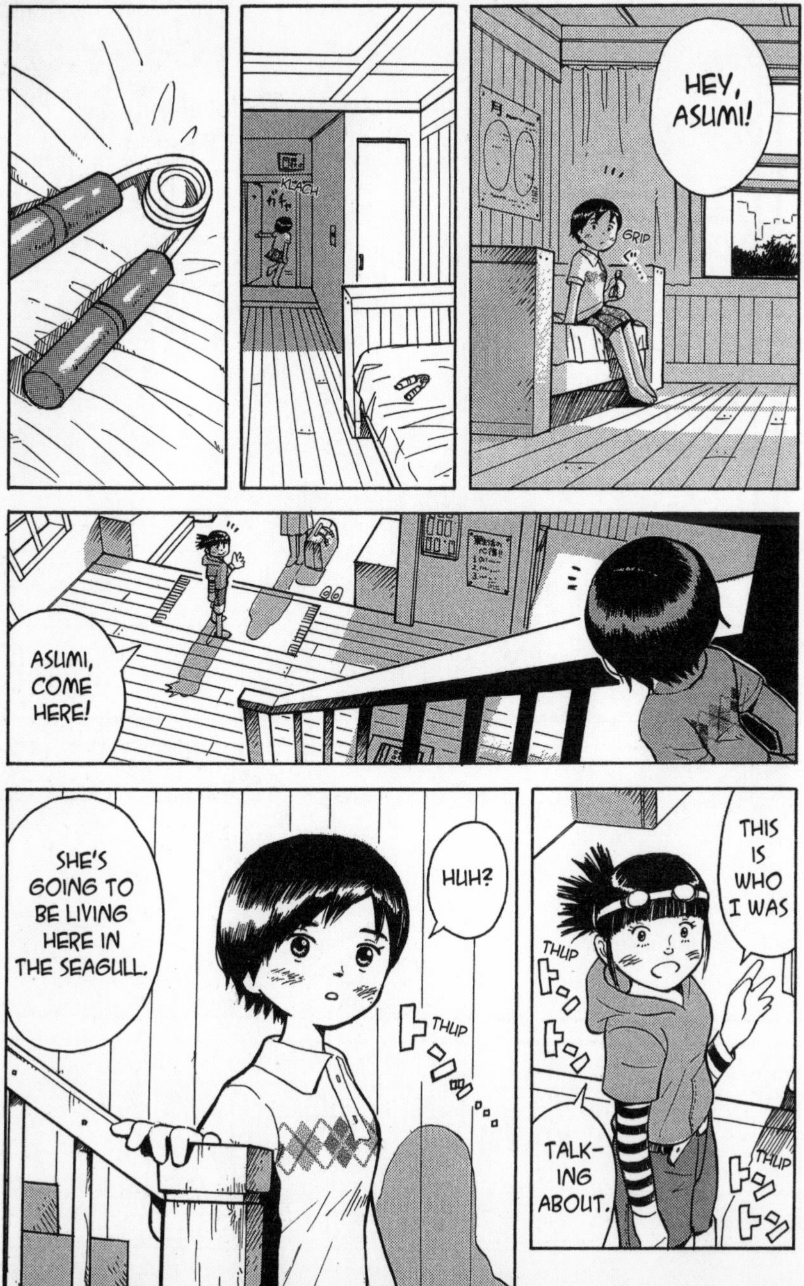
HEY, ASUMI!
GRIP
KLACH
ASUMI, COME HERE!
THIS IS WHO I WAS
THUP
TALK-ING ABOUT.
THUP
HUH?
SHE'S GOING TO BE LIVING HERE IN THE SEAGULL.
THUP

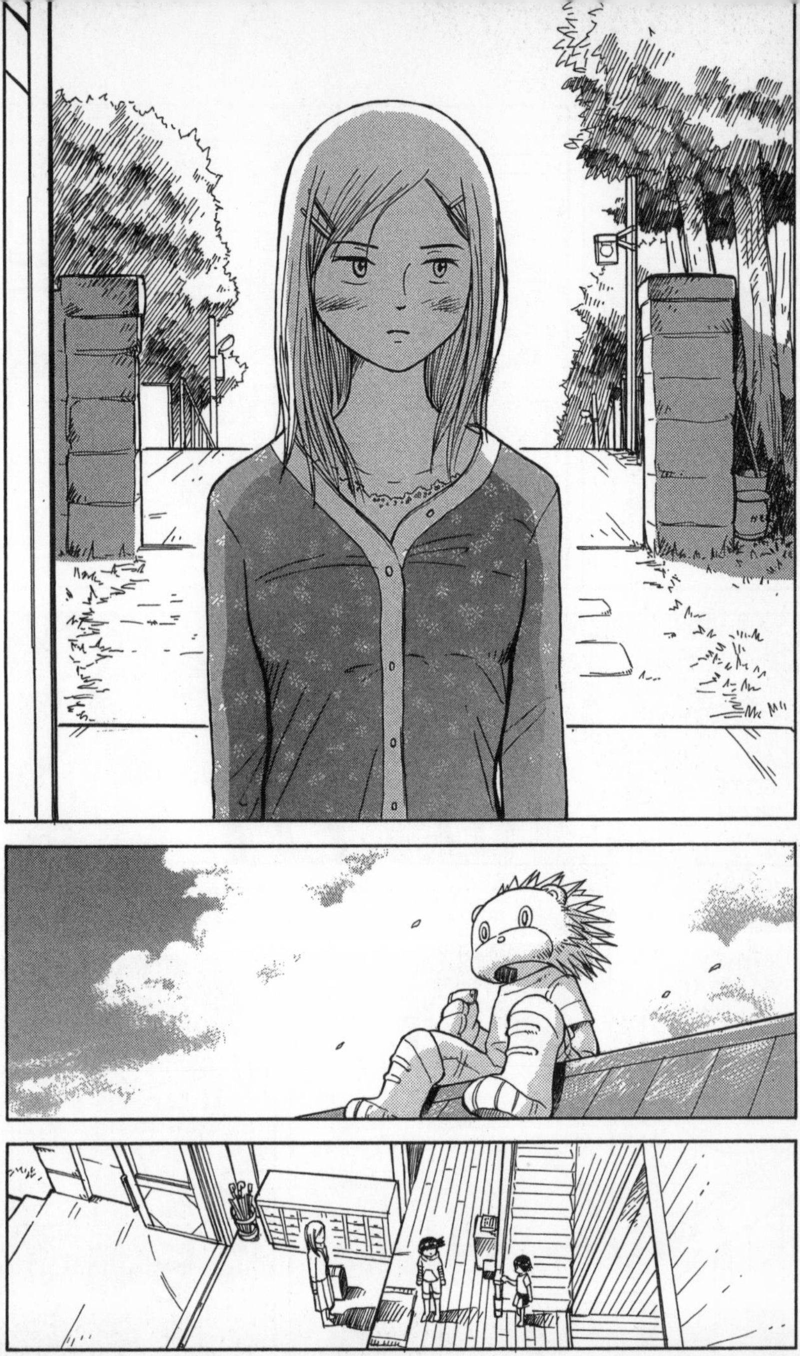

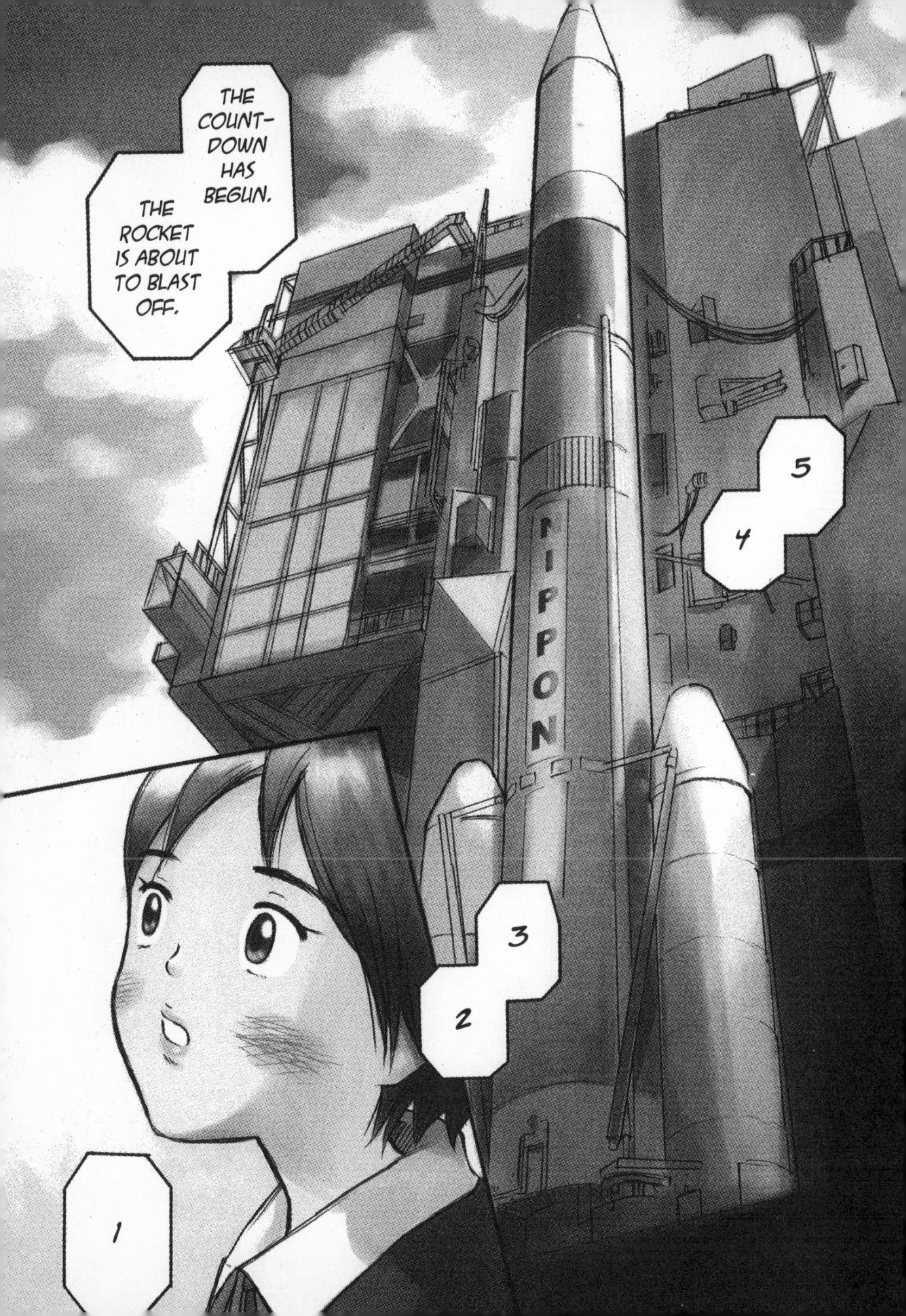
THE COUNT-DOWN HAS BEGUN.
THE ROCKET IS ABOUT TO BLAST OFF.
NIPPON
5
4
3
2
1

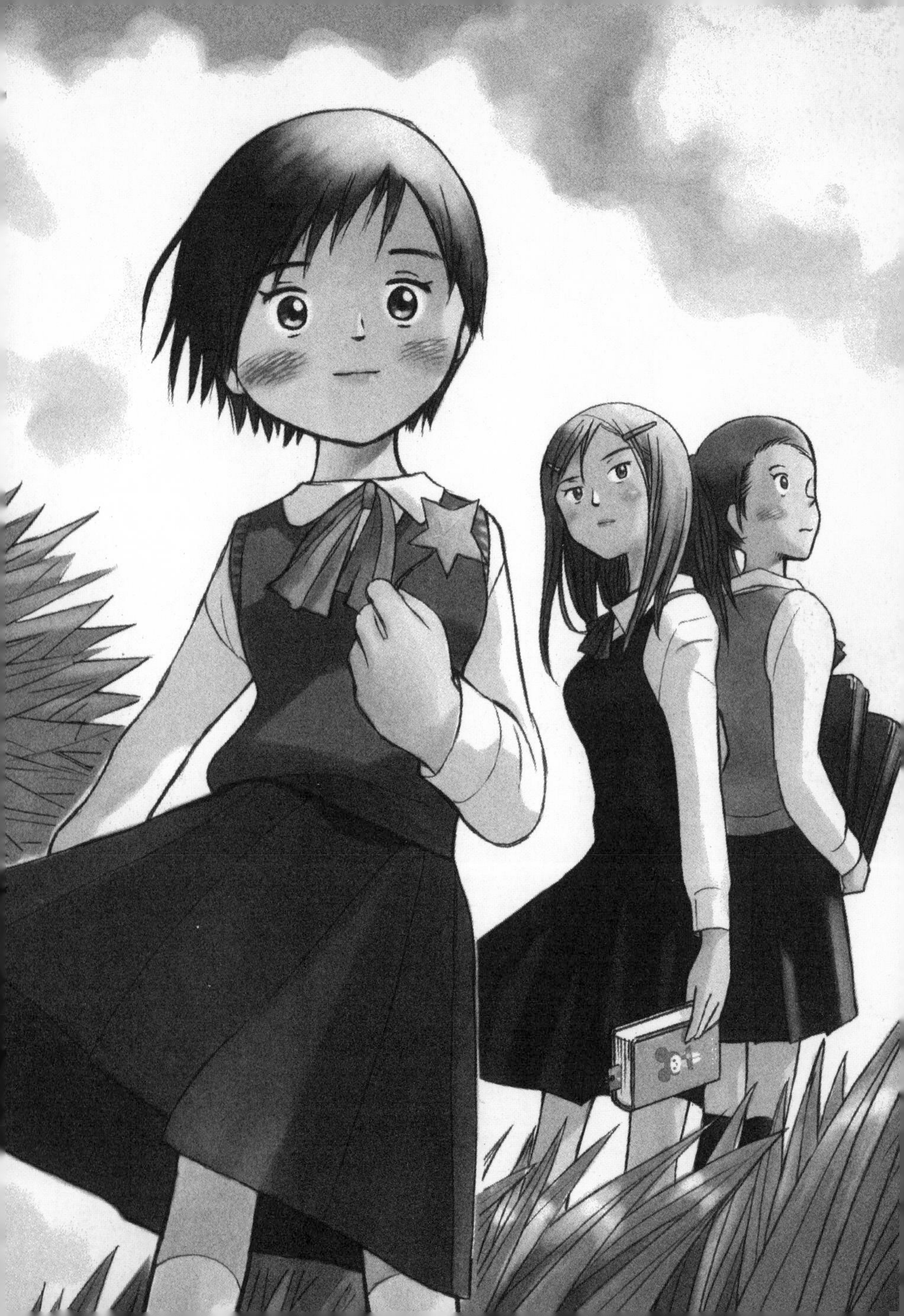

MISSION:15

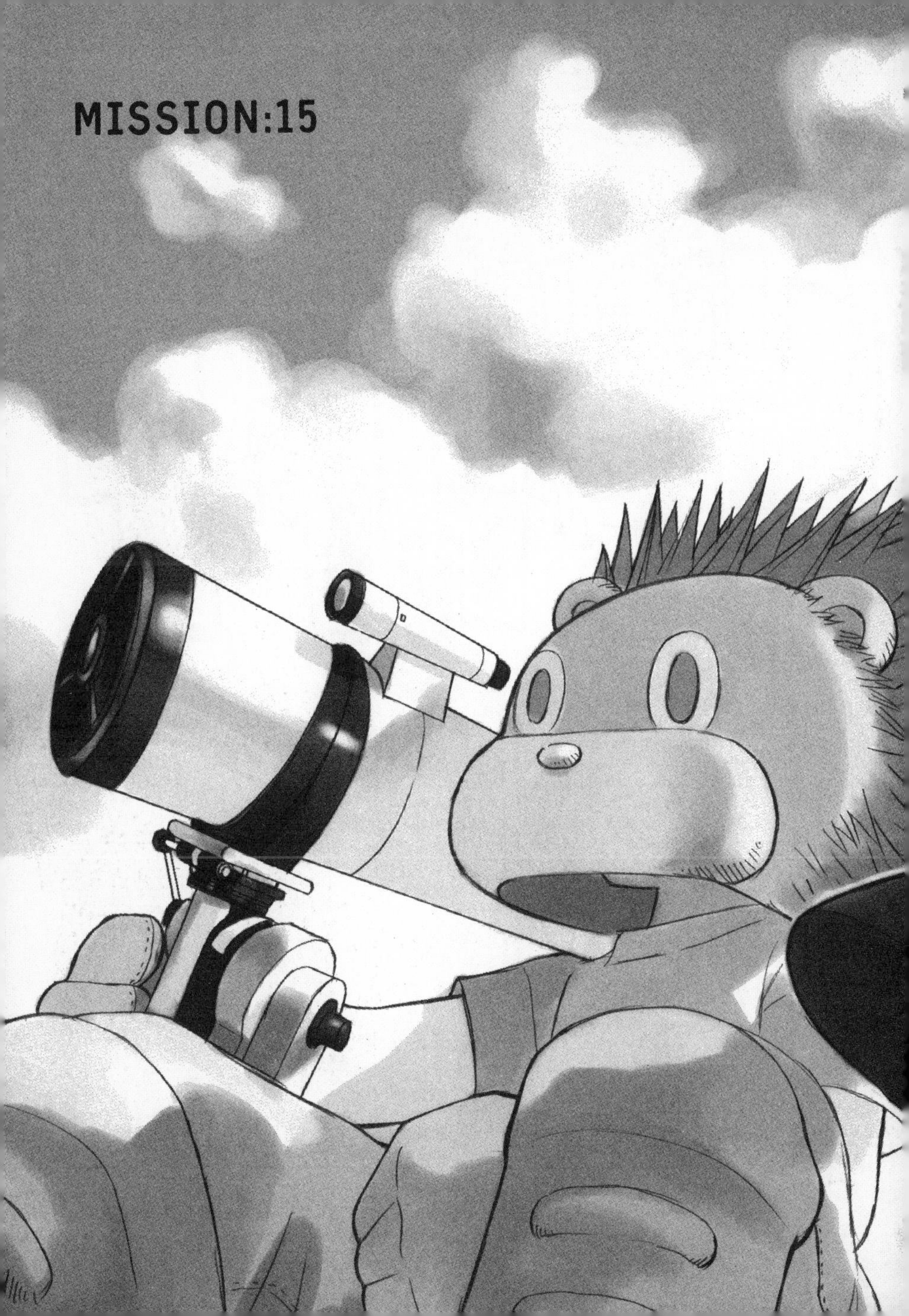

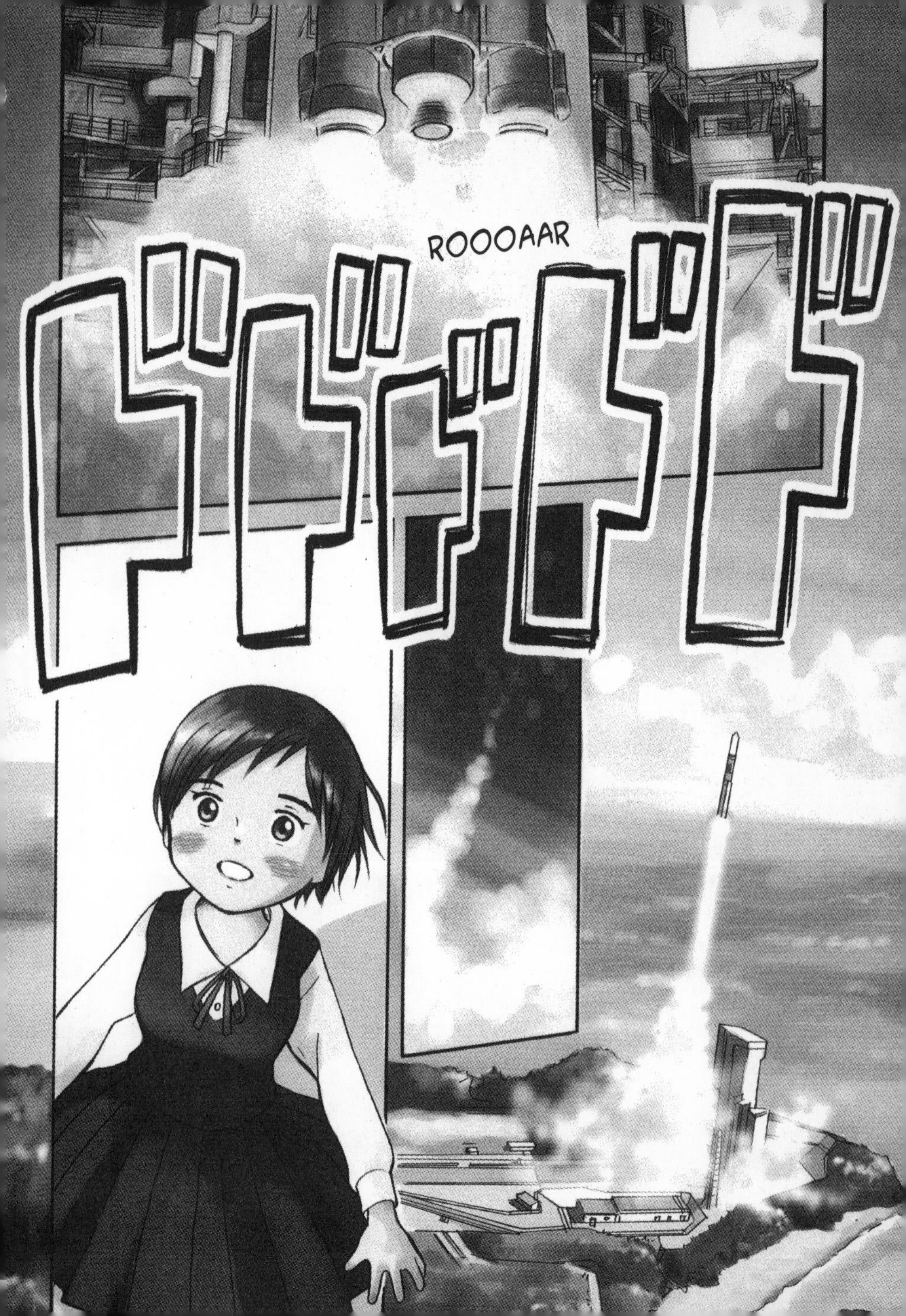
ROOOAAR
ドドドドドド

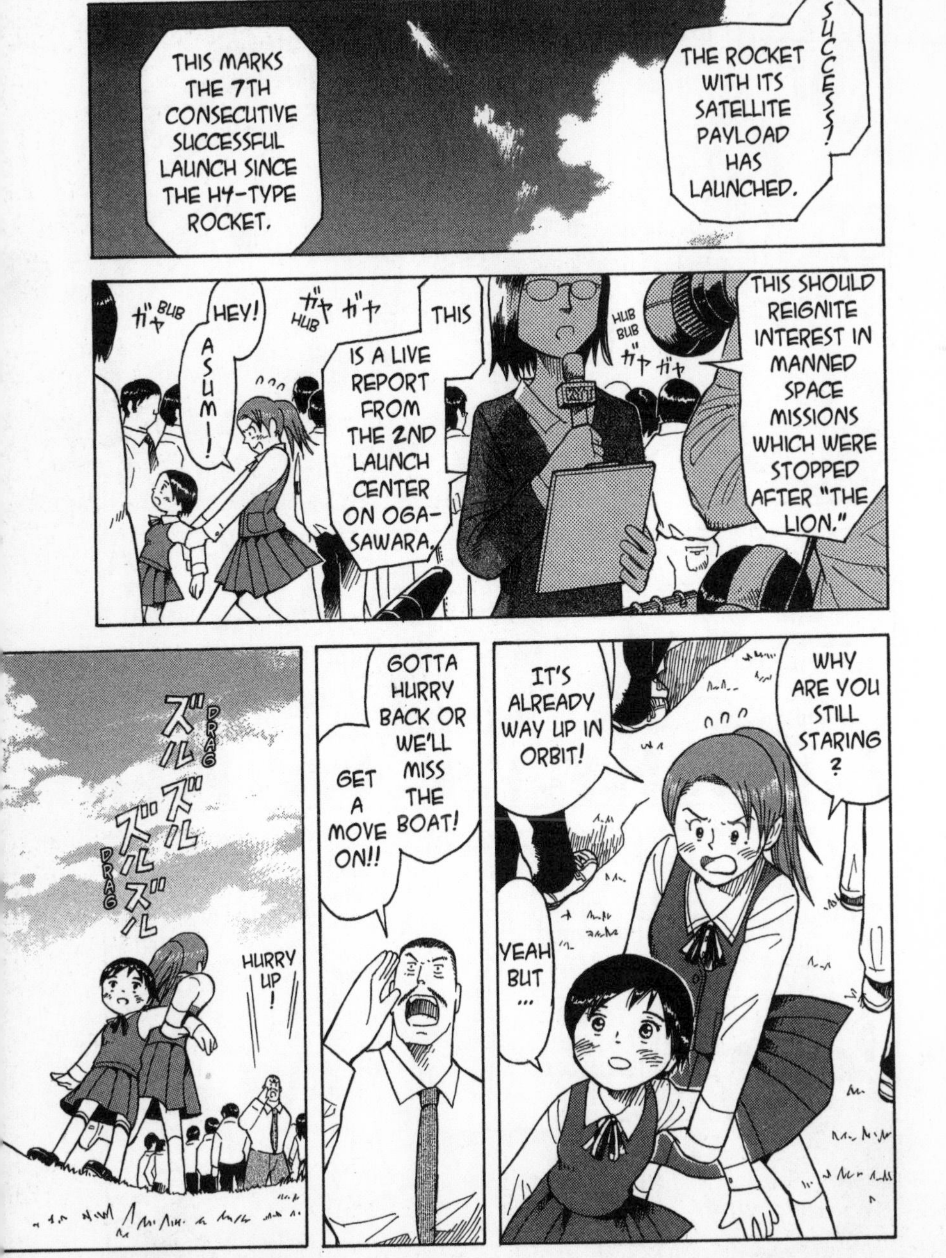
SUCCESS!
THE ROCKET WITH ITS SATELLITE PAYLOAD HAS LAUNCHED.
THIS MARKS THE 7TH CONSECUTIVE SUCCESSFUL LAUNCH SINCE THE H4-TYPE ROCKET.
THIS SHOULD REIGNITE INTEREST IN MANNED SPACE MISSIONS WHICH WERE STOPPED AFTER "THE LION."
ガヤガヤ HUB BUB
THIS IS A LIVE REPORT FROM THE 2ND LAUNCH CENTER ON OGA-SAWARA.
ガヤガヤ HUB
HEY! ASUMI!
ガヤ BUB
WHY ARE YOU STILL STARING?
IT'S ALREADY WAY UP IN ORBIT!
YEAH BUT ...
GOTTA HURRY BACK OR WE'LL MISS THE BOAT!
GET A MOVE ON!!
ズルズル DRAG
ズルズル DRAG
HURRY UP!

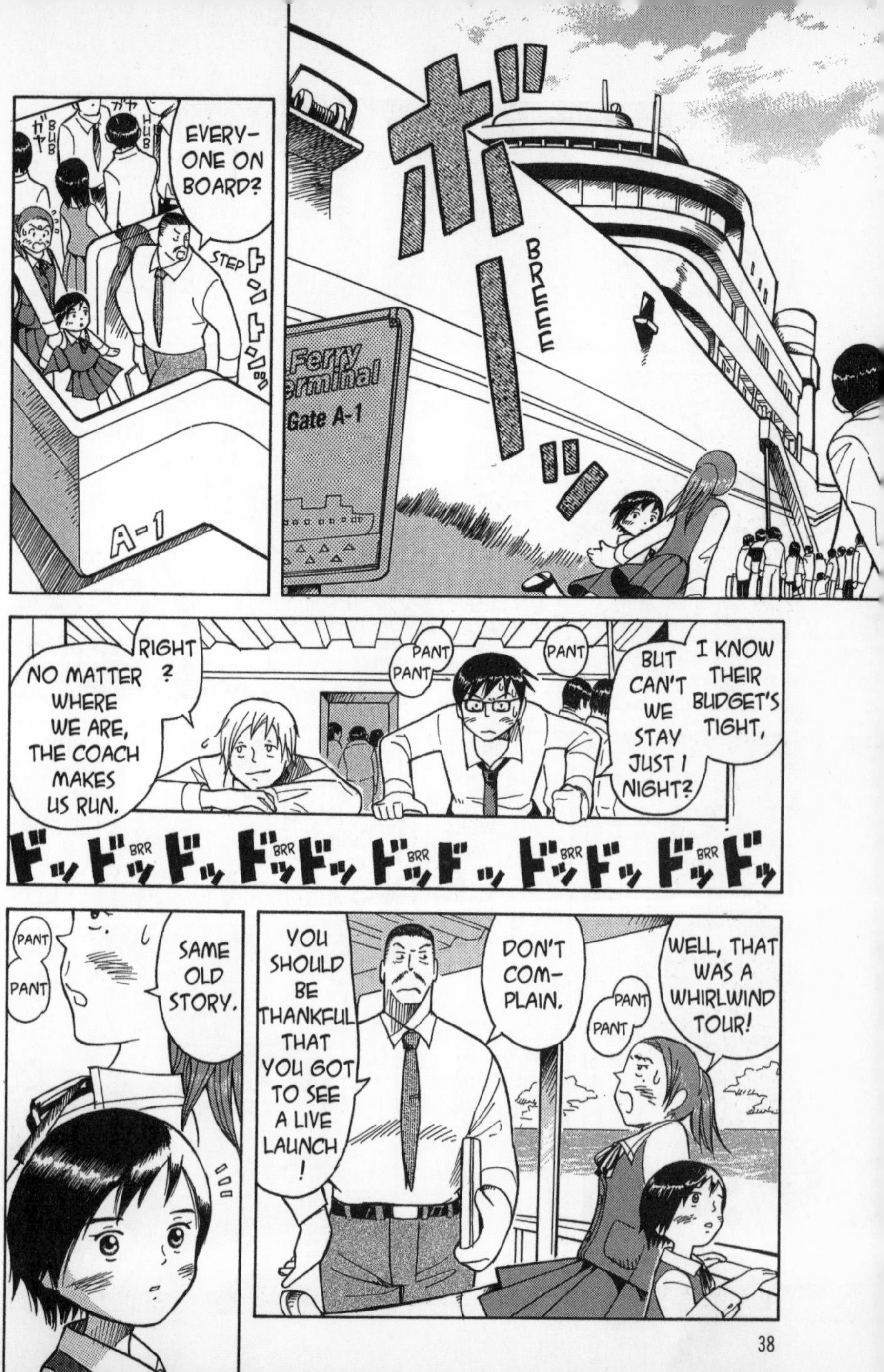
ボーッ
BREEE
ガヤ HUB
ガヤ BUB
EVERY-ONE ON BOARD?
STEP トットッ
I KNOW THEIR BUDGET'S TIGHT,
BUT CAN'T WE STAY JUST 1 NIGHT?
PANT
PANT PANT
RIGHT?
NO MATTER WHERE WE ARE, THE COACH MAKES US RUN.
ドッドッ BRR
WELL, THAT WAS A WHIRLWIND TOUR!
PANT PANT
DON'T COM-PLAIN.
YOU SHOULD BE THANKFUL THAT YOU GOT TO SEE A LIVE LAUNCH!
SAME OLD STORY.
PANT PANT

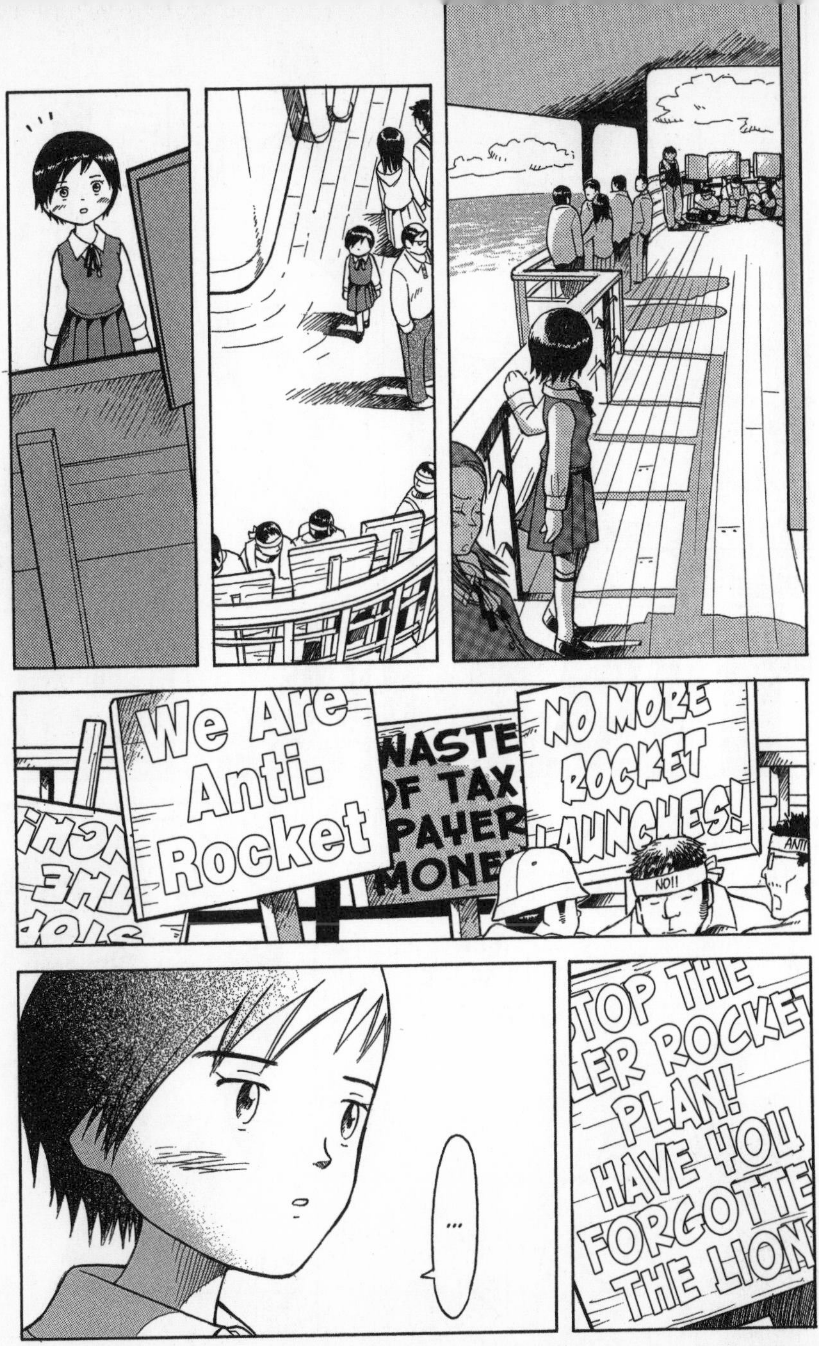
NO MORE ROCKET LAUNCHES!
WASTE OF TAX-PAYER MONE
We Are Anti-Rocket
ANTI
NO!!
TOP THE LER ROCKET PLAN! HAVE YOU FORGOTTE THE LION
...

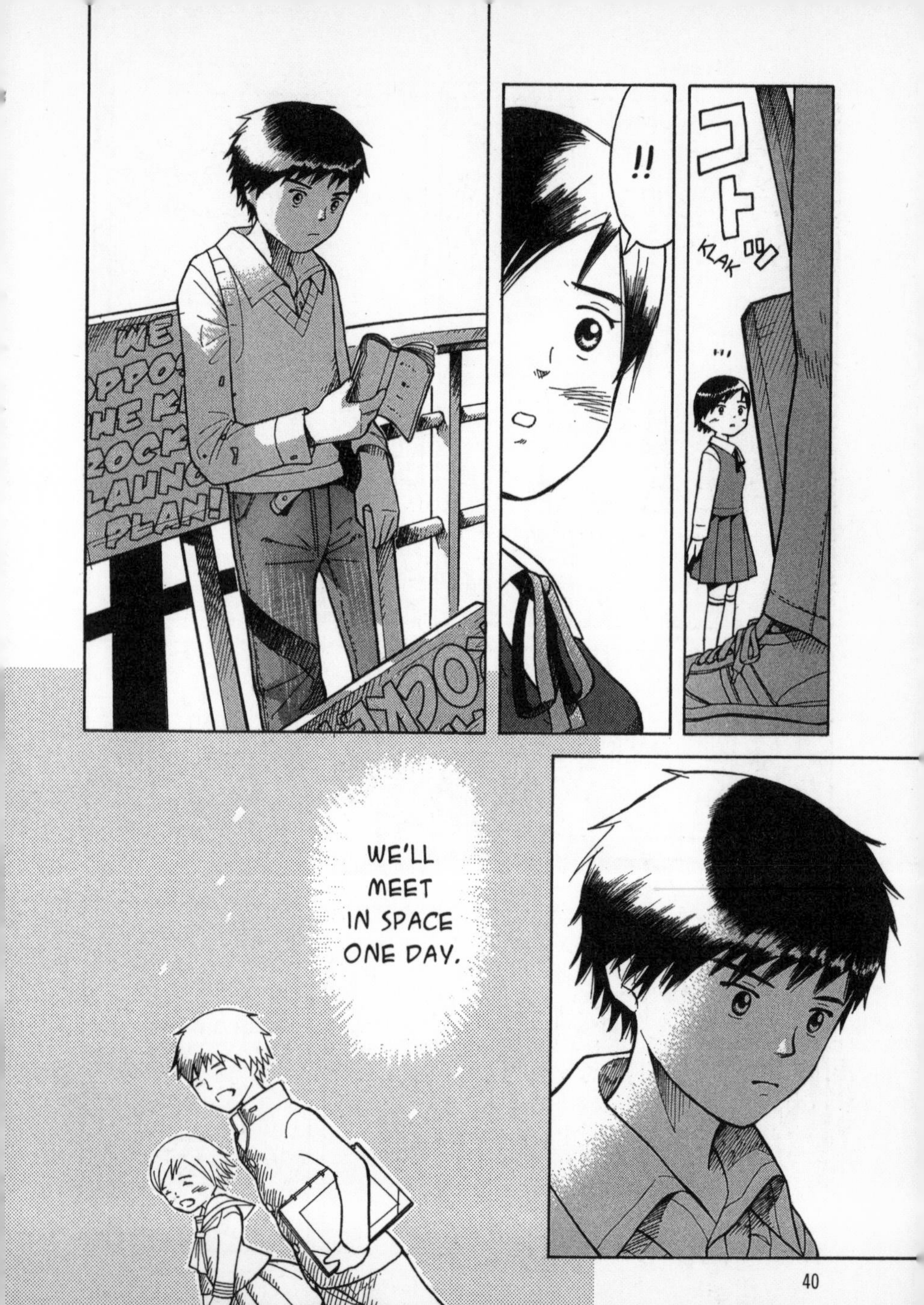
コト
KLAK
!!
WE
PLAN!
WE'LL MEET IN SPACE ONE DAY.

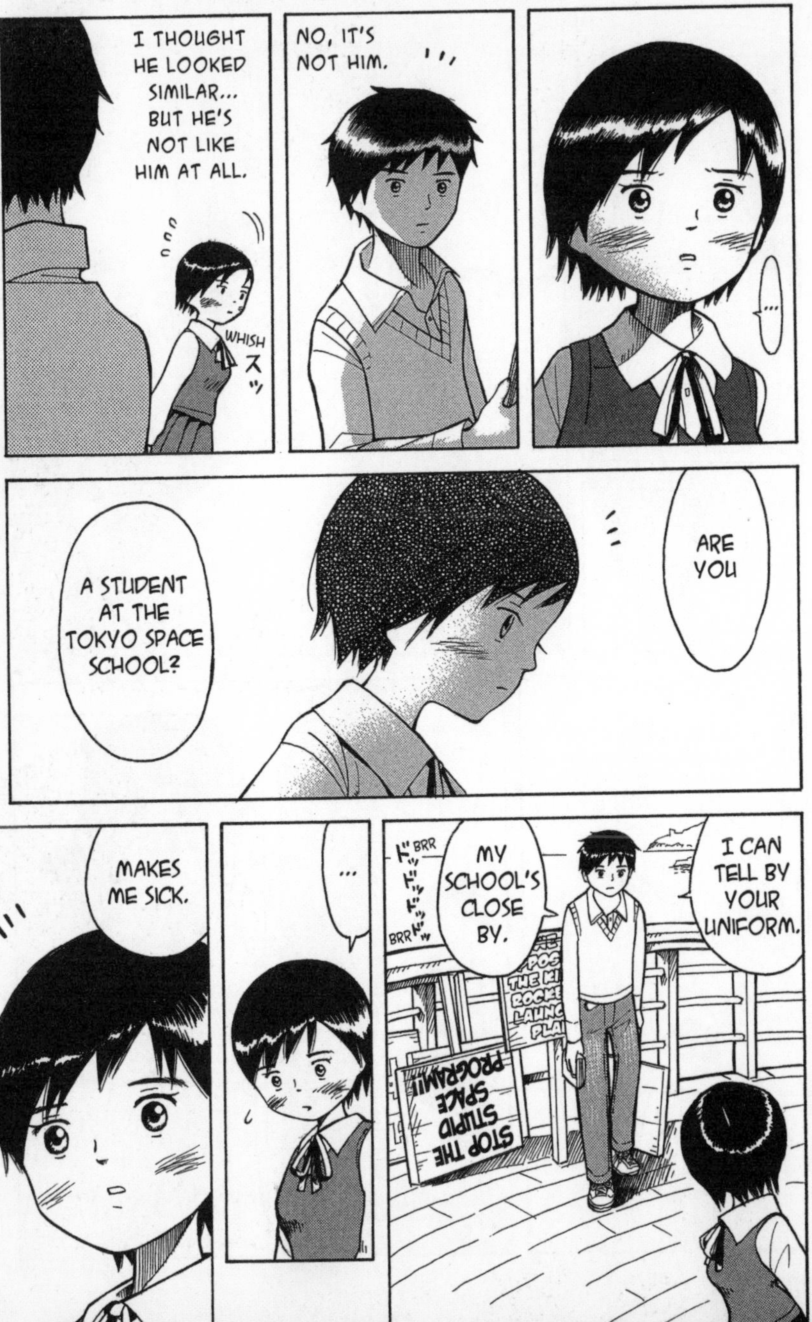
....
NO, IT'S NOT HIM.
I THOUGHT HE LOOKED SIMILAR... BUT HE'S NOT LIKE HIM AT ALL.
WHISH
スッ
ARE YOU
A STUDENT AT THE TOKYO SPACE SCHOOL?
I CAN TELL BY YOUR UNIFORM.
MY SCHOOL'S CLOSE BY.
BRR
ドッドッドッドッ
BRR
STOP THE STUPID SPACE PROGRAM!!
...
MAKES ME SICK.

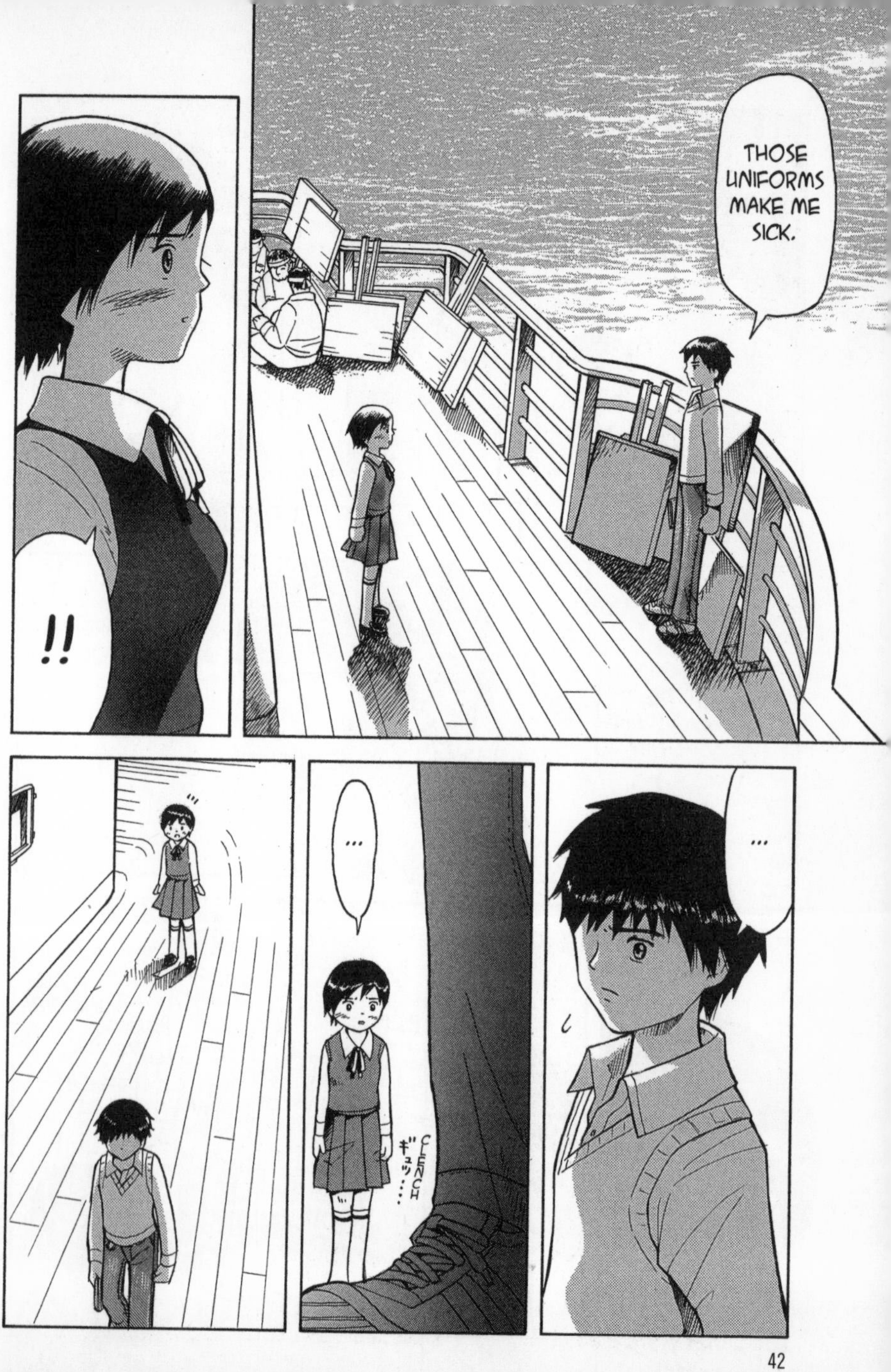
THOSE UNIFORMS MAKE ME SICK.
!!
...
...
CLENCH
ギュッ…

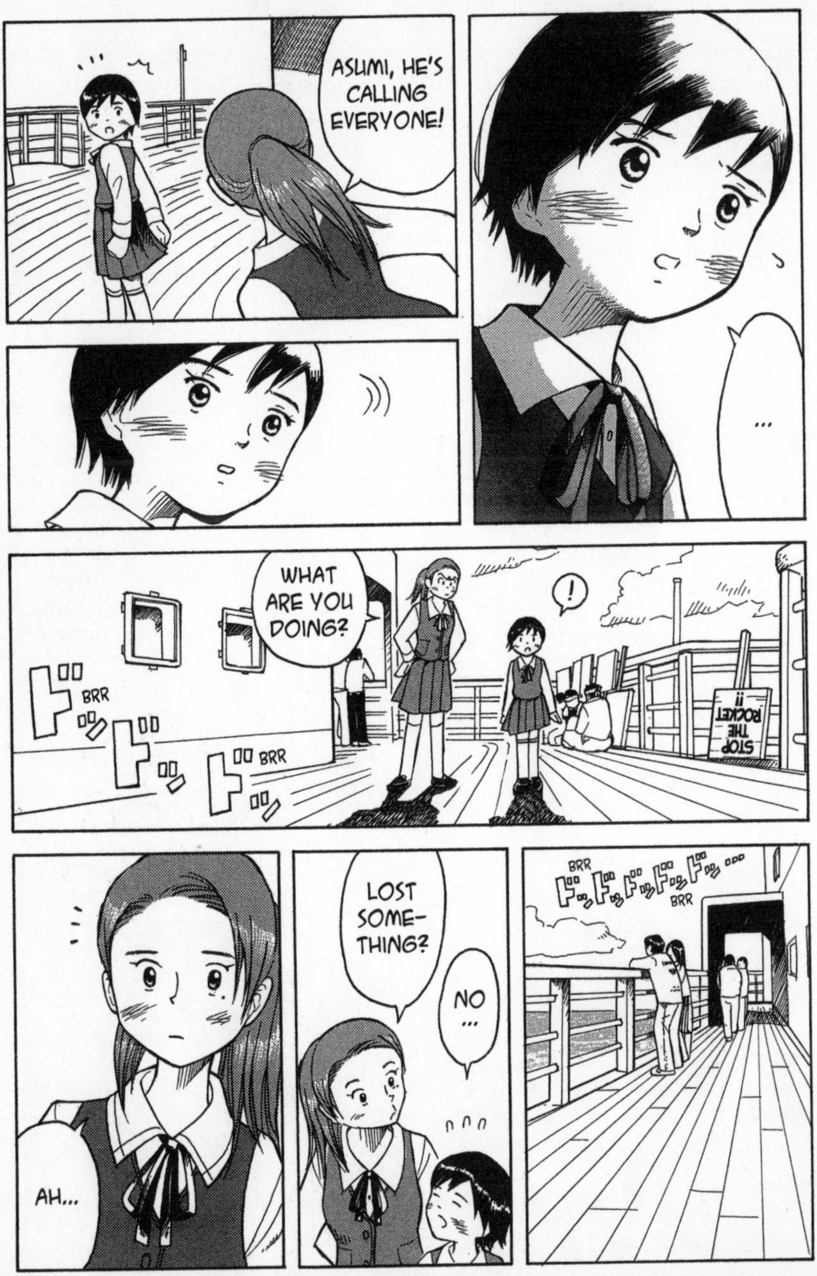
...
ASUMI, HE'S CALLING EVERYONE!
!
WHAT ARE YOU DOING?
STOP THE ROCKET!!
BRR
BRR
BRR
BRR
LOST SOME-THING?
NO ...
AH...

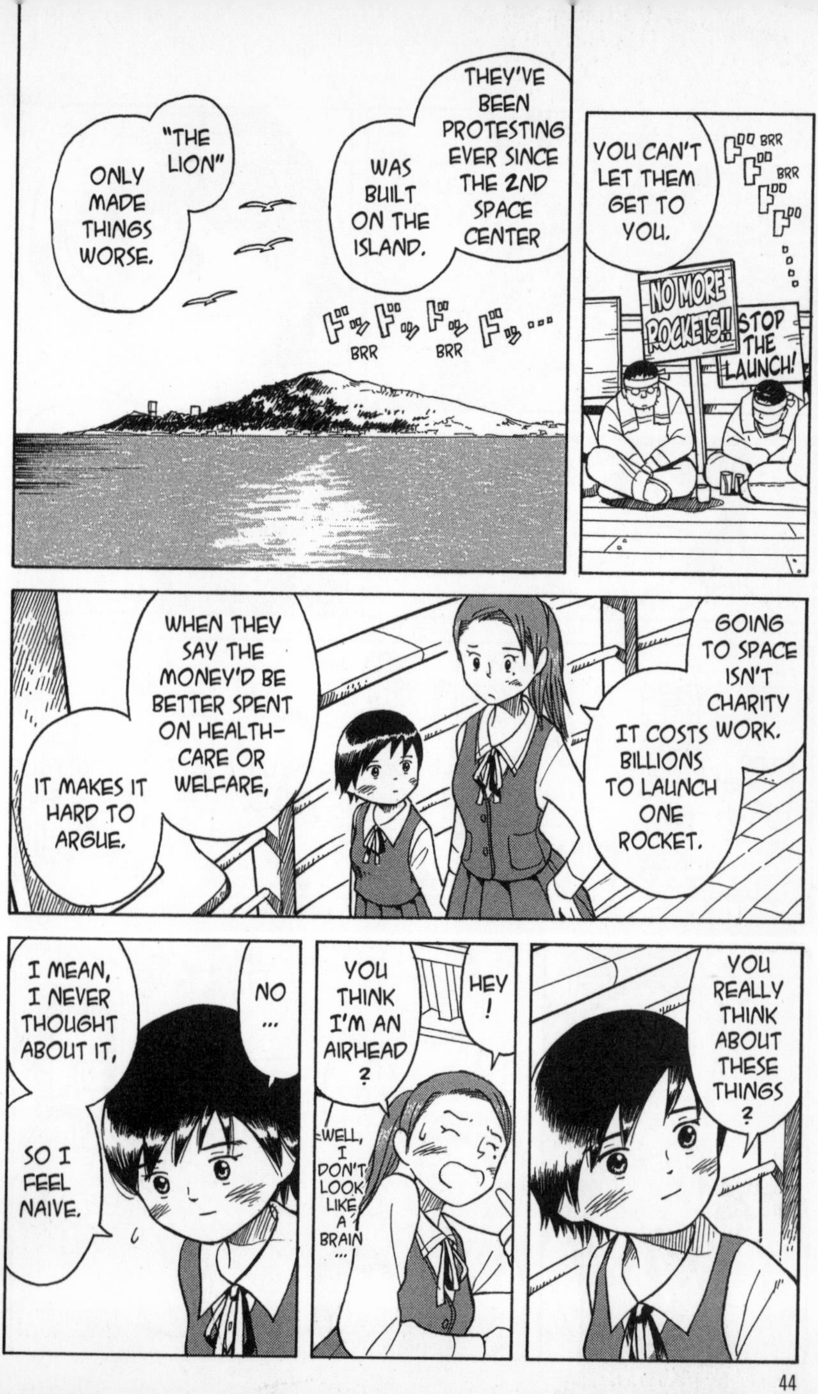
YOU CAN'T LET THEM GET TO YOU.
BRR BRR
NO MORE ROCKETS!!
STOP THE LAUNCH!
THEY'VE BEEN PROTESTING EVER SINCE THE 2ND SPACE CENTER
WAS BUILT ON THE ISLAND.
"THE LION"
ONLY MADE THINGS WORSE.
BRR BRR
GOING TO SPACE ISN'T CHARITY WORK.
IT COSTS BILLIONS TO LAUNCH ONE ROCKET.
WHEN THEY SAY THE MONEY'D BE BETTER SPENT ON HEALTH-CARE OR WELFARE,
IT MAKES IT HARD TO ARGUE.
YOU REALLY THINK ABOUT THESE THINGS?
HEY!
YOU THINK I'M AN AIRHEAD?
WELL, I DON'T LOOK LIKE A BRAIN...
NO...
I MEAN, I NEVER THOUGHT ABOUT IT,
SO I FEEL NAIVE.

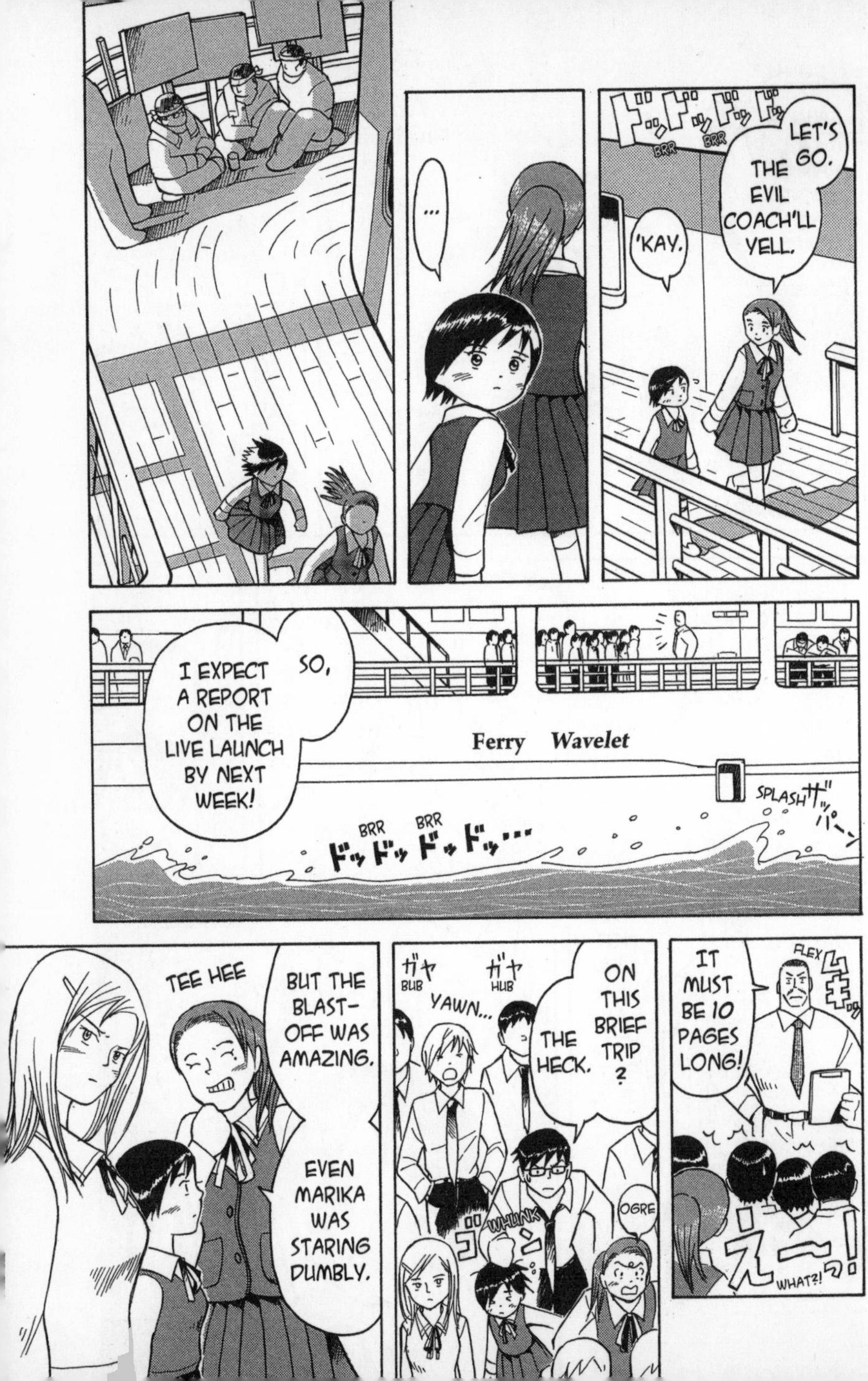

BRR BRR
LET'S GO. THE EVIL COACH'LL YELL.
'KAY.
...
SO,
I EXPECT A REPORT ON THE LIVE LAUNCH BY NEXT WEEK!
Ferry Wavelet
SPLASH
BRR BRR
FLEX
IT MUST BE 10 PAGES LONG!
WHAT?!
ON THIS BRIEF TRIP?
THE HECK.
BUB HUB
YAWN...
OGRE
WHUNK
BUT THE BLAST-OFF WAS AMAZING.
TEE HEE
EVEN MARIKA WAS STARING DUMBLY.

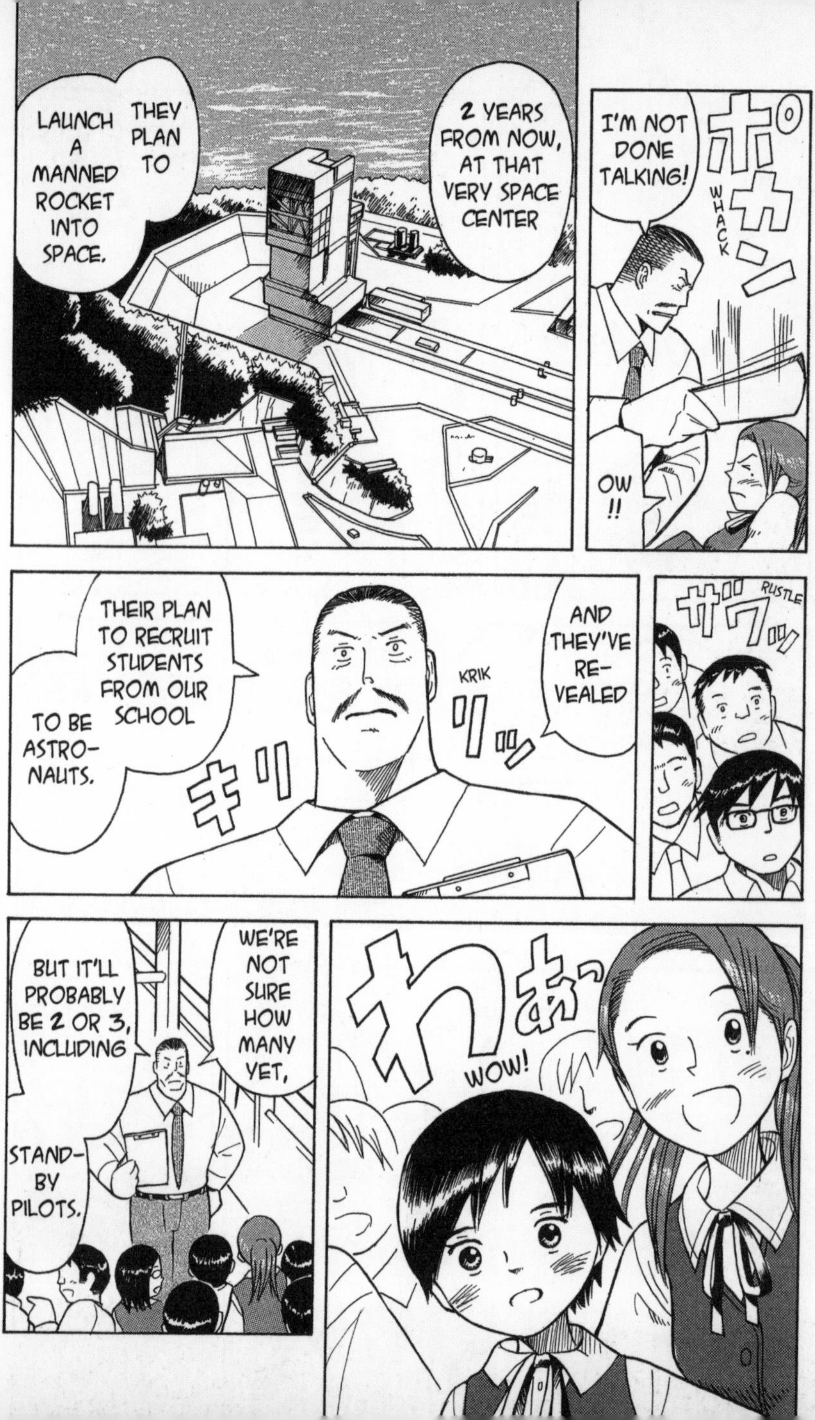
I'M NOT DONE TALKING!
ポカーン
WHACK
OW !!
2 YEARS FROM NOW, AT THAT VERY SPACE CENTER
THEY PLAN TO
LAUNCH A MANNED ROCKET INTO SPACE.
サワッ
RUSTLE
AND THEY'VE RE-VEALED
KRIK
キリッ
THEIR PLAN TO RECRUIT STUDENTS FROM OUR SCHOOL
TO BE ASTRO-NAUTS.
わあっ
WOW!
WE'RE NOT SURE HOW MANY YET,
BUT IT'LL PROBABLY BE 2 OR 3, INCLUDING
STAND-BY PILOTS.

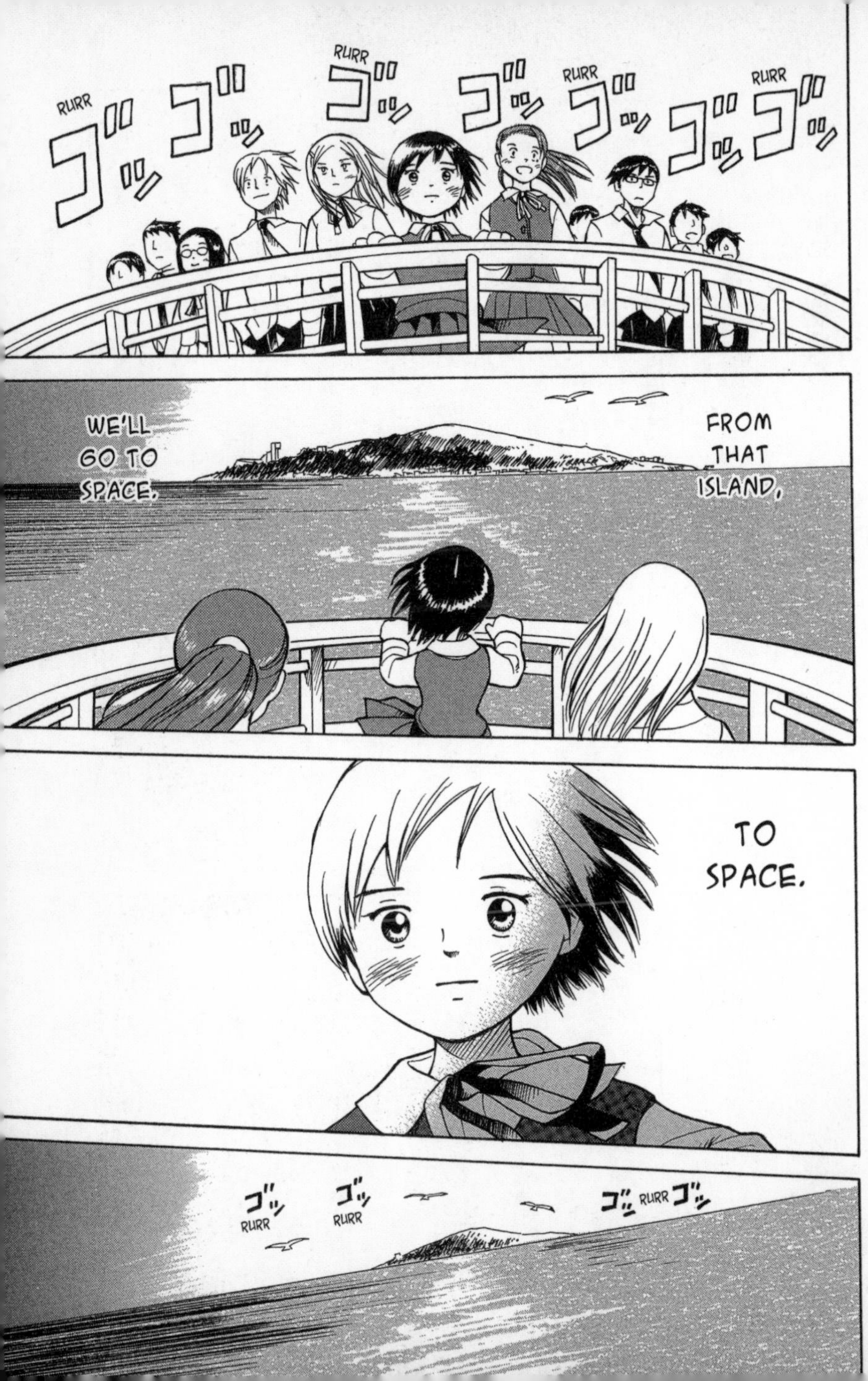
ゴッ ゴッ
RURR
ゴッ ゴッ
RURR
ゴッ
RURR
ゴッ
ゴッ ゴッ
RURR
FROM THAT ISLAND,
WE'LL GO TO SPACE.
TO SPACE.
ゴッ RURR ゴッ
ゴッ
RURR
ゴッ
RURR

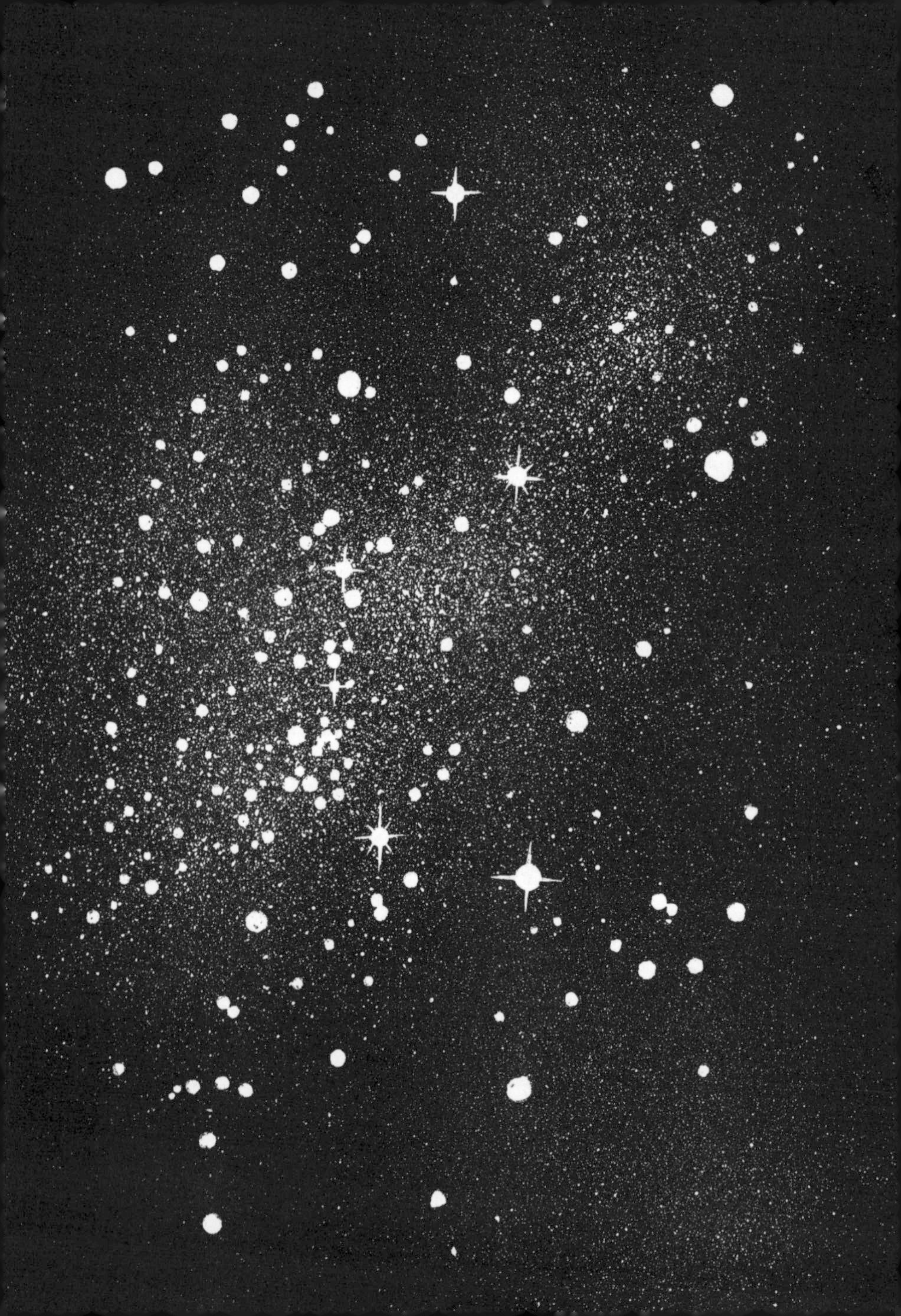

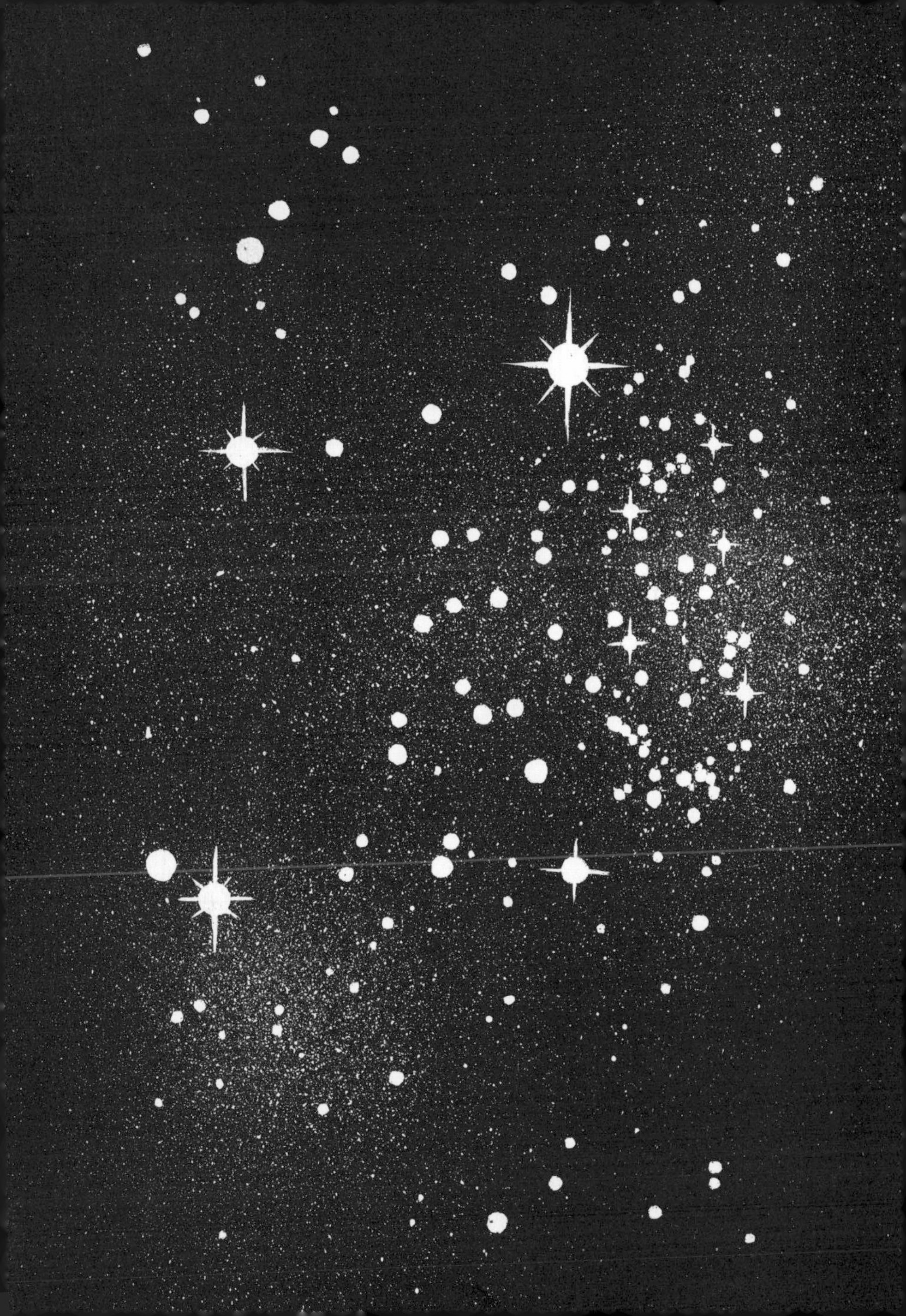

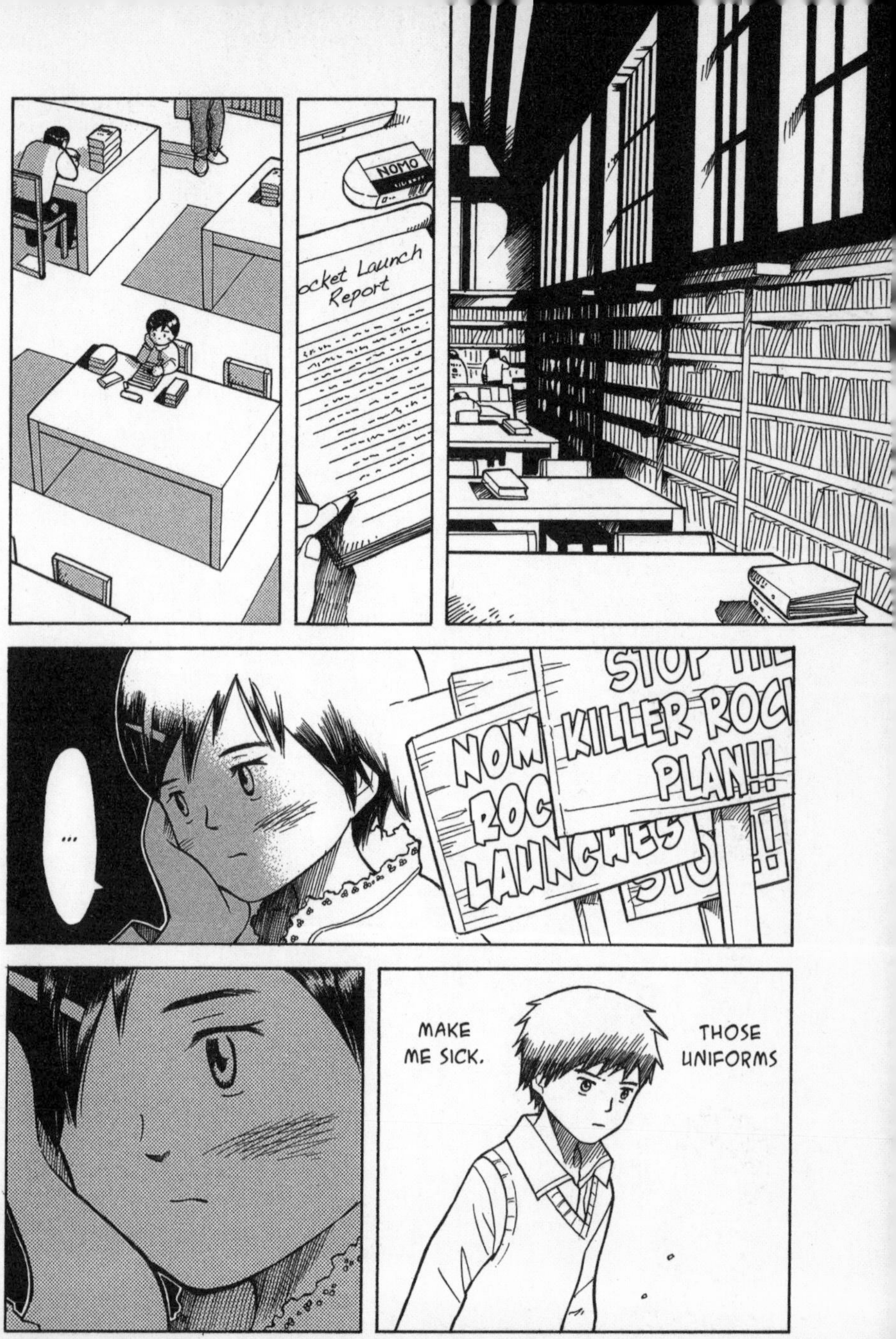

ocket Launch Report
NOMO
KILLER ROC PLAN!!
NOM ROC LAUNCHES
...
THOSE UNIFORMS
MAKE ME SICK.

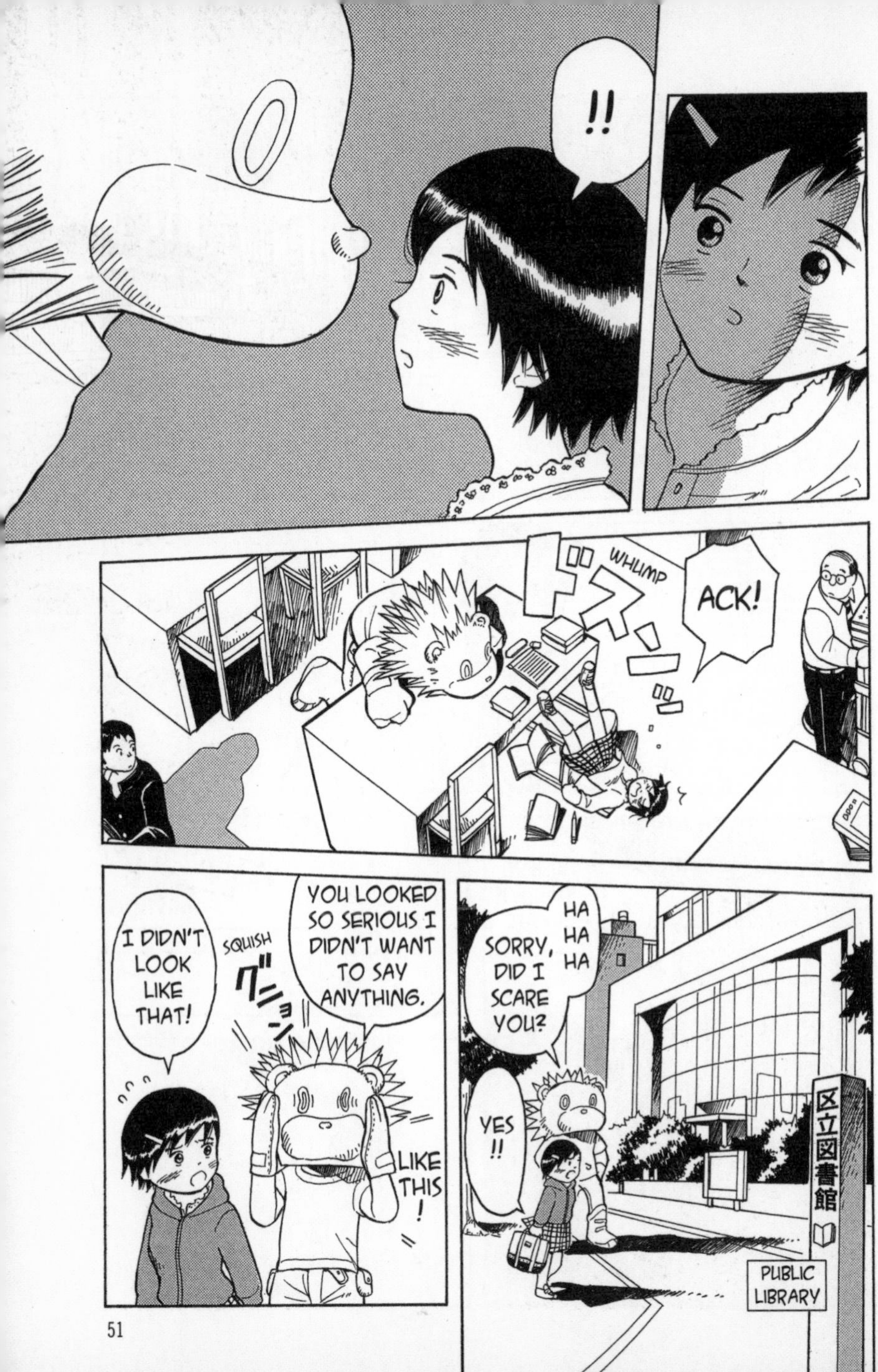
!!
WHUMP
ACK!
HA HA HA
SORRY, DID I SCARE YOU?
YES !!
区立図書館
PUBLIC LIBRARY
YOU LOOKED SO SERIOUS I DIDN'T WANT TO SAY ANYTHING.
SQUISH
I DIDN'T LOOK LIKE THAT!
LIKE THIS!

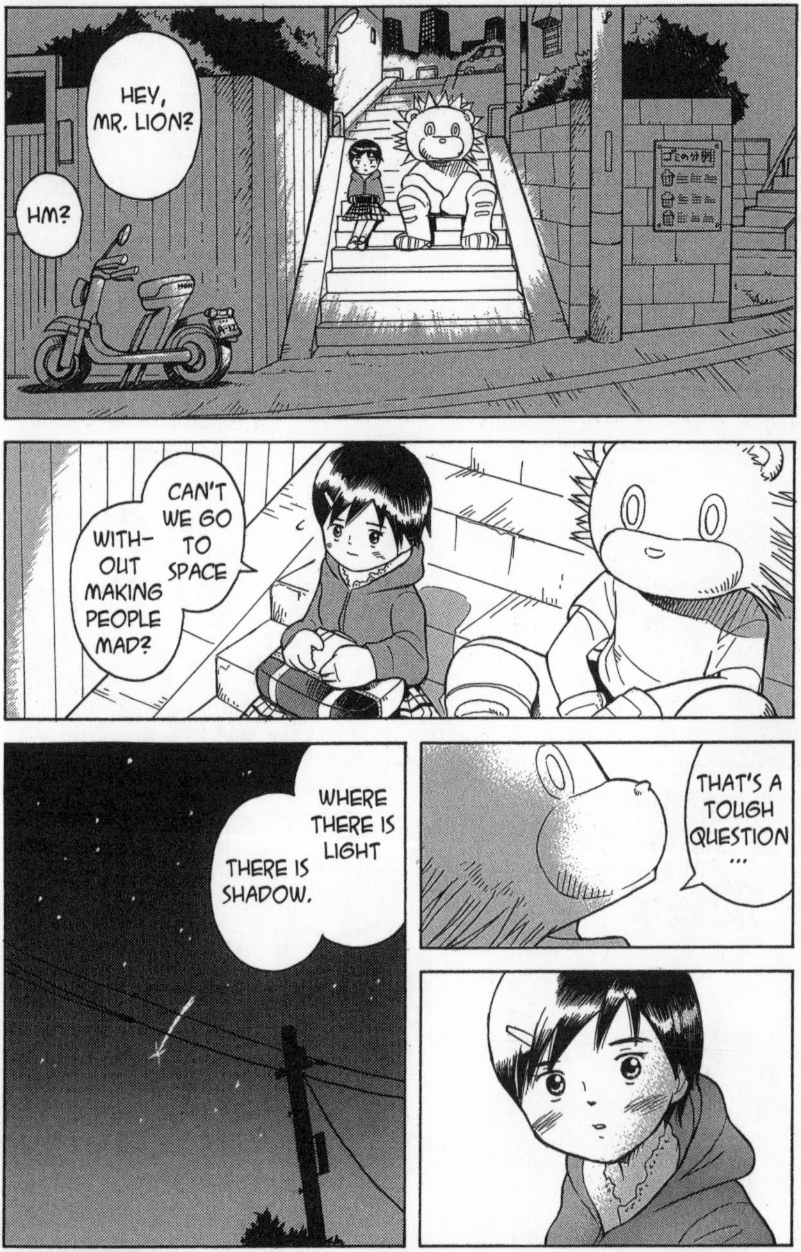
HEY, MR. LION?
HM?
CAN'T WE GO TO SPACE WITHOUT MAKING PEOPLE MAD?
THAT'S A TOUGH QUESTION ...
WHERE THERE IS LIGHT THERE IS SHADOW.

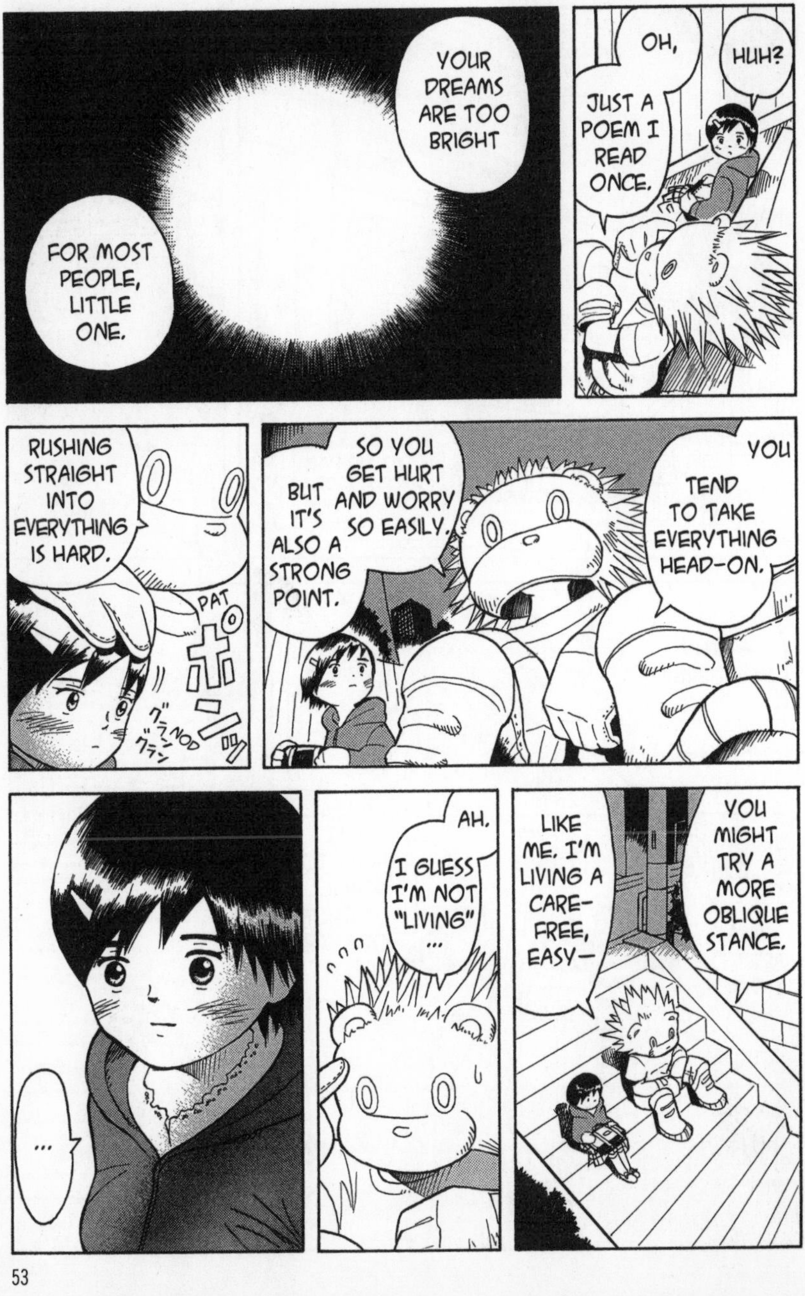
HUH?
OH, JUST A POEM I READ ONCE.
YOUR DREAMS ARE TOO BRIGHT
FOR MOST PEOPLE, LITTLE ONE.
YOU TEND TO TAKE EVERYTHING HEAD-ON.
SO YOU GET HURT AND WORRY SO EASILY.
BUT IT'S ALSO A STRONG POINT.
RUSHING STRAIGHT INTO EVERYTHING IS HARD.
PAT
ポン
NOD
グラングラン
YOU MIGHT TRY A MORE OBLIQUE STANCE.
LIKE ME. I'M LIVING A CARE-FREE, EASY—
AH, I GUESS I'M NOT "LIVING" ...
...

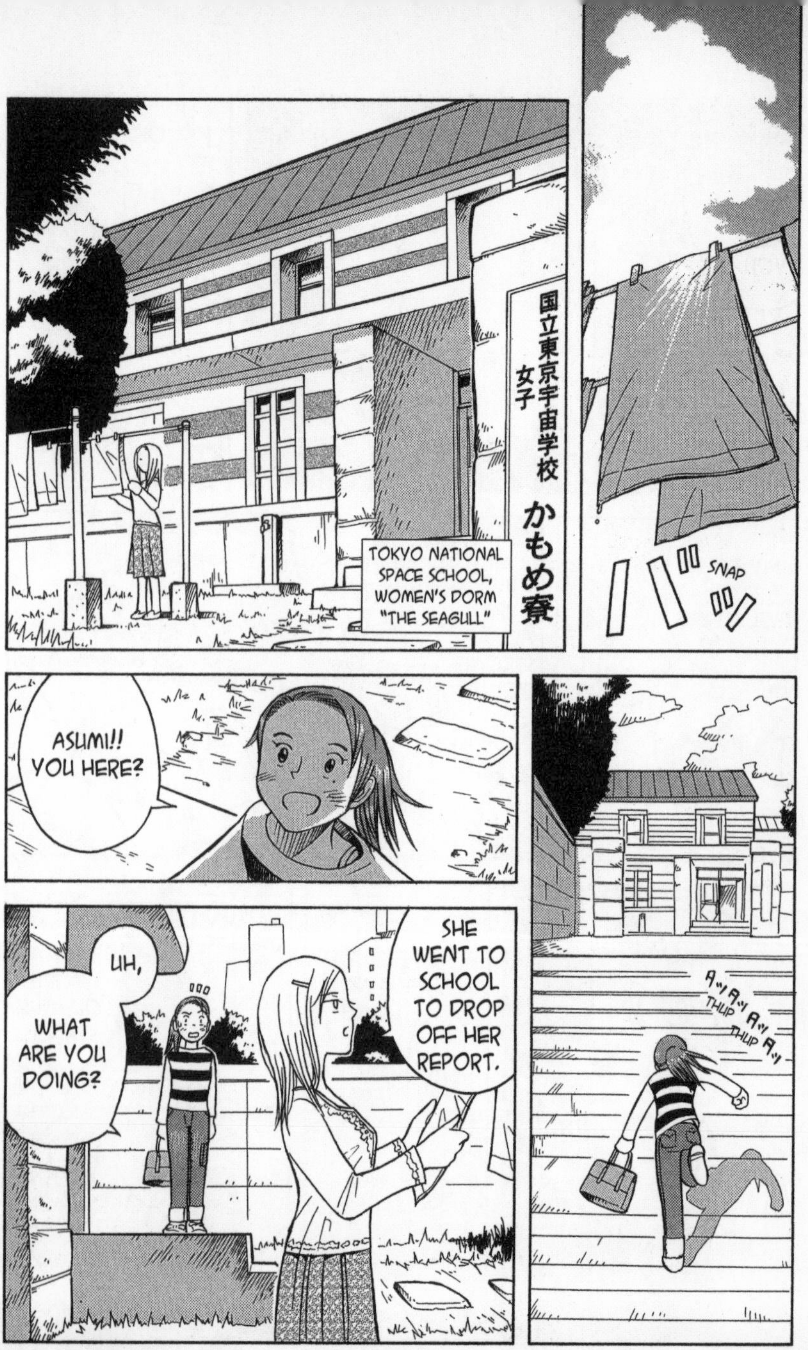
バッ
SNAP
国立東京宇宙学校
女子
かもめ寮
TOKYO NATIONAL SPACE SCHOOL, WOMEN'S DORM "THE SEAGULL"
タッタッタッタッ
THUP THUP
ASUMI!! YOU HERE?
SHE WENT TO SCHOOL TO DROP OFF HER REPORT.
UH,
WHAT ARE YOU DOING?

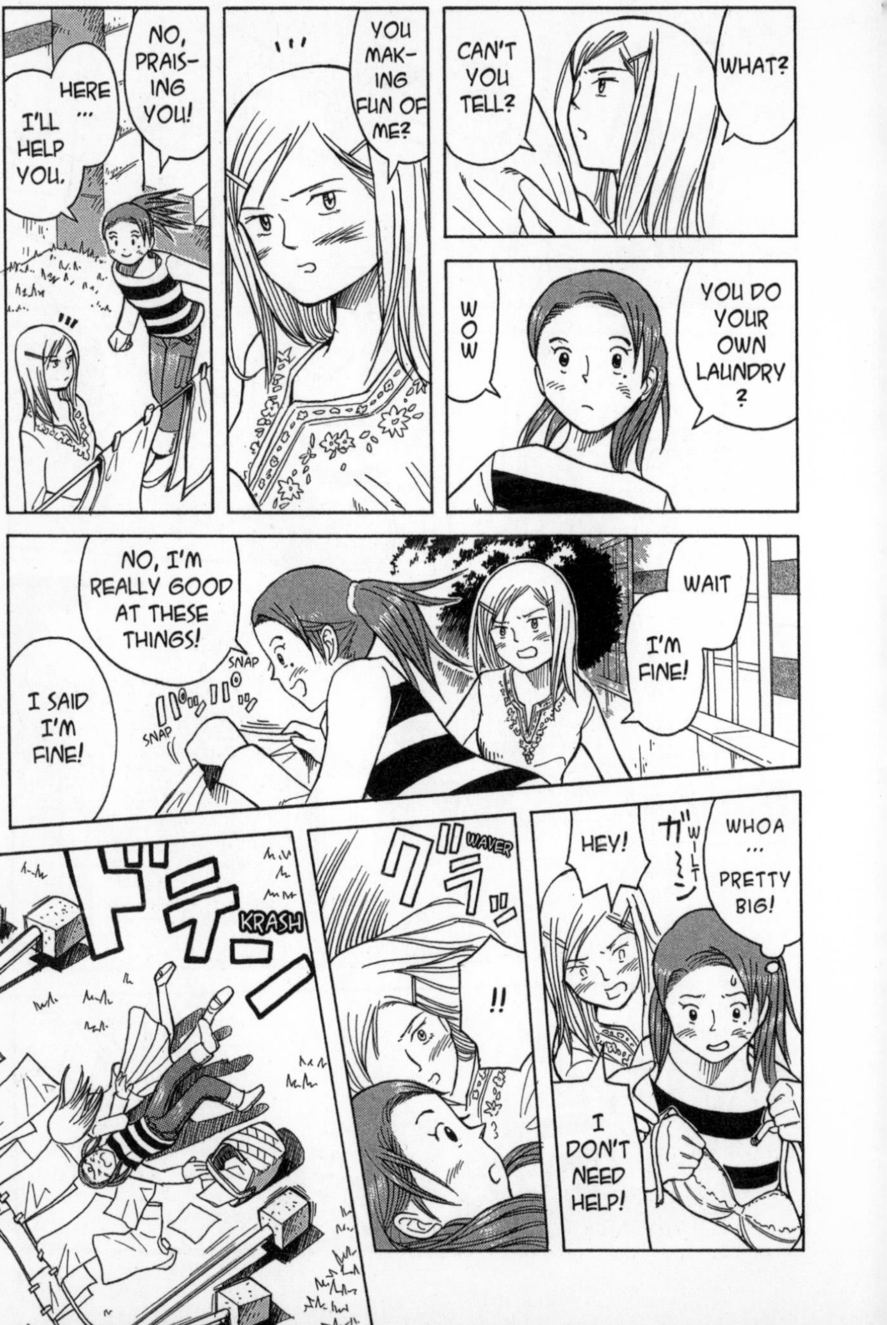
WHAT?
CAN'T YOU TELL?
YOU DO YOUR OWN LAUNDRY?
WOW
...
YOU MAKING FUN OF ME?
NO, PRAISING YOU!
HERE ... I'LL HELP YOU.
WAIT
I'M FINE!
NO, I'M REALLY GOOD AT THESE THINGS!
SNAP
SNAP
I SAID I'M FINE!
WHOA ... PRETTY BIG!
WILT
HEY!
I DON'T NEED HELP!
WAVER
!!
KRASH

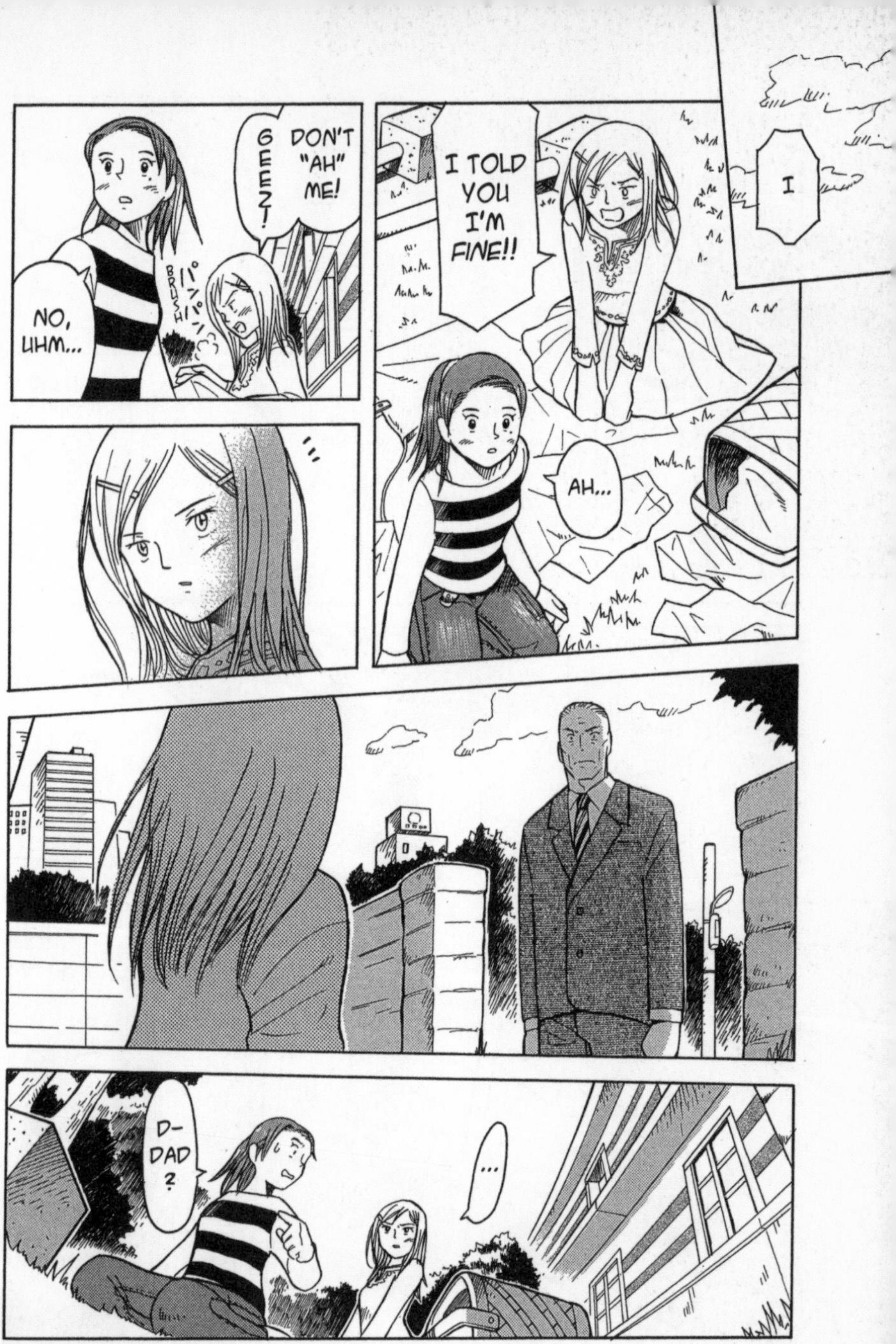
I
I TOLD YOU I'M FINE!!
AH...
DON'T "AH" ME!
GEEZ!
BRUSH
NO, UHM...
...
D-DAD?

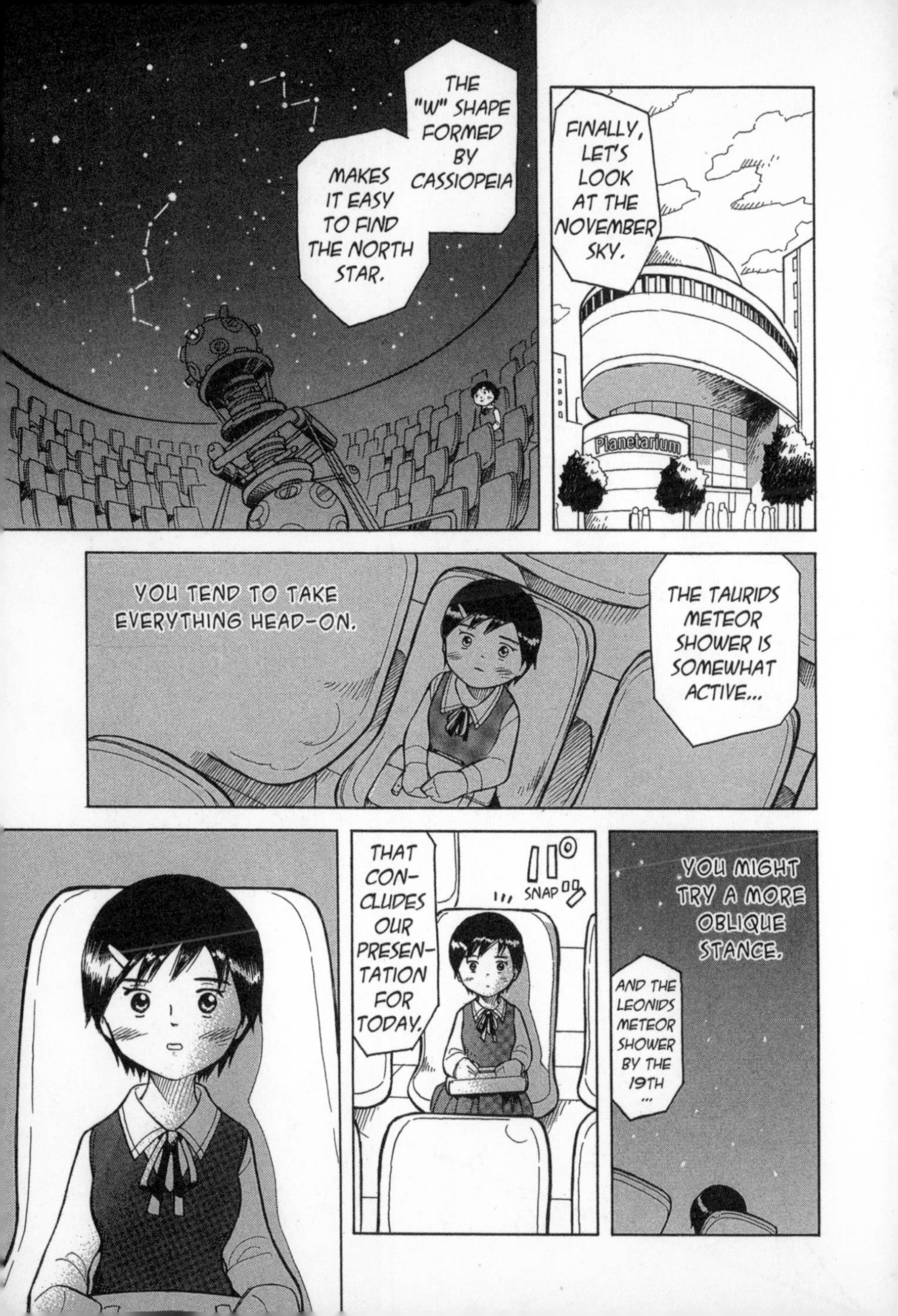
FINALLY, LET'S LOOK AT THE NOVEMBER SKY.
Planetarium
THE "W" SHAPE FORMED BY CASSIOPEIA
MAKES IT EASY TO FIND THE NORTH STAR.
THE TAURIDS METEOR SHOWER IS SOMEWHAT ACTIVE...
YOU TEND TO TAKE EVERYTHING HEAD-ON.
YOU MIGHT TRY A MORE OBLIQUE STANCE.
AND THE LEONIDS METEOR SHOWER BY THE 19TH ...
THAT CON-CLUDES OUR PRESEN-TATION FOR TODAY.
SNAP

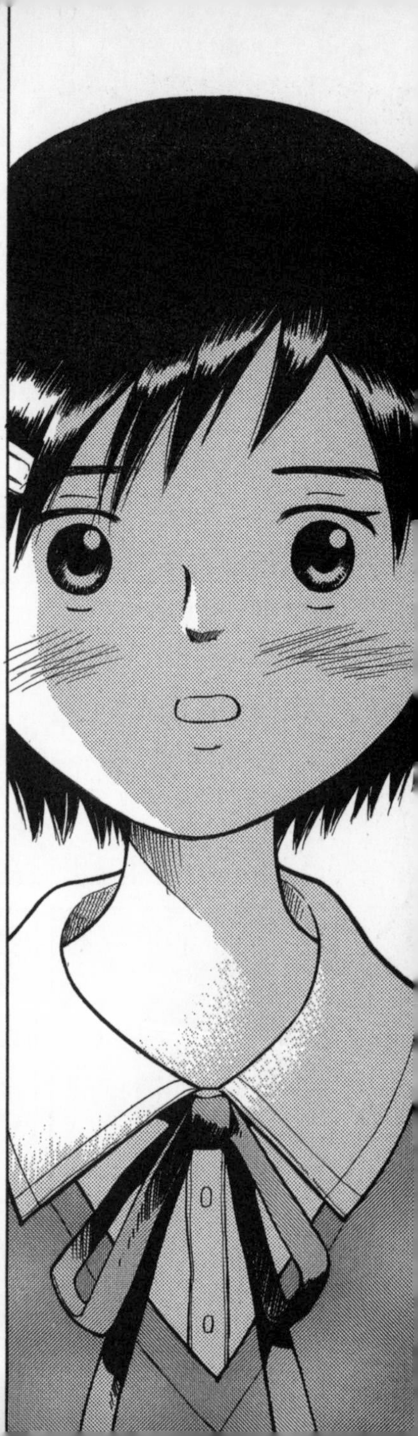
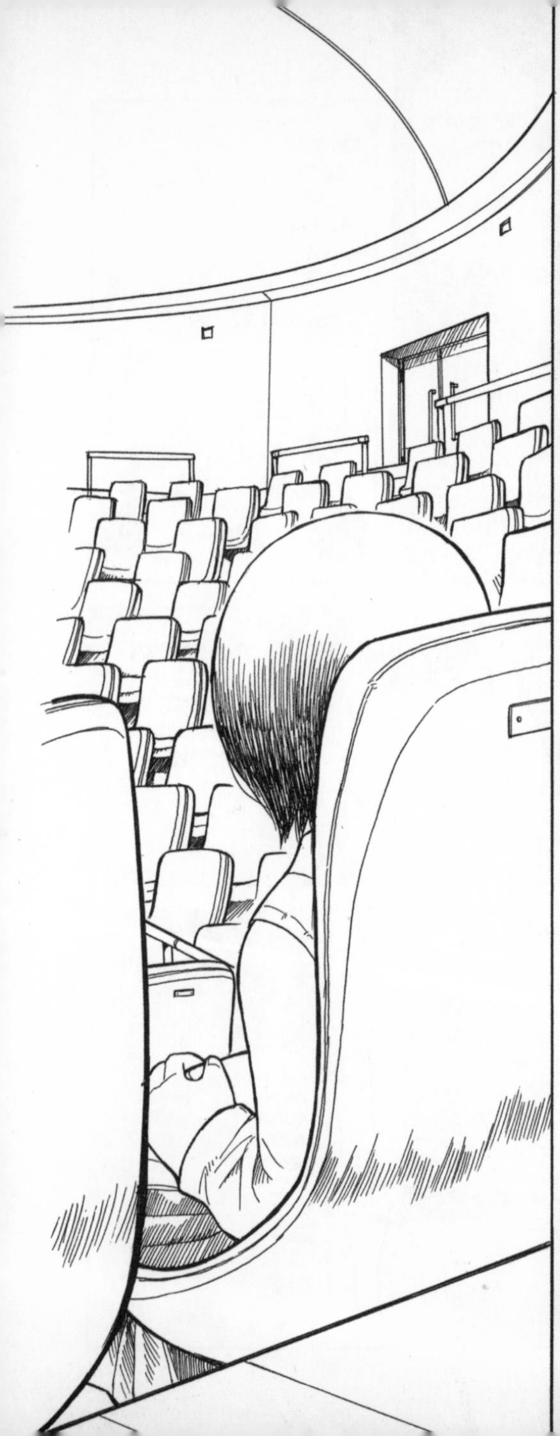

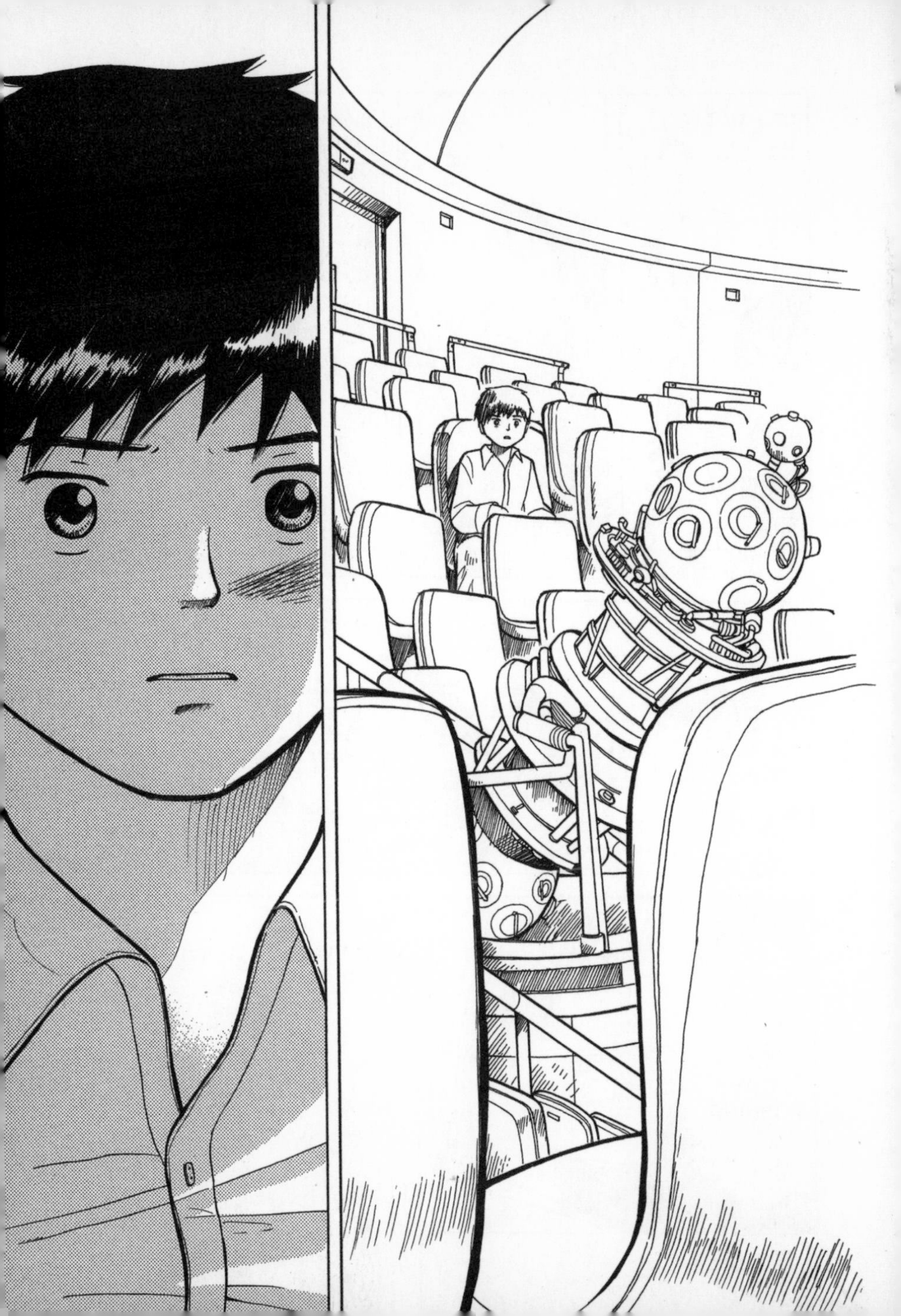

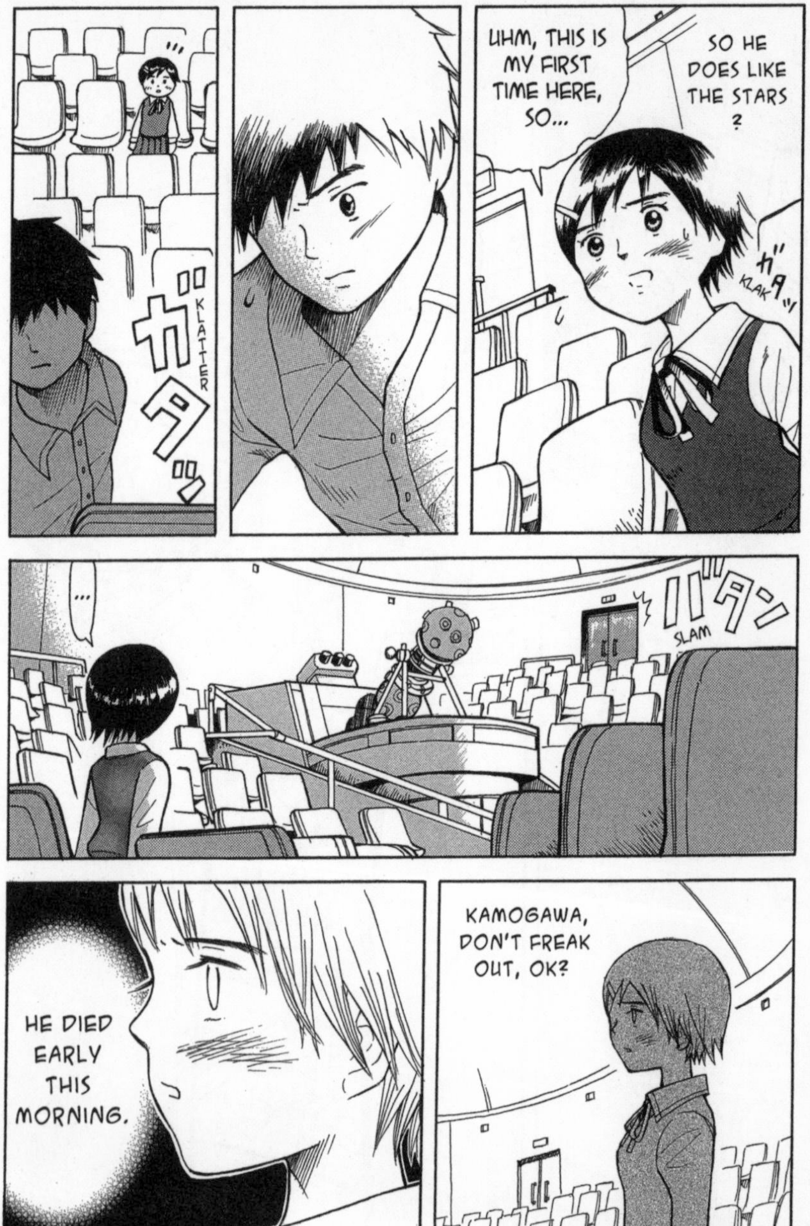
SO HE DOES LIKE THE STARS ?
UHM, THIS IS MY FIRST TIME HERE, SO...
ガタッ
KLAK
ガタッ
KLATTER
バタン
SLAM
...
KAMOGAWA, DON'T FREAK OUT, OK?
HE DIED EARLY THIS MORNING.

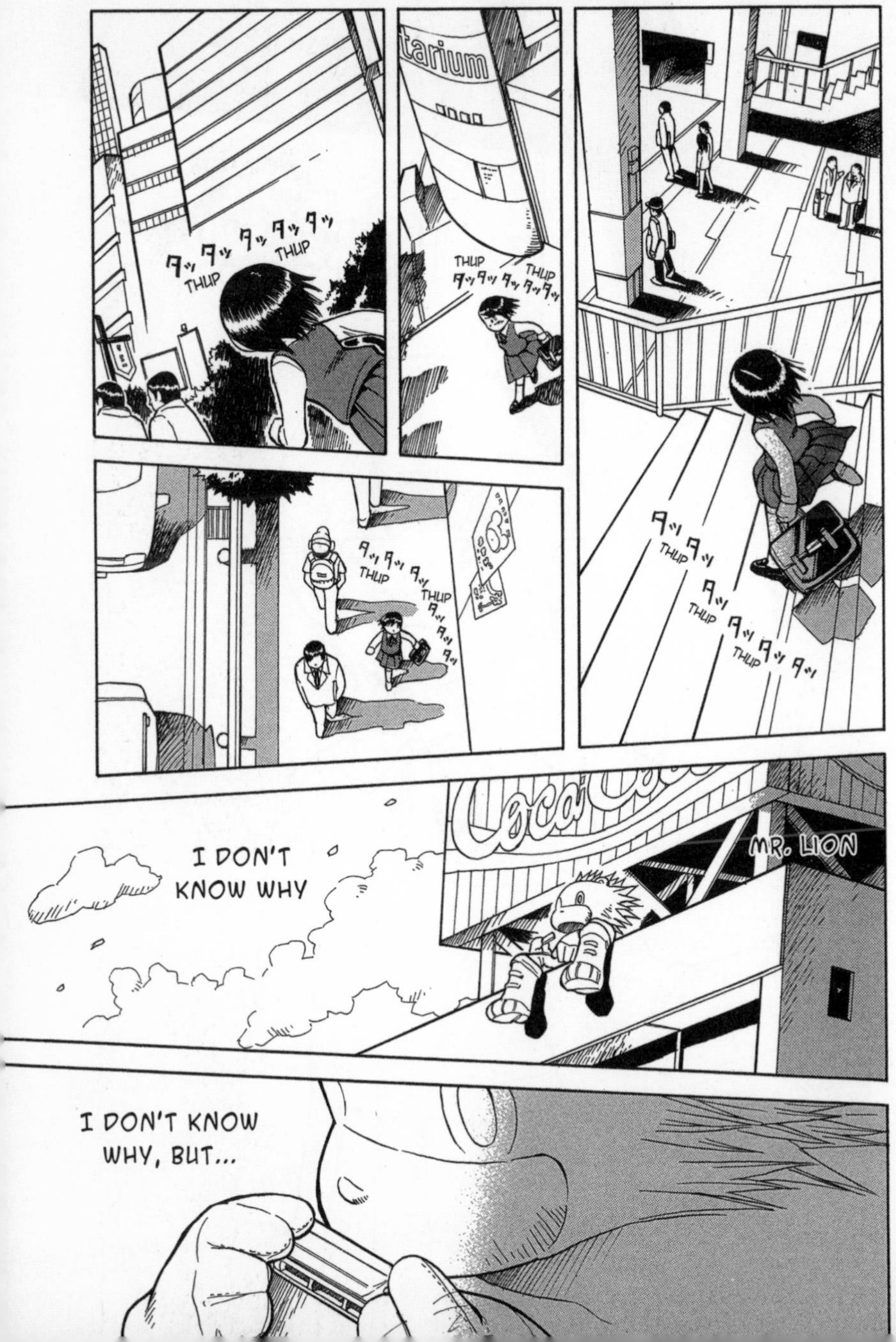

タッ THUP タッ
タッ THUP タッ
タッ THUP タッ タッ
tarium
THUP THUP
タッタッ タッ タッタッ
タッ タッ タッ タッ タッ
THUP THUP
タッ タッ タッ
THUP THUP
タッ タッ タッ
MR. LION
I DON'T KNOW WHY
I DON'T KNOW WHY, BUT...

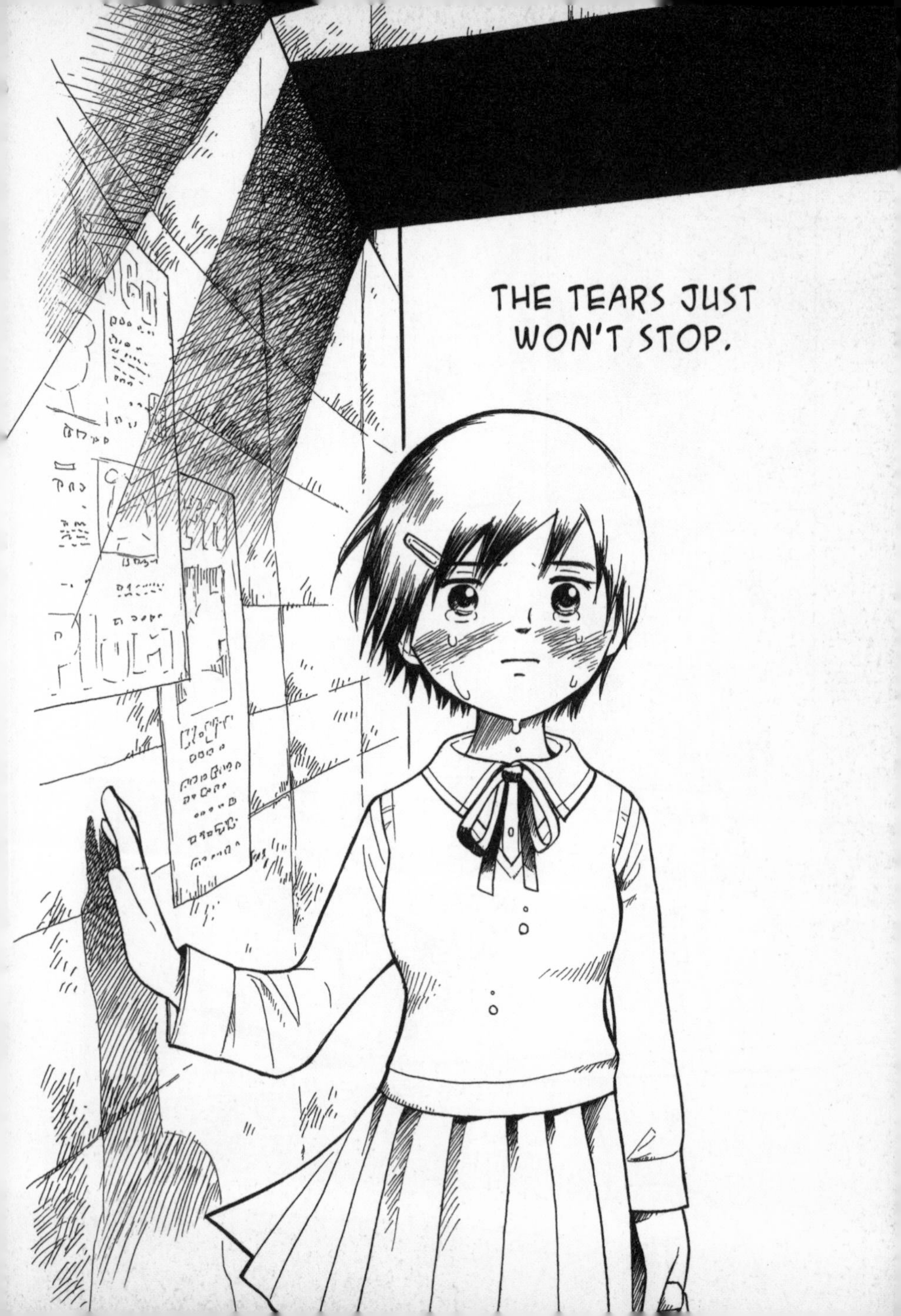
THE TEARS JUST WON'T STOP.

MISSION:16

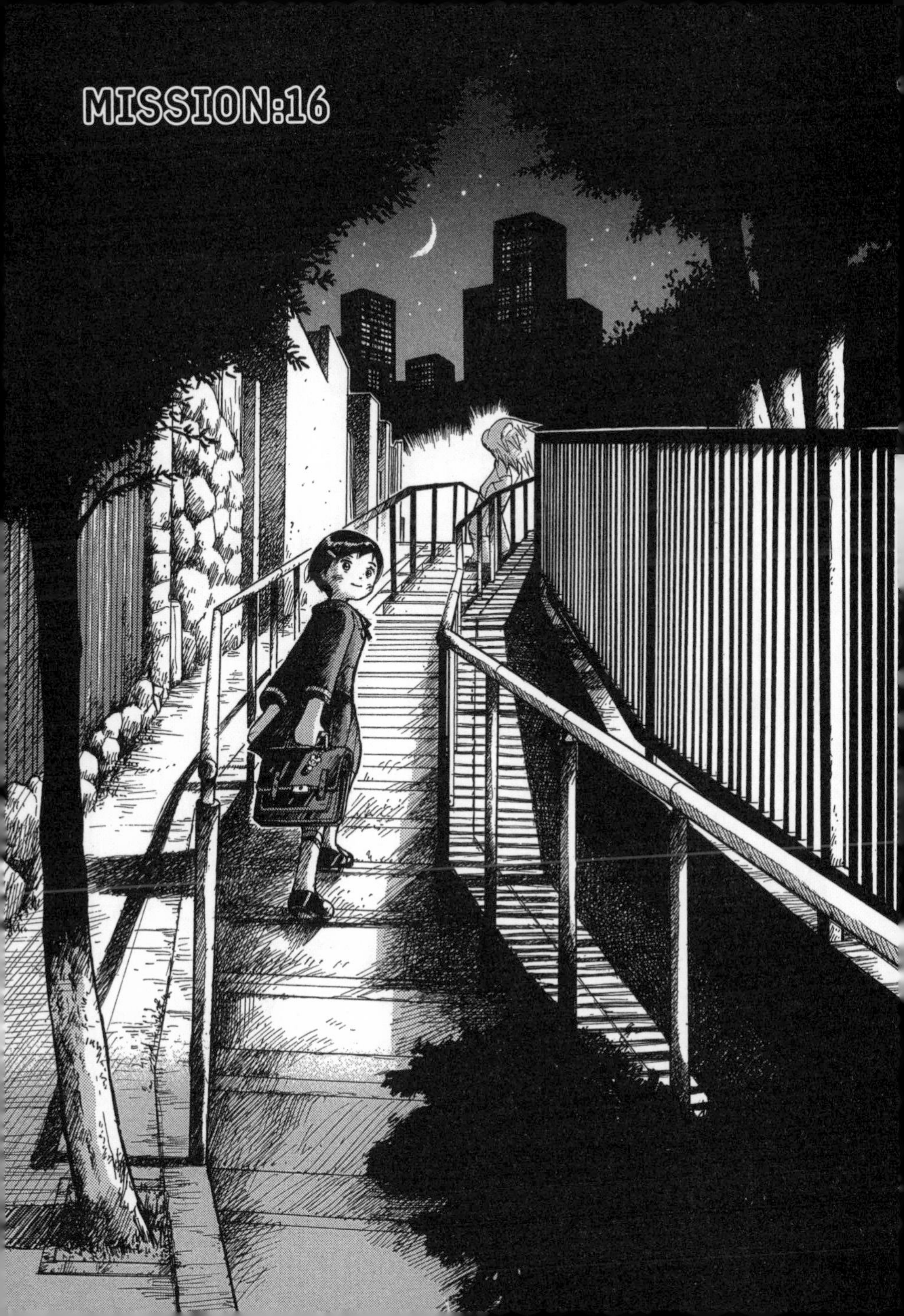

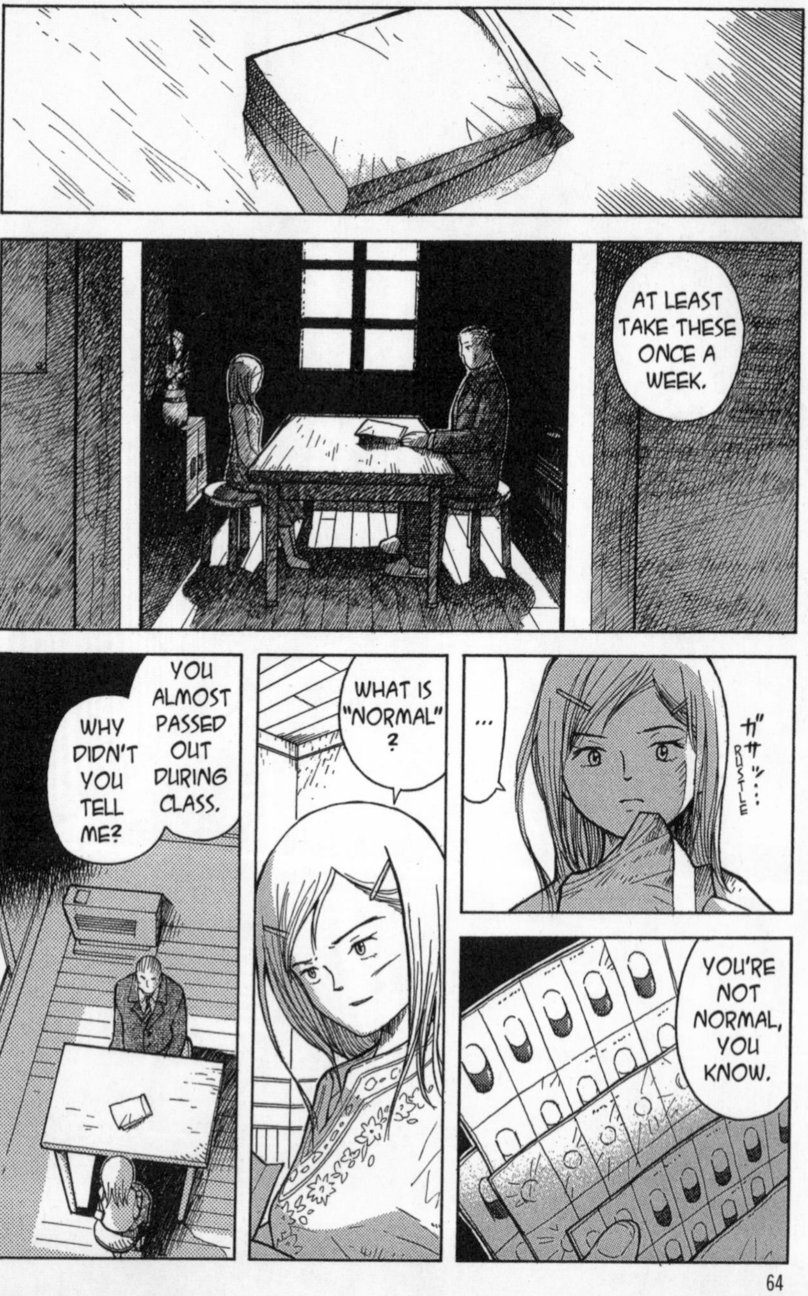
AT LEAST TAKE THESE ONCE A WEEK.
...
ガサッ…
RUSTLE
YOU'RE NOT NORMAL, YOU KNOW.
WHAT IS "NORMAL"?
YOU ALMOST PASSED OUT DURING CLASS.
WHY DIDN'T YOU TELL ME?

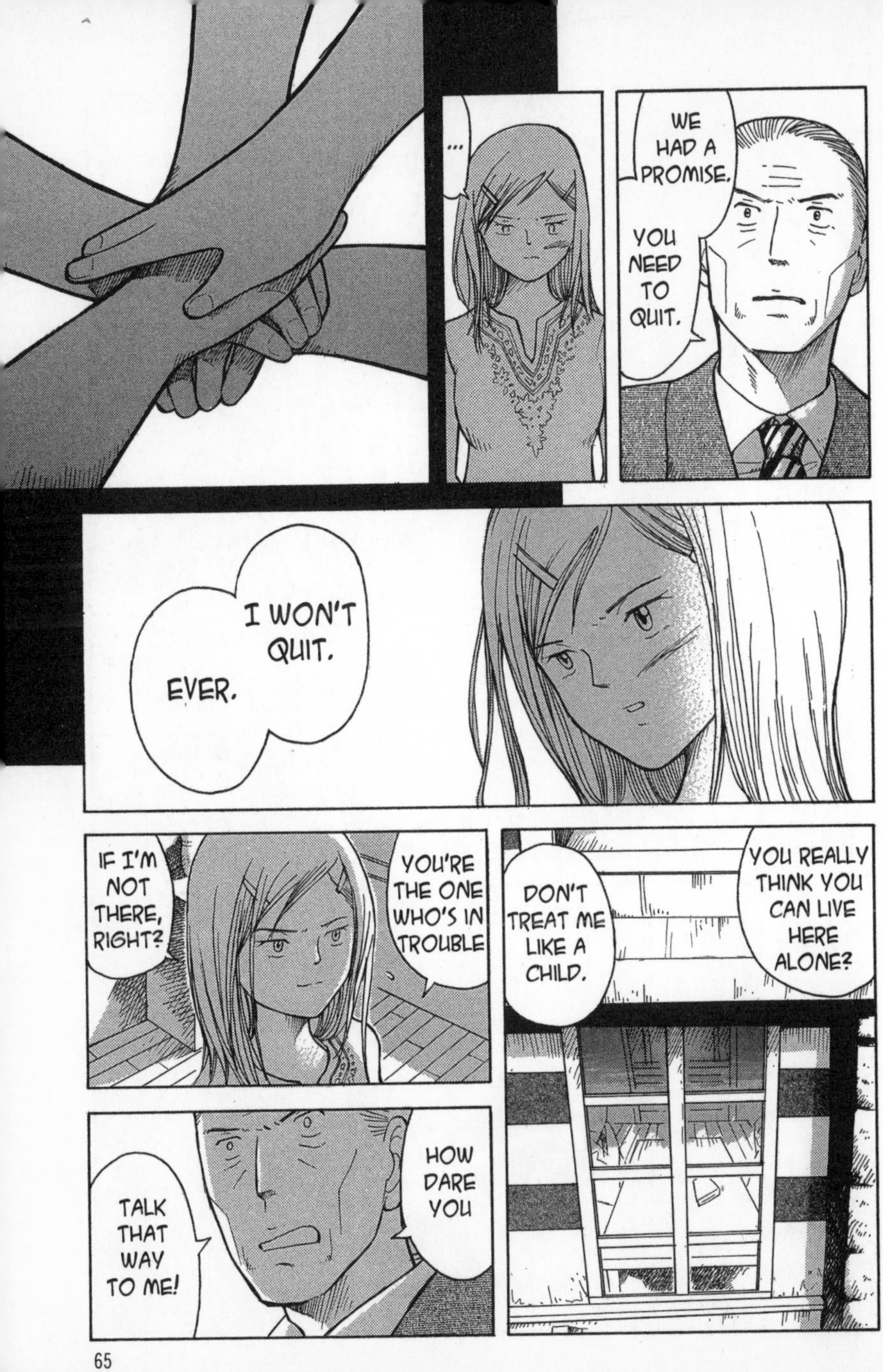
WE HAD A PROMISE.
YOU NEED TO QUIT.
...
I WON'T QUIT.
EVER.
YOU REALLY THINK YOU CAN LIVE HERE ALONE?
DON'T TREAT ME LIKE A CHILD.
YOU'RE THE ONE WHO'S IN TROUBLE
IF I'M NOT THERE, RIGHT?
HOW DARE YOU
TALK THAT WAY TO ME!

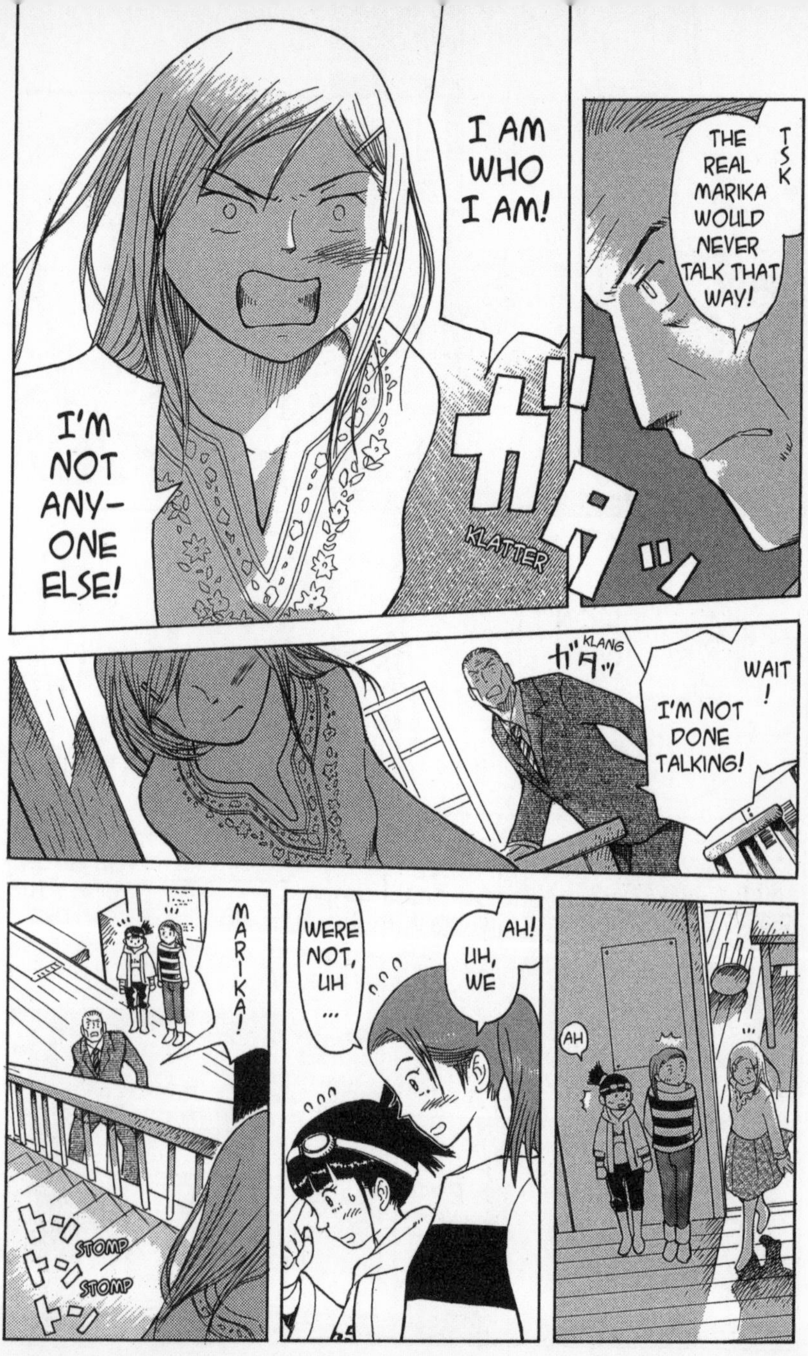
TSK
THE REAL MARIKA WOULD NEVER TALK THAT WAY!
I AM WHO I AM!
I'M NOT ANY-ONE ELSE!
ガタッ
KLATTER
WAIT! I'M NOT DONE TALKING!
ガタッ
KLANG
AH
AH! UH, WE
WERE NOT, UH ...
MARIKA!
STOMP
STOMP

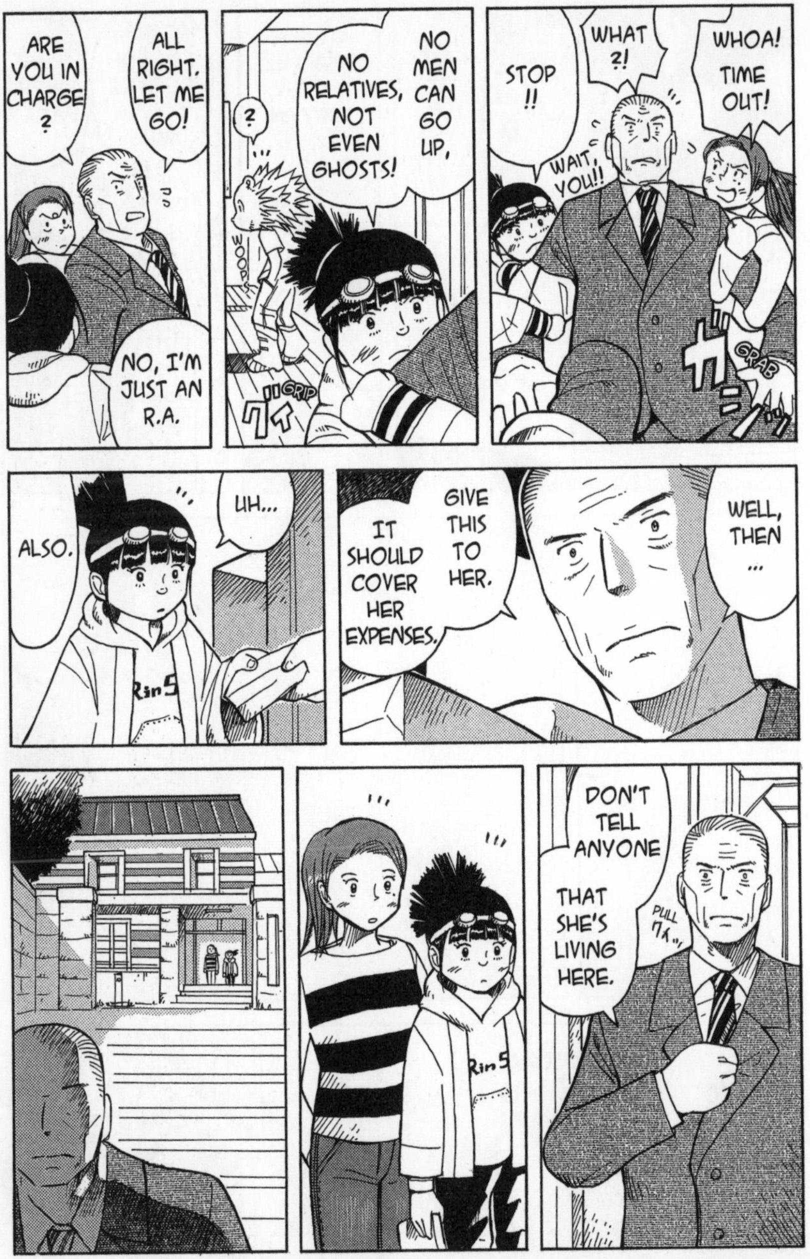
WHOA! TIME OUT!
WHAT ?!
STOP !!
WAIT, YOU!!
GRAB
NO MEN CAN GO UP,
NO RELATIVES, NOT EVEN GHOSTS!
?
WOOPS
GRIP
ALL RIGHT. LET ME GO!
ARE YOU IN CHARGE ?
NO, I'M JUST AN R.A.
WELL, THEN ...
GIVE THIS TO HER.
IT SHOULD COVER HER EXPENSES.
UH...
ALSO.
DON'T TELL ANYONE
THAT SHE'S LIVING HERE.
PULL

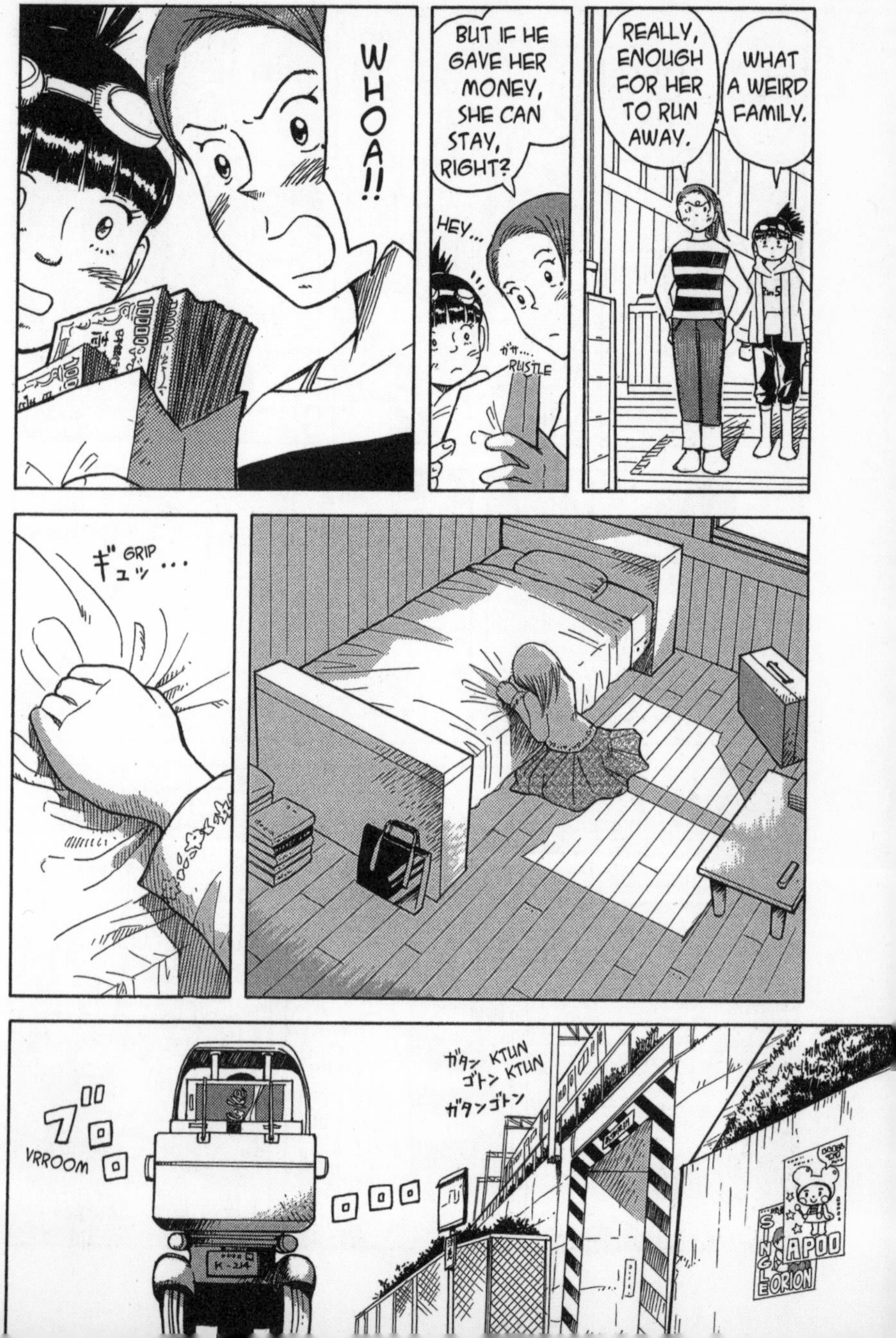
WHAT A WEIRD FAMILY.
REALLY, ENOUGH FOR HER TO RUN AWAY.
BUT IF HE GAVE HER MONEY, SHE CAN STAY, RIGHT?
HEY...
ガサ…
RUSTLE
WHOA!!
ギュッ…
GRIP
ガタン KTUN
ゴトン KTUN
ガタンゴトン
APOO
ブロロロロ
VRROOM

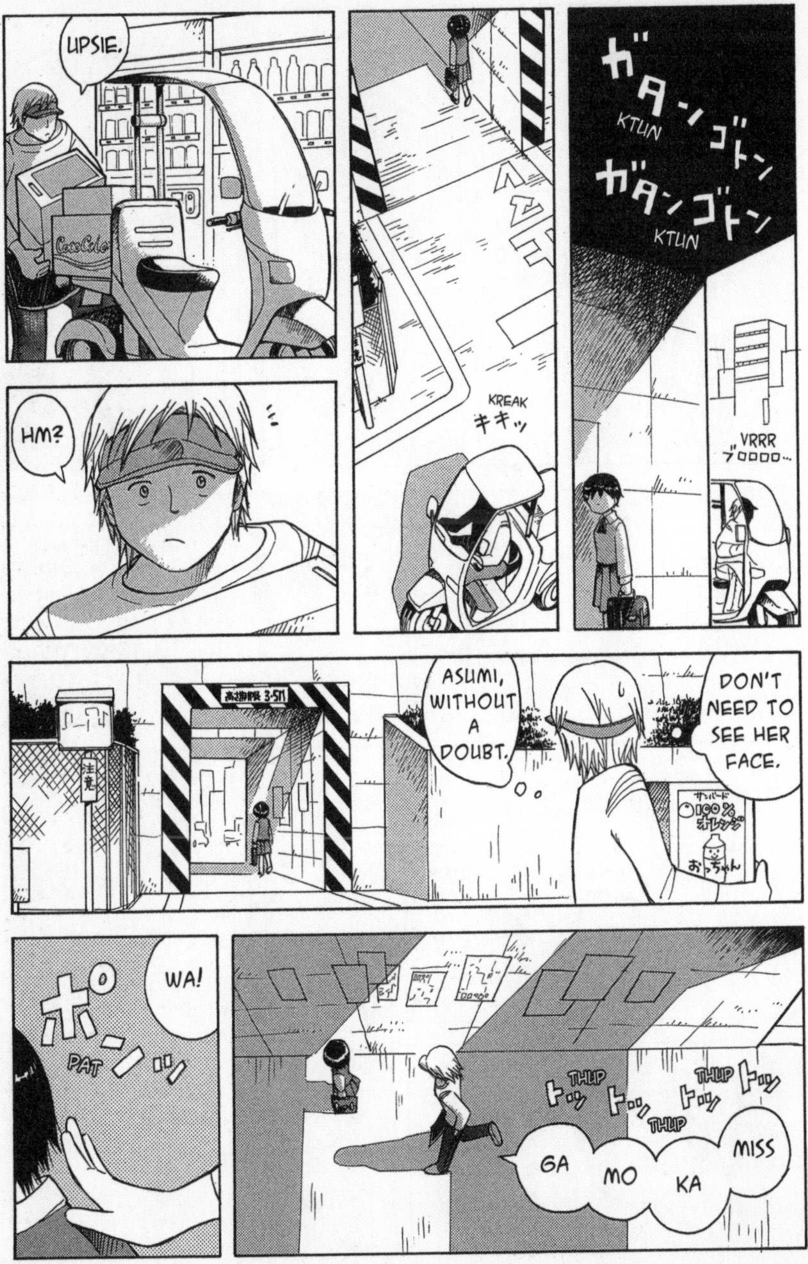

ガタンゴトン
KTUN
ガタンゴトン
KTUN
VRRR
ブロロロロ…
KREAK
キキッ
UPSIE.
HM?
DON'T NEED TO SEE HER FACE.
ASUMI, WITHOUT A DOUBT.
THUP
トッ
GA MO KA MISS
WA!
ポンッ
PAT

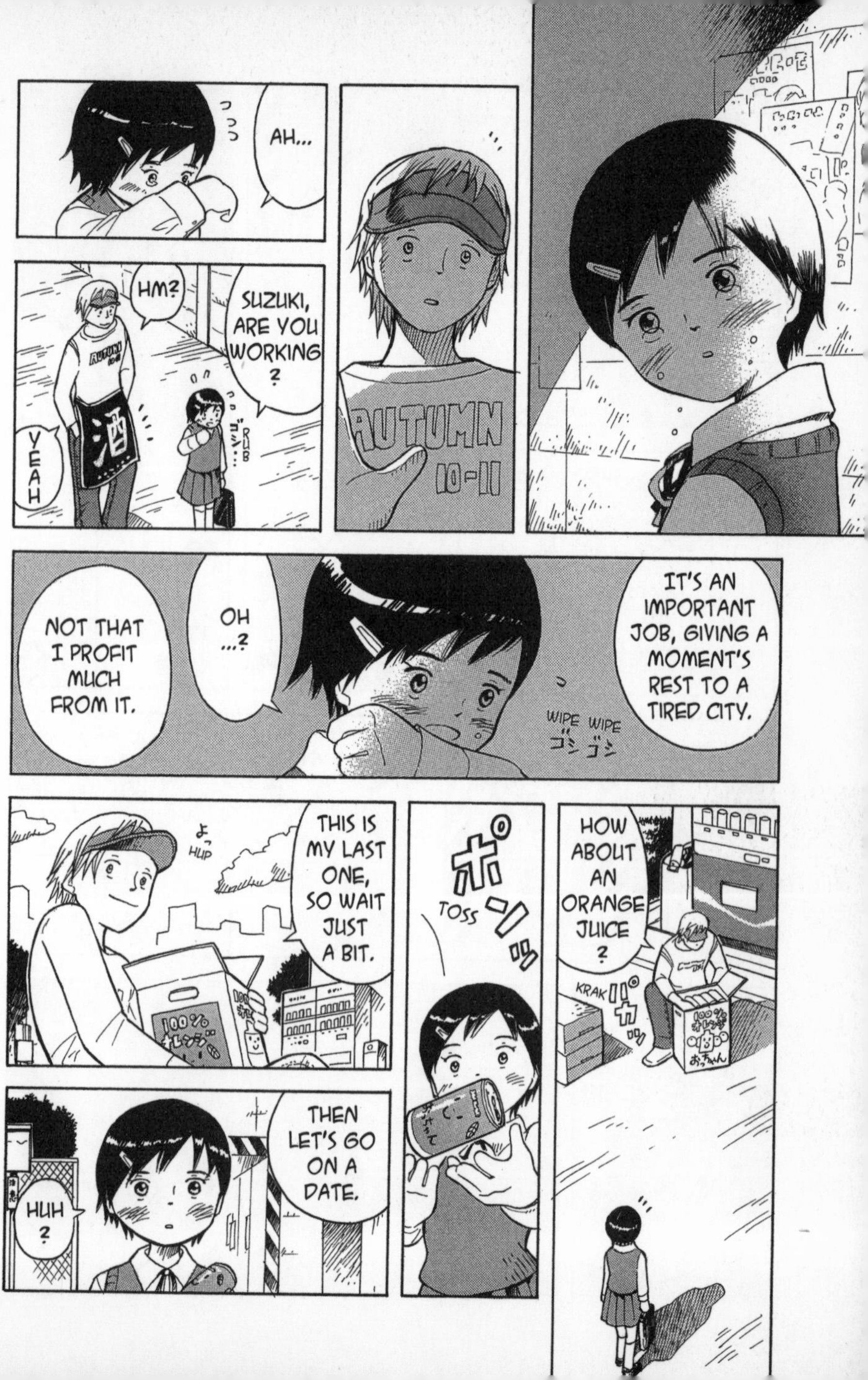
AH...
SUZUKI, ARE YOU WORKING?
HM?
YEAH
RUB
IT'S AN IMPORTANT JOB, GIVING A MOMENT'S REST TO A TIRED CITY.
WIPE WIPE
ゴシゴシ
OH ...?
NOT THAT I PROFIT MUCH FROM IT.
HOW ABOUT AN ORANGE JUICE?
KRAK
TOSS
THIS IS MY LAST ONE, SO WAIT JUST A BIT.
HUP
THEN LET'S GO ON A DATE.
HUH?

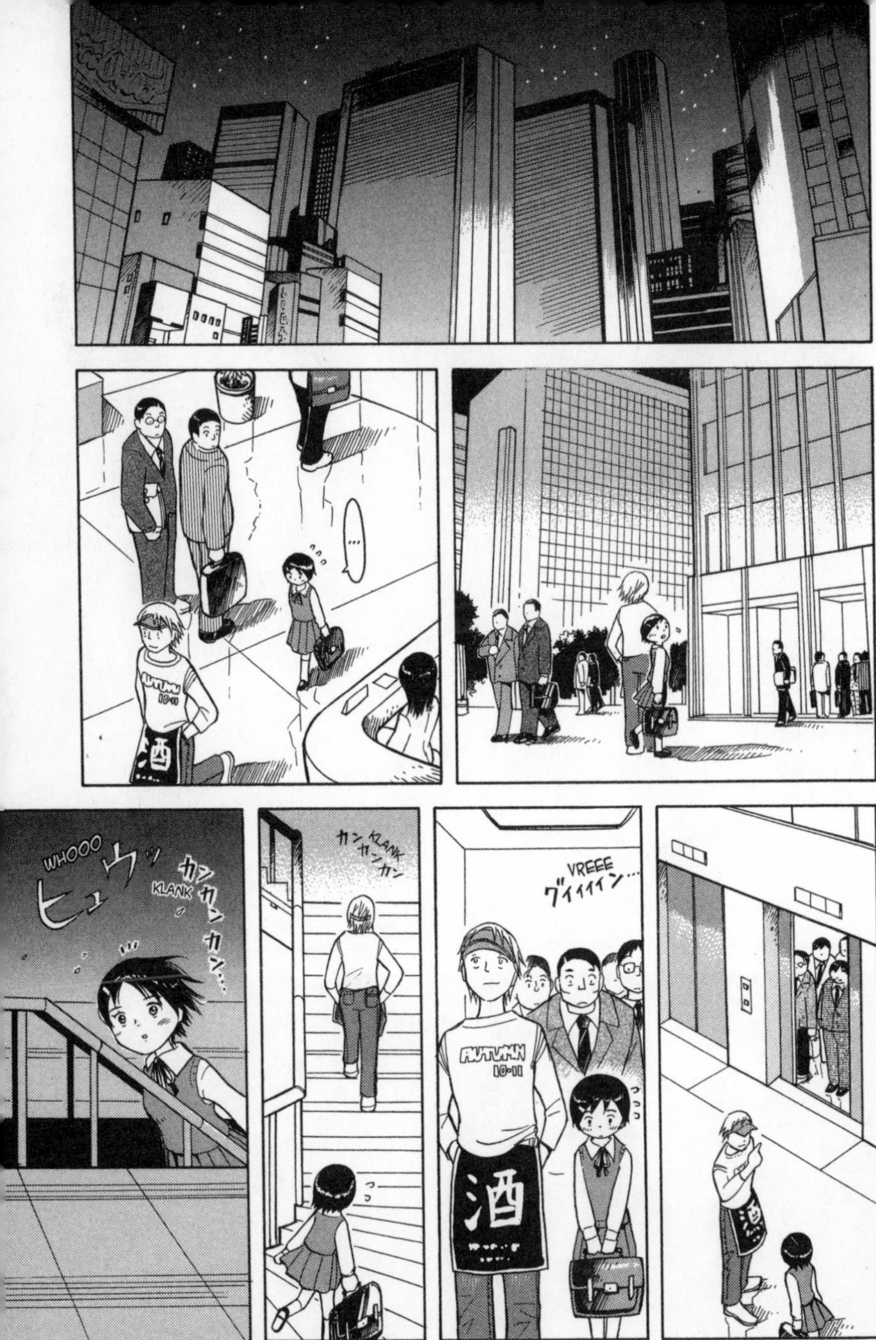
...
VREEE
グイイイイン…
カン KLANK
カンカンカン
WHOOO
ヒュウッ
KLANK
カンカンカン…

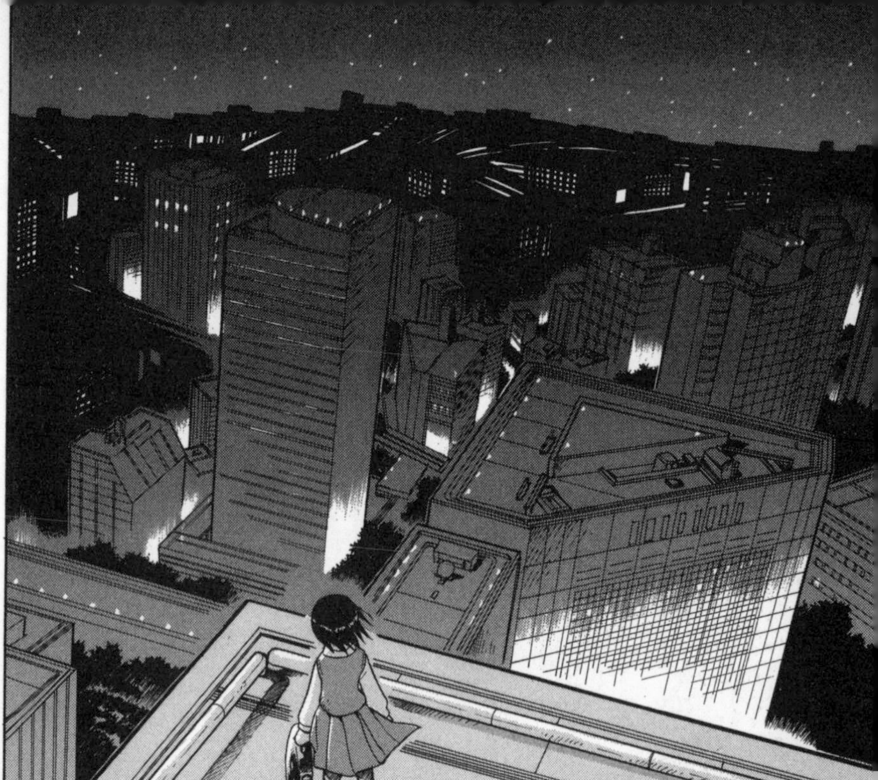

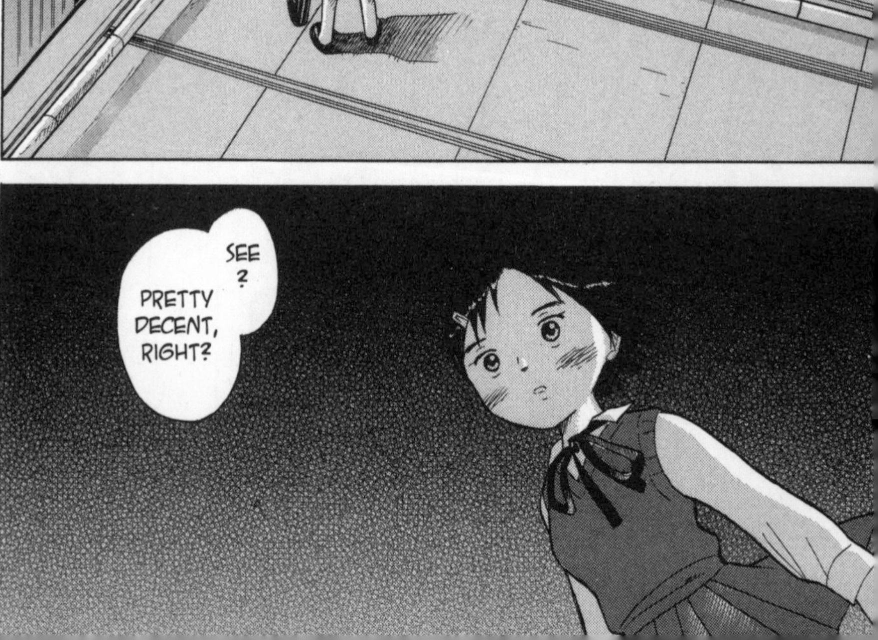
SEE?
PRETTY DECENT, RIGHT?

ASUMI
UP HERE.
カチャ KLAK
カチャ KLAK
A TELESCOPE?
YUP.
I HIDE IT UNDER THE VENTILATOR.
SHOULD BE EAST-SOUTH-EAST NOW...
カチッ KLIK
HMM...
?
FOUND IT. SEE?

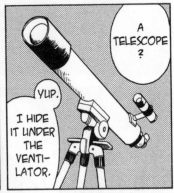

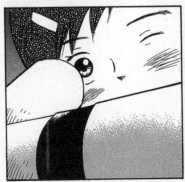

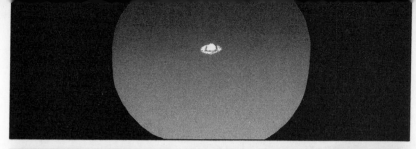

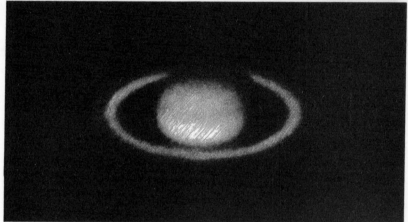

SATURN!!
PRETTY CLEAR FOR AN OLD MODEL, EH?
YEAH!
I CAN EVEN SEE THE RINGS!
ATLAS, PROMETHEUS, PANDORA
EPIMETHEUS, JANUS, MIMAS ...
I USED TO RATTLE OFF THE NAMES OF SATURN'S MOONS.
UMN
10-11

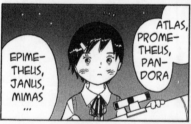

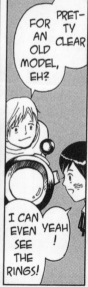

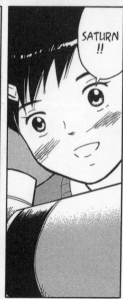

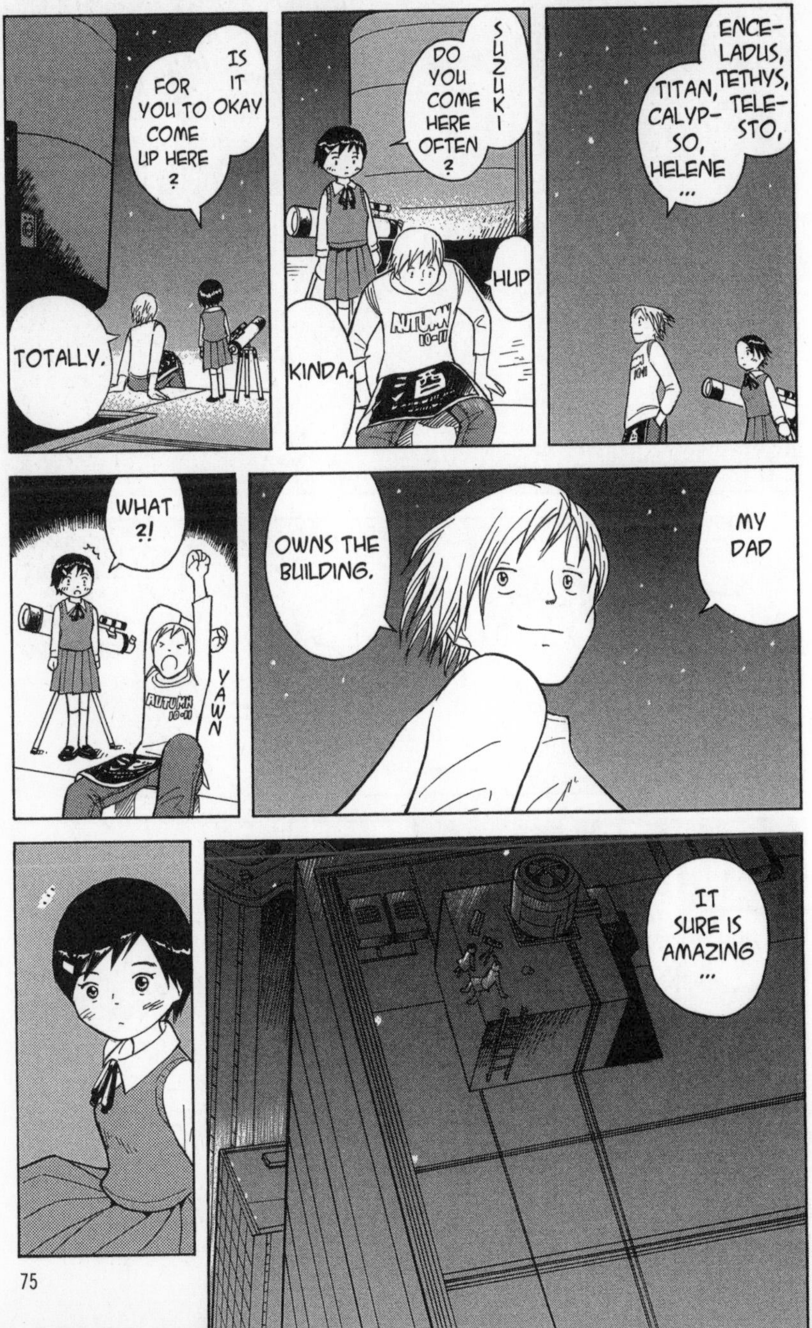
ENCE-LADUS, TETHYS, TELE-STO, TITAN, CALYP-SO, HELENE ...
SUZUKI
DO YOU COME HERE OFTEN ?
HUP
KINDA.
IS IT OKAY FOR YOU TO COME UP HERE ?
TOTALLY.
MY DAD
OWNS THE BUILDING.
WHAT ?!
YAWN
IT SURE IS AMAZING ...

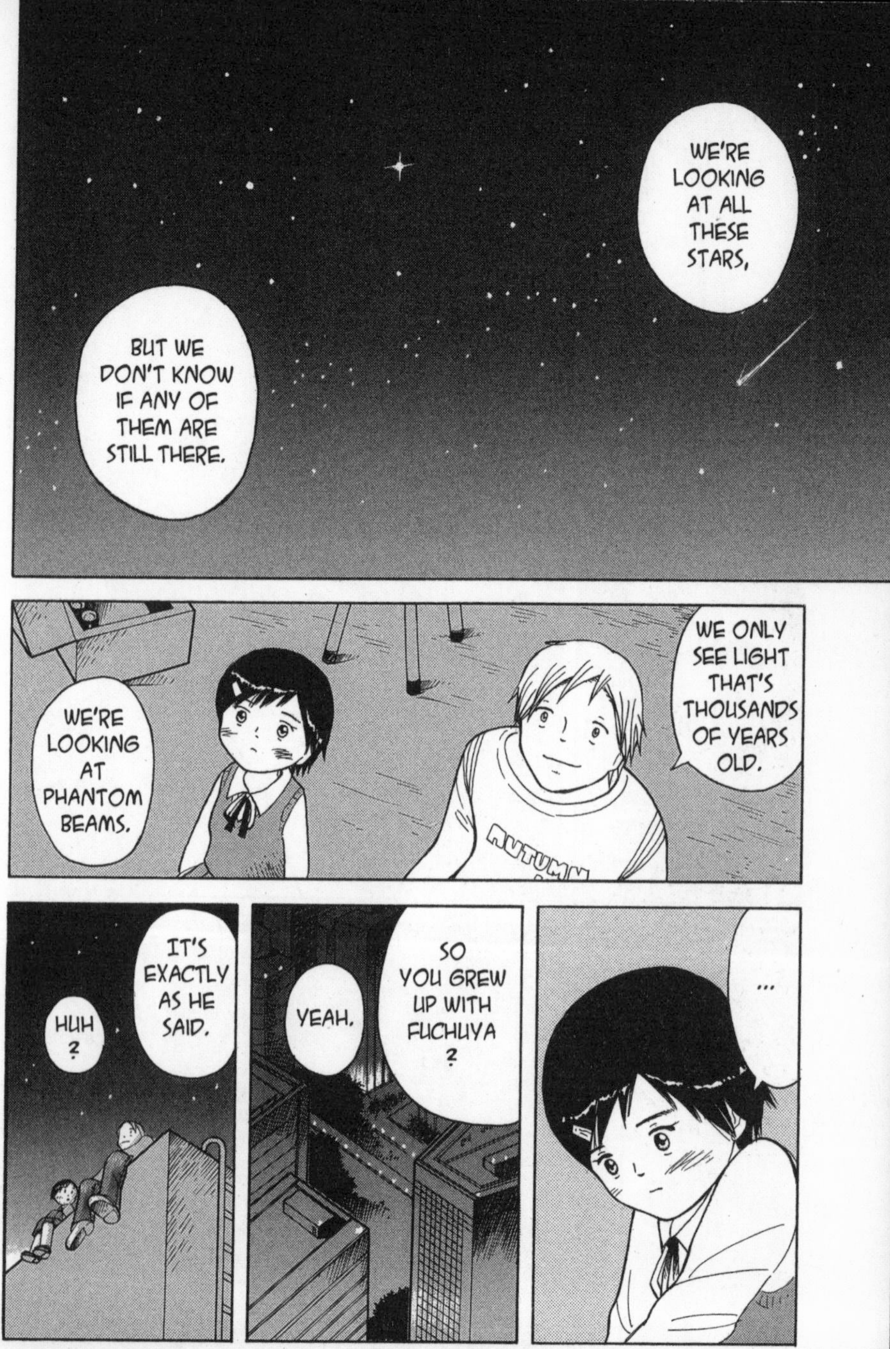
WE'RE LOOKING AT ALL THESE STARS,
BUT WE DON'T KNOW IF ANY OF THEM ARE STILL THERE.
WE ONLY SEE LIGHT THAT'S THOUSANDS OF YEARS OLD.
WE'RE LOOKING AT PHANTOM BEAMS.
...
SO YOU GREW UP WITH FUCHUYA?
YEAH.
IT'S EXACTLY AS HE SAID.
HUH?

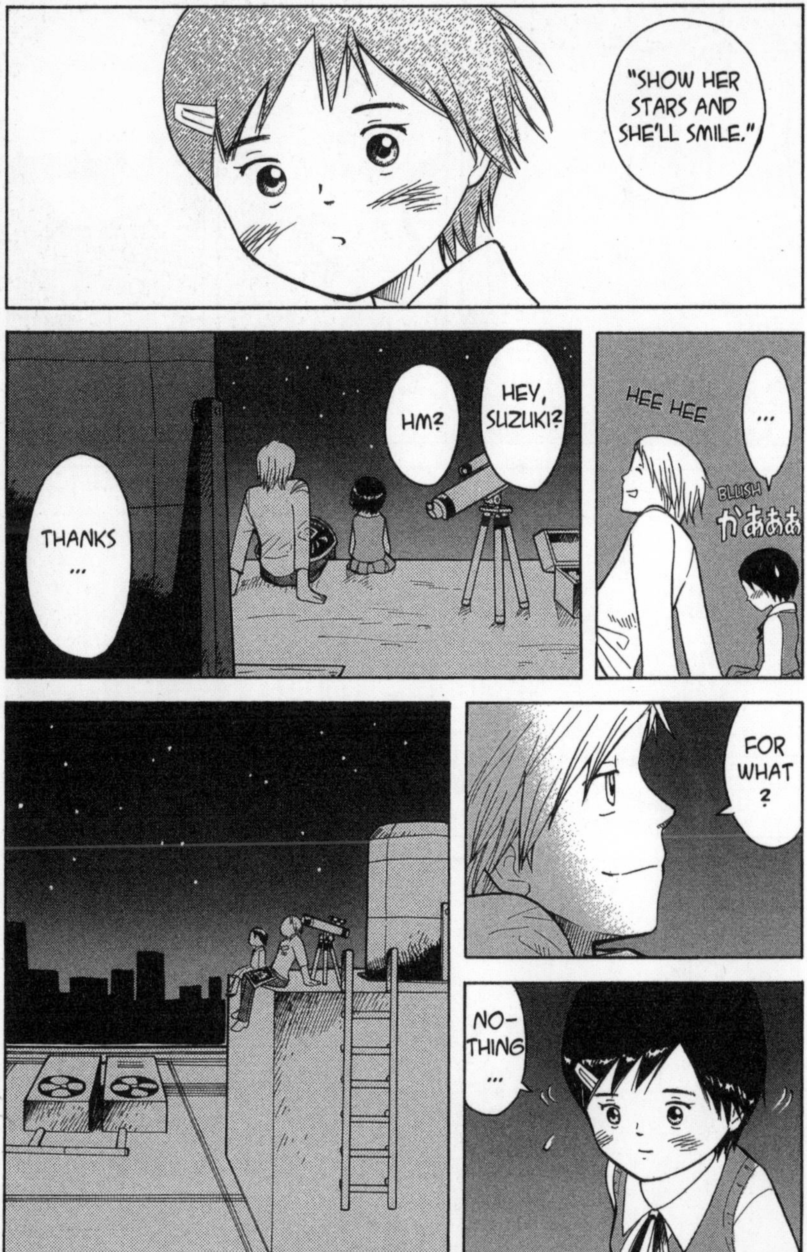
"SHOW HER STARS AND SHE'LL SMILE."
...
HEE HEE
BLUSH かあああ
HEY, SUZUKI?
HM?
THANKS ...
FOR WHAT ?
NO-THING ...

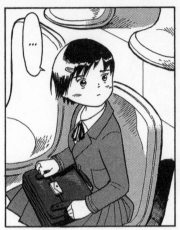

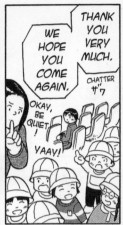

Planetarium
THANK YOU VERY MUCH.
WE HOPE YOU COME AGAIN.
CHATTER ザワ
OKAY, BE QUIET!
YAAY!
...
HEY RINGO, I'M BACK.
OH
GOOD TIMING!
I THINK THIS IS FOR MISS UKITA. CAN YOU GIVE IT TO HER?
LEFT IT IN THE PARLOR
IS SHE IN POOR HEALTH?
HUH?

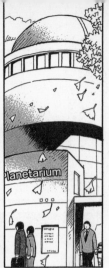

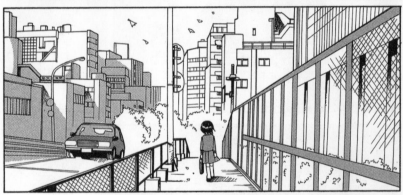

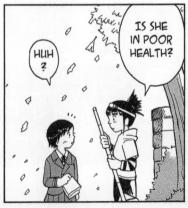

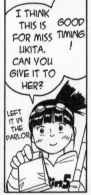

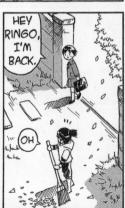

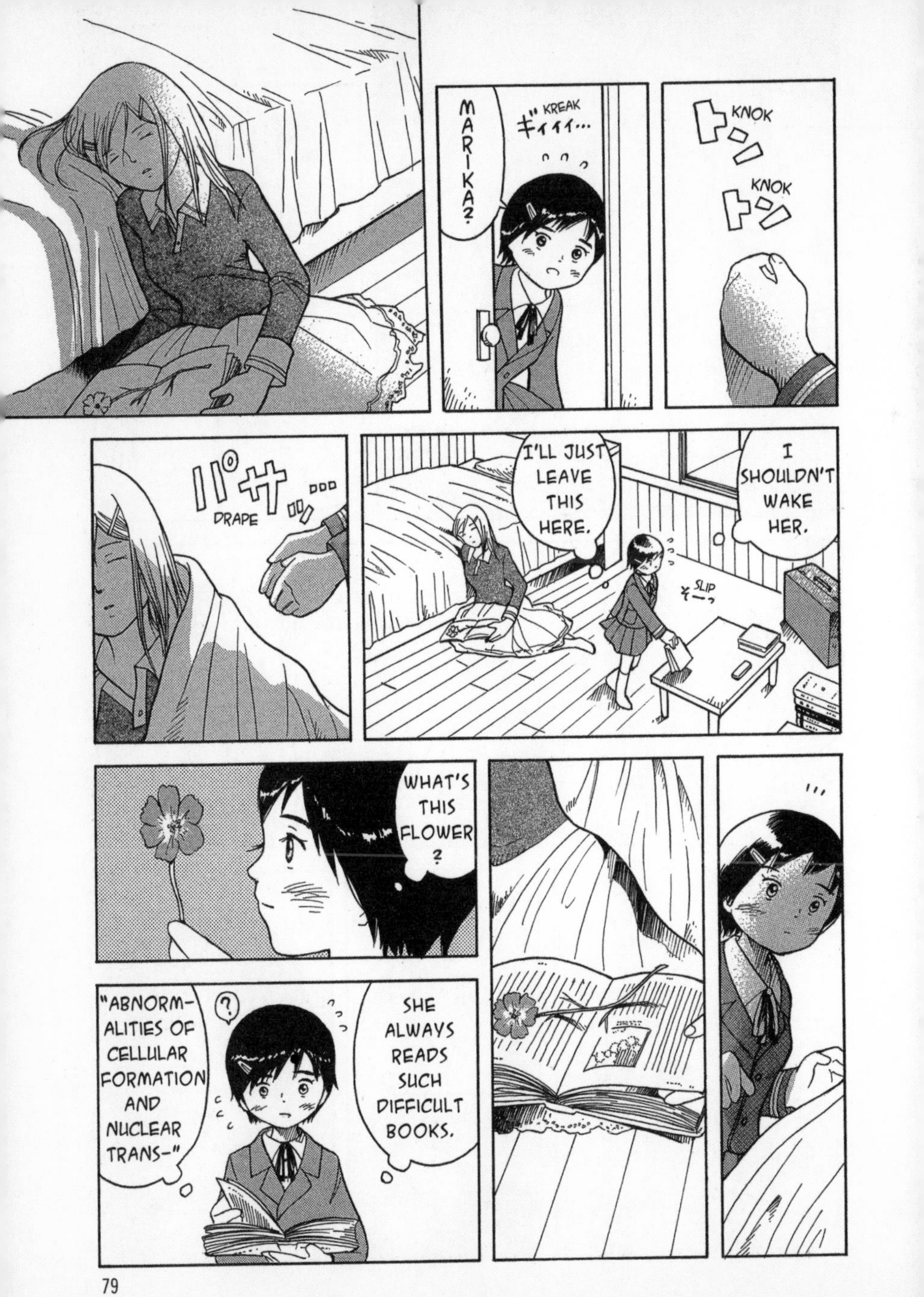
KNOK
トン
KNOK
トン
KREAK
ギィィィ…
MARIKA?
I SHOULDN'T WAKE HER.
I'LL JUST LEAVE THIS HERE.
SLIP
DRAPE
パサ
...
WHAT'S THIS FLOWER?
SHE ALWAYS READS SUCH DIFFICULT BOOKS.
?
"ABNORMALITIES OF CELLULAR FORMATION AND NUCLEAR TRANS-"

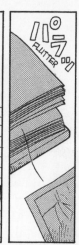

COME TO THINK OF IT, I'VE NEVER SEEN MARIKA SMILE.

...

THE DATE IS WRONG.

HUH.

2007.3.1

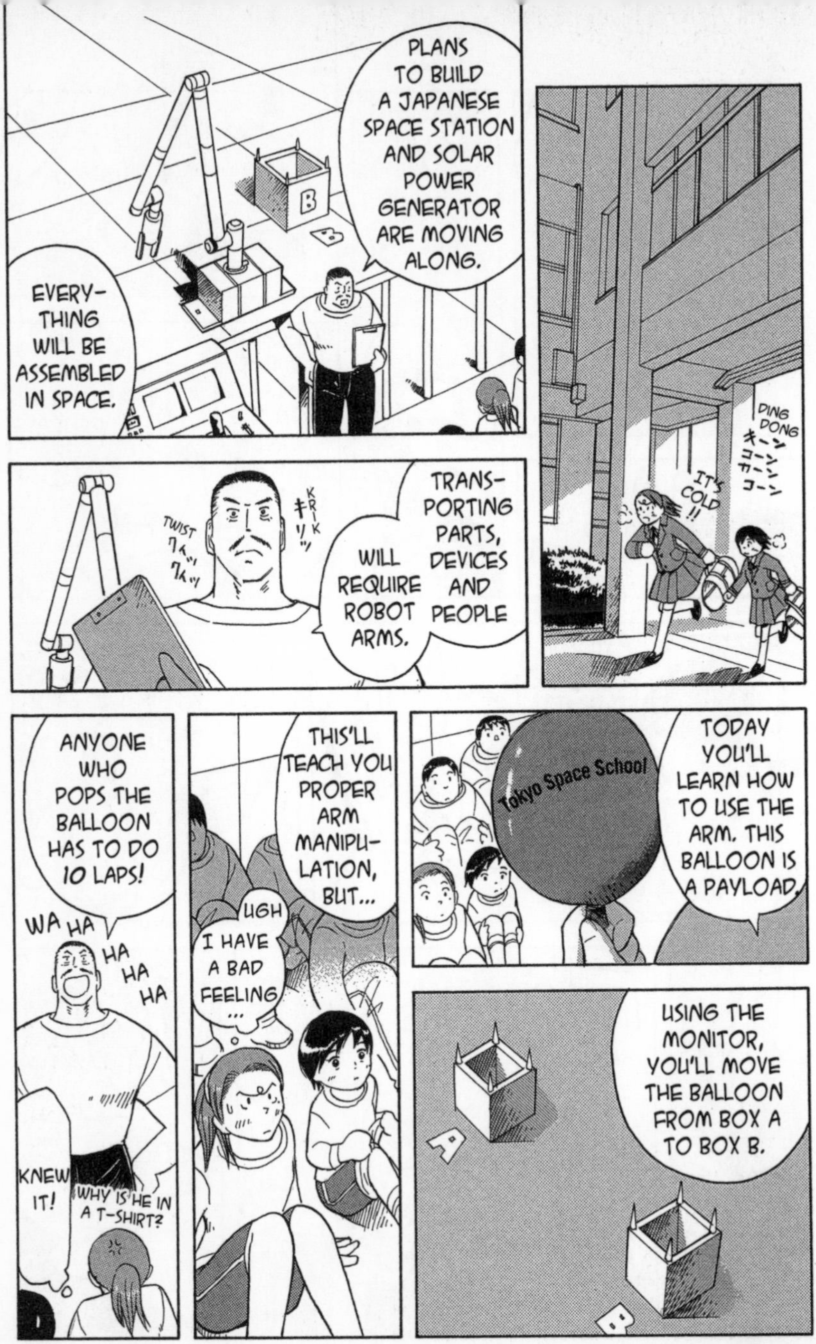
DING DONG
キーン コーン カーン コーン
IT'S COLD!!
PLANS TO BUILD A JAPANESE SPACE STATION AND SOLAR POWER GENERATOR ARE MOVING ALONG.
EVERY-THING WILL BE ASSEMBLED IN SPACE.
B
KRIK キリッ
TWIST クイッ クイッ
TRANS-PORTING PARTS, DEVICES AND PEOPLE
WILL REQUIRE ROBOT ARMS.
TODAY YOU'LL LEARN HOW TO USE THE ARM. THIS BALLOON IS A PAYLOAD.
Tokyo Space School
USING THE MONITOR, YOU'LL MOVE THE BALLOON FROM BOX A TO BOX B.
A
B
THIS'LL TEACH YOU PROPER ARM MANIPU-LATION, BUT...
UGH
I HAVE A BAD FEELING...
ANYONE WHO POPS THE BALLOON HAS TO DO 10 LAPS!
WA HA HA HA HA
KNEW IT!
WHY IS HE IN A T-SHIRT?

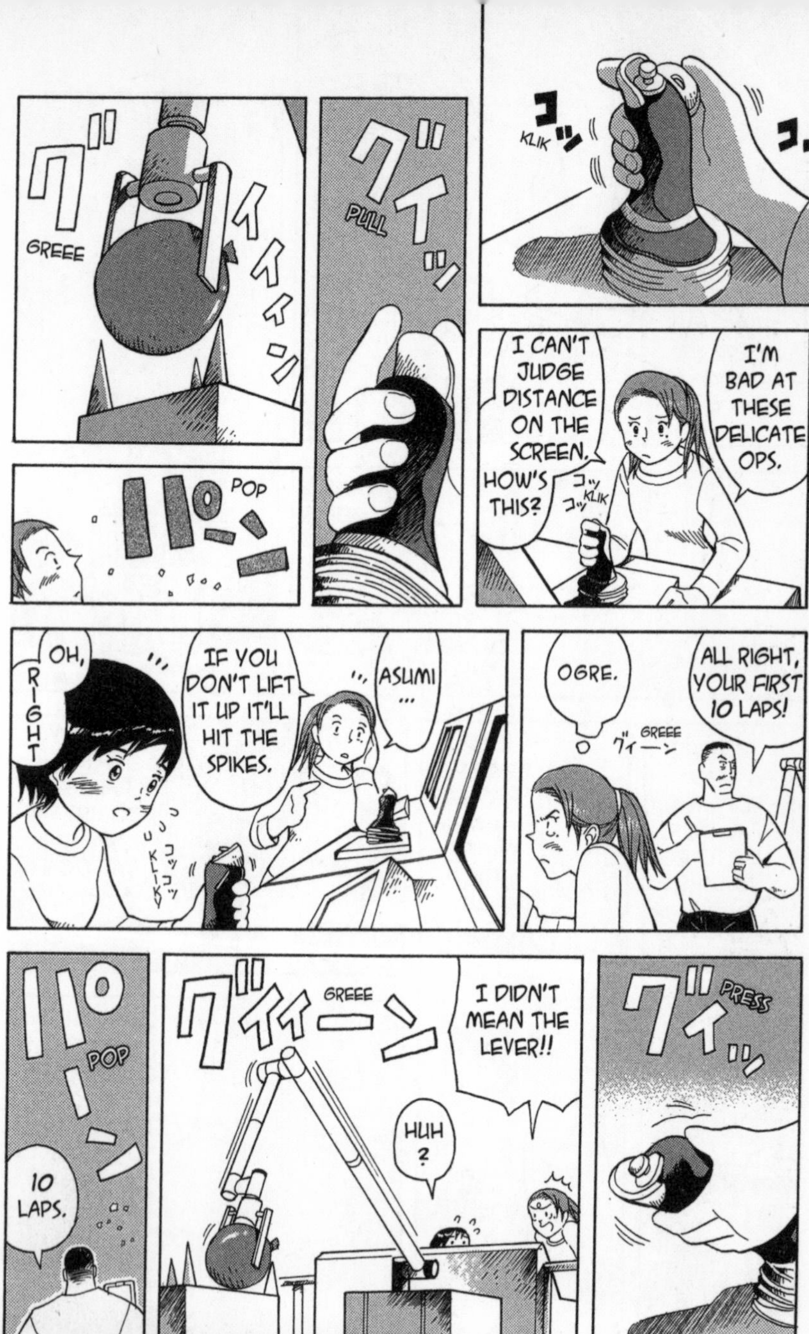
KLIK
KLIK
I'M BAD AT THESE DELICATE OPS.
I CAN'T JUDGE DISTANCE ON THE SCREEN.
HOW'S THIS?
KLIK
PULL
GREEE
POP
ALL RIGHT, YOUR FIRST 10 LAPS!
OGRE.
GREEE
ASUMI ...
IF YOU DON'T LIFT IT UP IT'LL HIT THE SPIKES.
OH, RIGHT
KLIK
PRESS
GREEE
I DIDN'T MEAN THE LEVER!!
HUH?
POP
10 LAPS.

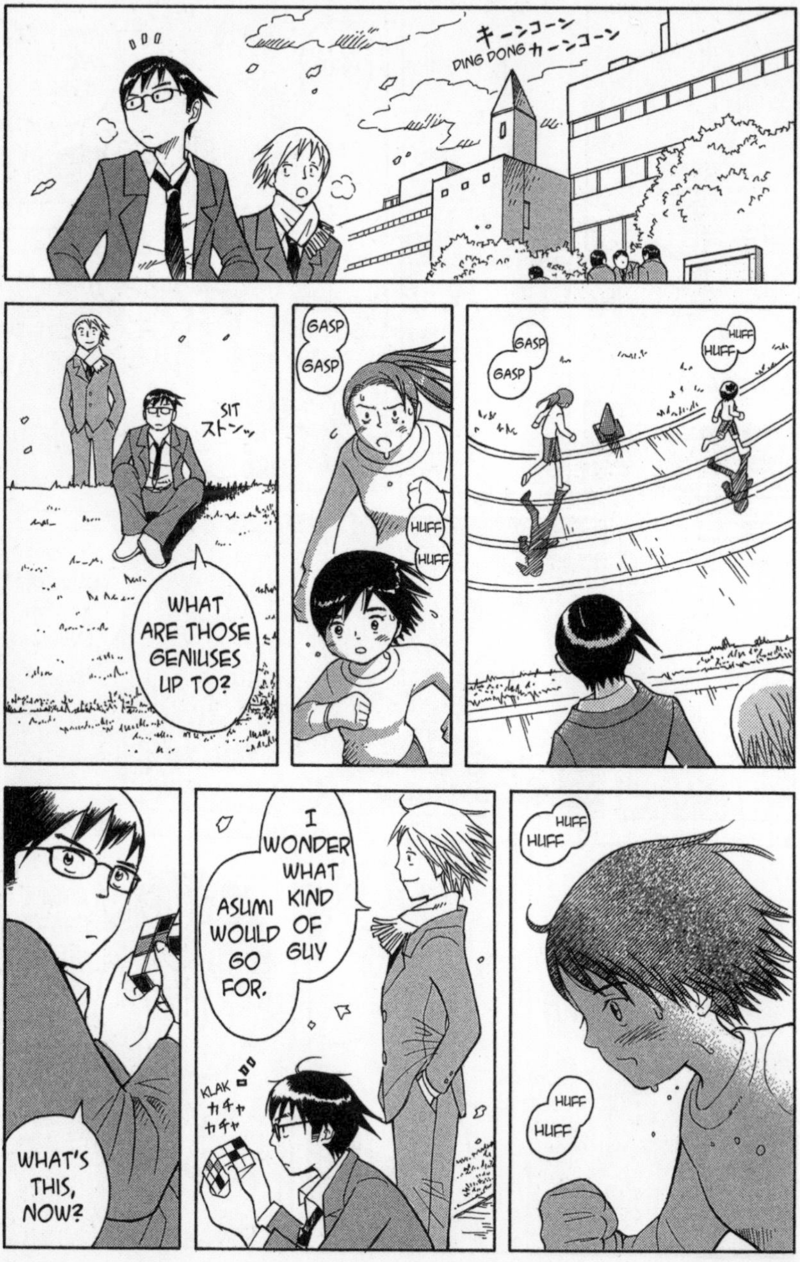
キーンコーン
DING DONG
カーンコーン
HUFF HUFF
GASP GASP
GASP GASP
HUFF HUFF
SIT
ストンッ
WHAT ARE THOSE GENIUSES UP TO?
HUFF HUFF
HUFF HUFF
I WONDER WHAT KIND OF GUY ASUMI WOULD GO FOR.
KLAK
カチャカチャ
WHAT'S THIS, NOW?

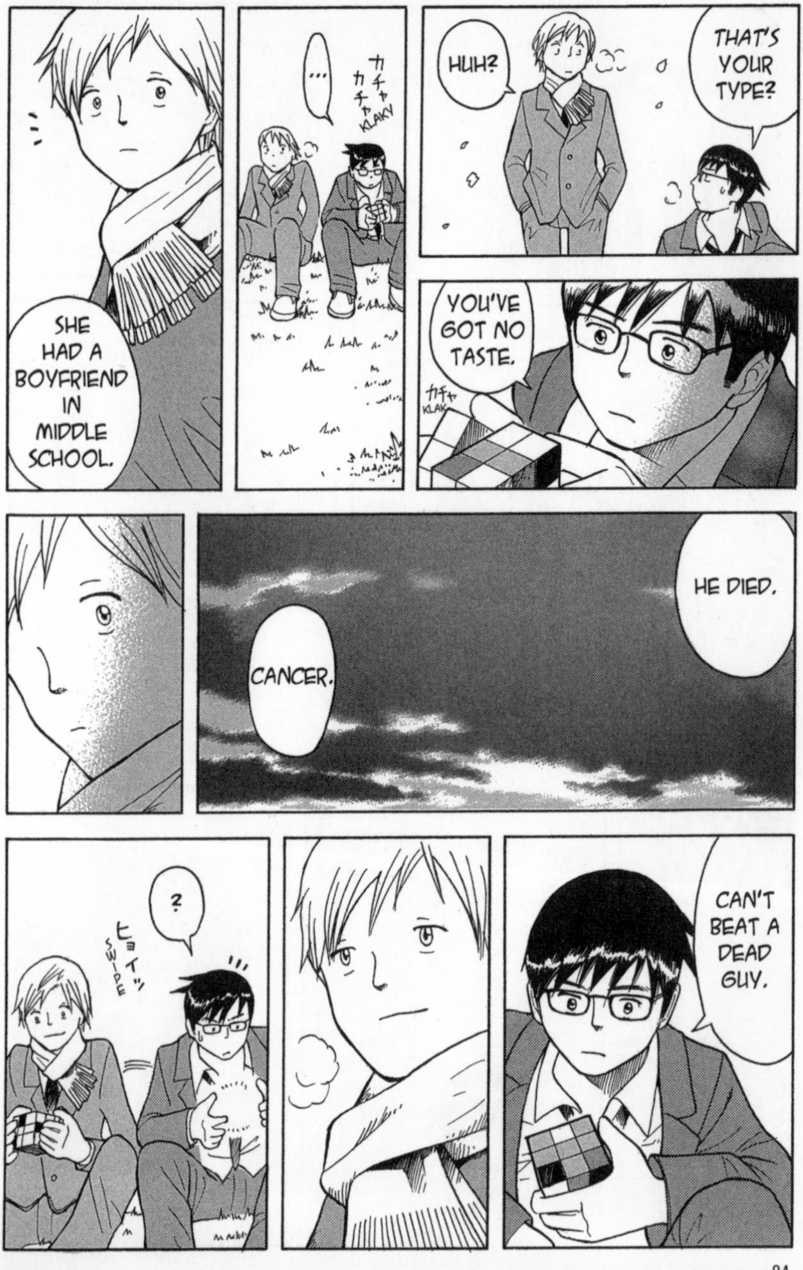
THAT'S YOUR TYPE?
HUH?
YOU'VE GOT NO TASTE.
カチャ KLAK
...
カチャカチャ KLAKY
SHE HAD A BOYFRIEND IN MIDDLE SCHOOL.
HE DIED.
CANCER.
CAN'T BEAT A DEAD GUY.
?
ヒョイッ SWIPE

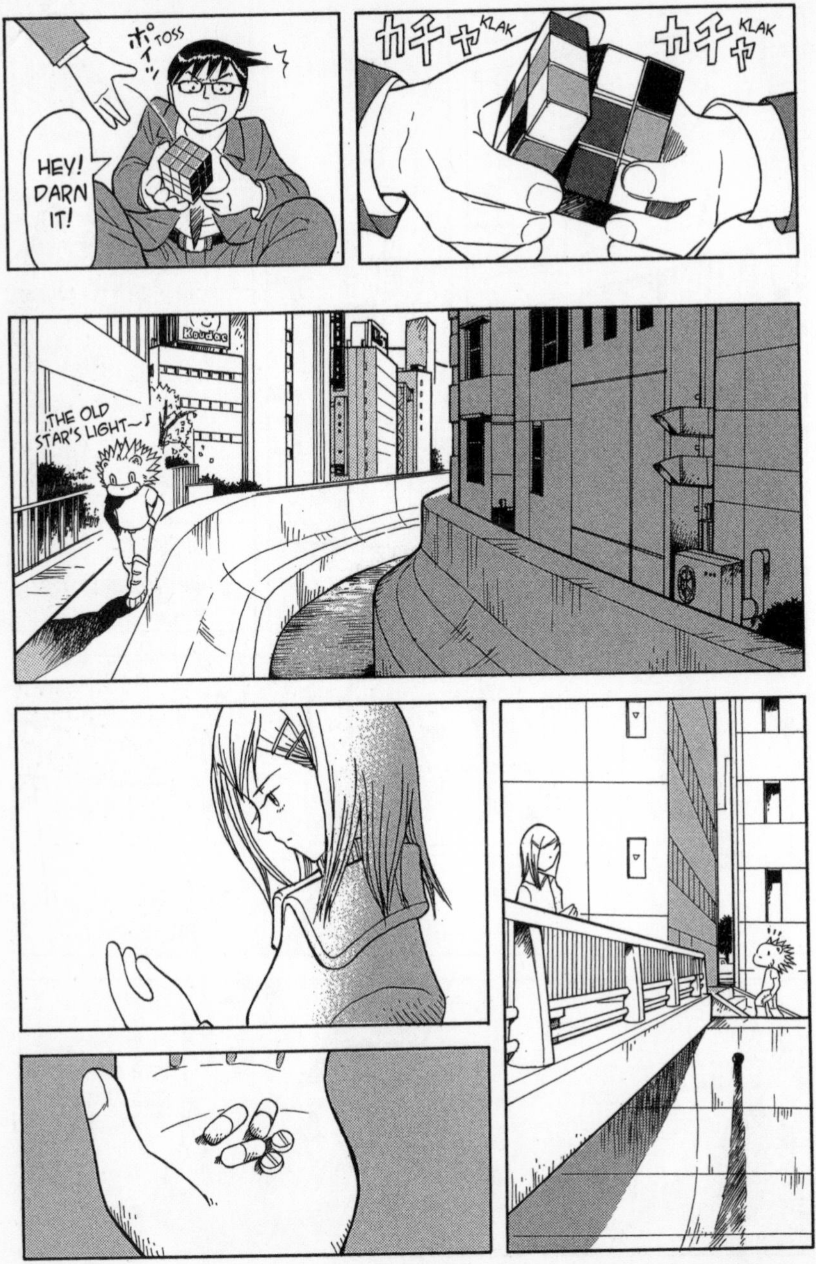
カチャ KLAK
カチャ KLAK
ポイッ TOSS
HEY! DARN IT!
THE OLD STAR'S LIGHT~♪

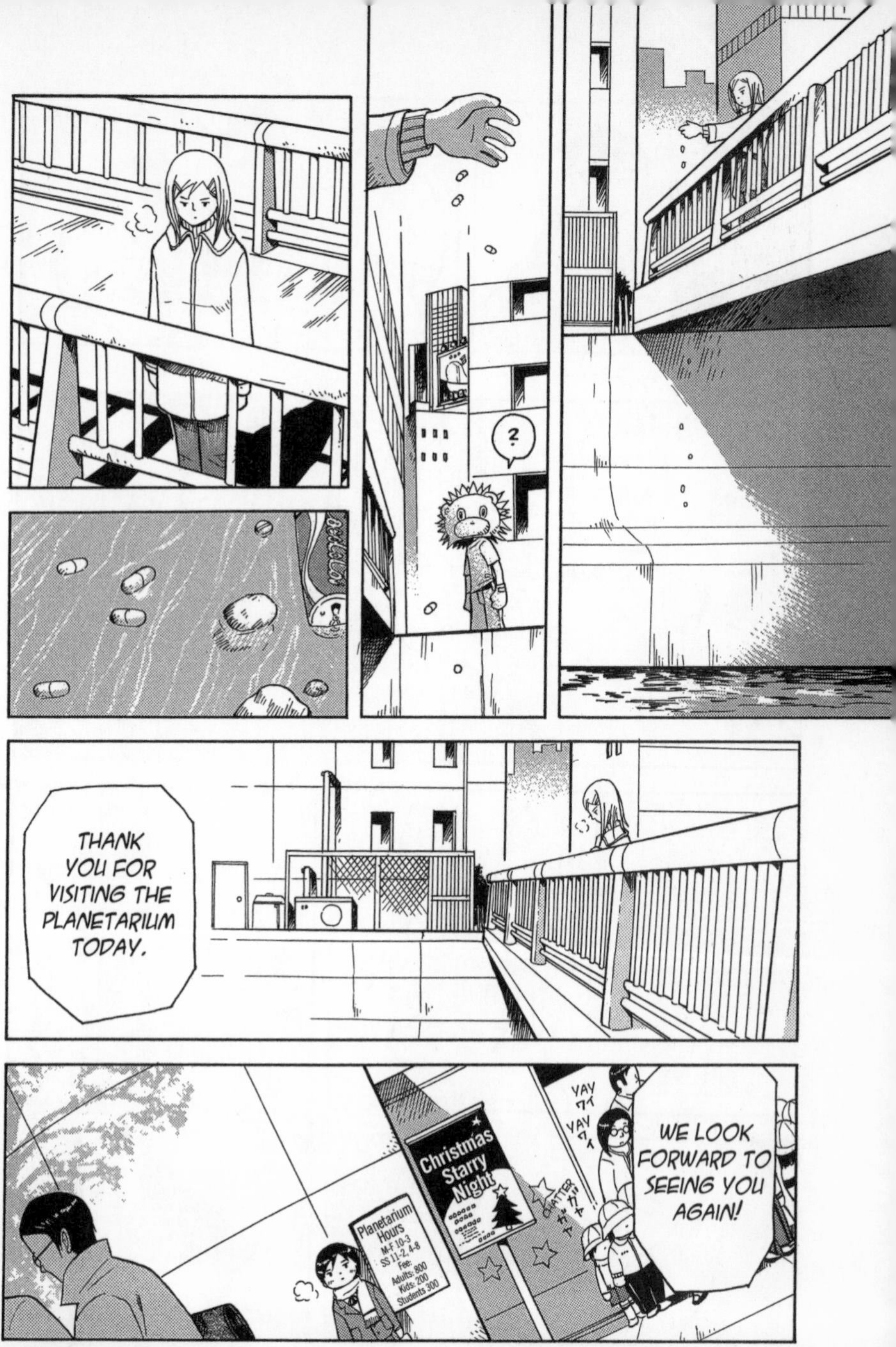
?
THANK YOU FOR VISITING THE PLANETARIUM TODAY.
WE LOOK FORWARD TO SEEING YOU AGAIN!
YAY ワイ
YAY ワイ
CHATTER ガヤ ガヤ
Christmas Starry Night
Planetarium Hours
M-F 10-3
SS 11-2, 4-8
Fee:
Adults: 800
Kids: 200
Students 300

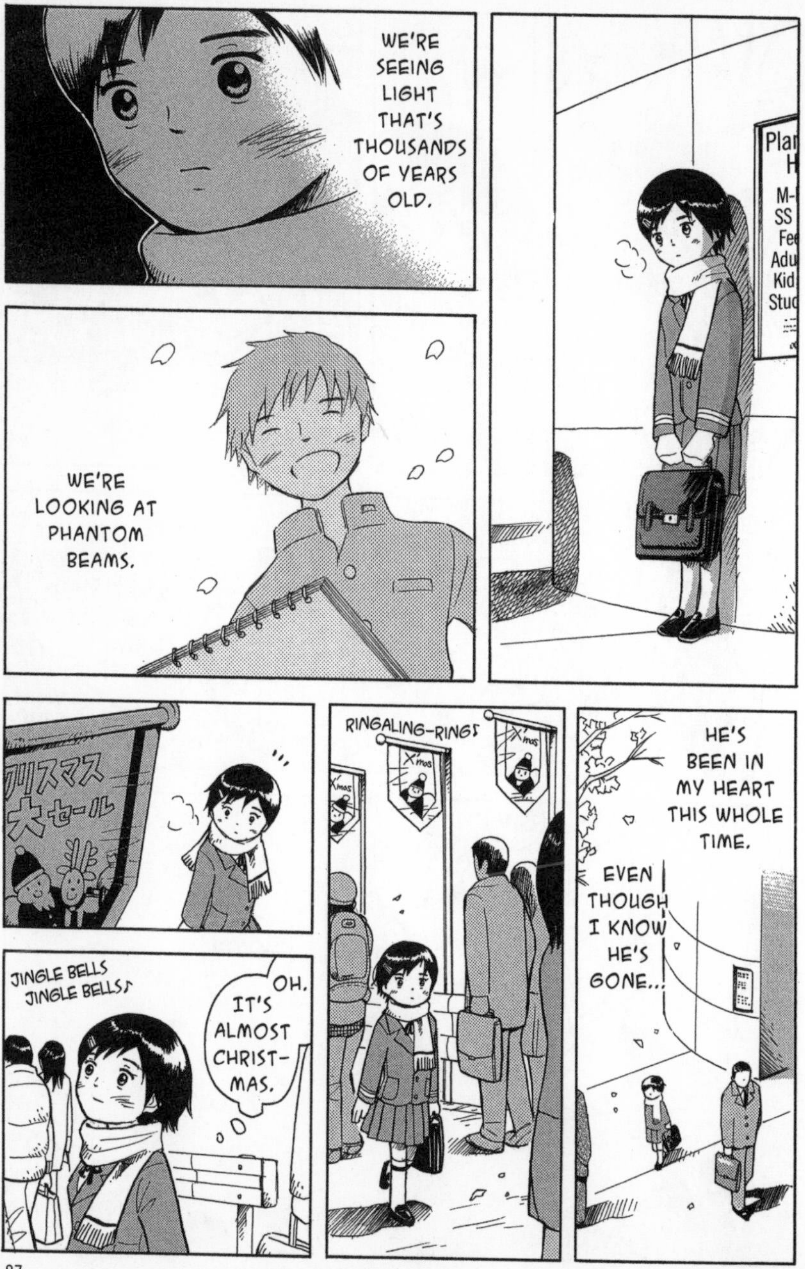
WE'RE SEEING LIGHT THAT'S THOUSANDS OF YEARS OLD.
WE'RE LOOKING AT PHANTOM BEAMS.
HE'S BEEN IN MY HEART THIS WHOLE TIME.
EVEN THOUGH I KNOW HE'S GONE...
RINGALING-RINGS♪
X'mas
X'mas
X'mas
クリスマス大セール
JINGLE BELLS JINGLE BELLS♪
OH.
IT'S ALMOST CHRIST-MAS.

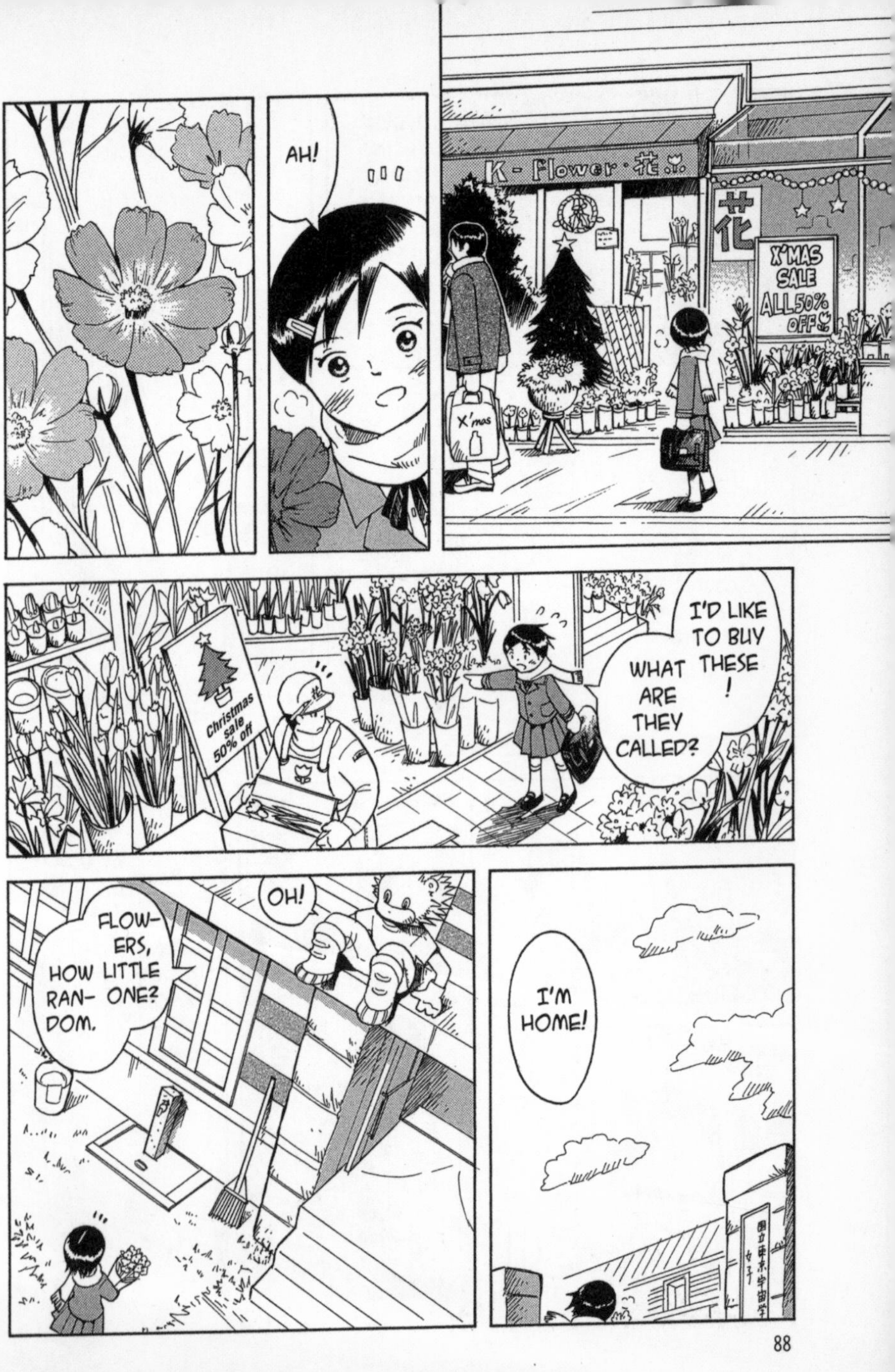
K-Flower·花
花
X'MAS SALE ALL 50% OFF
X'mas
AH!
I'D LIKE TO BUY THESE!
WHAT ARE THEY CALLED?
Christmas sale 50% off
I'M HOME!
OH!
HOW LITTLE ONE?
FLOW-ERS, RAN-DOM.

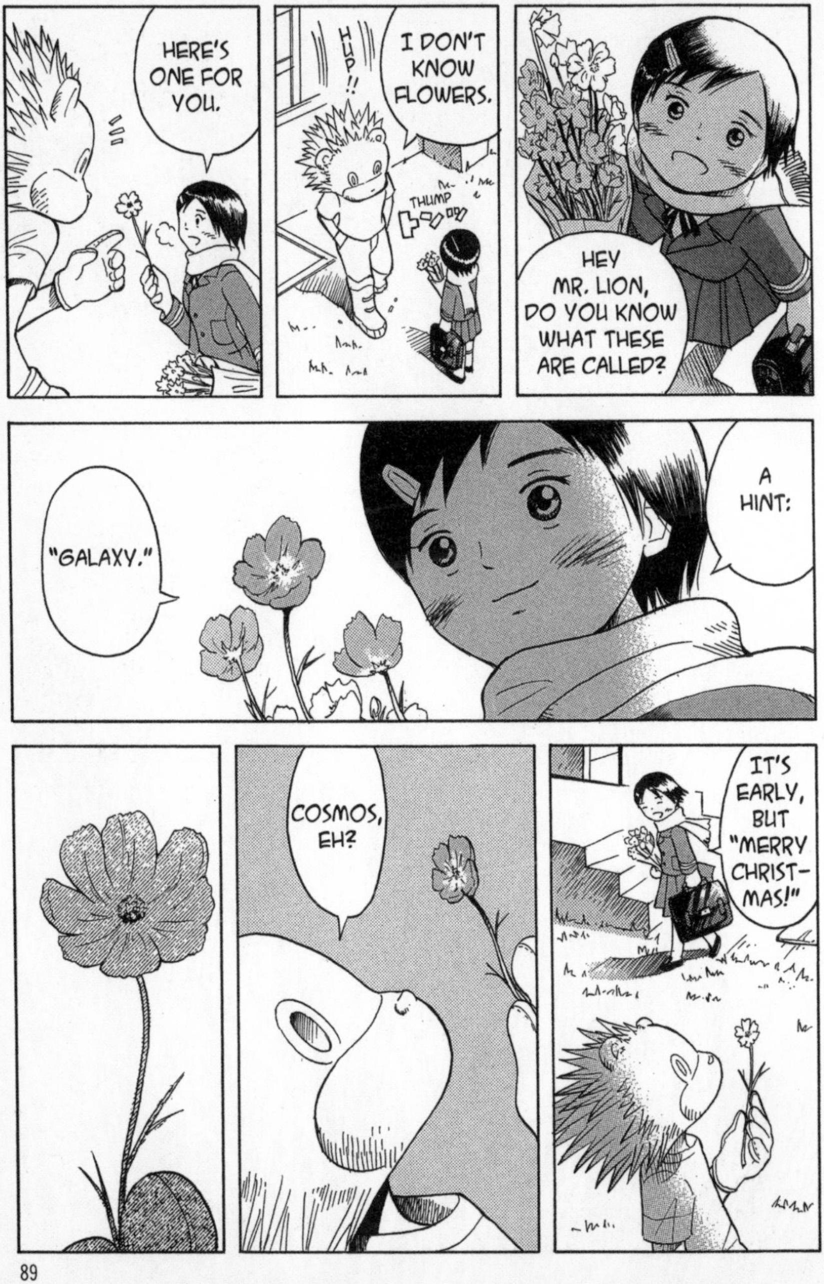
HEY MR. LION, DO YOU KNOW WHAT THESE ARE CALLED?
I DON'T KNOW FLOWERS.
HUP!!
THUMP
HERE'S ONE FOR YOU.
A HINT:
"GALAXY."
IT'S EARLY, BUT "MERRY CHRIST-MAS!"
COSMOS, EH?

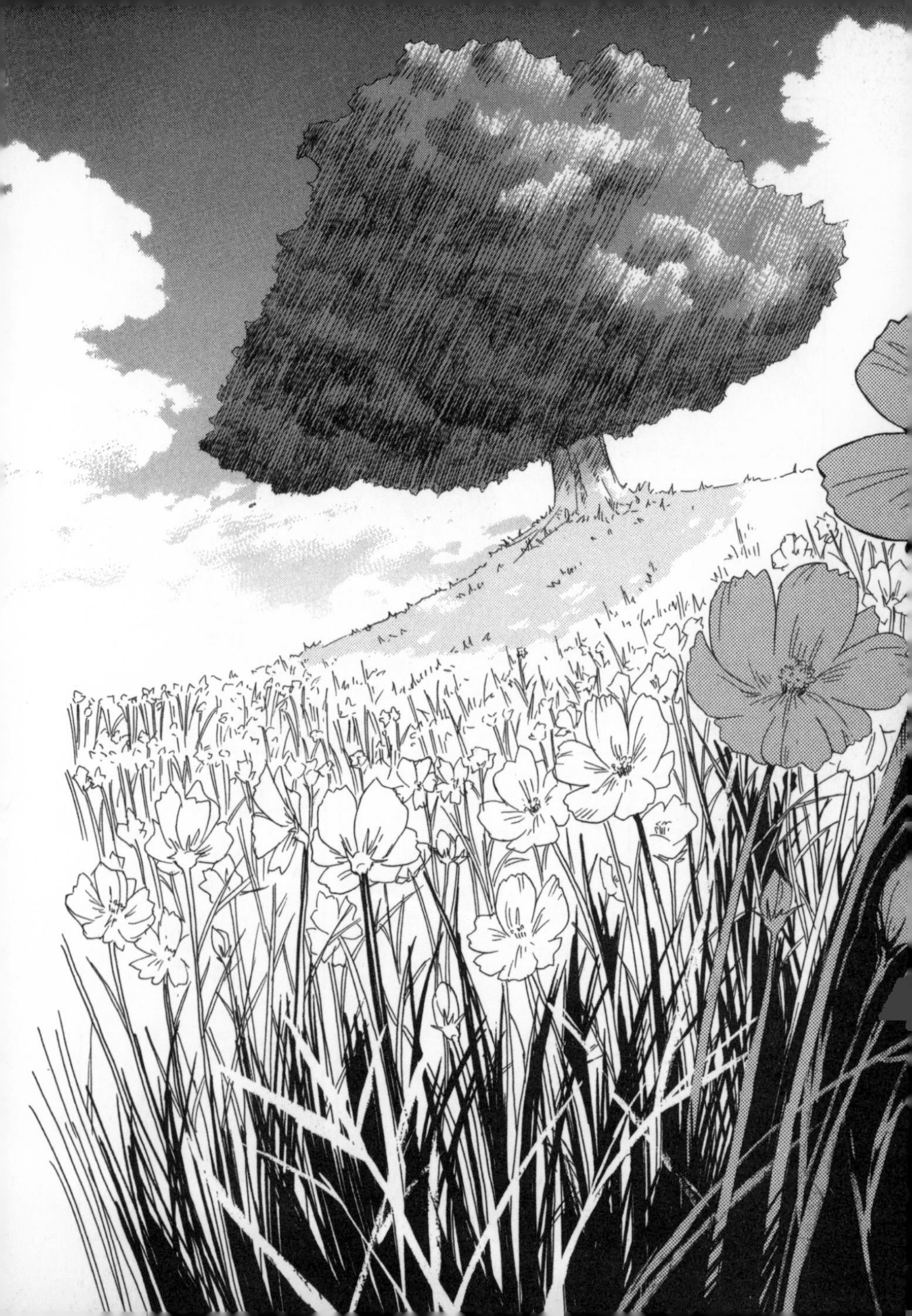

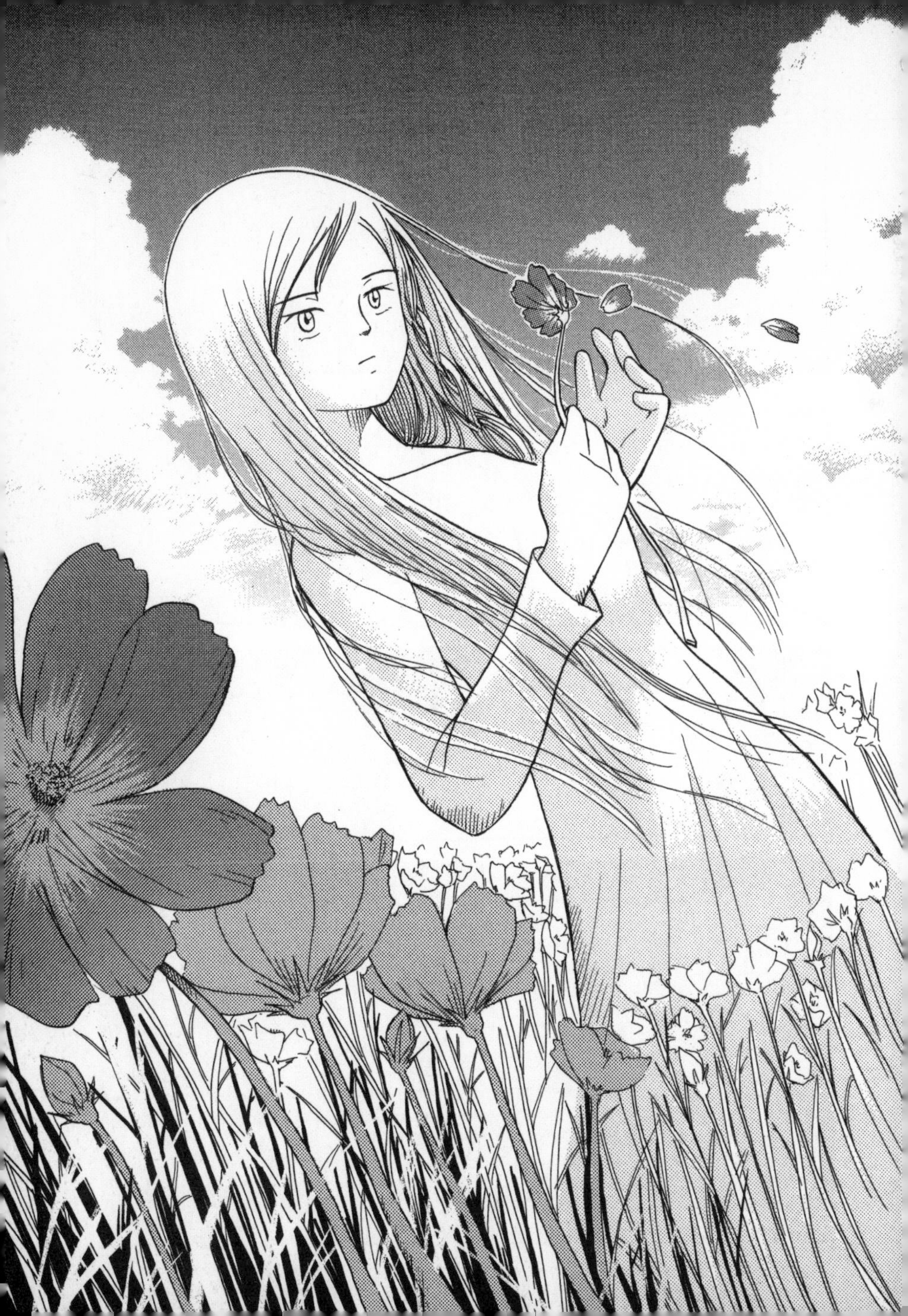

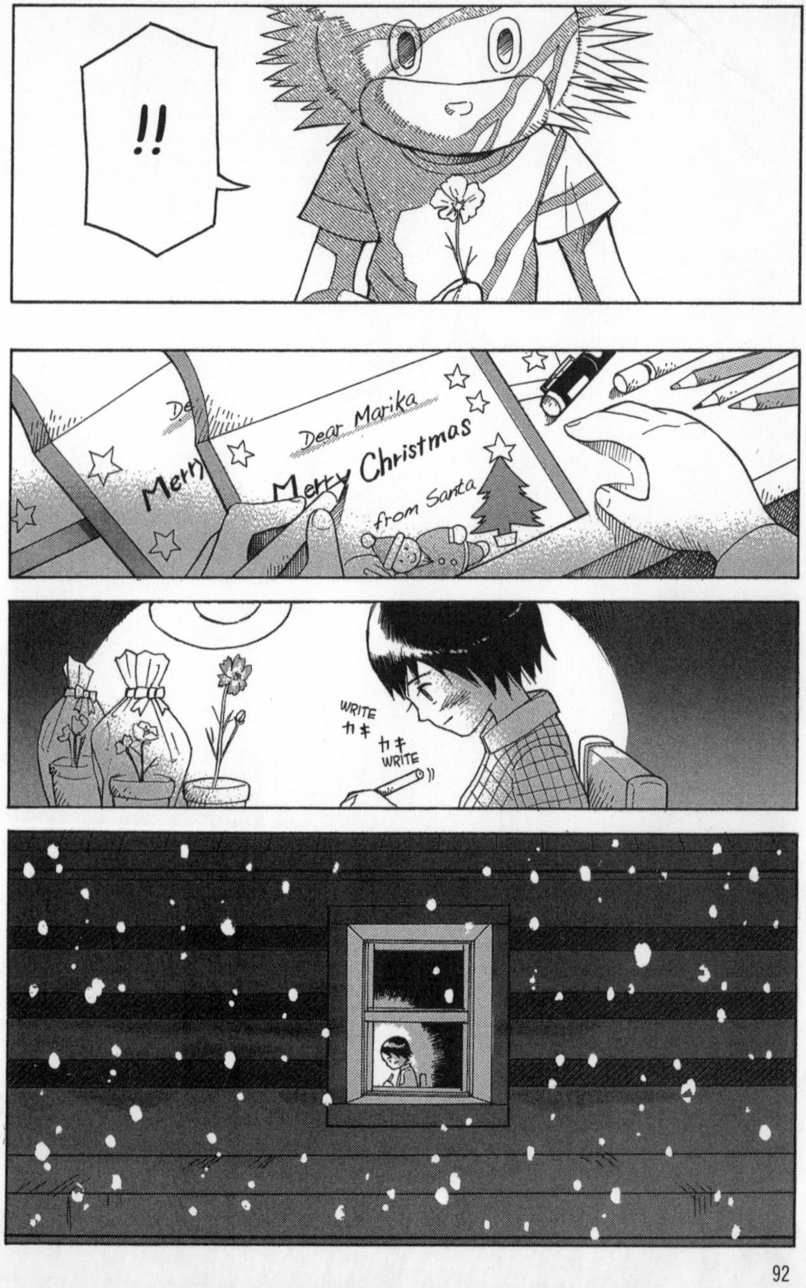
!!
Dear Marika
Merry Christmas
from Santa
De
Merry
WRITE
カキ
カキ
WRITE

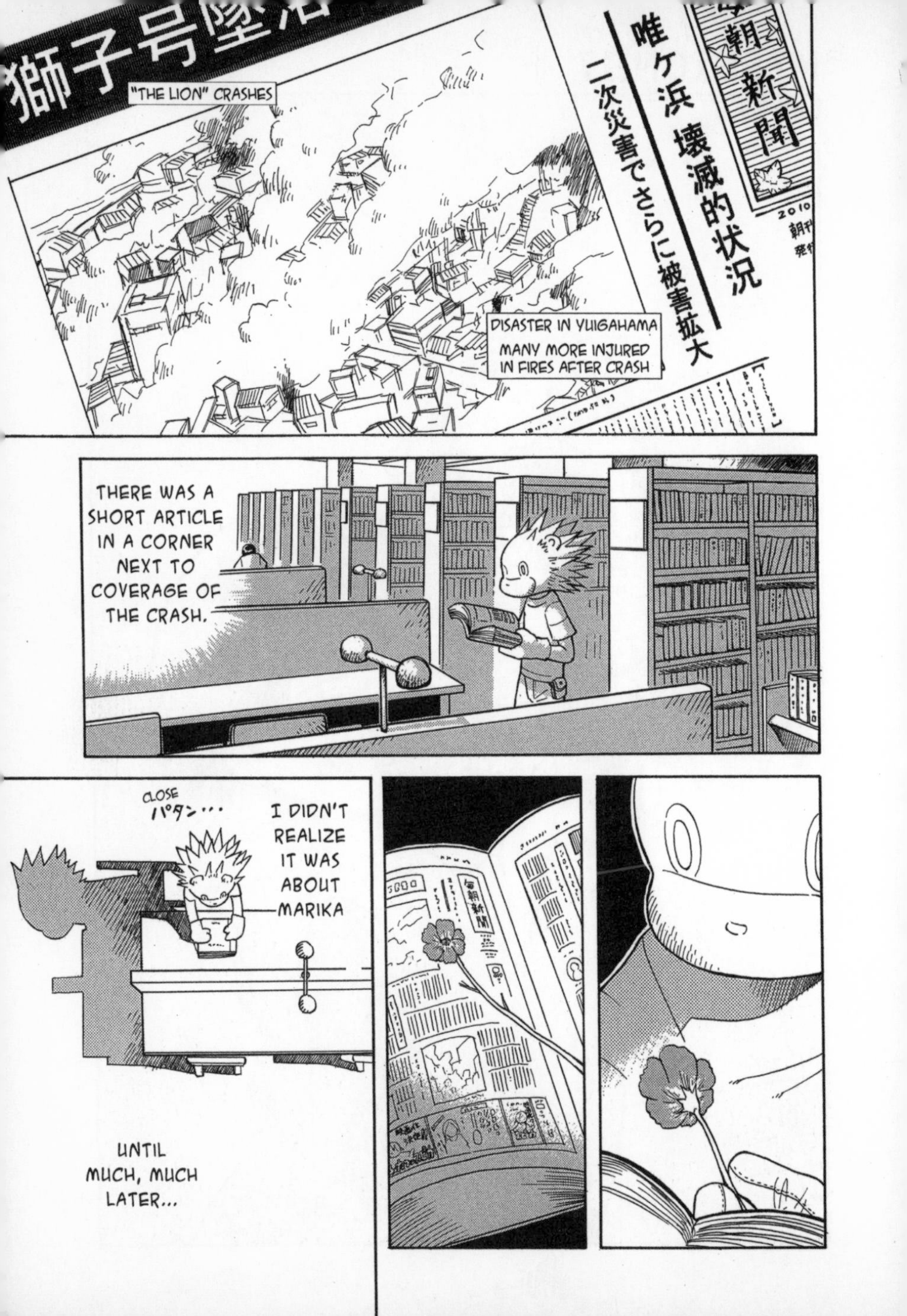

朝新聞
2010
朝刊
唯ケ浜 壊滅的状況
二次災害でさらに被害拡大
獅子号墜
"THE LION" CRASHES
DISASTER IN YUIGAHAMA
MANY MORE INJURED IN FIRES AFTER CRASH
THERE WAS A SHORT ARTICLE IN A CORNER NEXT TO COVERAGE OF THE CRASH.
CLOSE
パタン・・・
I DIDN'T REALIZE IT WAS ABOUT MARIKA
UNTIL MUCH, MUCH LATER...

MISSION:17

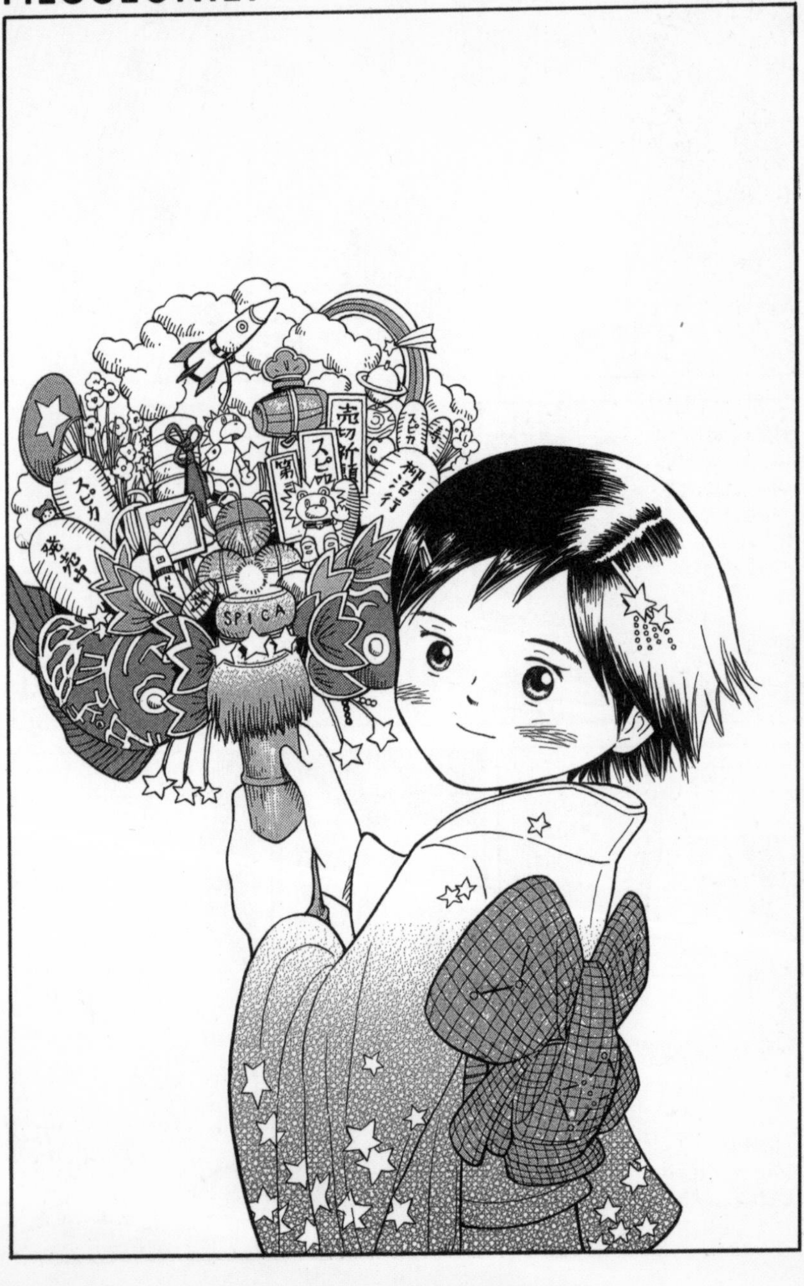
スピカ
SPICA

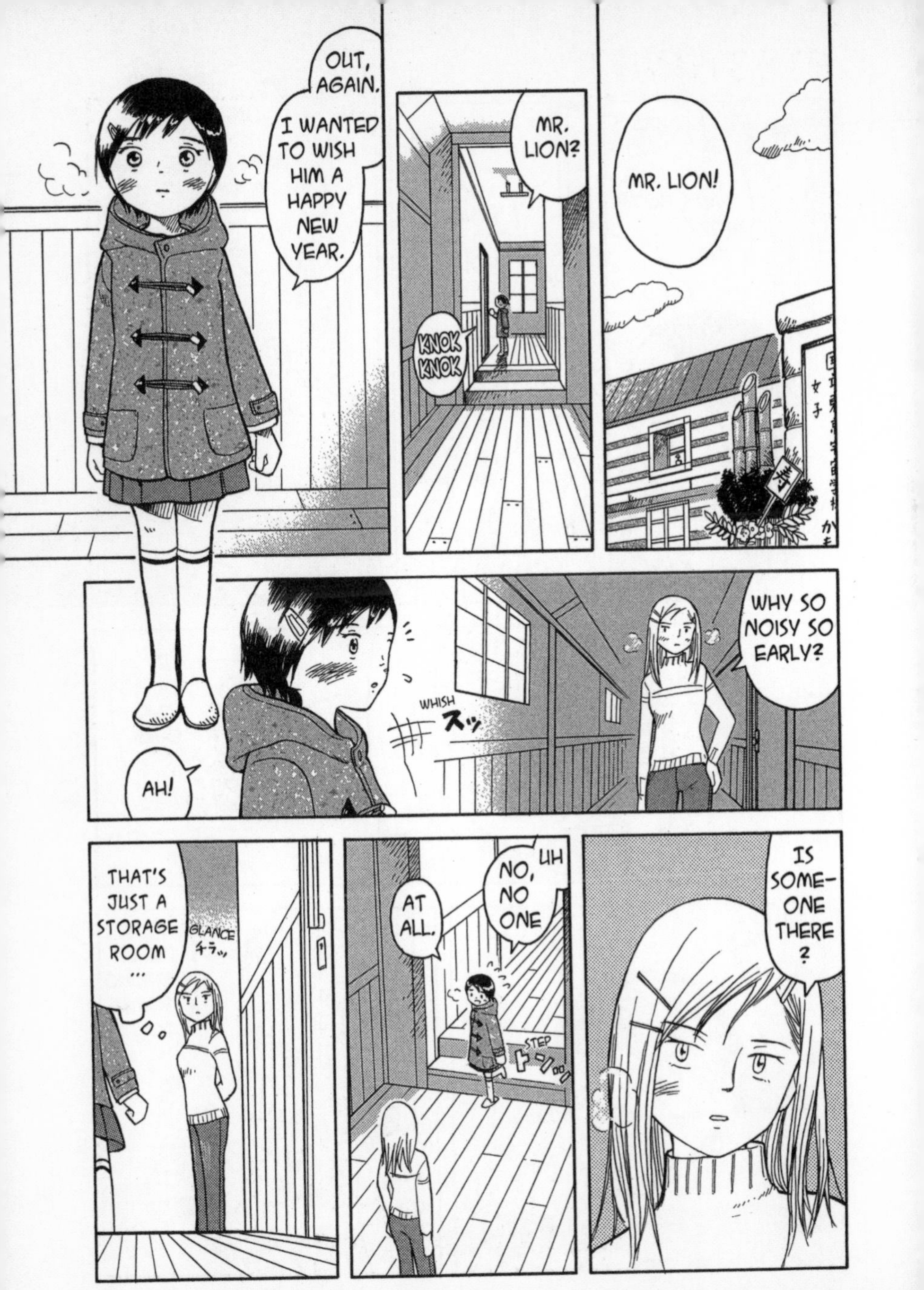
MR. LION!
MR. LION?
KNOK KNOK
OUT, AGAIN.
I WANTED TO WISH HIM A HAPPY NEW YEAR.
WHY SO NOISY SO EARLY?
WHISH スッ
AH!
IS SOME-ONE THERE?
UH
NO, NO ONE
AT ALL.
STEP
THAT'S JUST A STORAGE ROOM ...
GLANCE チラッ

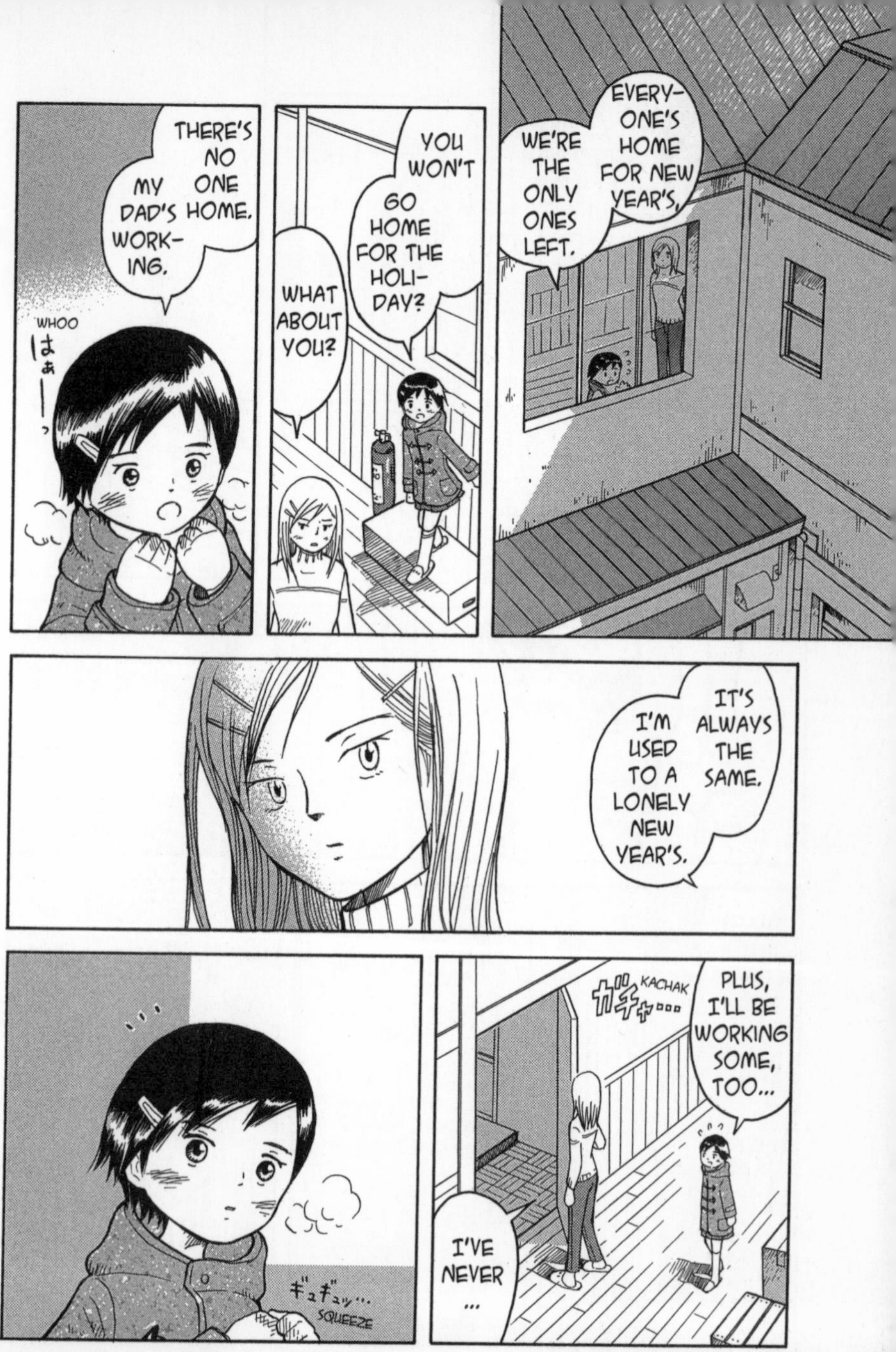
EVERY-ONE'S HOME FOR NEW YEAR'S,
WE'RE THE ONLY ONES LEFT.
YOU WON'T GO HOME FOR THE HOLIDAY?
WHAT ABOUT YOU?
THERE'S NO ONE HOME.
MY DAD'S WORKING.
WHOO
はぁ—っ
IT'S ALWAYS THE SAME.
I'M USED TO A LONELY NEW YEAR'S.
ガチャ…
KACHAK
PLUS, I'LL BE WORKING SOME, TOO...
I'VE NEVER ...
ギュギュッ‥
SQUEEZE

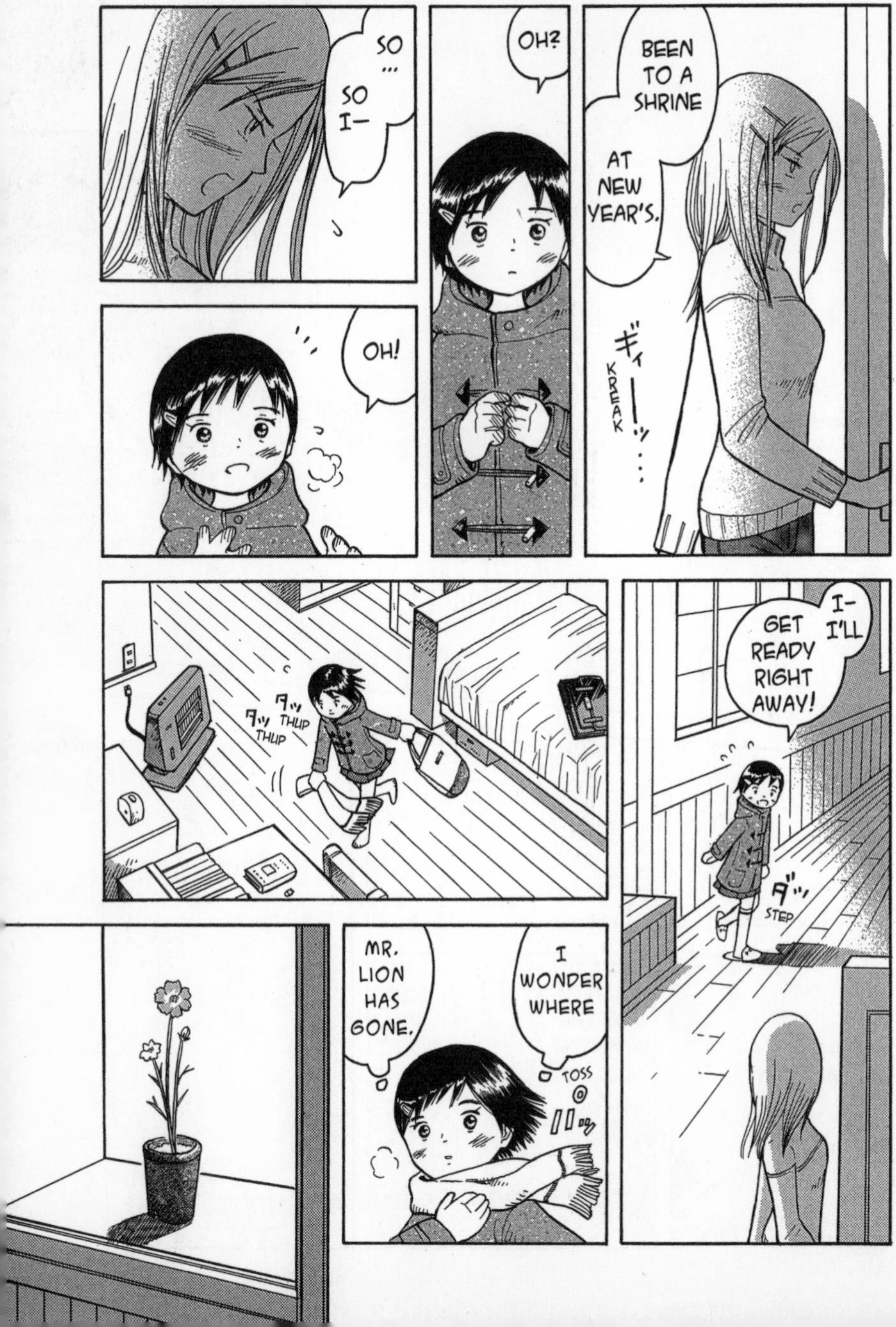
BEEN TO A SHRINE AT NEW YEAR'S.
ギィーッ…
KREAK
OH?
SO… SO I—
OH!
I— I'LL GET READY RIGHT AWAY!
タッ
STEP
タッ THUP
タッ THUP
I WONDER WHERE
MR. LION HAS GONE.
TOSS

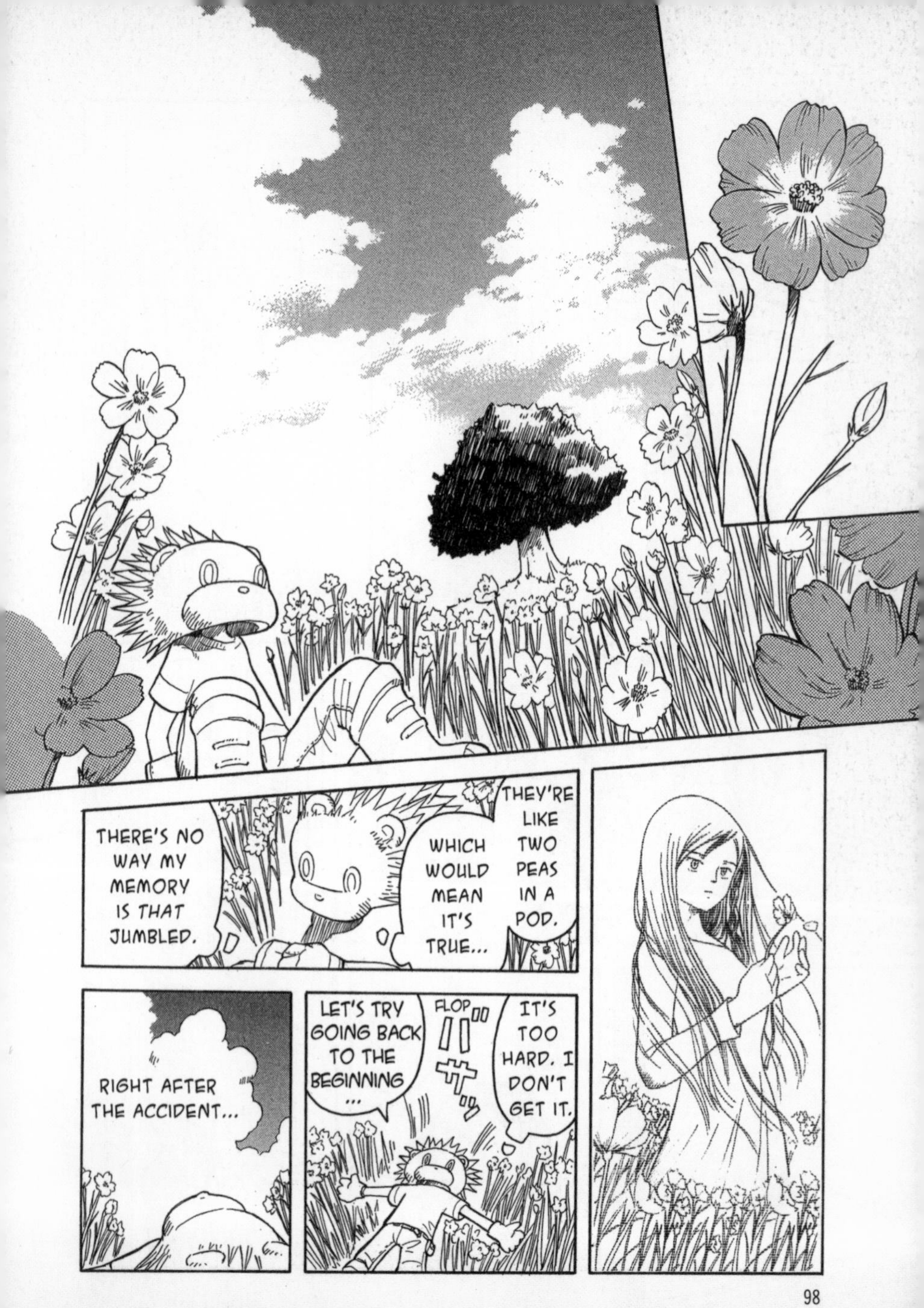
THEY'RE LIKE TWO PEAS IN A POD.
WHICH WOULD MEAN IT'S TRUE...
THERE'S NO WAY MY MEMORY IS THAT JUMBLED.
IT'S TOO HARD. I DON'T GET IT.
FLOP
LET'S TRY GOING BACK TO THE BEGINNING...
RIGHT AFTER THE ACCIDENT...

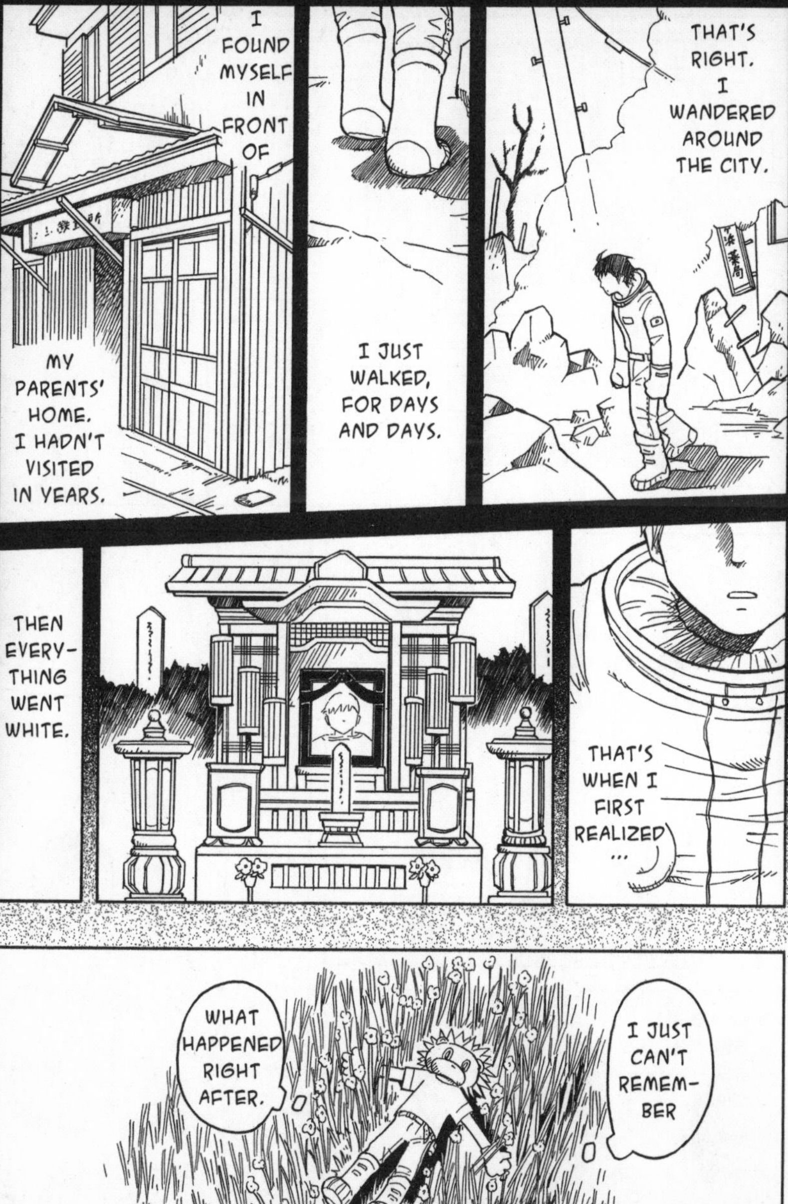
THAT'S RIGHT. I WANDERED AROUND THE CITY.
I JUST WALKED, FOR DAYS AND DAYS.
I FOUND MYSELF IN FRONT OF
MY PARENTS' HOME. I HADN'T VISITED IN YEARS.
THAT'S WHEN I FIRST REALIZED ...
THEN EVERY-THING WENT WHITE.
I JUST CAN'T REMEM-BER
WHAT HAPPENED RIGHT AFTER.

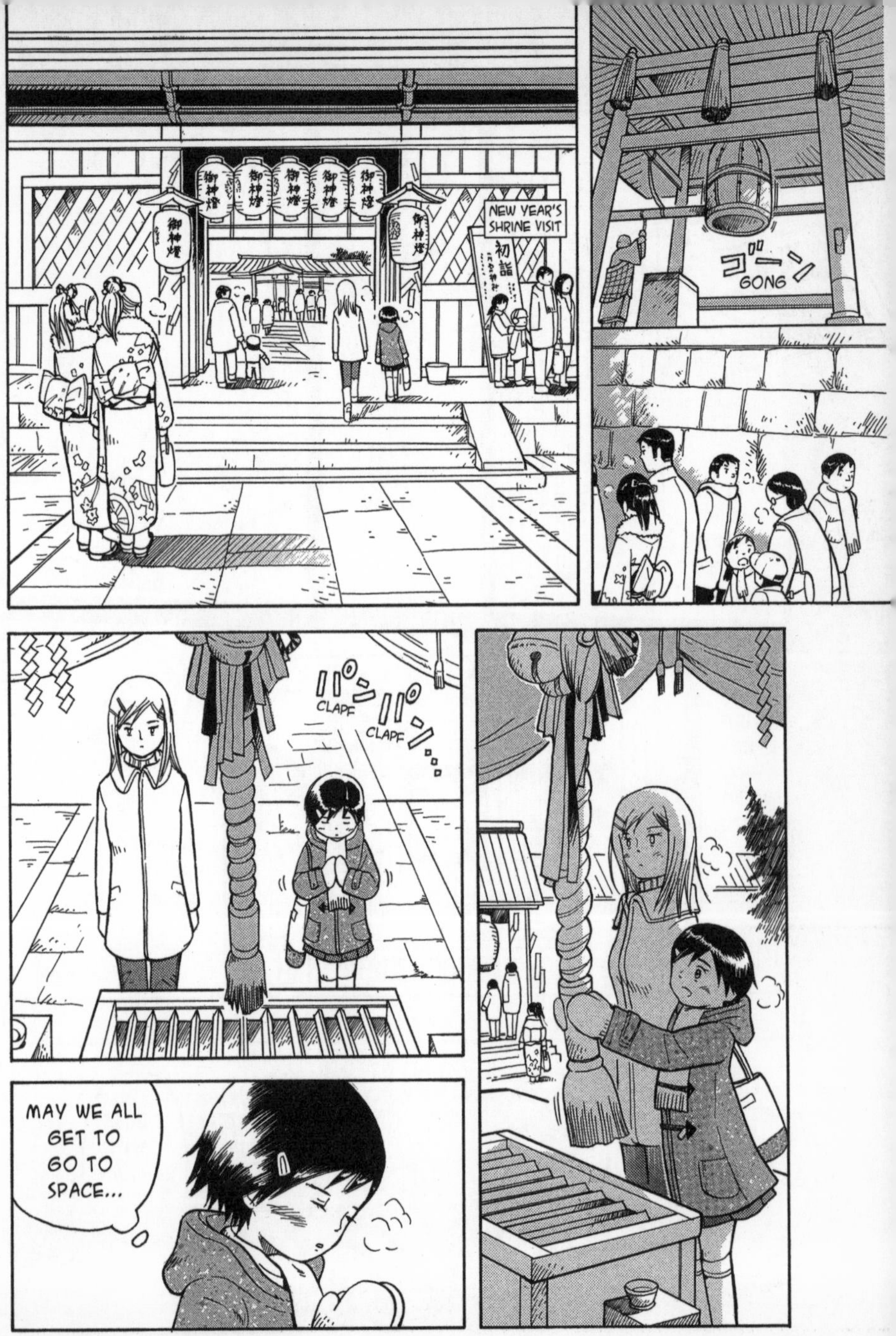
ゴーン
GONG
御神燈
NEW YEAR'S SHRINE VISIT
初詣
パン
CLAPF
パン
CLAPF
MAY WE ALL GET TO GO TO SPACE...

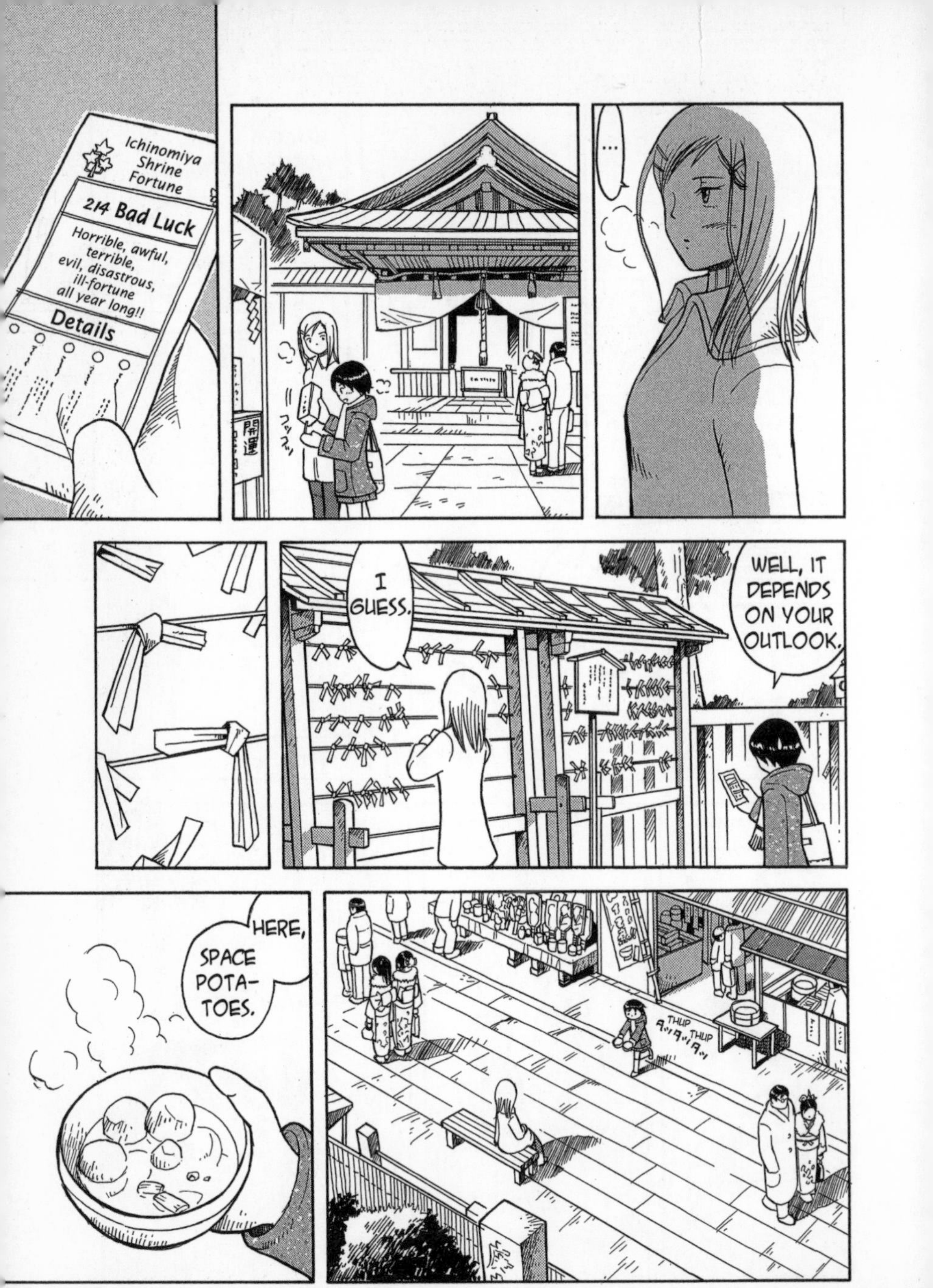
...
Ichinomiya Shrine Fortune
214 Bad Luck
Horrible, awful, terrible, evil, disastrous, ill-fortune all year long!!
Details
WELL, IT DEPENDS ON YOUR OUTLOOK.
I GUESS.
THUP THUP
HERE, SPACE POTA-TOES.

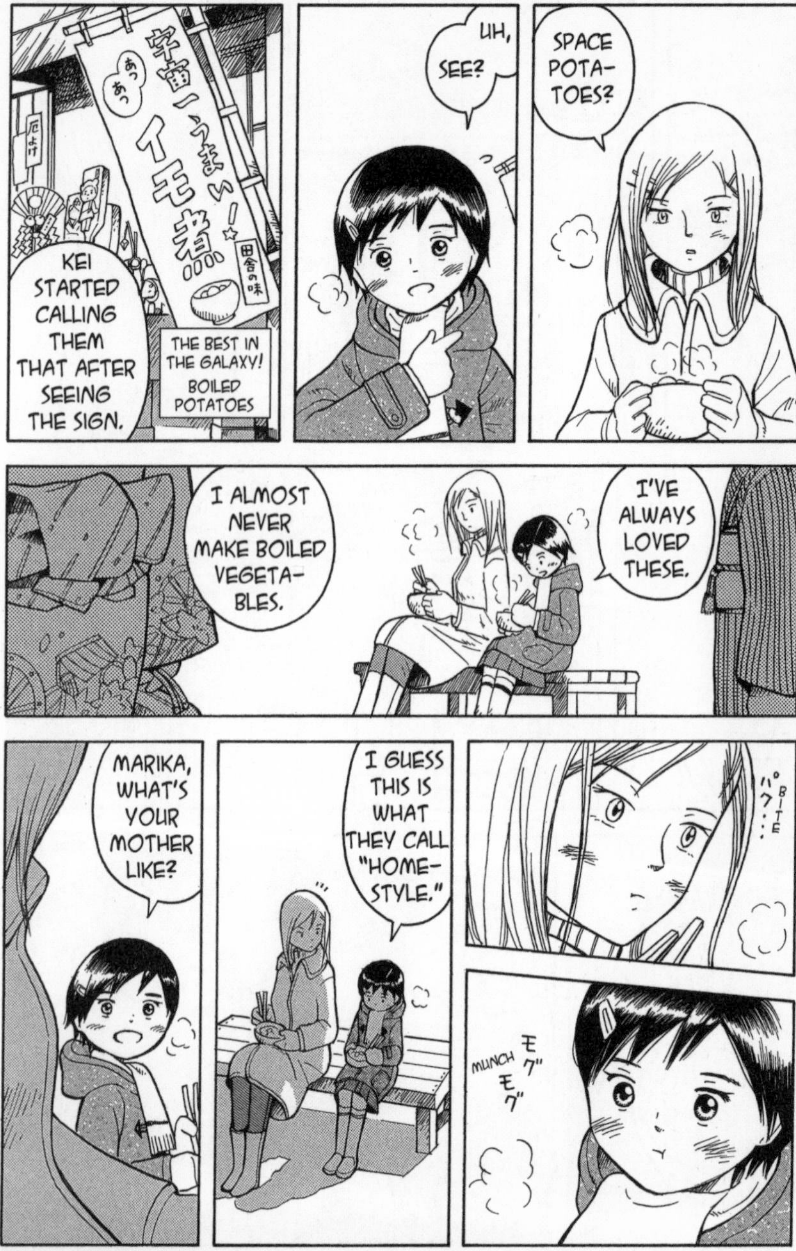
SPACE POTATOES?
UH, SEE?
宇宙一うまい！☆
イモ煮
あっ あっ
田舎の味
厄よけ
THE BEST IN THE GALAXY! BOILED POTATOES
KEI STARTED CALLING THEM THAT AFTER SEEING THE SIGN.
I'VE ALWAYS LOVED THESE.
I ALMOST NEVER MAKE BOILED VEGETABLES.
パク…
BITE
モグ モグ
MUNCH
I GUESS THIS IS WHAT THEY CALL "HOME-STYLE."
MARIKA, WHAT'S YOUR MOTHER LIKE?

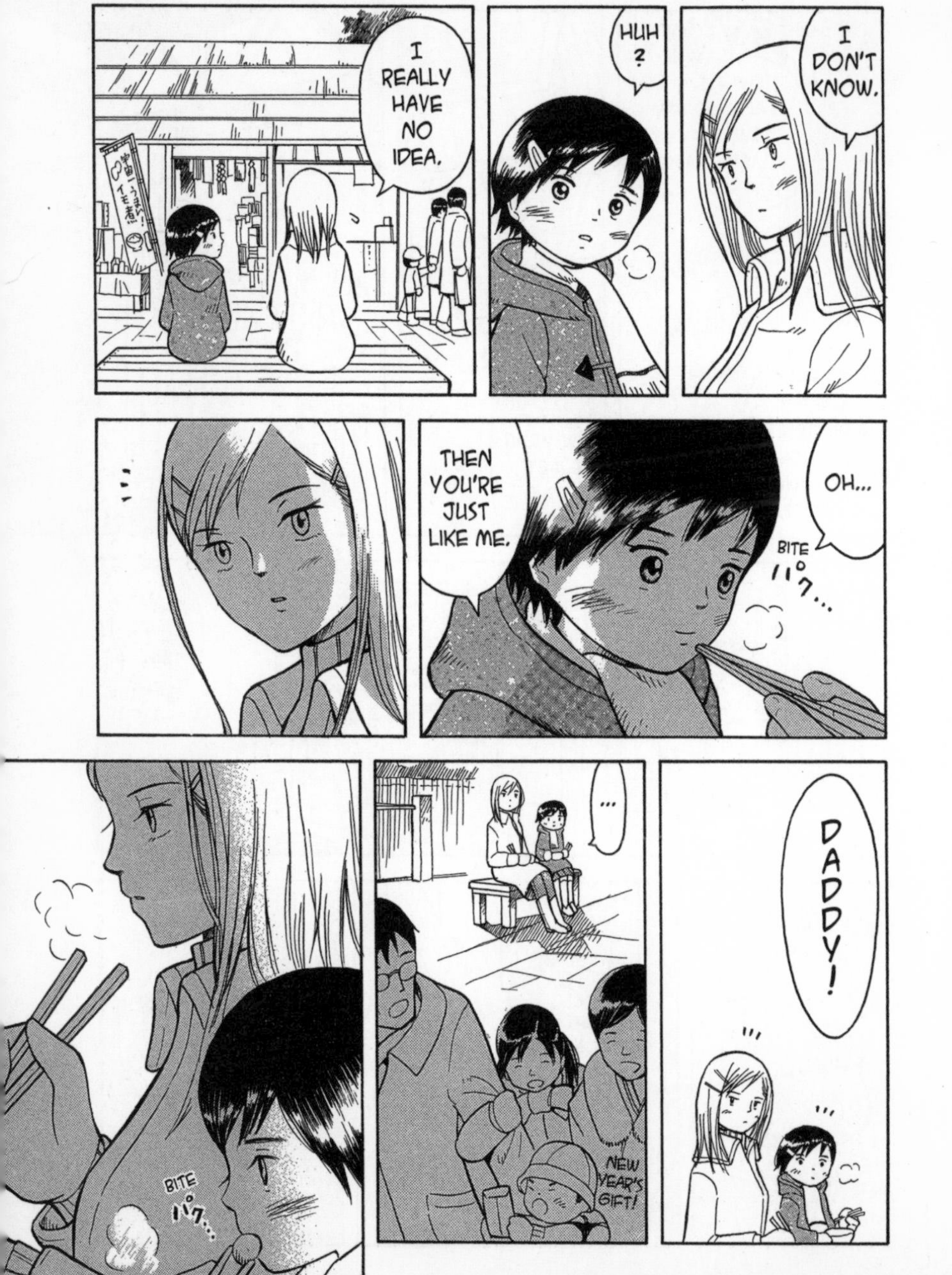
I DON'T KNOW.
HUH ?
I REALLY HAVE NO IDEA.
OH...
BITE
パク...
THEN YOU'RE JUST LIKE ME.
DADDY!
...
NEW YEAR'S GIFT!
BITE
パク...

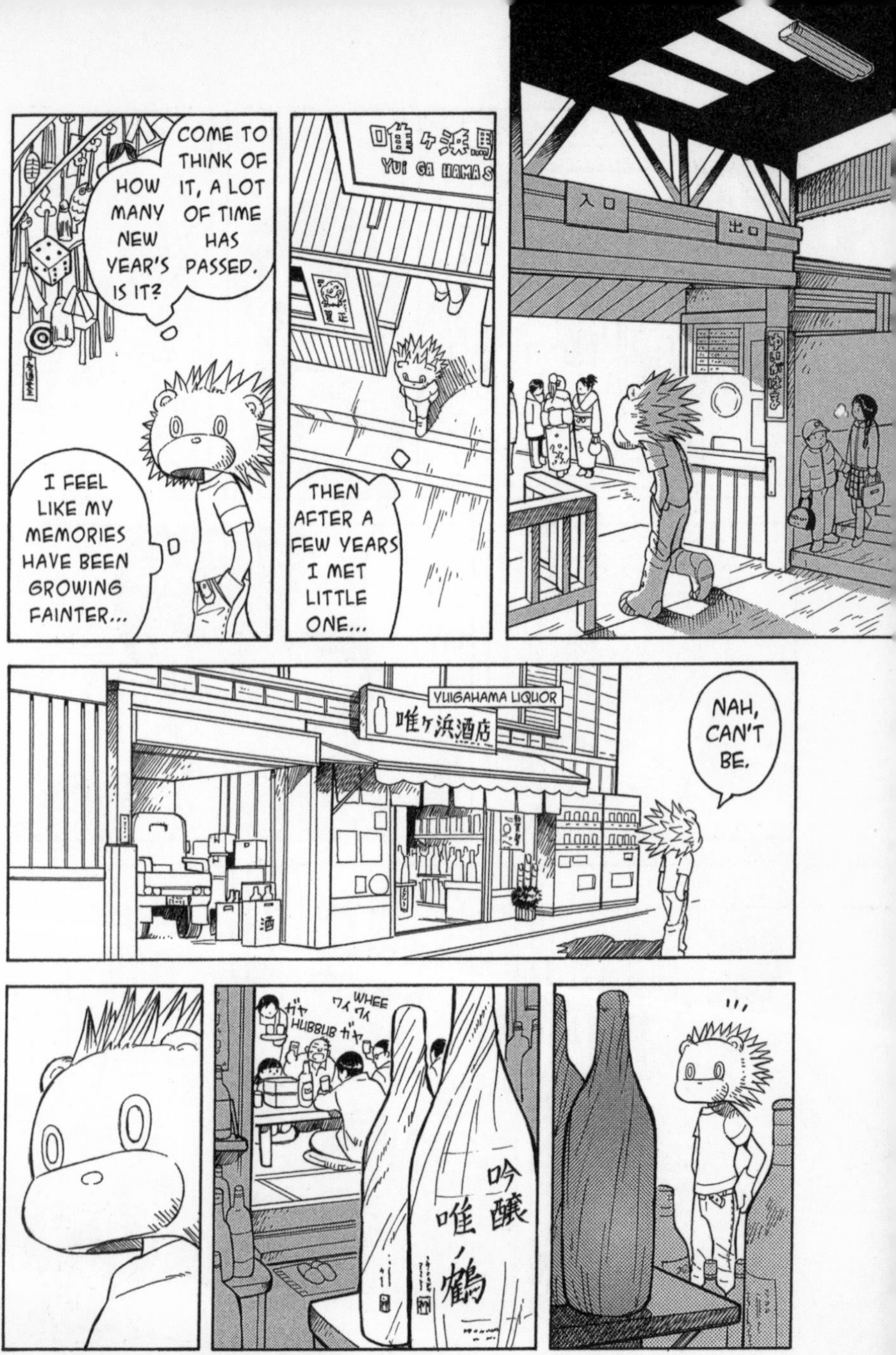
入口
出口
唯ヶ浜駅
YUI GA HAMA S
THEN AFTER A FEW YEARS I MET LITTLE ONE...
COME TO THINK OF IT, A LOT OF TIME HAS PASSED.
HOW MANY NEW YEAR'S IS IT?
I FEEL LIKE MY MEMORIES HAVE BEEN GROWING FAINTER...
NAH, CAN'T BE.
YUIGAHAMA LIQUOR
唯ヶ浜酒店
WHEE ワイワイ
HUBBUB ガヤガヤ
吟醸
唯ノ鶴

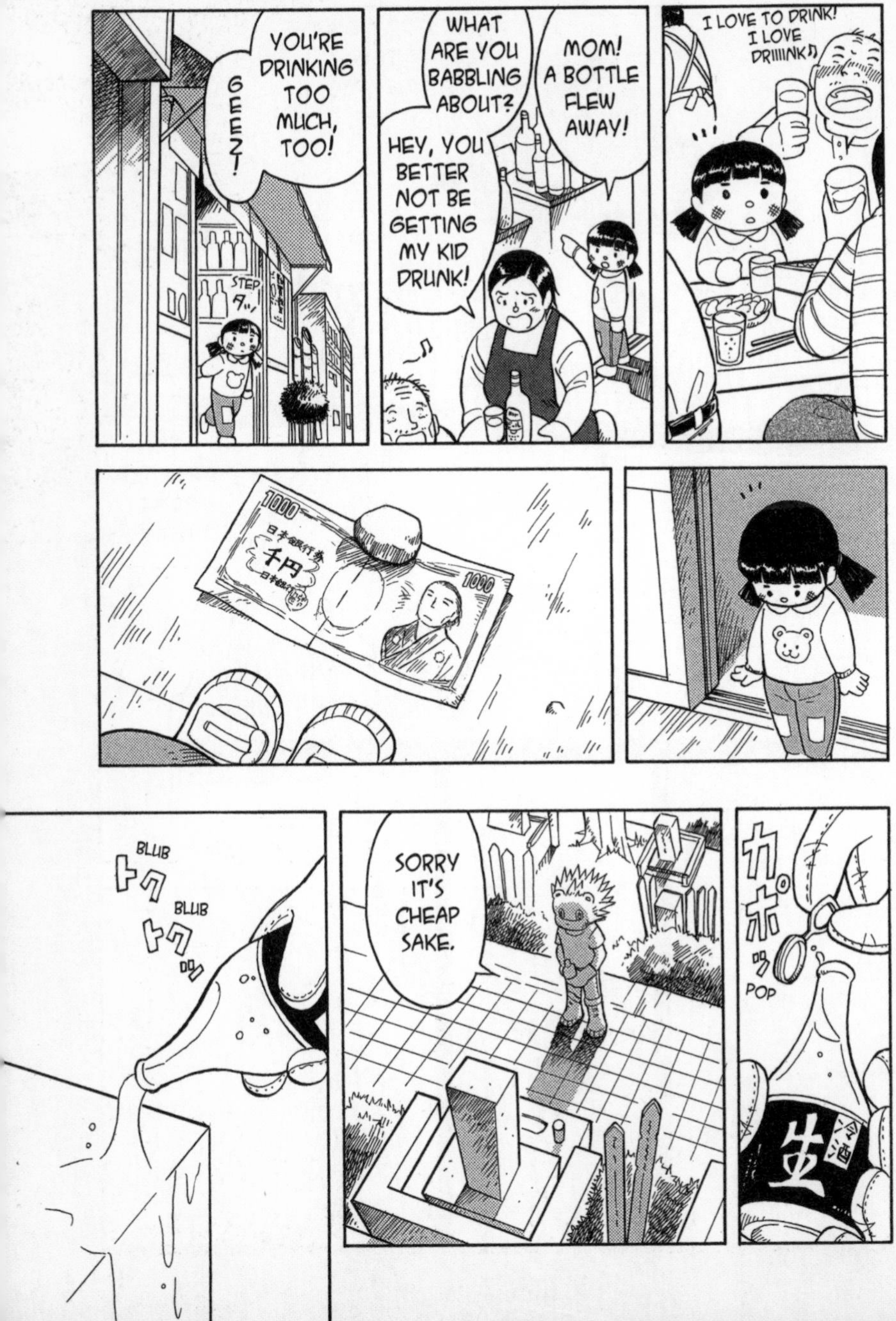
I LOVE TO DRINK! I LOVE DRIIIINK♫
MOM! A BOTTLE FLEW AWAY!
WHAT ARE YOU BABBLING ABOUT?
HEY, YOU BETTER NOT BE GETTING MY KID DRUNK!
YOU'RE DRINKING TOO MUCH, TOO!
GEEZ!
STEP タッ
カポッ
POP
SORRY IT'S CHEAP SAKE.
BLUB トク
BLUB トクッ

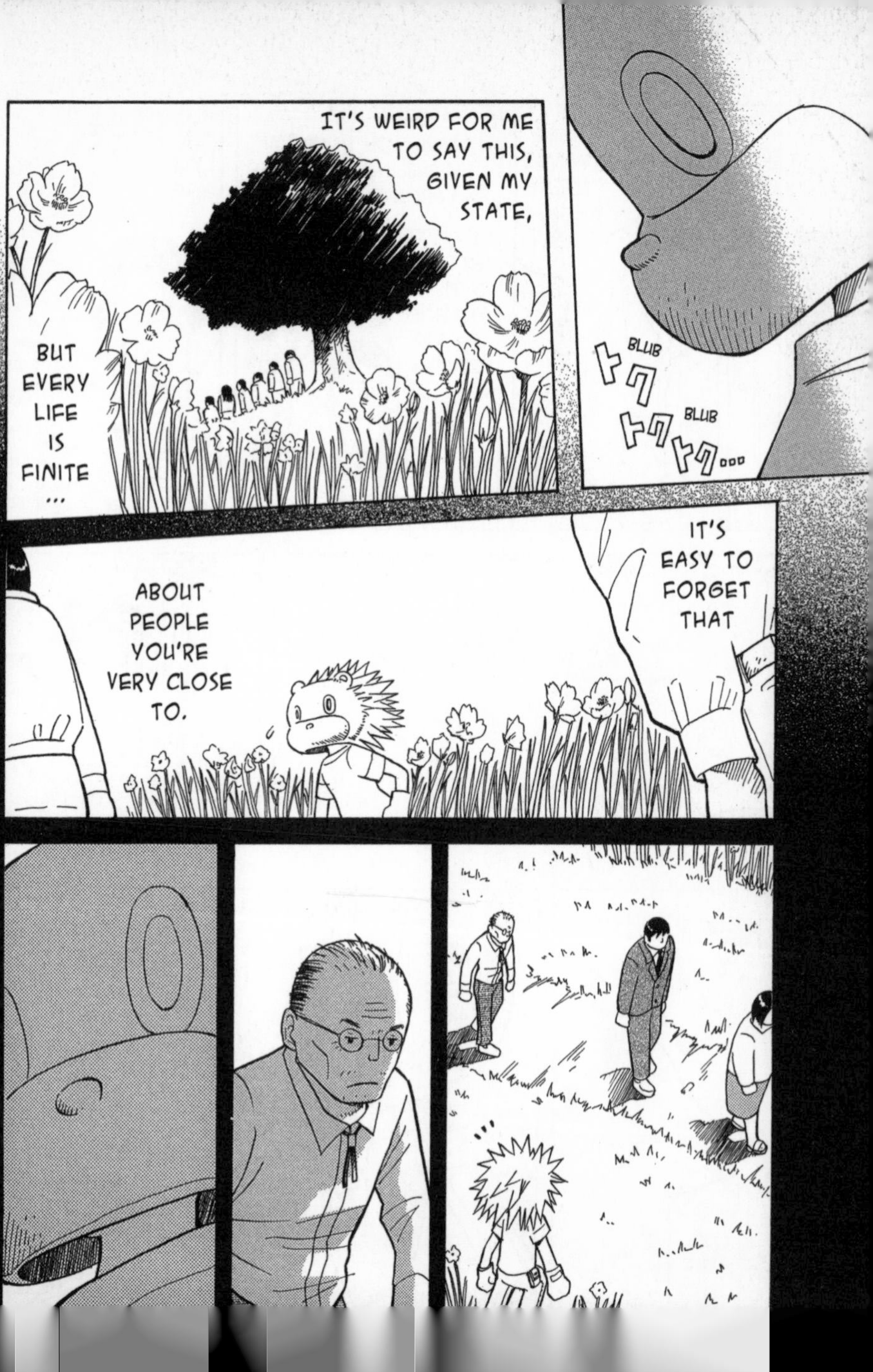
トク
BLUB
トクトク...
BLUB
IT'S WEIRD FOR ME TO SAY THIS, GIVEN MY STATE,
BUT EVERY LIFE IS FINITE...
IT'S EASY TO FORGET THAT
ABOUT PEOPLE YOU'RE VERY CLOSE TO.

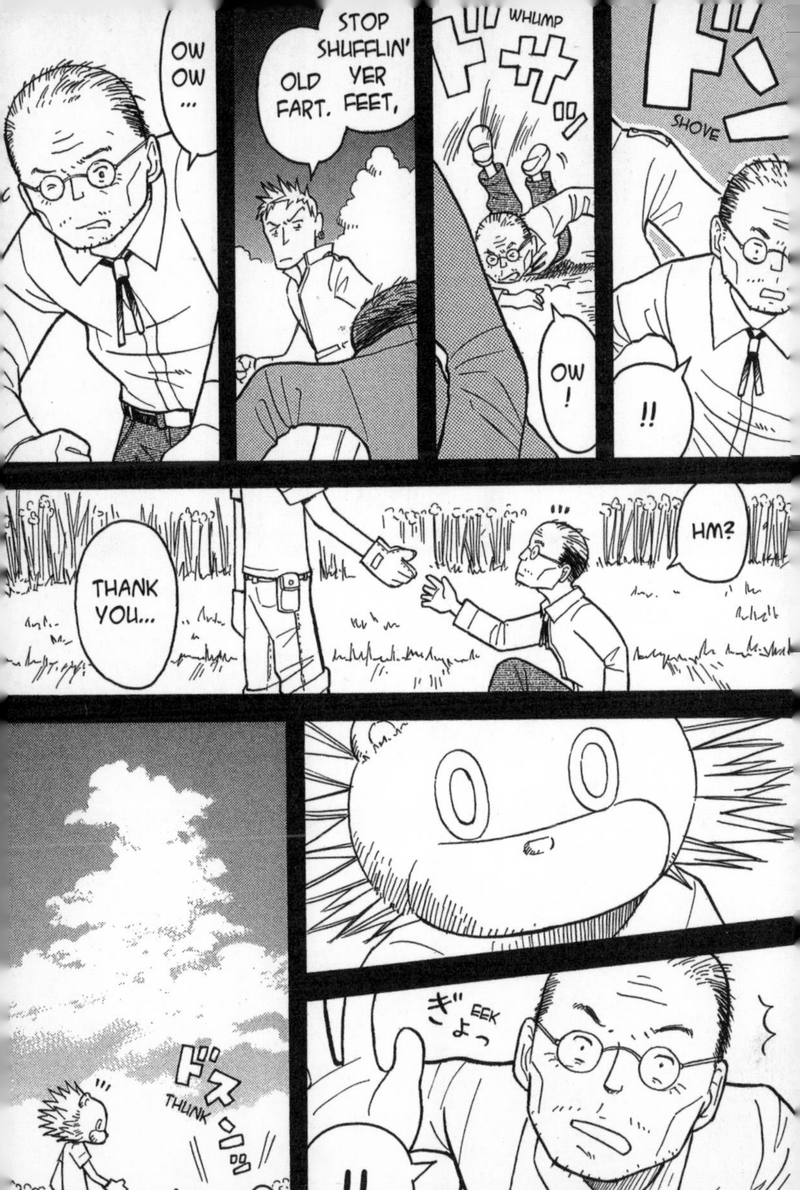
ドン
SHOVE
!!
ドサッ
WHUMP
OW!
STOP SHUFFLIN' YER FEET,
OLD FART.
OW OW ...
HM?
THANK YOU...
ぎょっ
EEK
!!
ドスッ
THUNK
OW

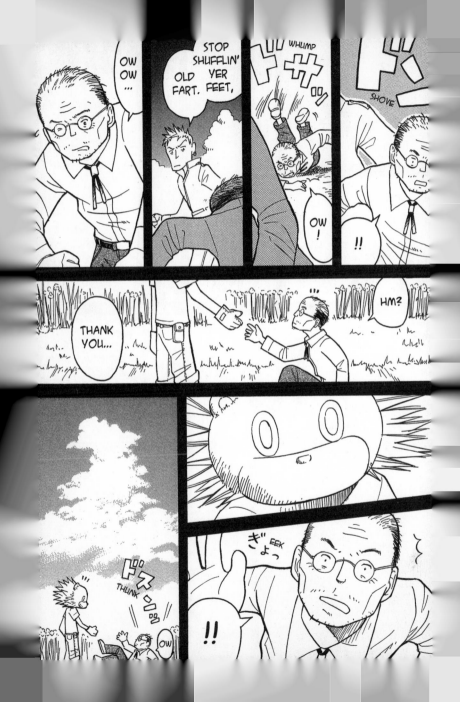

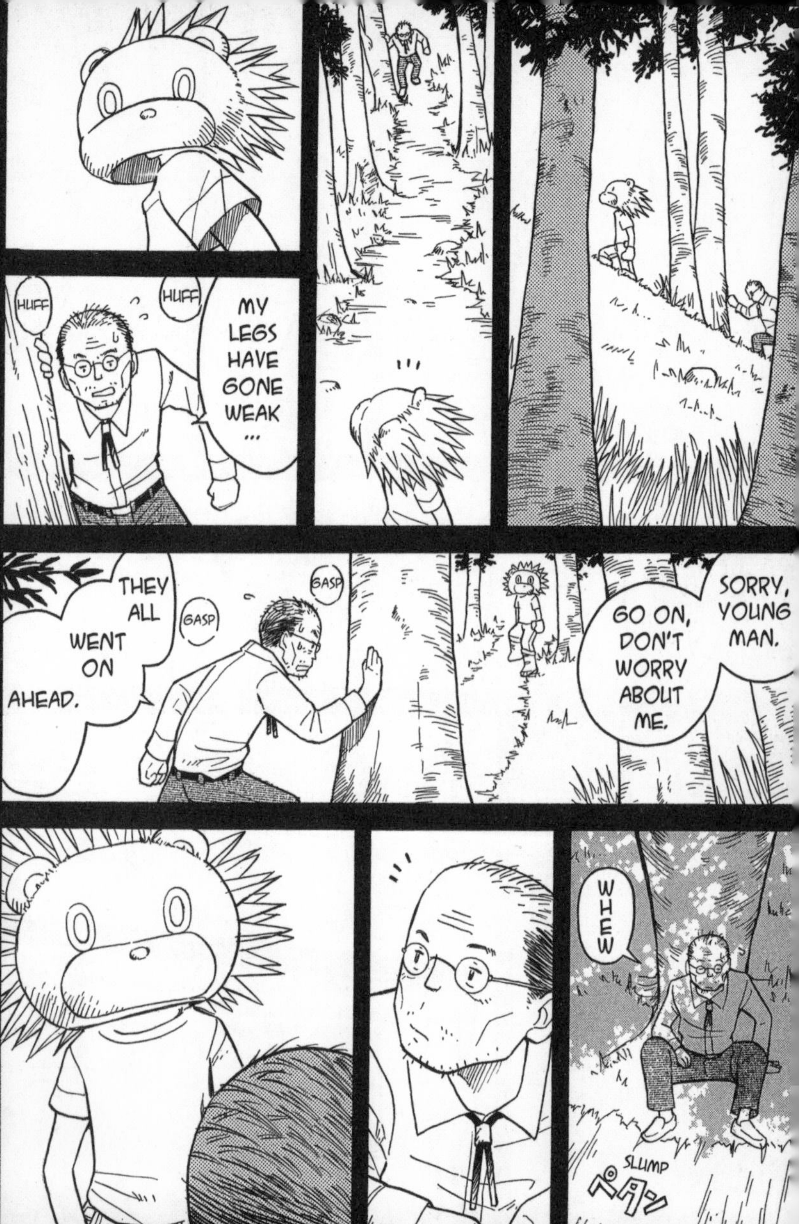
HUFF
HUFF
MY LEGS HAVE GONE WEAK ...
SORRY, YOUNG MAN.
GO ON, DON'T WORRY ABOUT ME.
GASP
GASP
THEY ALL WENT ON AHEAD.
WHEW
SLUMP
ペタン

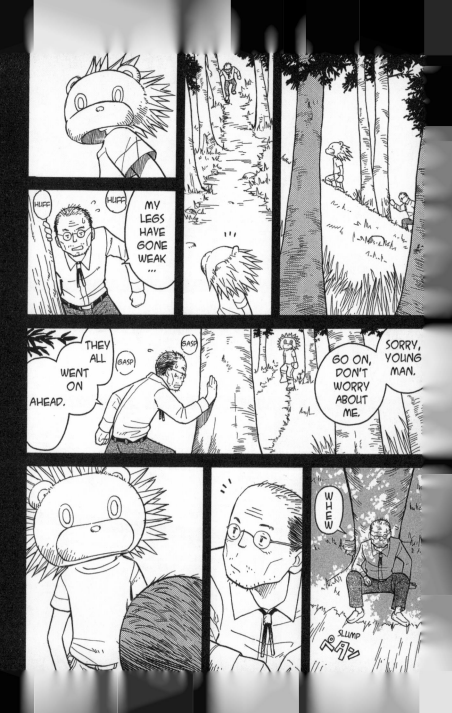

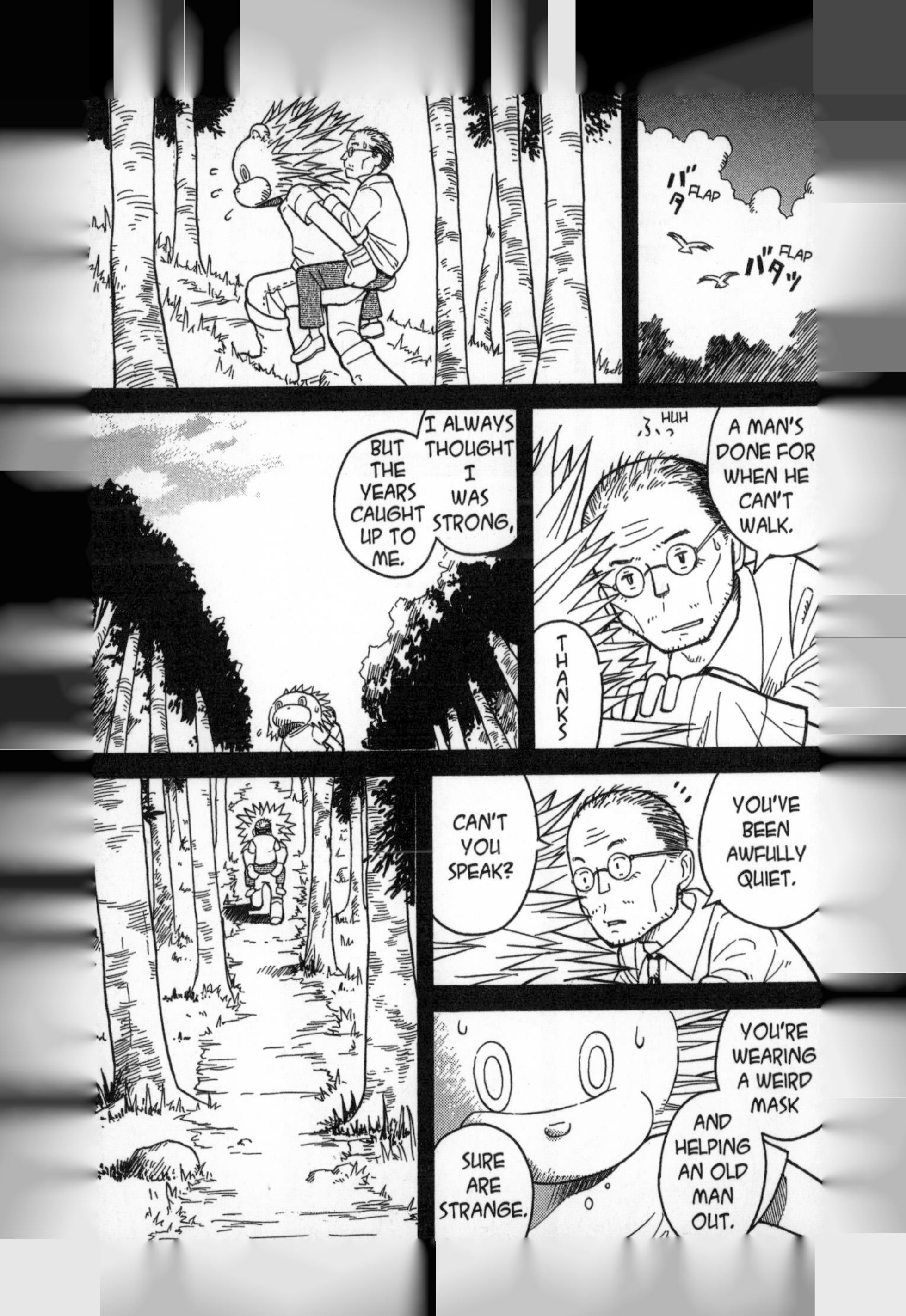
バタ FLAP
バタッ FLAP
ふっ HUH
A MAN'S DONE FOR WHEN HE CAN'T WALK.
THANKS
I ALWAYS THOUGHT I WAS STRONG,
BUT THE YEARS CAUGHT UP TO ME.
YOU'VE BEEN AWFULLY QUIET.
CAN'T YOU SPEAK?
YOU'RE WEARING A WEIRD MASK
AND HELPING AN OLD MAN OUT.
SURE ARE STRANGE.

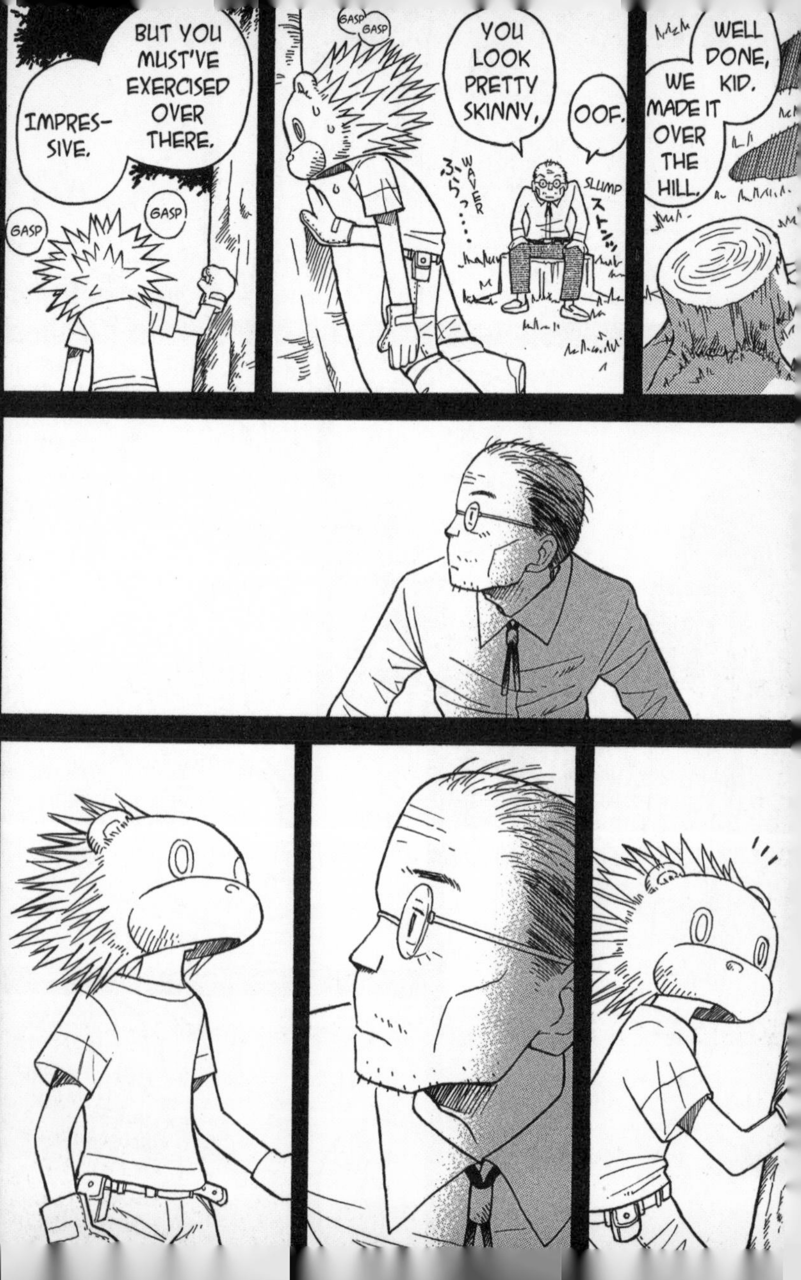
WELL DONE, KID.
WE MADE IT OVER THE HILL.
GASP GASP
YOU LOOK PRETTY SKINNY,
OOF.
SLUMP
ストンッ
ふらっ
WAVER
IMPRES-SIVE.
BUT YOU MUST'VE EXERCISED OVER THERE.
GASP
GASP

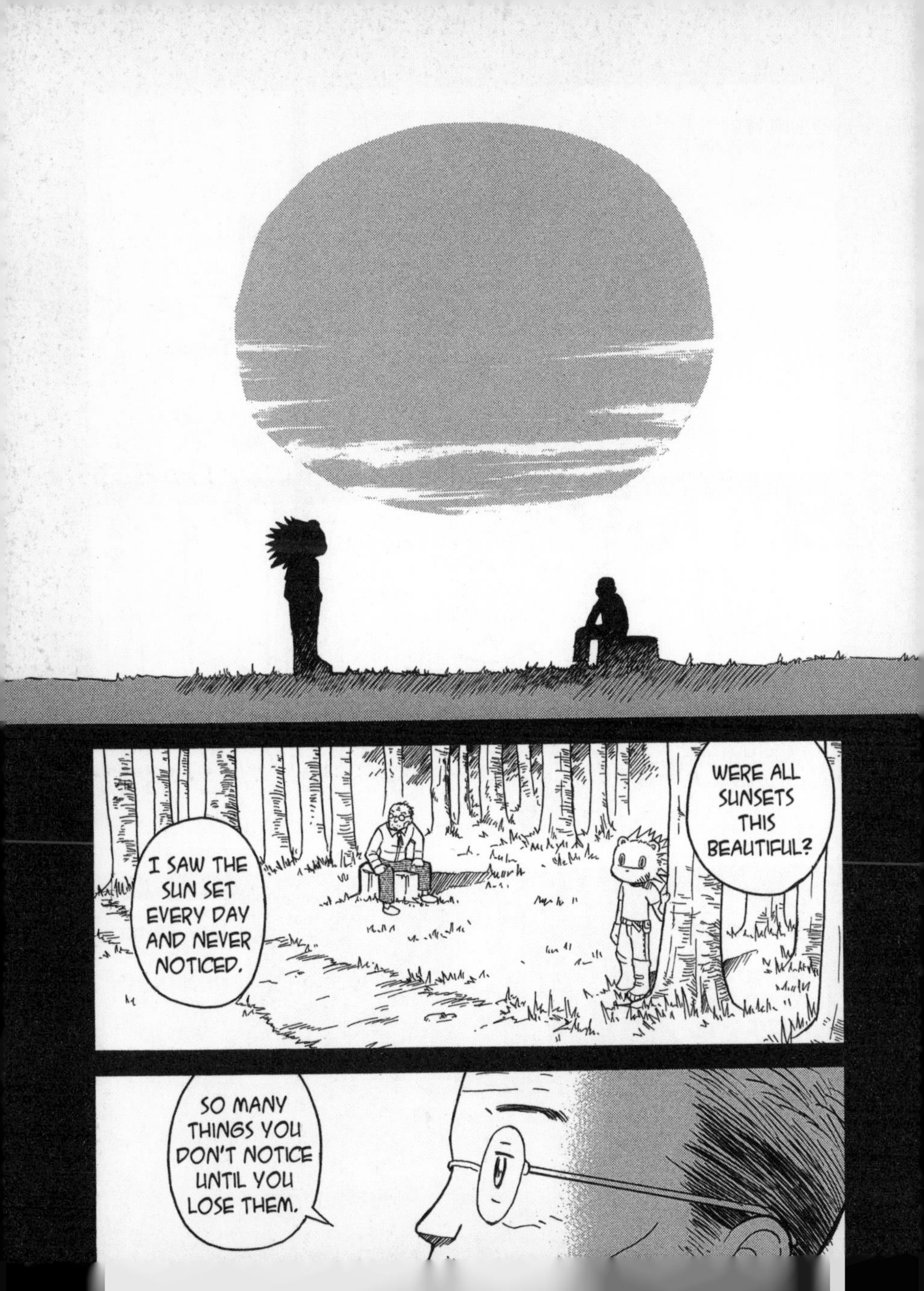
WERE ALL SUNSETS THIS BEAUTIFUL?
I SAW THE SUN SET EVERY DAY AND NEVER NOTICED.
SO MANY THINGS YOU DON'T NOTICE UNTIL YOU LOSE THEM.

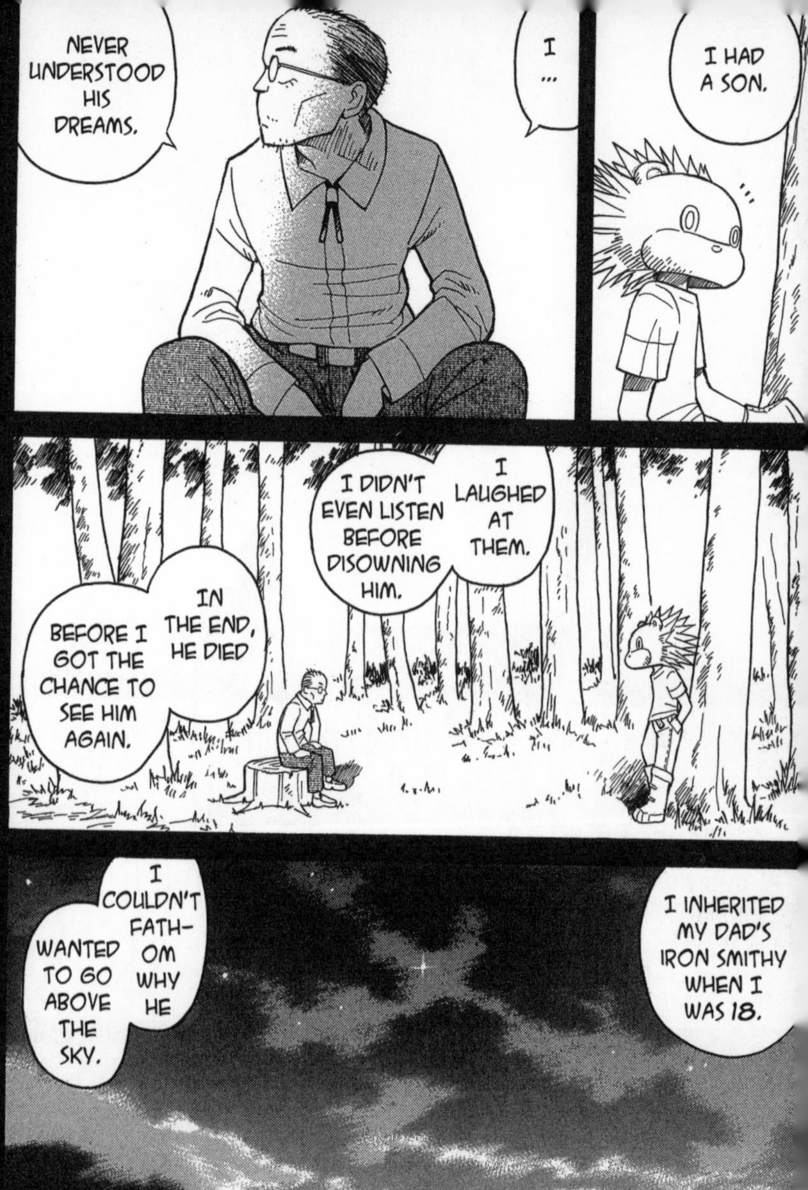
I HAD A SON.
I ...
NEVER UNDERSTOOD HIS DREAMS.
I LAUGHED AT THEM.
I DIDN'T EVEN LISTEN BEFORE DISOWNING HIM.
IN THE END, HE DIED
BEFORE I GOT THE CHANCE TO SEE HIM AGAIN.
I INHERITED MY DAD'S IRON SMITHY WHEN I WAS 18.
I COULDN'T FATH-OM WHY HE
WANTED TO GO ABOVE THE SKY.

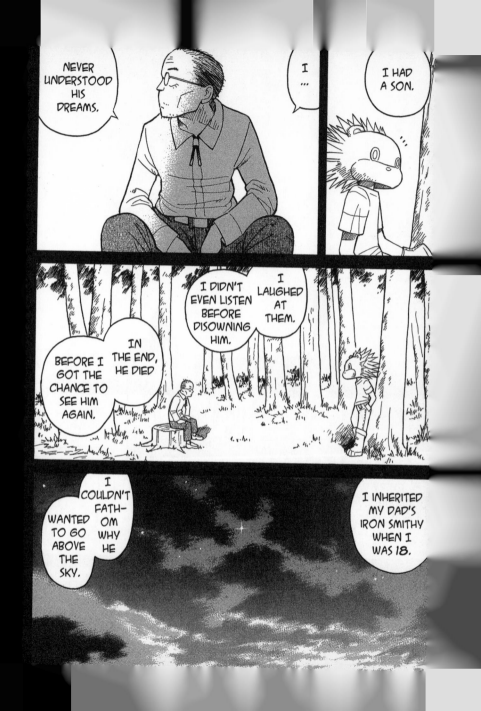

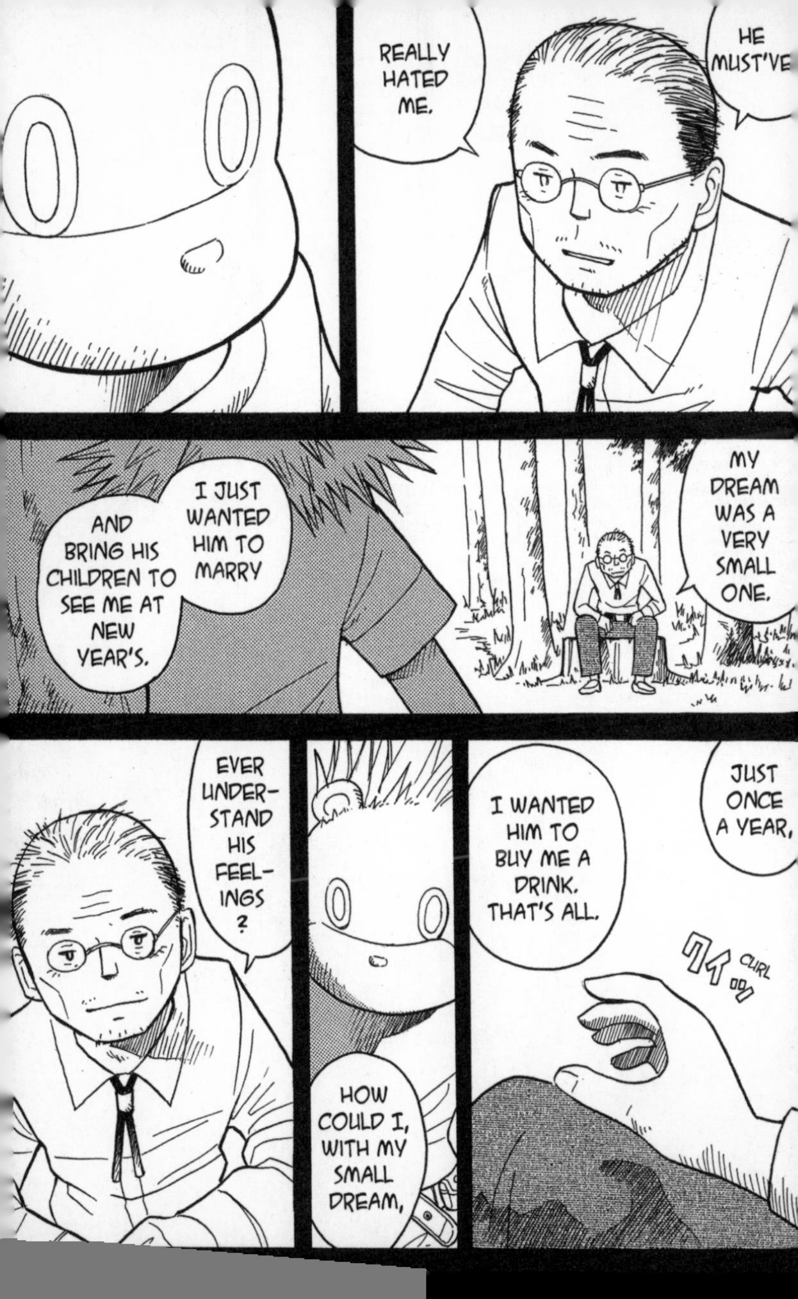
HE MUST'VE
REALLY HATED ME.
MY DREAM WAS A VERY SMALL ONE.
I JUST WANTED HIM TO MARRY
AND BRING HIS CHILDREN TO SEE ME AT NEW YEAR'S.
JUST ONCE A YEAR,
I WANTED HIM TO BUY ME A DRINK. THAT'S ALL.
クイッ
CURL
HOW COULD I, WITH MY SMALL DREAM,
EVER UNDER-STAND HIS FEEL-INGS?

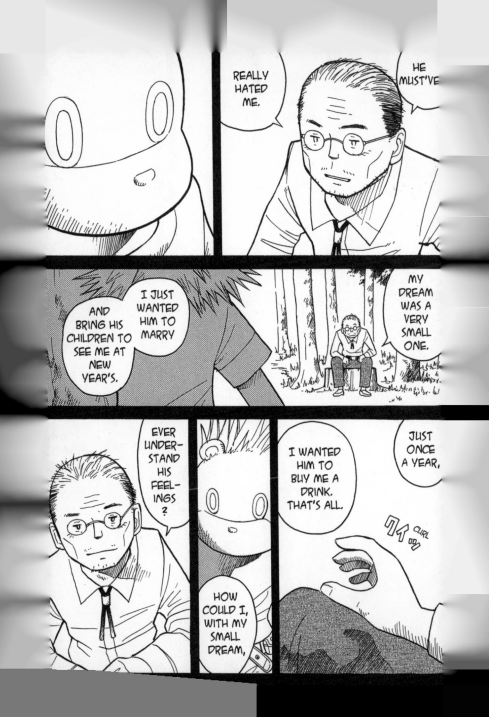

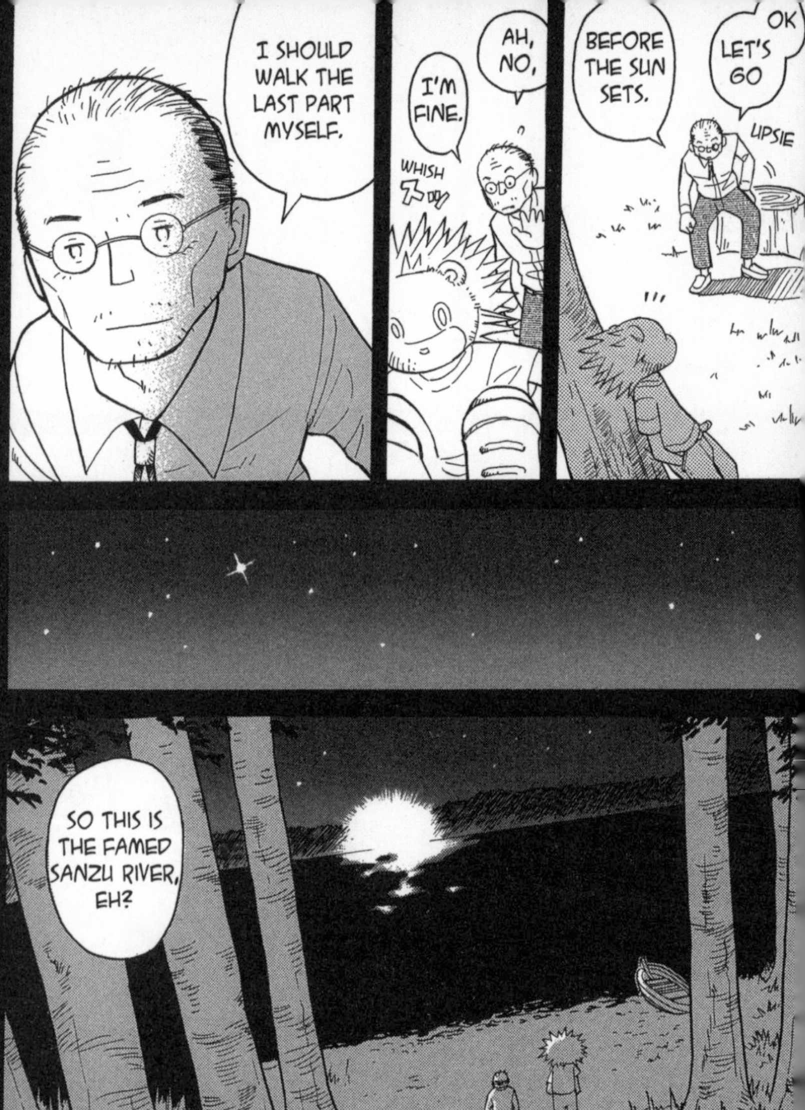
OK LET'S GO
UPSIE
BEFORE THE SUN SETS.
AH, NO,
I'M FINE.
WHISH
I SHOULD WALK THE LAST PART MYSELF.
SO THIS IS THE FAMED SANZU RIVER, EH?

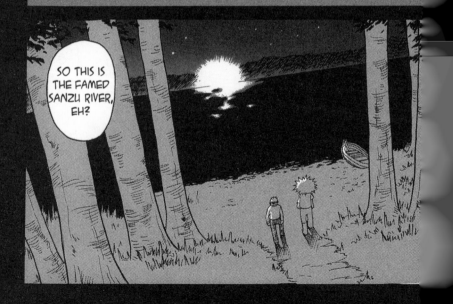

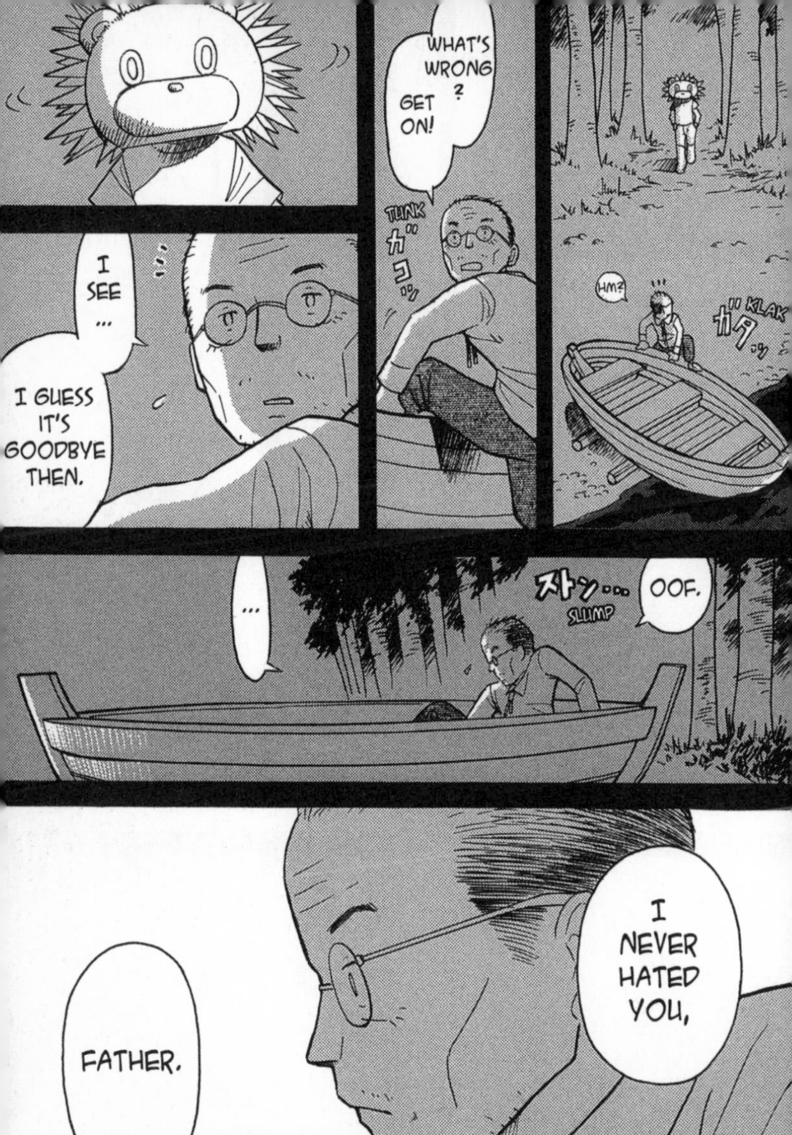
HM?
カタッ KLAK
WHAT'S WRONG? GET ON!
ガゴッ TUNK
I SEE...
I GUESS IT'S GOODBYE THEN.
OOF.
ストン... SLUMP
...
I NEVER HATED YOU,
FATHER.

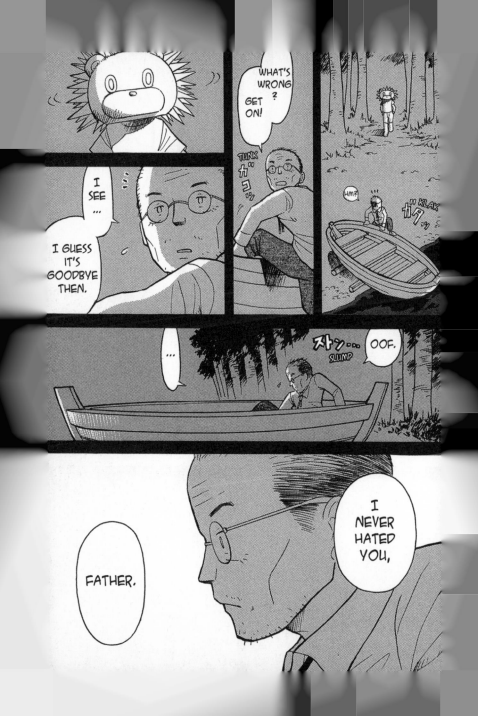

!!
YOU ...
ROLL
コロコロ...
KLATTER
ガタッ
くるっ....
TURN
...

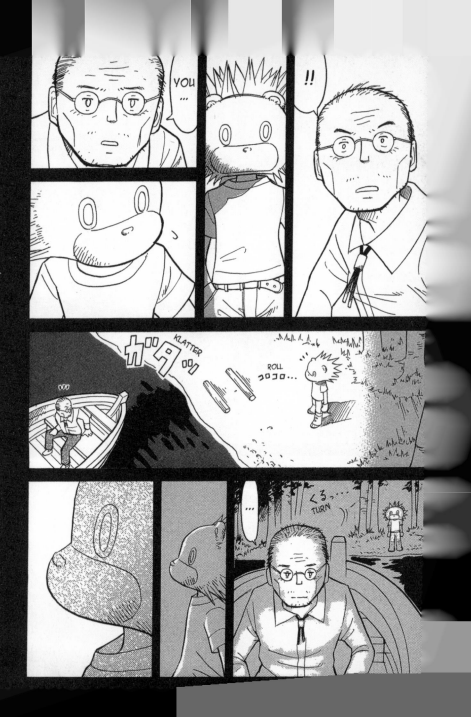

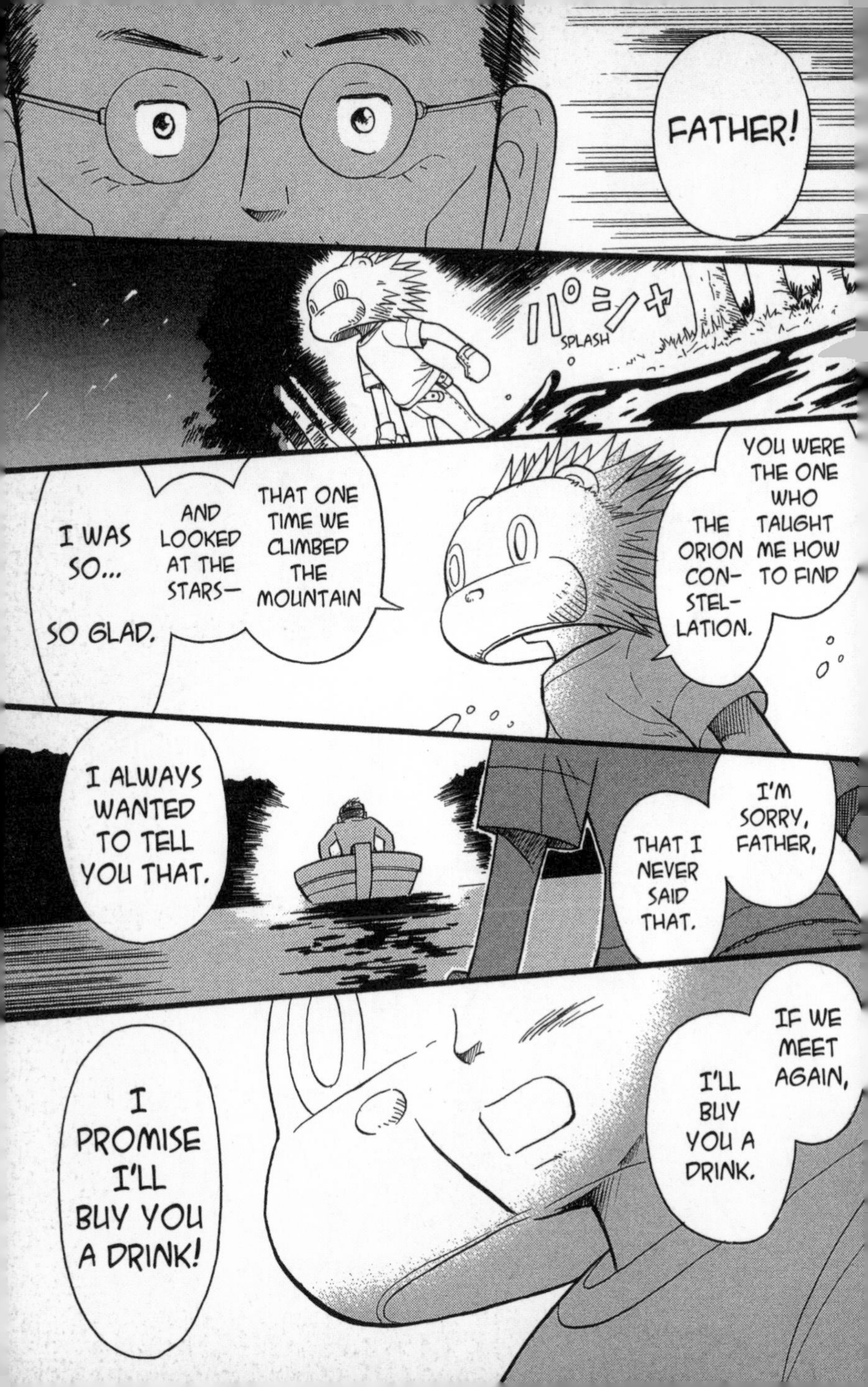
FATHER!
SPLASH
YOU WERE THE ONE WHO TAUGHT ME HOW TO FIND THE ORION CON-STEL-LATION.
THAT ONE TIME WE CLIMBED THE MOUNTAIN AND LOOKED AT THE STARS—
I WAS SO... SO GLAD.
I'M SORRY, FATHER, THAT I NEVER SAID THAT.
I ALWAYS WANTED TO TELL YOU THAT.
IF WE MEET AGAIN, I'LL BUY YOU A DRINK.
I PROMISE I'LL BUY YOU A DRINK!

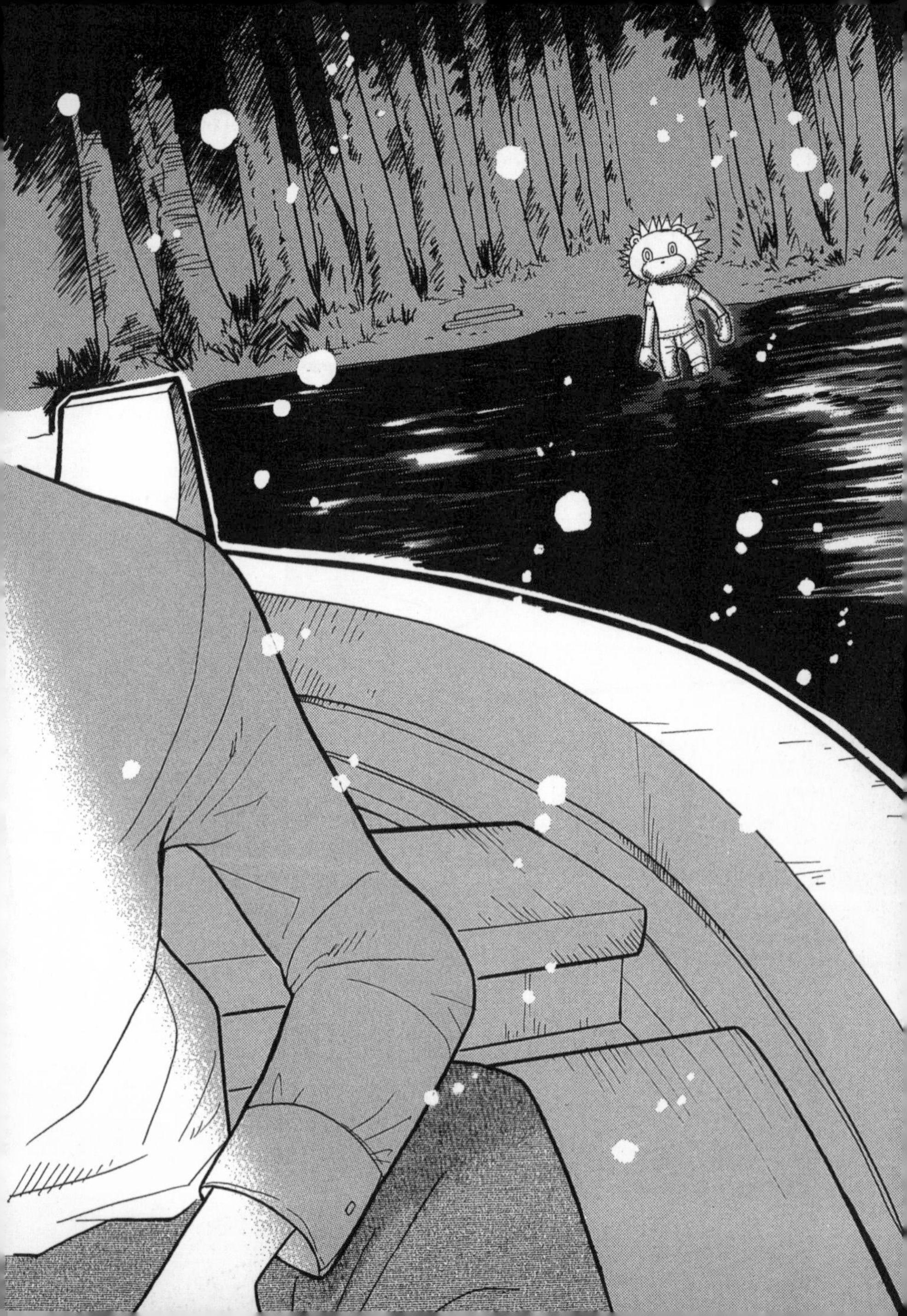

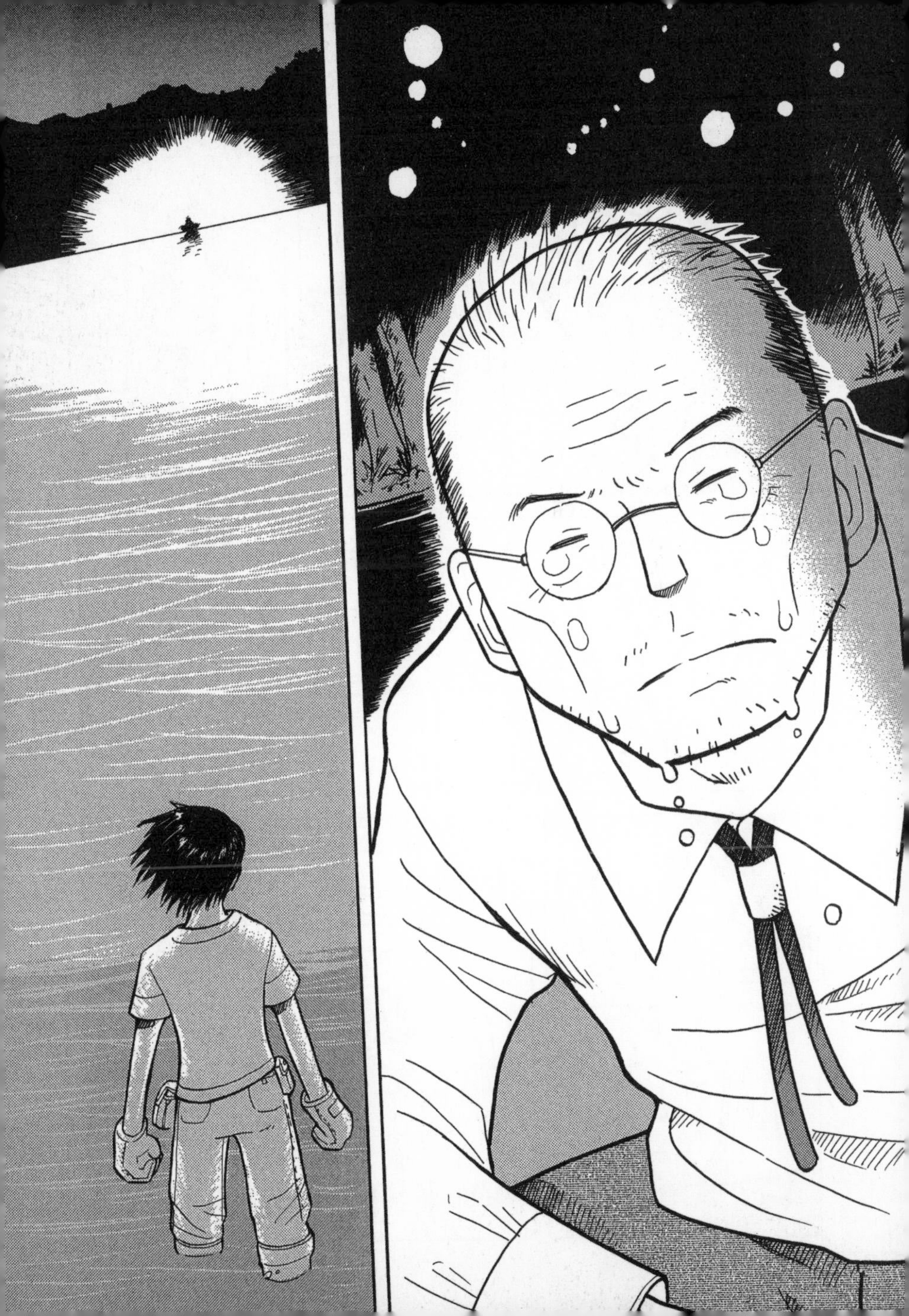

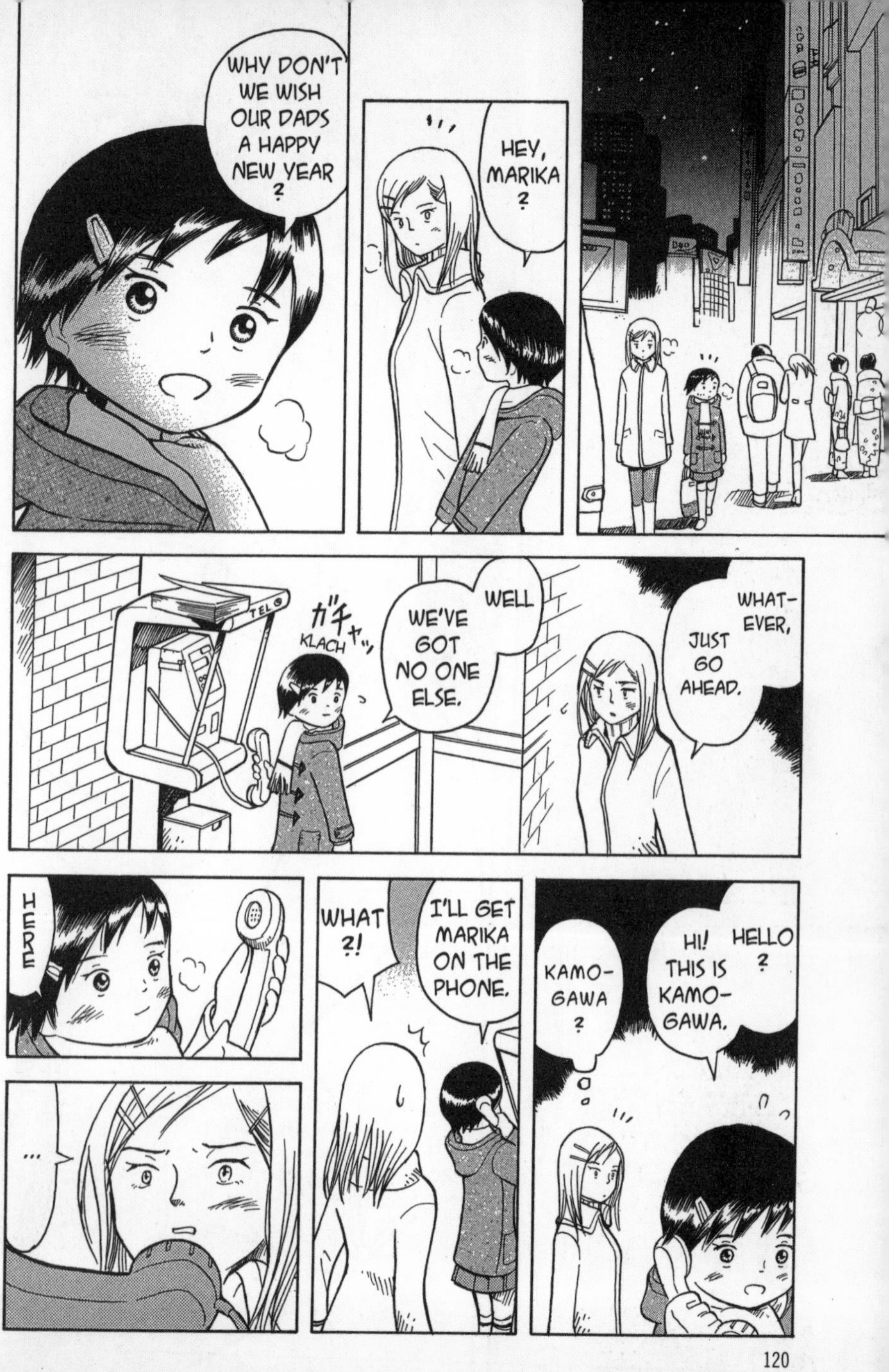
HEY, MARIKA?
WHY DON'T WE WISH OUR DADS A HAPPY NEW YEAR?
WHATEVER, JUST GO AHEAD.
WELL
WE'VE GOT NO ONE ELSE.
ガチャッ
KLACH
HELLO?
HI! THIS IS KAMOGAWA.
KAMOGAWA?
I'LL GET MARIKA ON THE PHONE.
WHAT?!
HERE
...

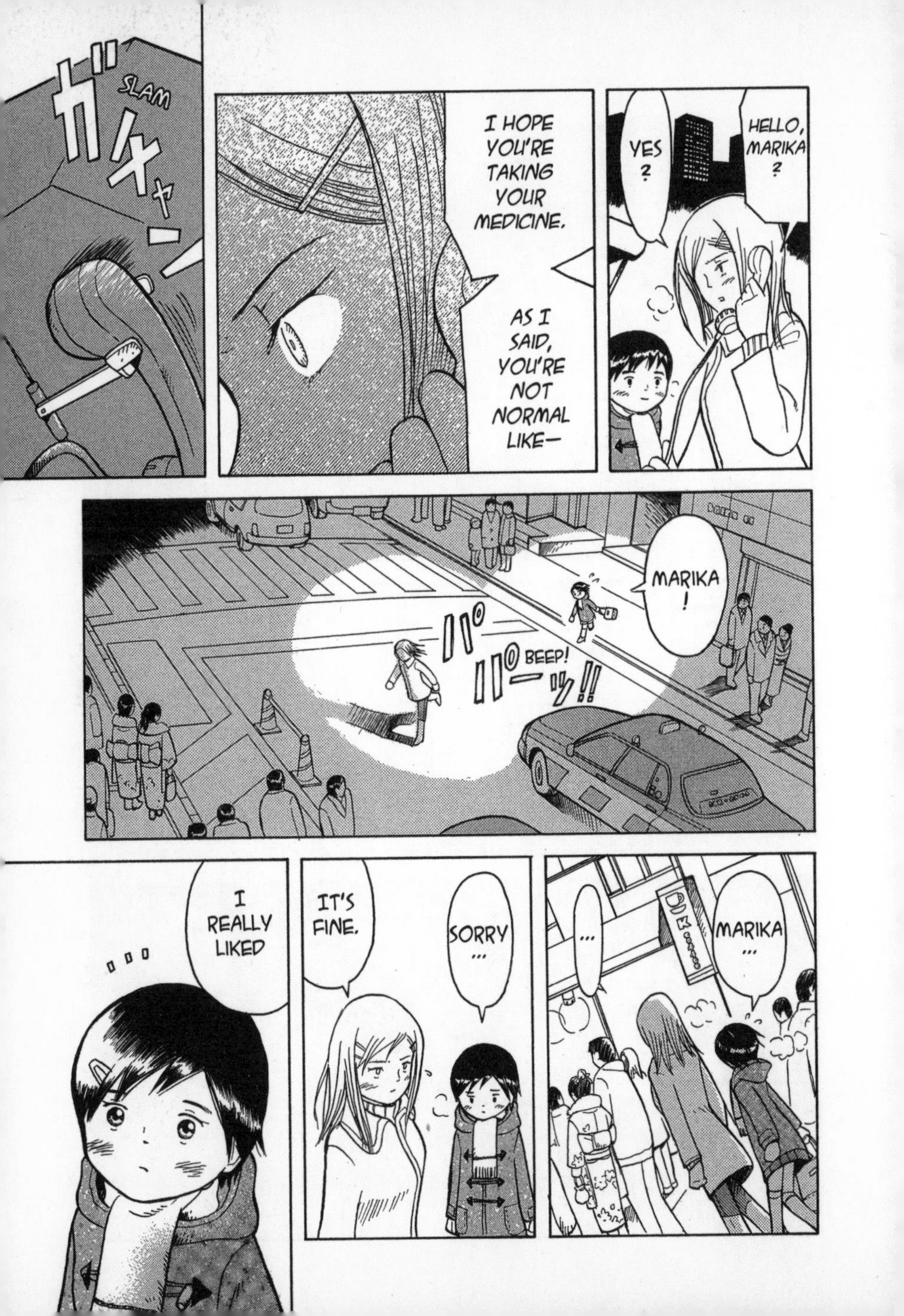
HELLO, MARIKA?
YES?
I HOPE YOU'RE TAKING YOUR MEDICINE.
AS I SAID, YOU'RE NOT NORMAL LIKE—
SLAM
MARIKA!
パパーッ!!
BEEP!
MARIKA...
...
SORRY...
IT'S FINE.
I REALLY LIKED
...

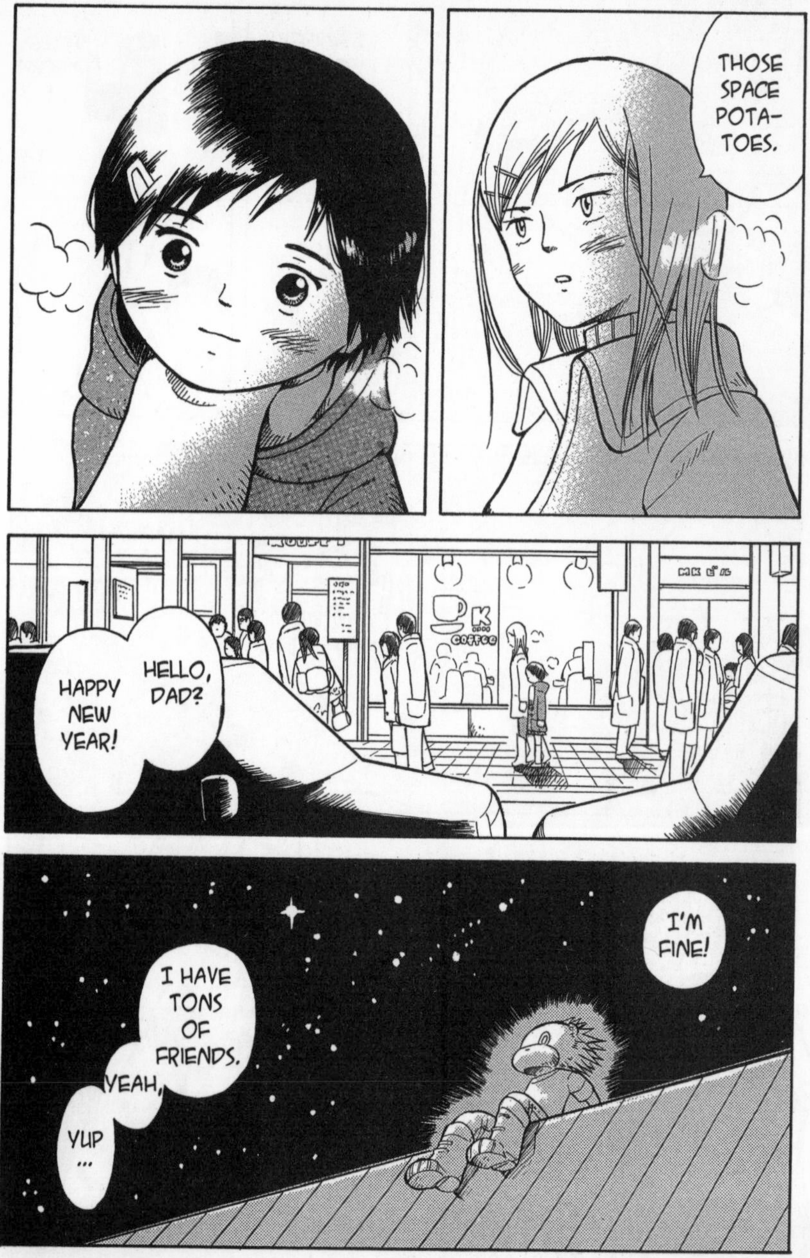
THOSE SPACE POTA-TOES.
HELLO, DAD?
HAPPY NEW YEAR!
I'M FINE!
I HAVE TONS OF FRIENDS.
YEAH,
YUP ...

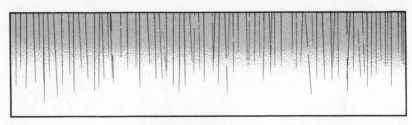

ザーッ
ZHAA

ザー
ZHAA

はぁっ
WHOO

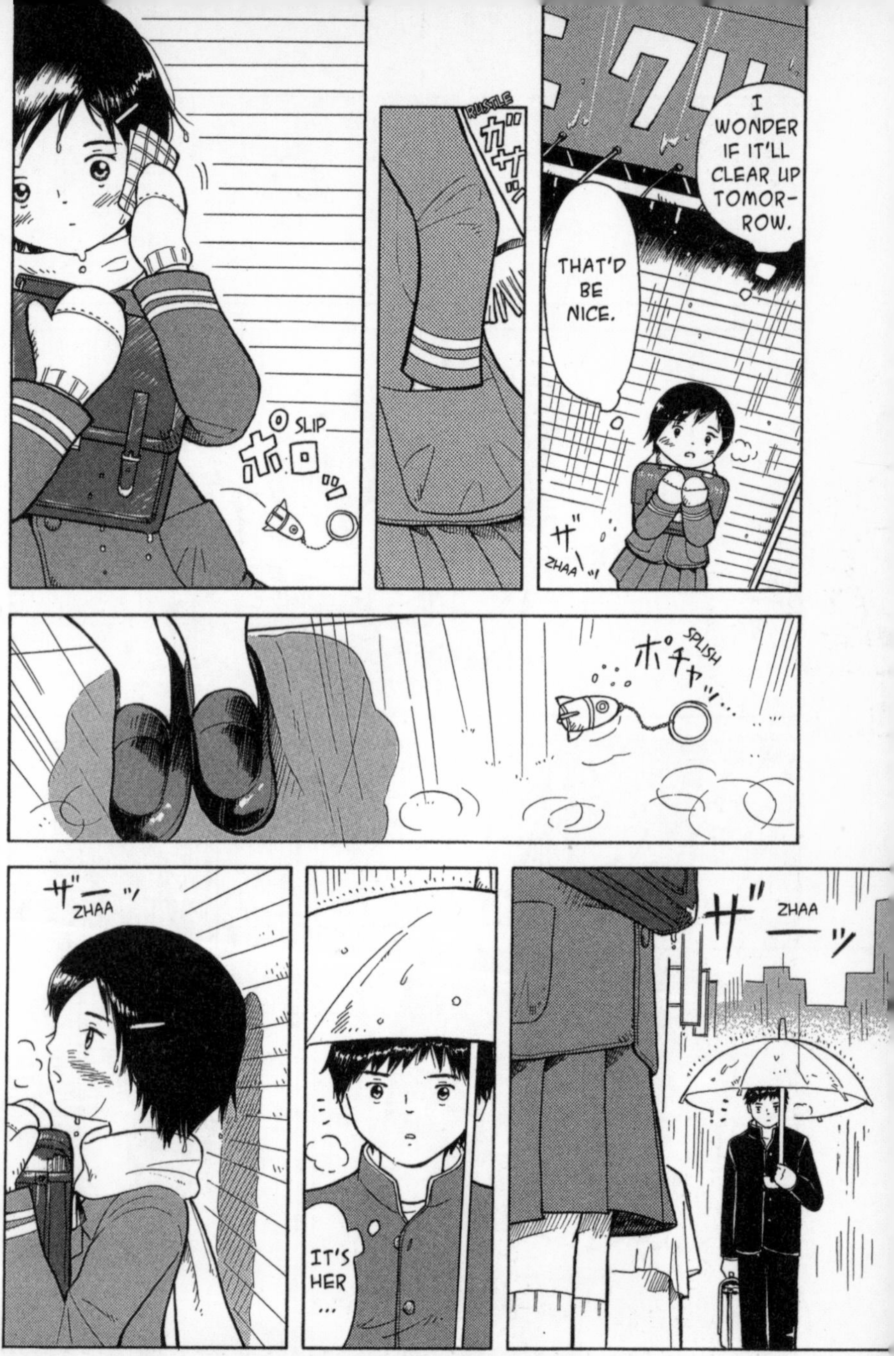
I WONDER IF IT'LL CLEAR UP TOMOR-ROW.
THAT'D BE NICE.
ザッ
ZHAA
ガサッ
RUSTLE
ポロッ
SLIP
ポチャッ…
SPLISH
ザーッ
ZHAA
IT'S HER …
ザーッ
ZHAA

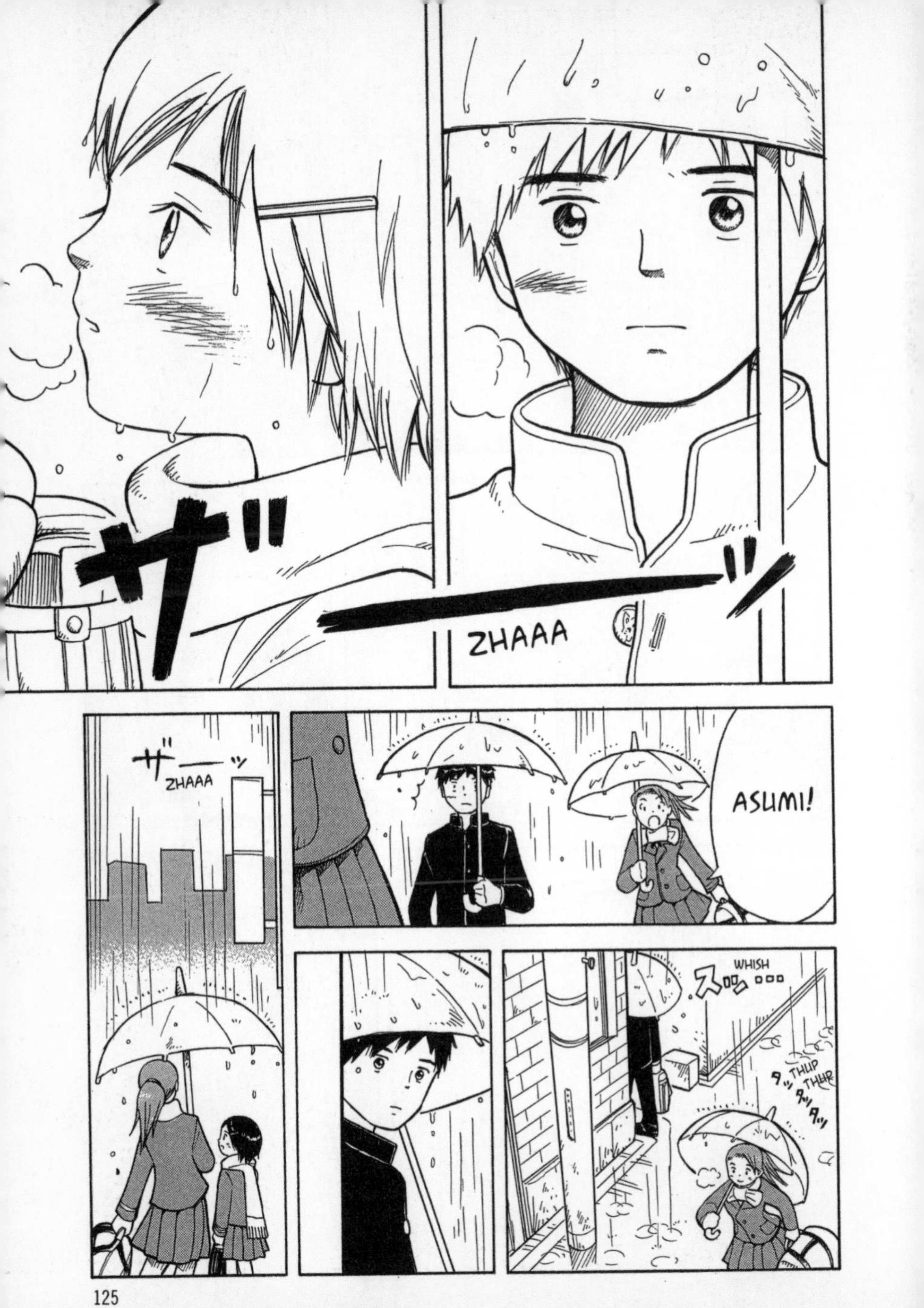
ザーッ
ZHAAA
ASUMI!
スッ
WHISH
タッ タッ タッ
THUP THUP
ザーッ
ZHAAA

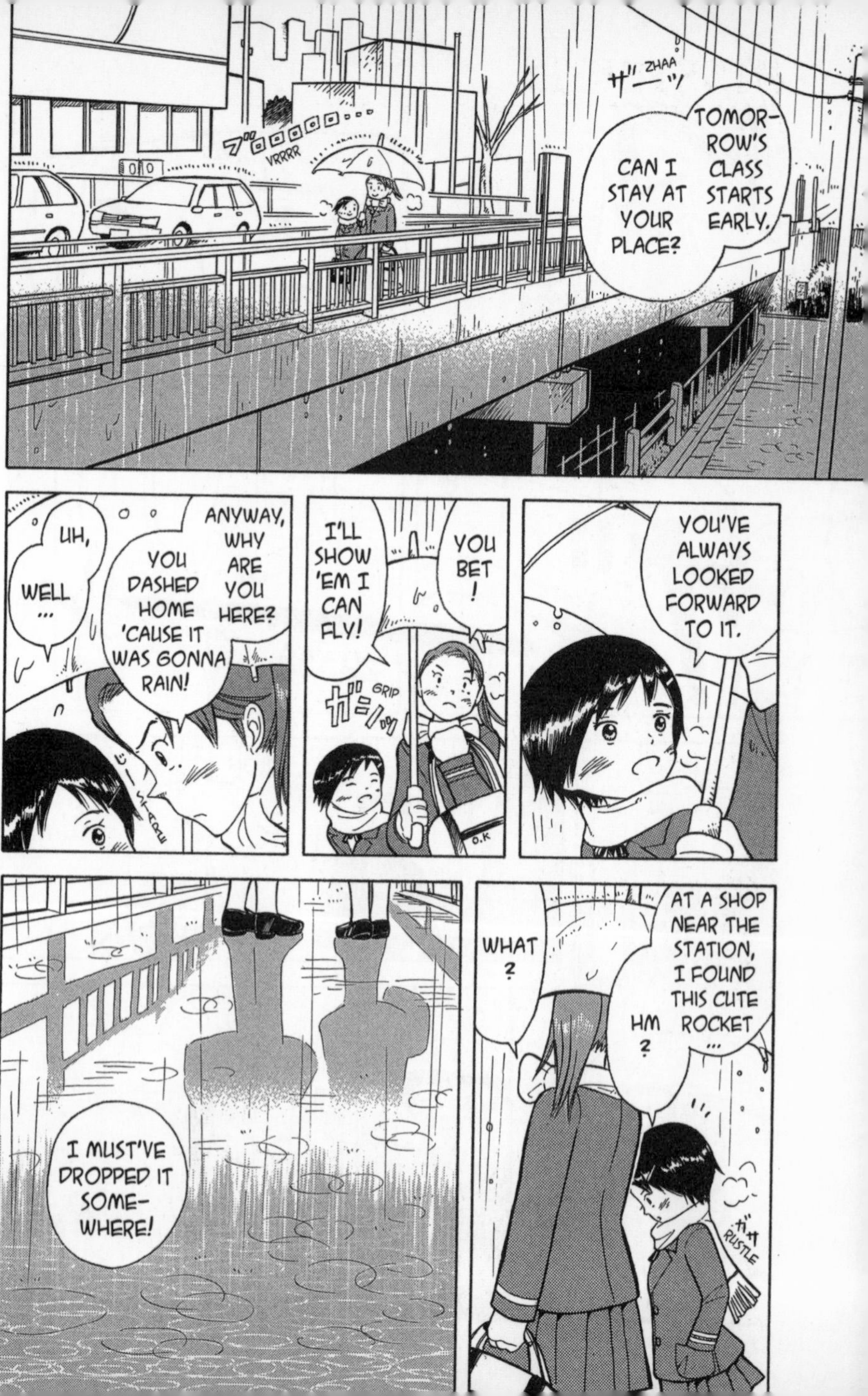
ZHAA
TOMORROW'S CLASS STARTS EARLY.
CAN I STAY AT YOUR PLACE?
VRRRR
YOU'VE ALWAYS LOOKED FORWARD TO IT.
YOU BET!
I'LL SHOW 'EM I CAN FLY!
GRIP
ANYWAY, WHY ARE YOU HERE?
YOU DASHED HOME 'CAUSE IT WAS GONNA RAIN!
UH, WELL...
AT A SHOP NEAR THE STATION, I FOUND THIS CUTE ROCKET...
HM?
WHAT?
RUSTLE
I MUST'VE DROPPED IT SOMEWHERE!

MISSION:18

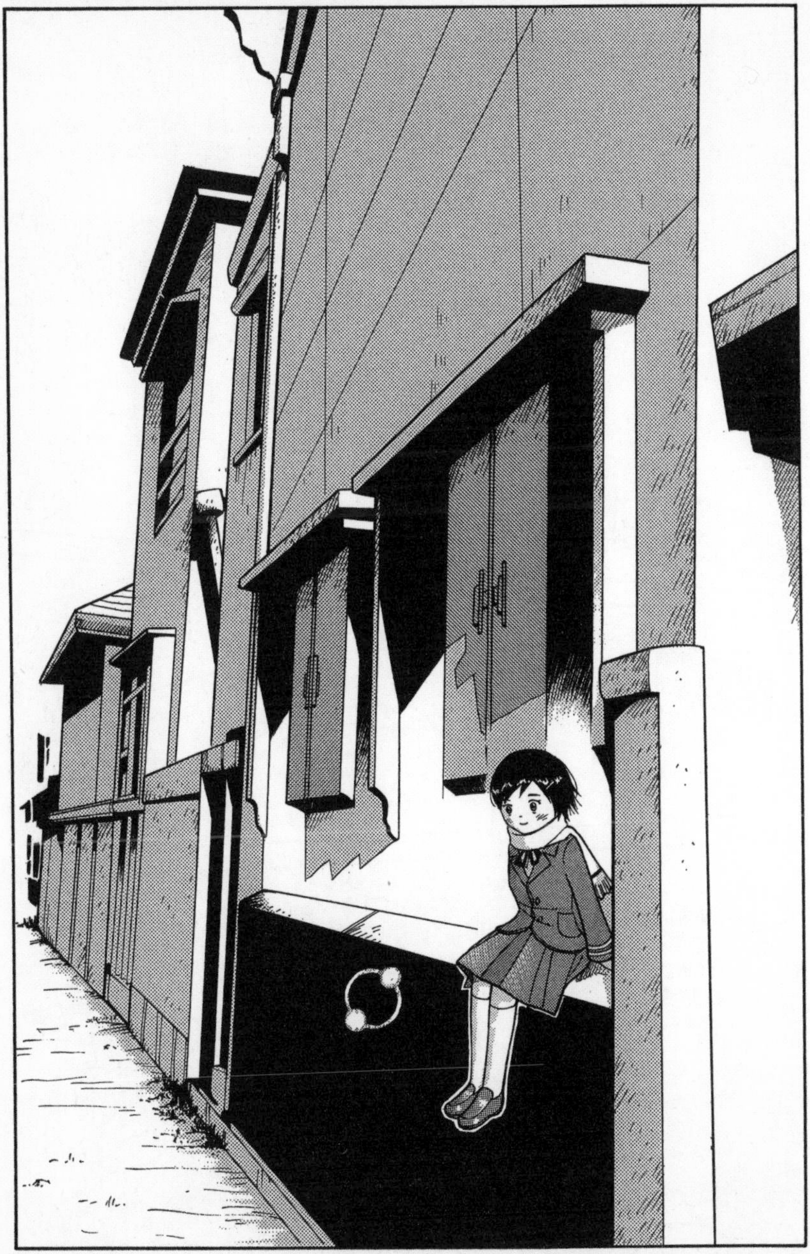

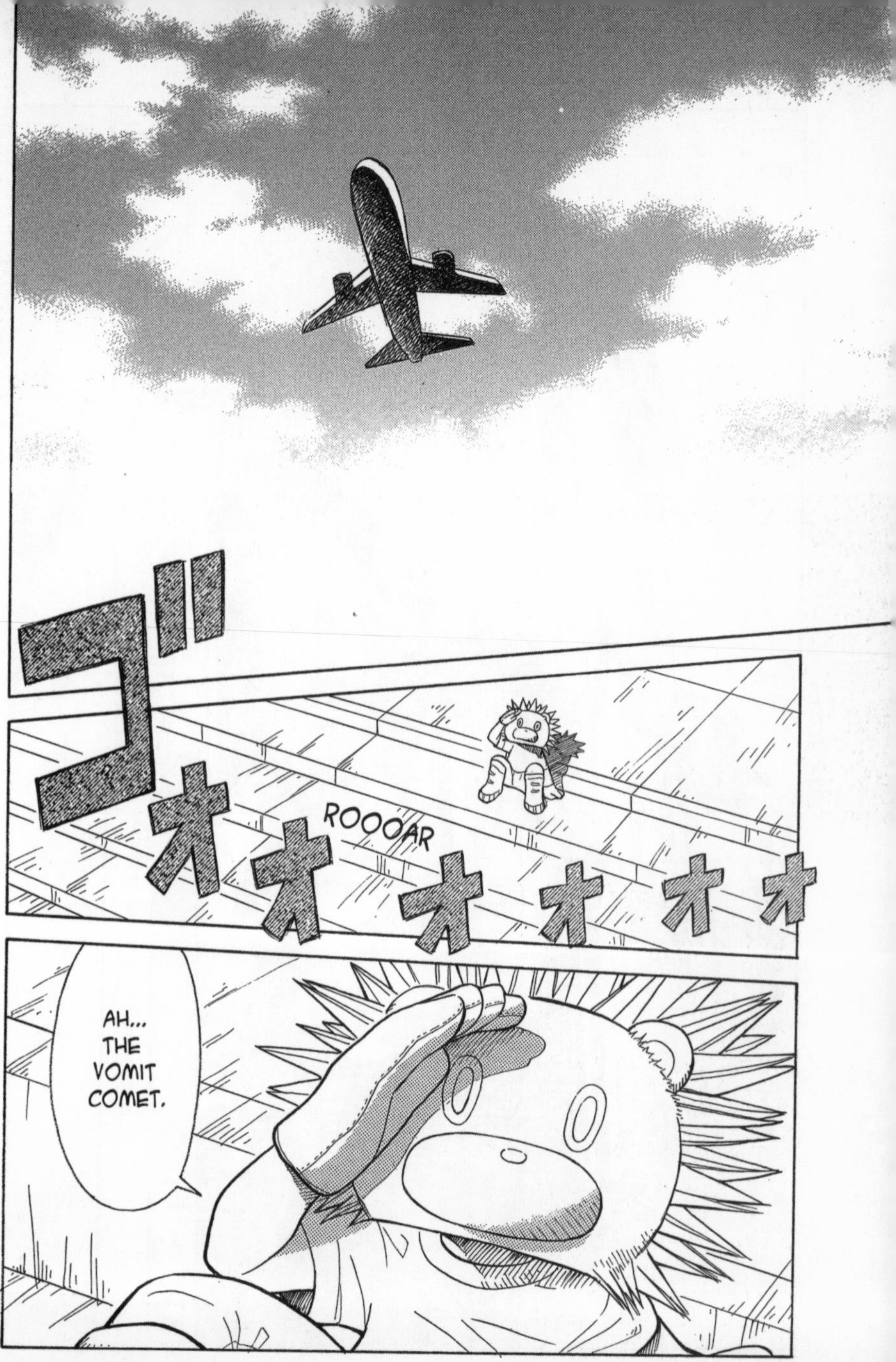
ゴオオオオオ
ROOOAR
AH... THE VOMIT COMET.

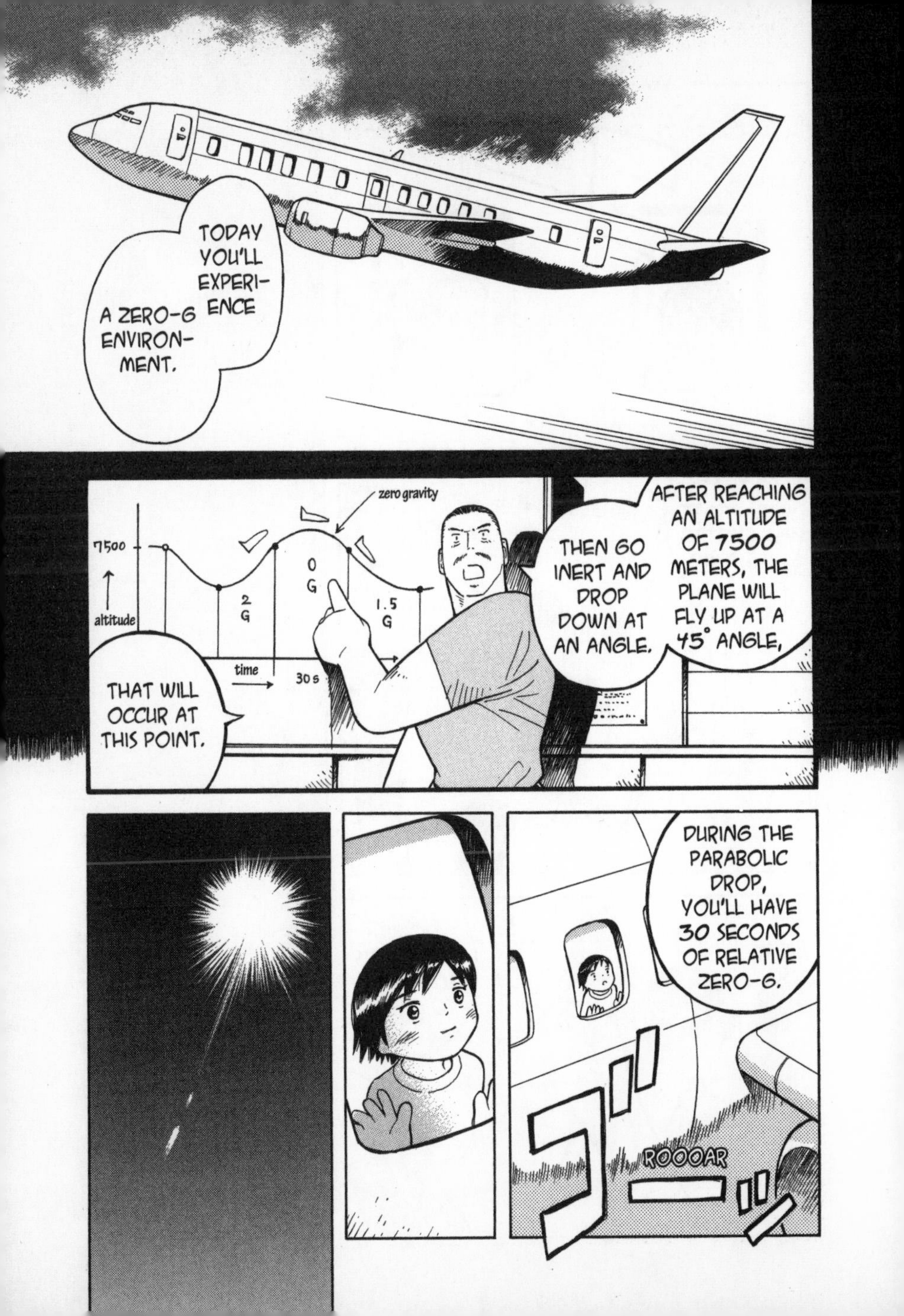
TODAY YOU'LL EXPERIENCE A ZERO-G ENVIRONMENT.
AFTER REACHING AN ALTITUDE OF 7500 METERS, THE PLANE WILL FLY UP AT A 45° ANGLE,
THEN GO INERT AND DROP DOWN AT AN ANGLE.
zero gravity
7500
altitude
2 G
0 G
1.5 G
time
30 s
THAT WILL OCCUR AT THIS POINT.
DURING THE PARABOLIC DROP, YOU'LL HAVE 30 SECONDS OF RELATIVE ZERO-G.
ROOOAR

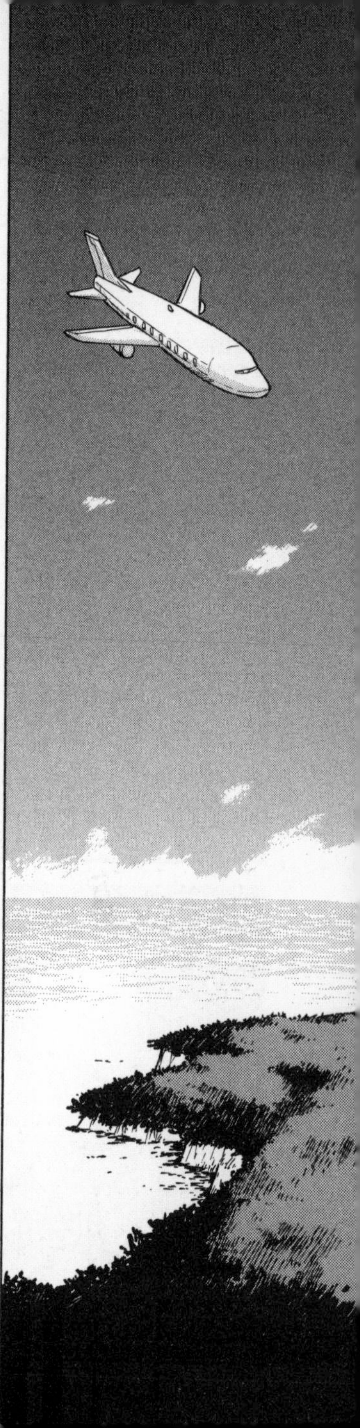

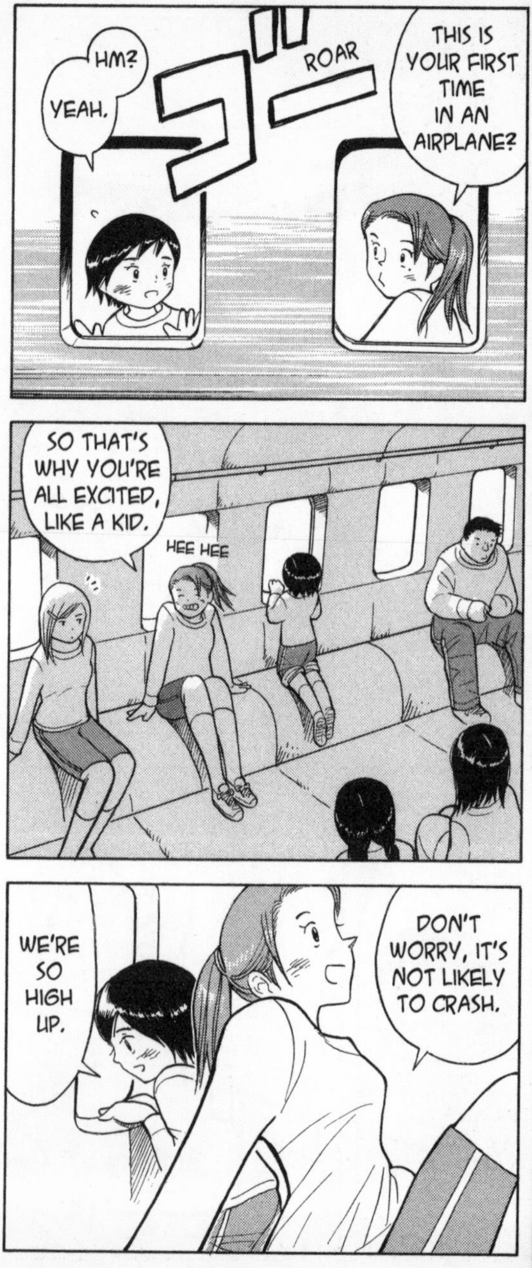
THIS IS YOUR FIRST TIME IN AN AIRPLANE?
ROAR
HM?
YEAH.
SO THAT'S WHY YOU'RE ALL EXCITED, LIKE A KID.
HEE HEE
DON'T WORRY, IT'S NOT LIKELY TO CRASH.
WE'RE SO HIGH UP.

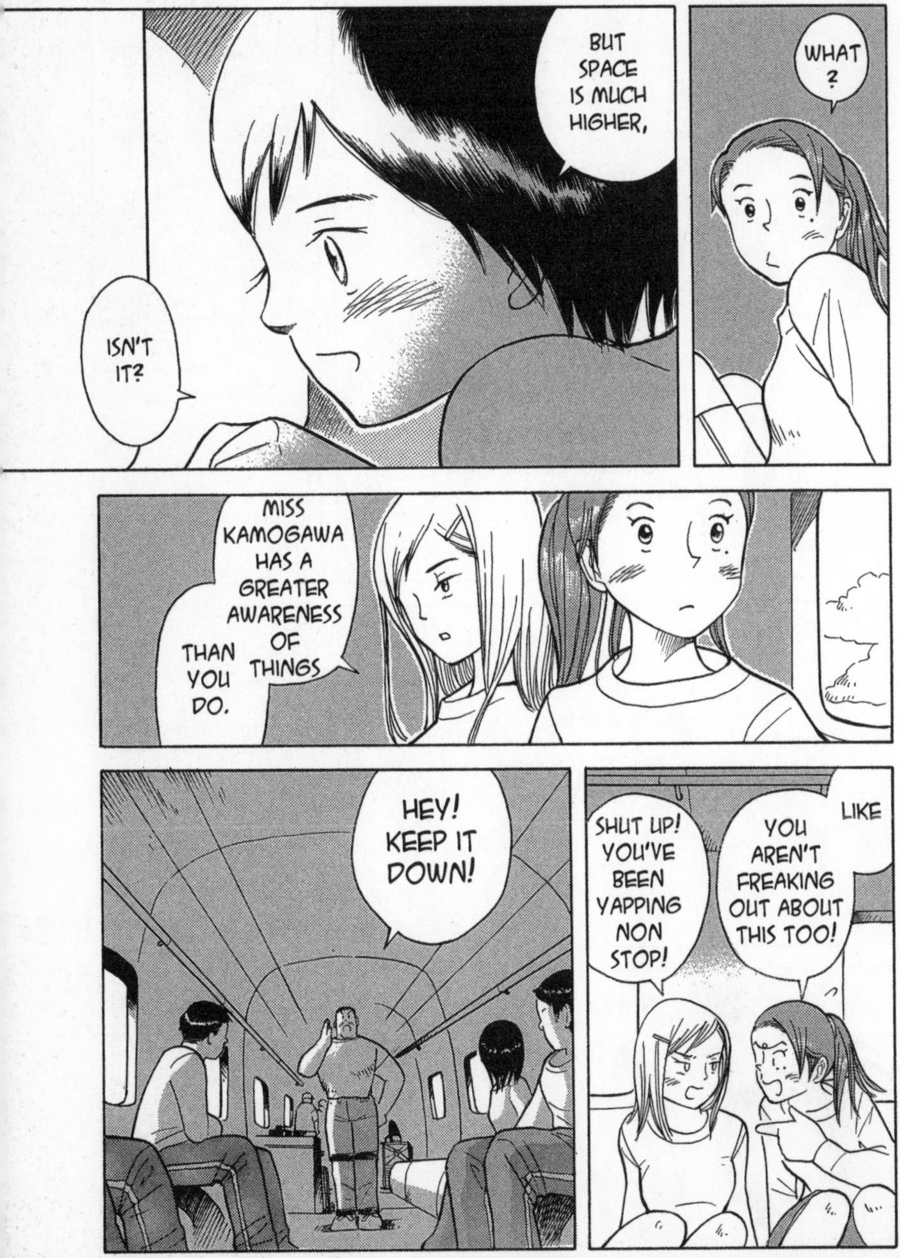
WHAT?
BUT SPACE IS MUCH HIGHER,
ISN'T IT?
MISS KAMOGAWA HAS A GREATER AWARENESS OF THINGS THAN YOU DO.
LIKE YOU AREN'T FREAKING OUT ABOUT THIS TOO!
SHUT UP! YOU'VE BEEN YAPPING NON STOP!
HEY! KEEP IT DOWN!

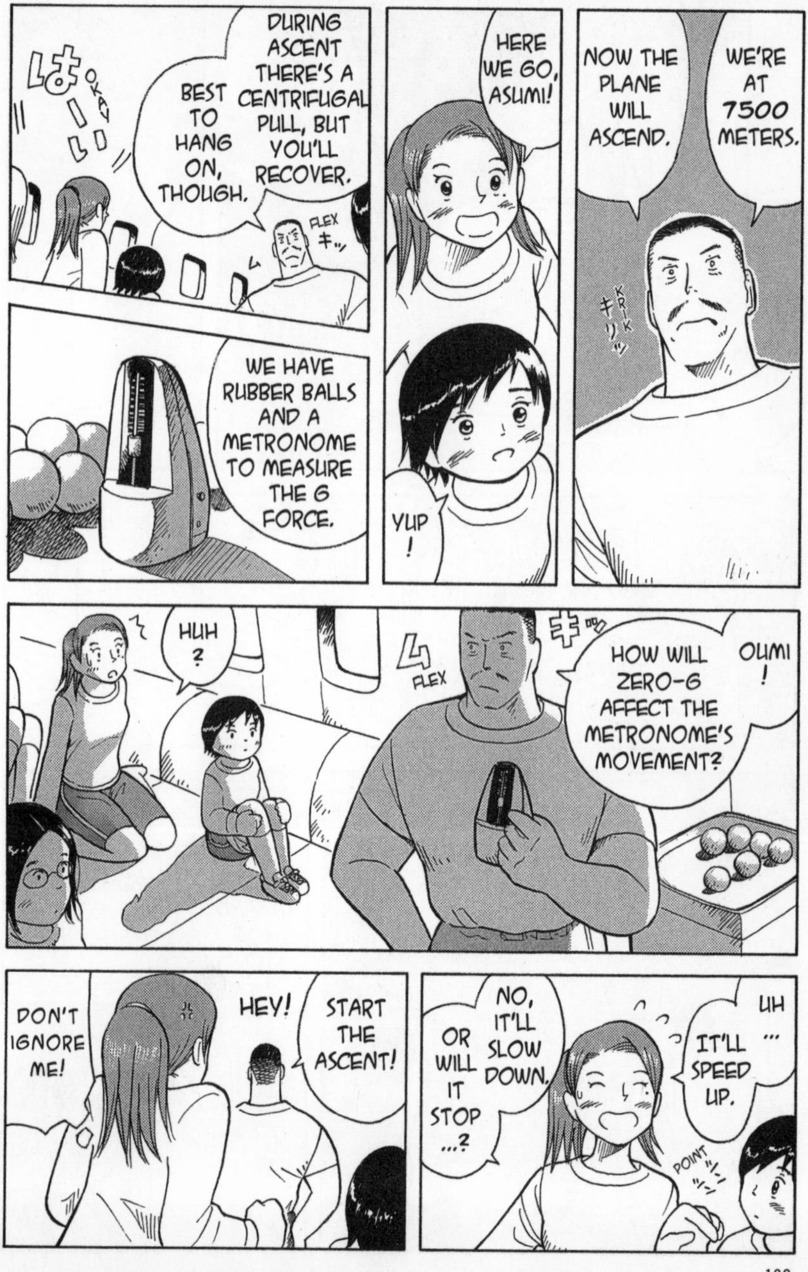
WE'RE AT 7500 METERS.
NOW THE PLANE WILL ASCEND.
KRIK
キリッ
HERE WE GO, ASUMI!
YUP!
DURING ASCENT THERE'S A CENTRIFUGAL PULL, BUT YOU'LL RECOVER.
BEST TO HANG ON, THOUGH.
FLEX
キッ
ム
OKAY
はーい
WE HAVE RUBBER BALLS AND A METRONOME TO MEASURE THE G FORCE.
OUMI!
HOW WILL ZERO-G AFFECT THE METRONOME'S MOVEMENT?
キッ
ム
FLEX
HUH?
UH ...
IT'LL SPEED UP.
NO, IT'LL SLOW DOWN.
OR WILL IT STOP ...?
POINT
START THE ASCENT!
HEY!
DON'T IGNORE ME!

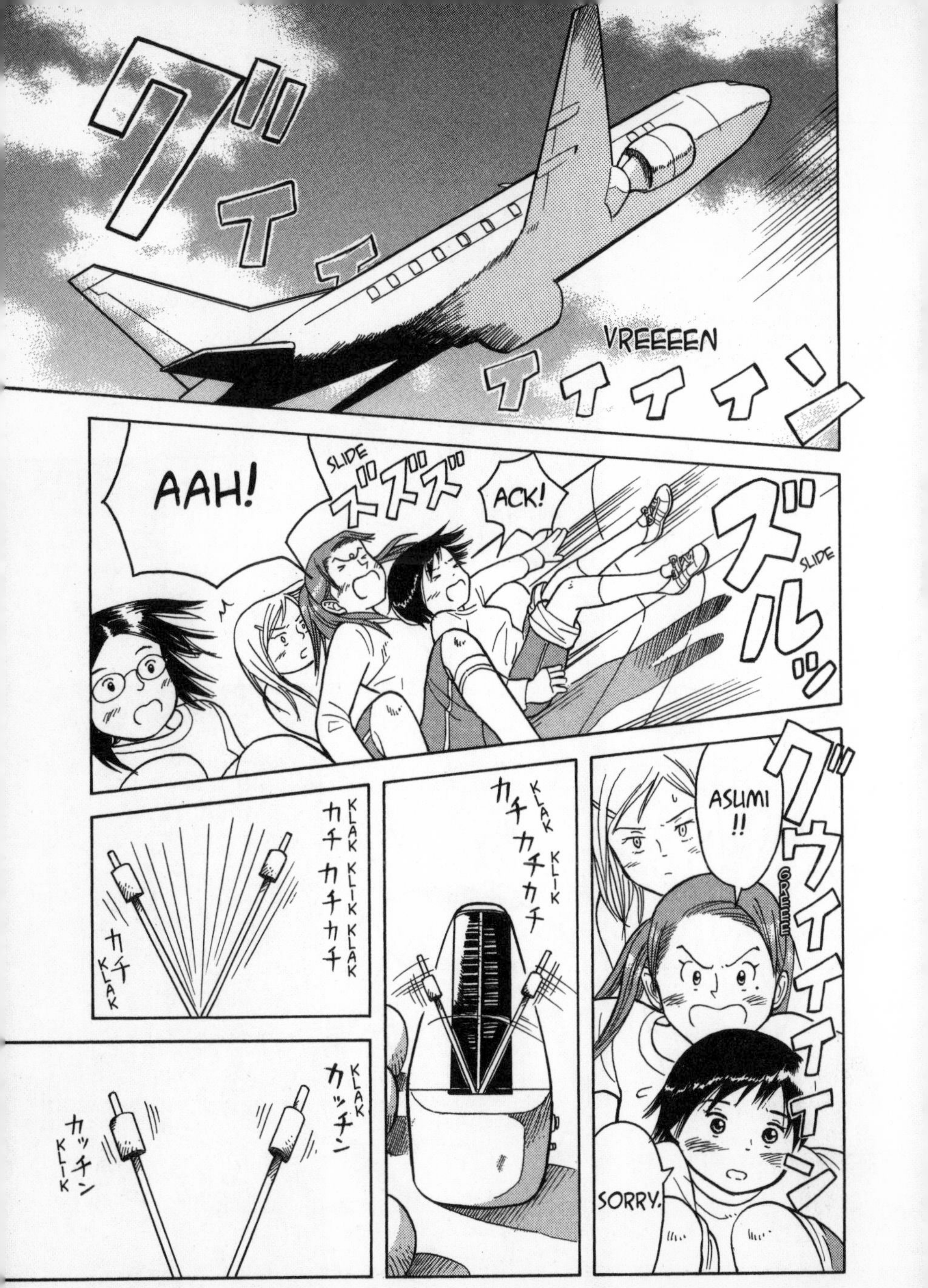
グイィイイイイン
VREEEEEN
AAH!
ズズズ
SLIDE
ACK!
ズルッ
SLIDE
ASUMI!!
グウィイイイーン
GREEEE
SORRY.
カチカチカチカチ
KLAK KLIK
カチカチカチカチ
KLAK KLIK KLAK
カチ
KLAK
カッチン
KLAK
カッチン
KLIK

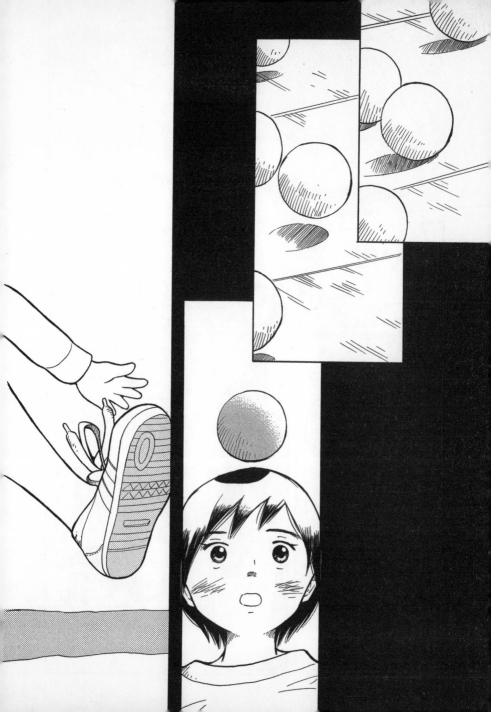

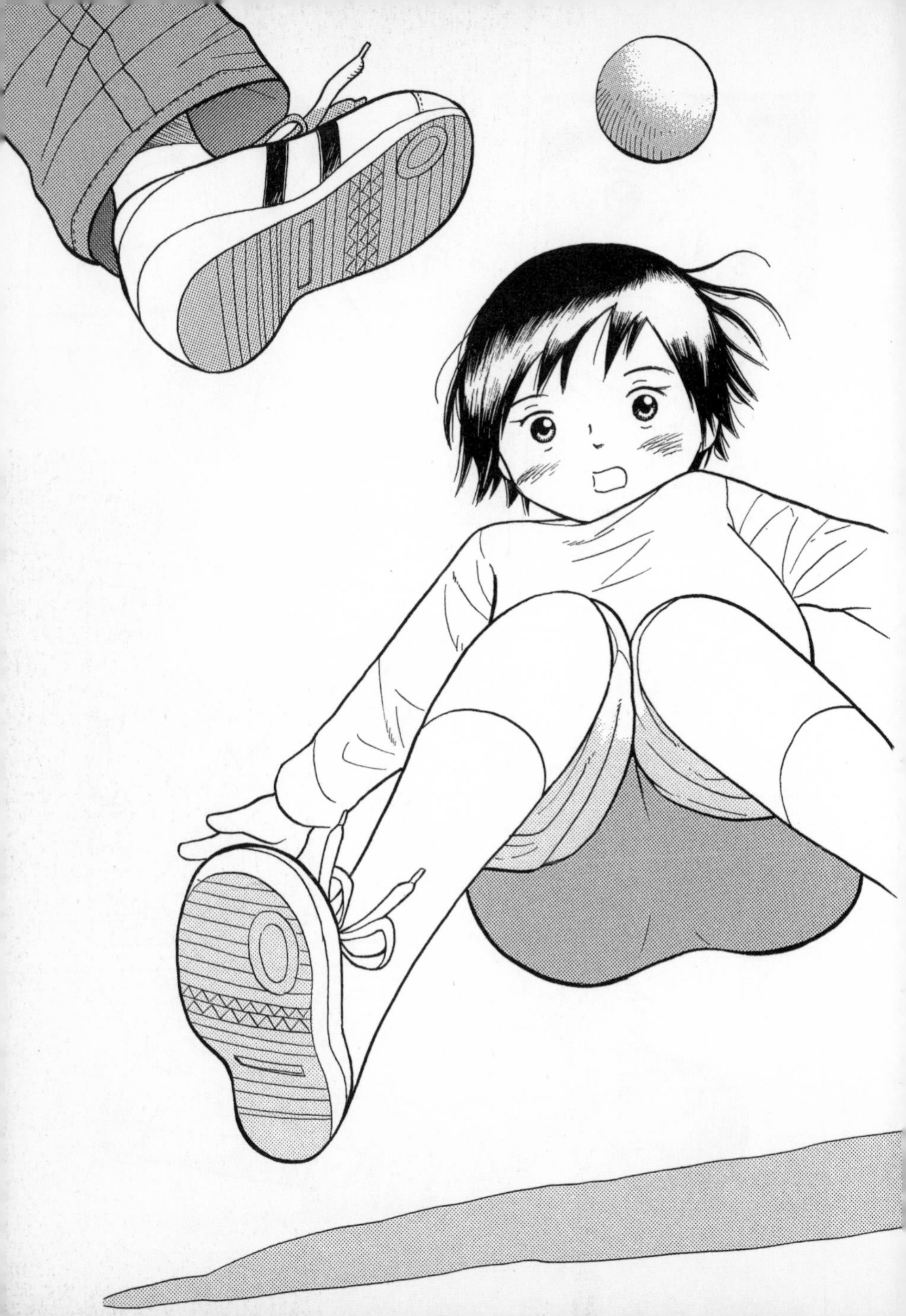

I'M FLYING!

FLOAT ふわっ

ROAR ゴー ーッ

WOW! WOW! WOW!

WOW!

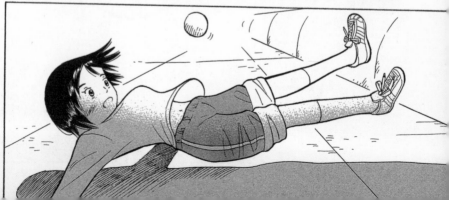

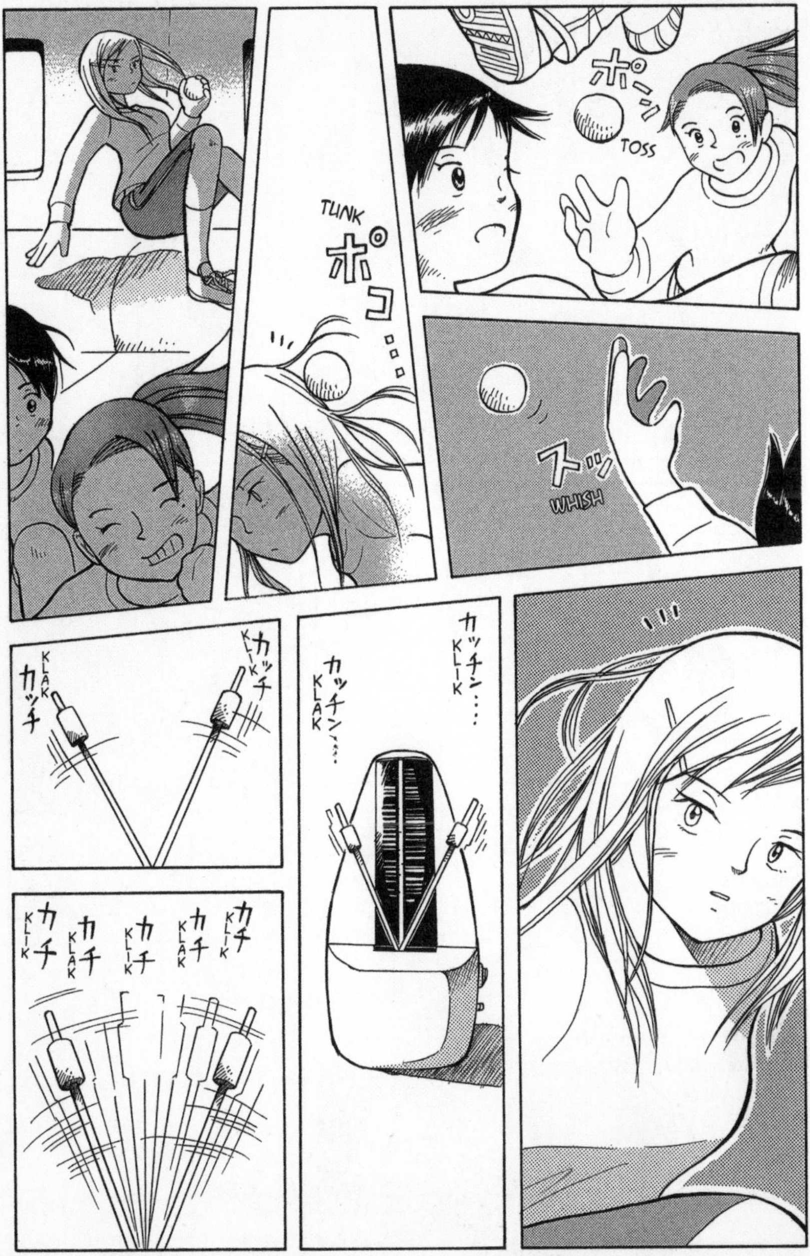
ポーン
TOSS
スッ
WHISH
TUNK
ポコ
カッチン…
KLIK
カッチン…
KLAK
カッチ
KLIK
カッチ
KLAK
カチ
KLIK
カチ
KLAK
カチ
KLIK
カチ
KLAK
カチ
KLIK

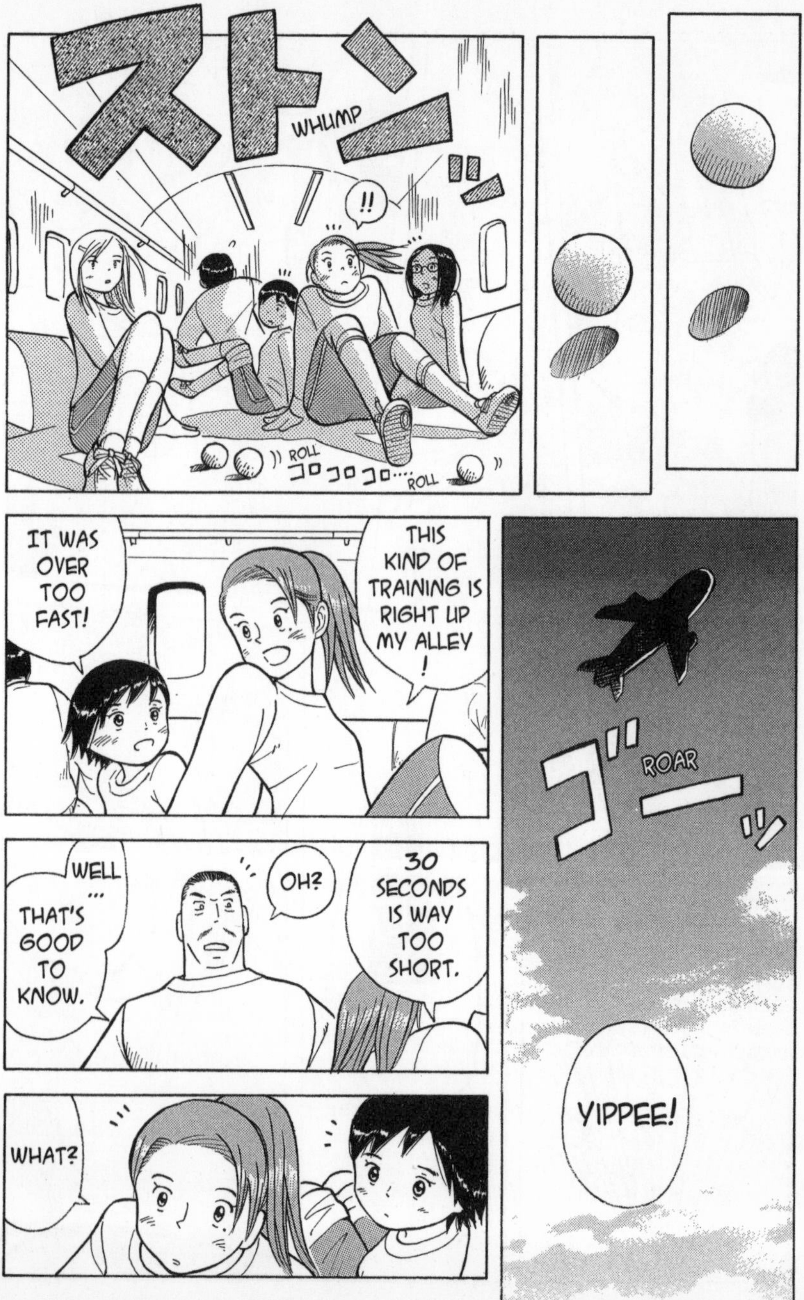
ストン
WHUMP
!!
ROLL
コロコロコロ....
ROLL
ゴーッ
ROAR
YIPPEE!
THIS KIND OF TRAINING IS RIGHT UP MY ALLEY!
IT WAS OVER TOO FAST!
30 SECONDS IS WAY TOO SHORT.
OH?
WELL... THAT'S GOOD TO KNOW.
WHAT?

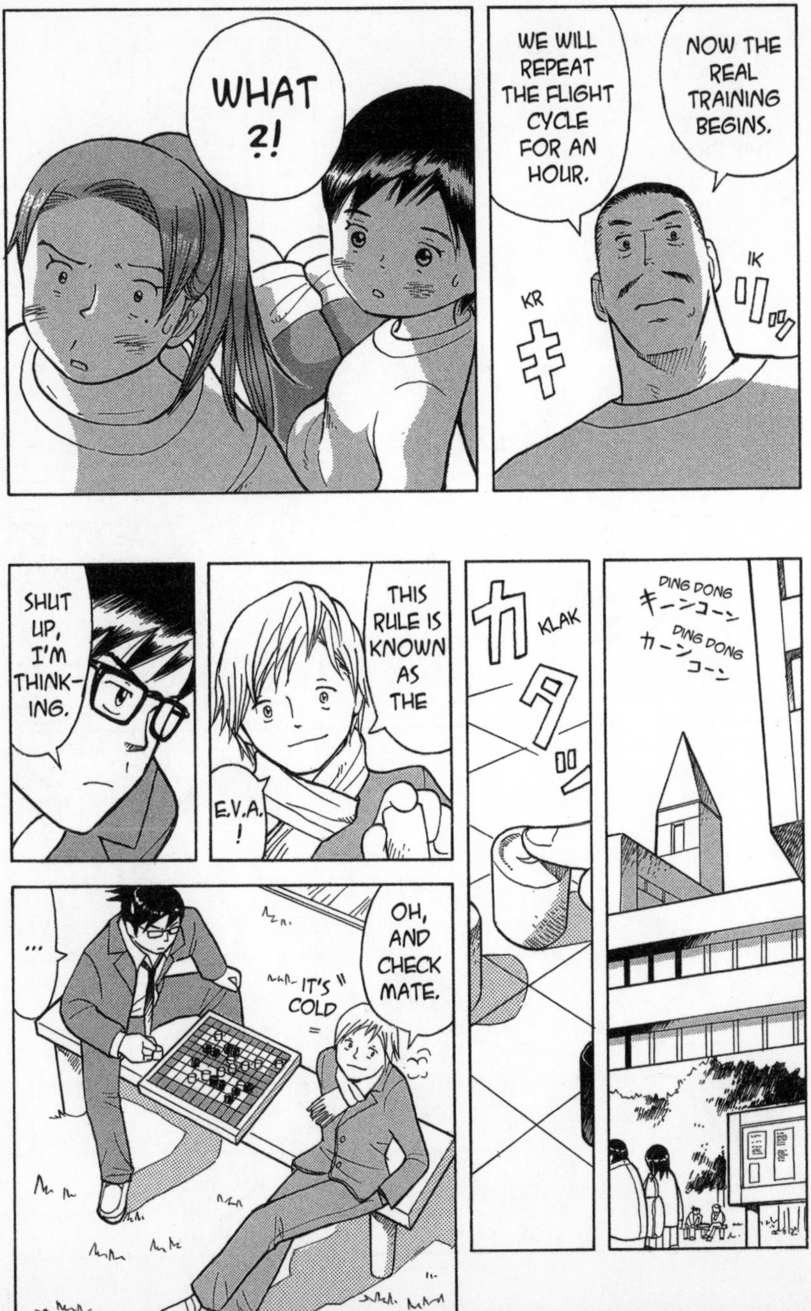
NOW THE REAL TRAINING BEGINS.
WE WILL REPEAT THE FLIGHT CYCLE FOR AN HOUR.
IK
リッ
KR
キ
WHAT ?!
DING DONG
キーンコーン
DING DONG
カーンコーン
カタッ
KLAK
THIS RULE IS KNOWN AS THE
E.V.A. !
SHUT UP, I'M THINK-ING.
OH, AND CHECK MATE.
IT'S COLD
...

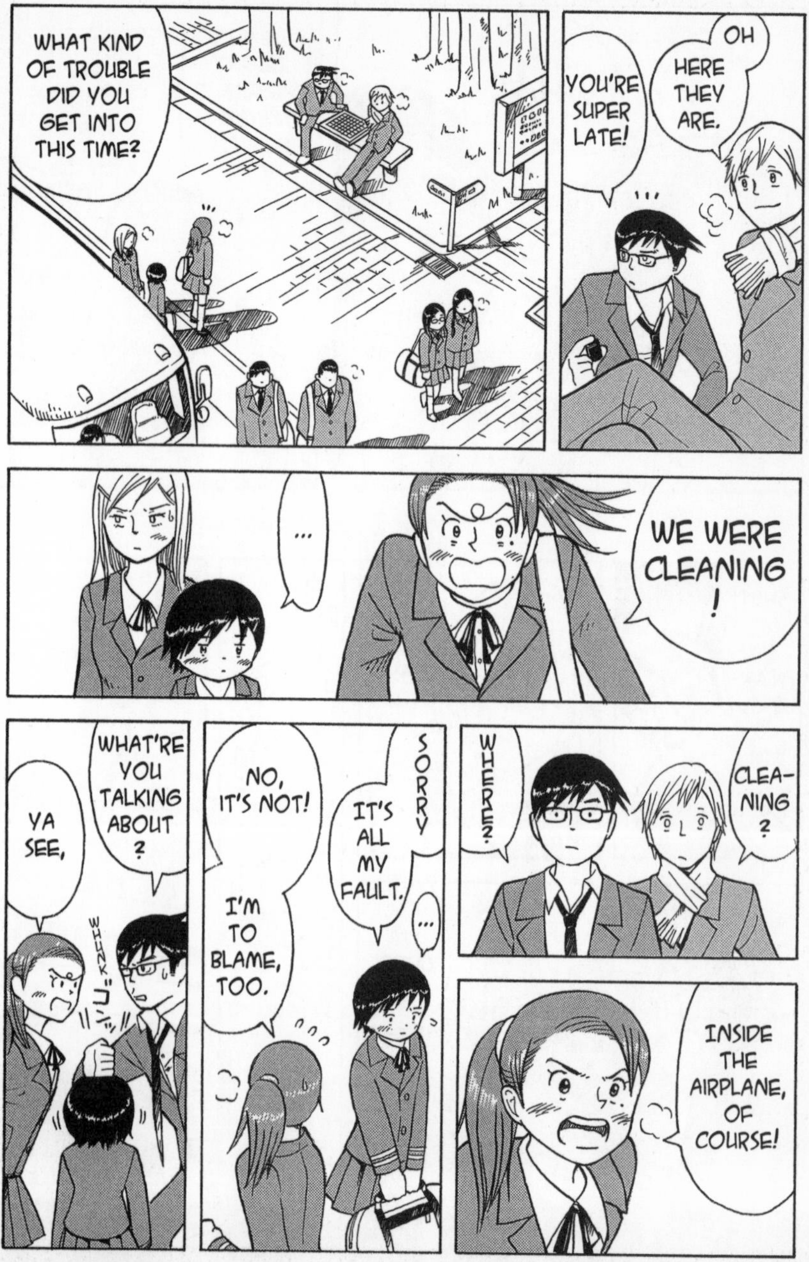
OH
HERE THEY ARE.
YOU'RE SUPER LATE!
WHAT KIND OF TROUBLE DID YOU GET INTO THIS TIME?
WE WERE CLEANING!
...
CLEA-NING?
WHERE?
INSIDE THE AIRPLANE, OF COURSE!
SORRY
IT'S ALL MY FAULT.
NO, IT'S NOT!
...
I'M TO BLAME, TOO.
WHAT'RE YOU TALKING ABOUT?
YA SEE,
WHUNK

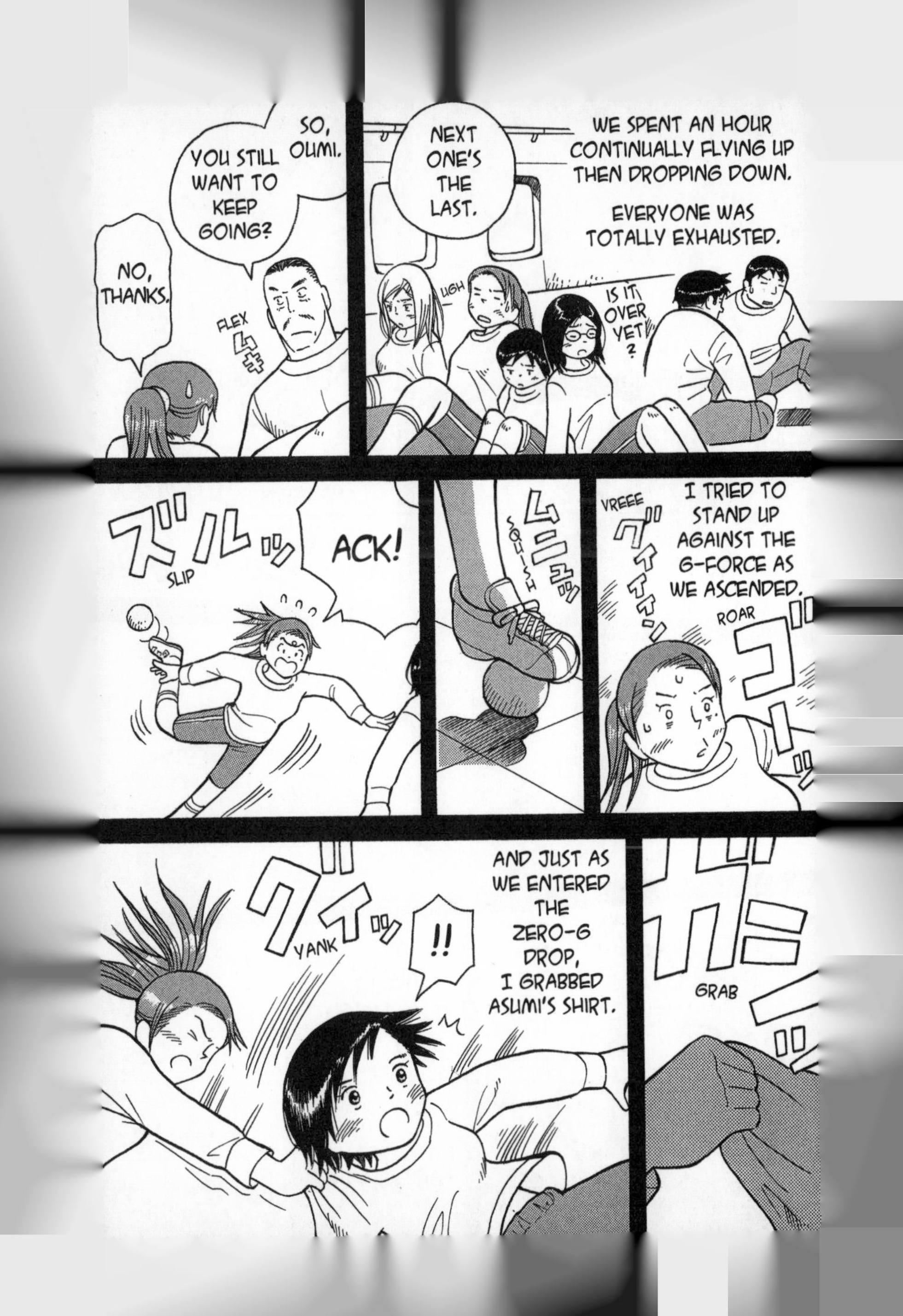
WE SPENT AN HOUR CONTINUALLY FLYING UP THEN DROPPING DOWN.
EVERYONE WAS TOTALLY EXHAUSTED.
NEXT ONE'S THE LAST.
UGH
IS IT OVER YET?
SO, OUMI.
YOU STILL WANT TO KEEP GOING?
FLEX
ムキ
NO, THANKS.
I TRIED TO STAND UP AGAINST THE G-FORCE AS WE ASCENDED.
VREEE
グイイイッ
ROAR
ゴーッ
ムニュッ
SQUISH
ACK!
ズルッ
SLIP
ガシーッ
GRAB
AND JUST AS WE ENTERED THE ZERO-G DROP, I GRABBED ASUMI'S SHIRT.
!!
クイッ
YANK

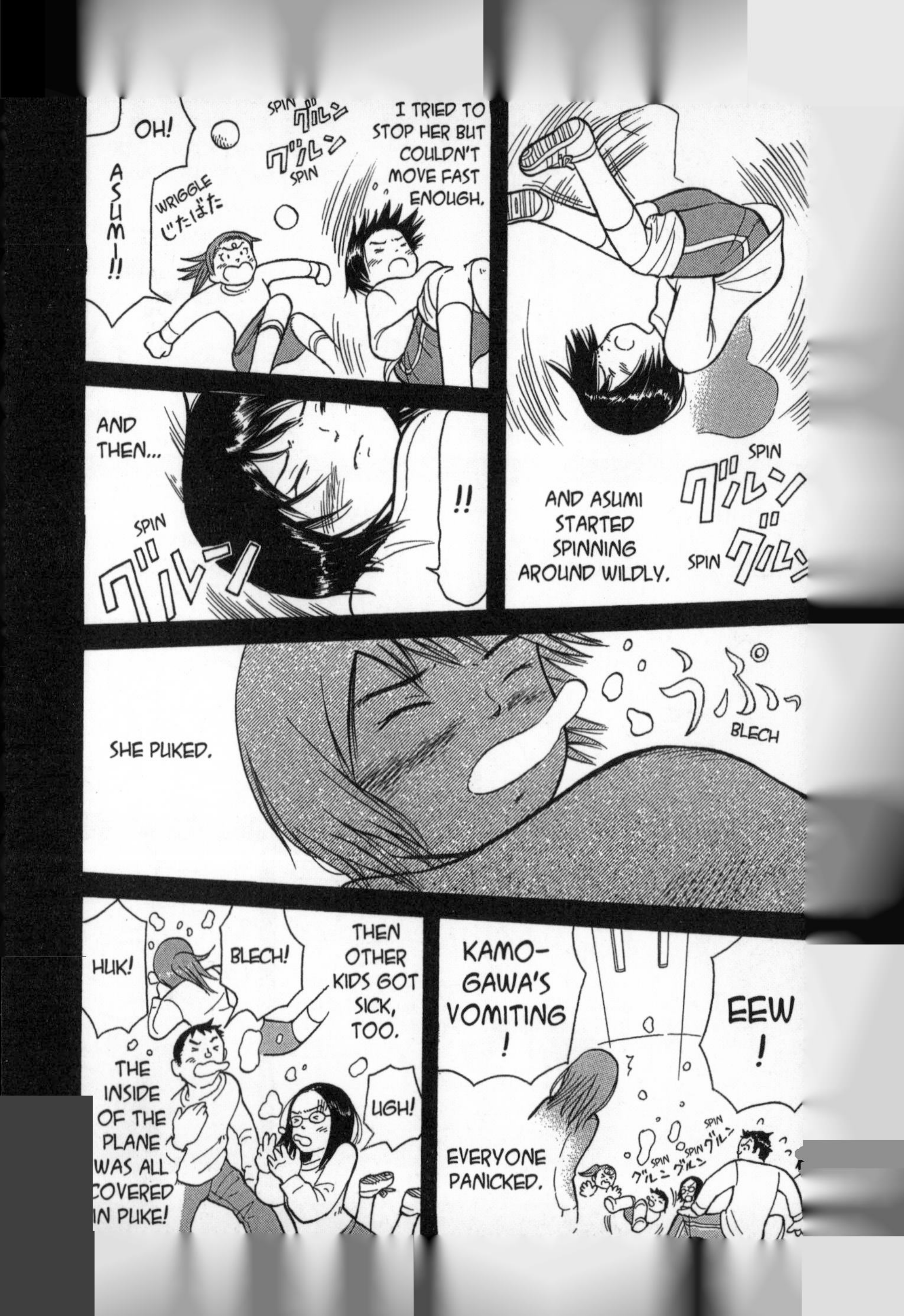
SPIN グルン
AND ASUMI STARTED SPINNING AROUND WILDLY.
SPIN グルン
I TRIED TO STOP HER BUT COULDN'T MOVE FAST ENOUGH.
SPIN グルン
グルン SPIN
OH!
ASUMI!!
WRIGGLE じたばた
!!
AND THEN...
SPIN グルーン
うぷっ BLECH
SHE PUKED.
EEW!
KAMO-GAWA'S VOMITING!
SPIN グルン
SPIN グルン
SPIN グルン
EVERYONE PANICKED.
THEN OTHER KIDS GOT SICK, TOO.
BLECH!
HUK!
UGH!
THE INSIDE OF THE PLANE WAS ALL COVERED IN PUKE!

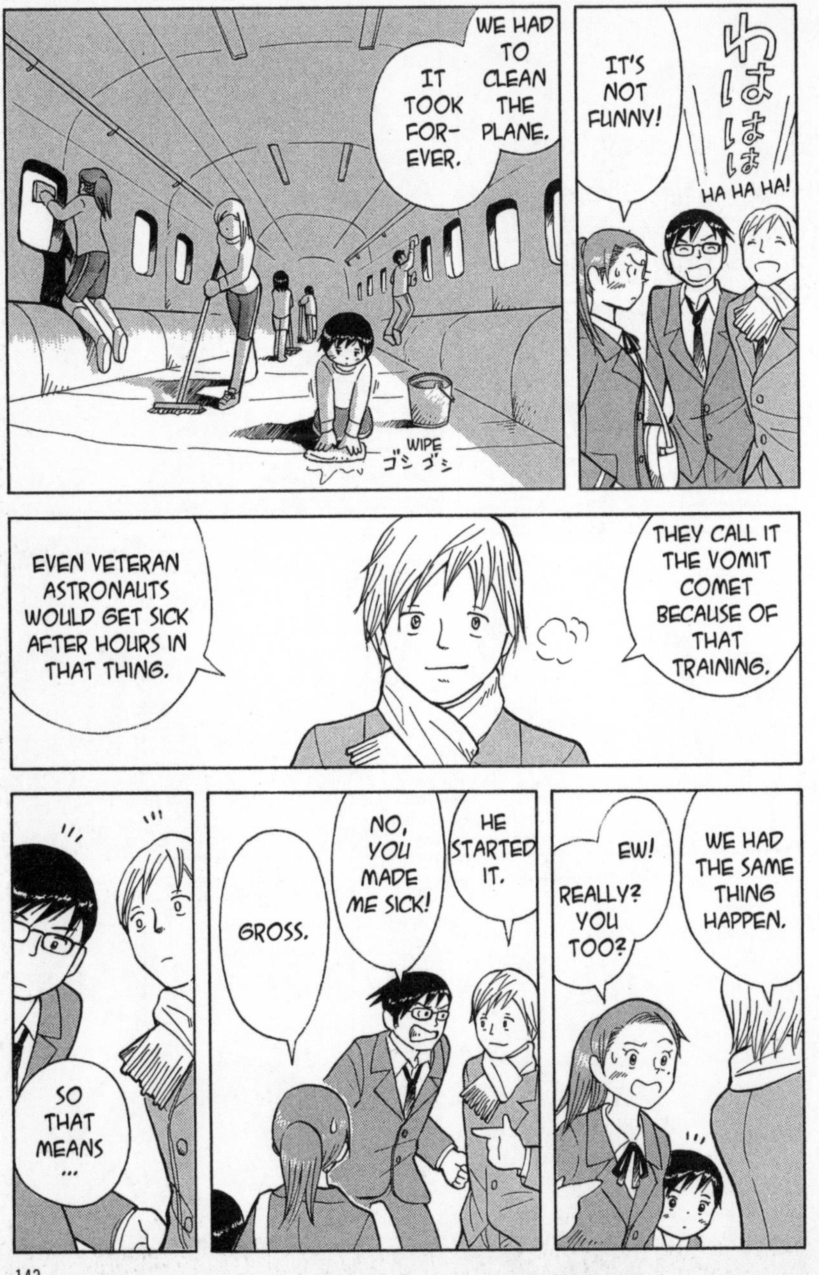
わははは
HA HA HA!
IT'S NOT FUNNY!
WE HAD TO CLEAN THE PLANE.
IT TOOK FOR-EVER.
WIPE
ゴシゴシ
THEY CALL IT THE VOMIT COMET BECAUSE OF THAT TRAINING.
EVEN VETERAN ASTRONAUTS WOULD GET SICK AFTER HOURS IN THAT THING.
WE HAD THE SAME THING HAPPEN.
EW!
REALLY? YOU TOO?
HE STARTED IT.
NO, YOU MADE ME SICK!
GROSS.
SO THAT MEANS ...

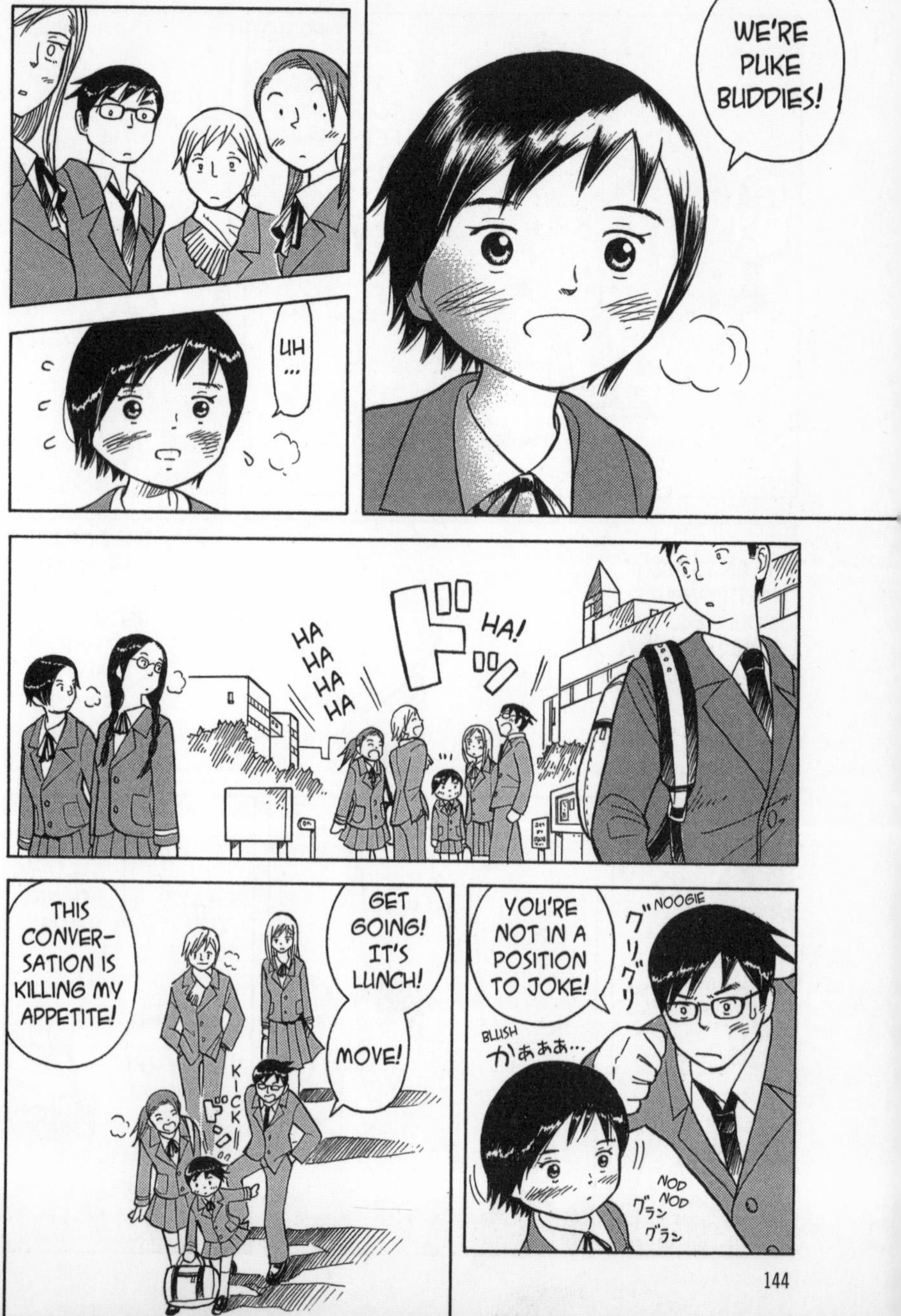
WE'RE PUKE BUDDIES!
UH ...
HA!
ドッ
HA HA HA HA
YOU'RE NOT IN A POSITION TO JOKE!
NOOGIE
グリグリ
BLUSH
かあああ…
NOD NOD
グラン グラン
GET GOING! IT'S LUNCH!
MOVE!
KICK
ドッ
THIS CONVER-SATION IS KILLING MY APPETITE!

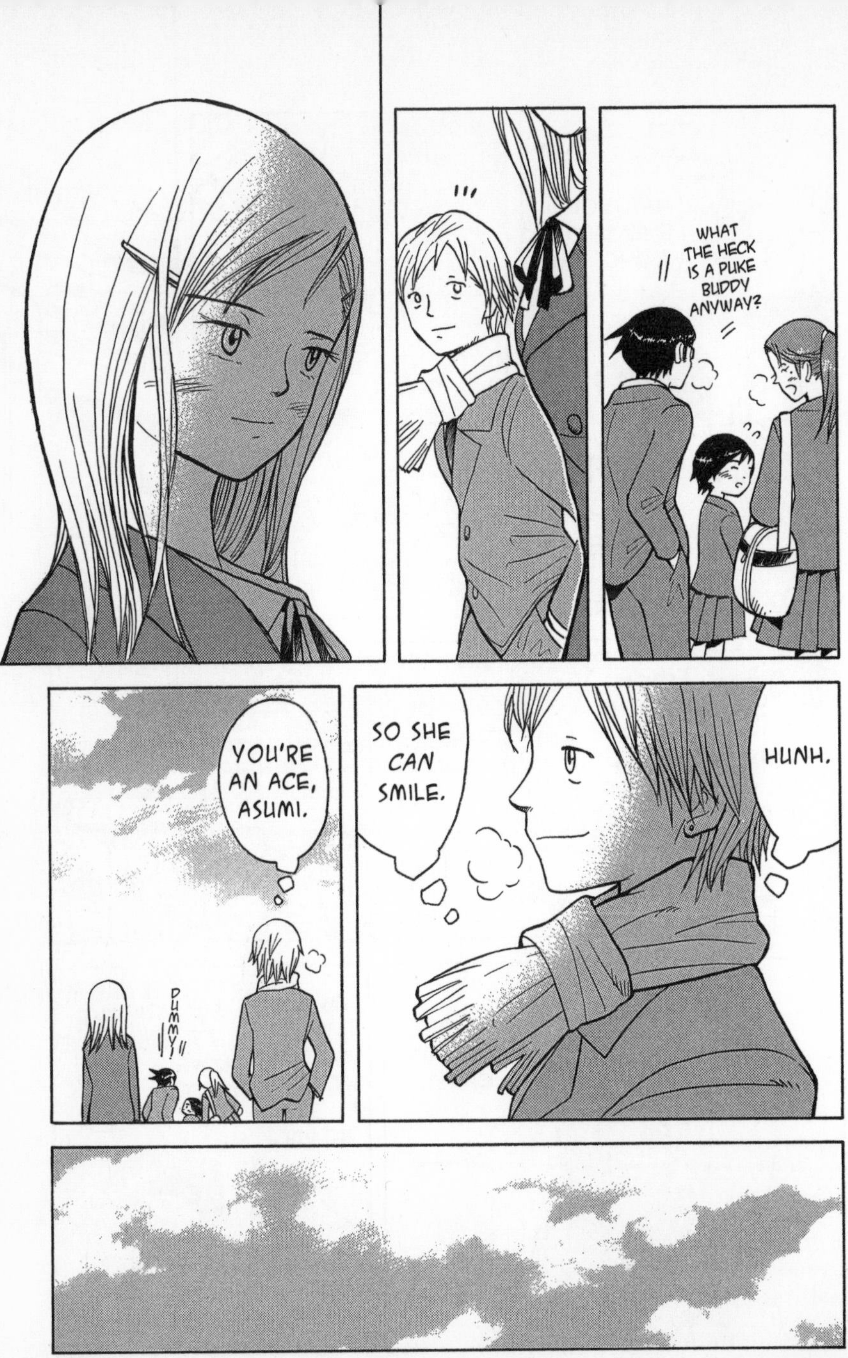
WHAT THE HECK IS A PUKE BUDDY ANYWAY?
HUNH.
SO SHE CAN SMILE.
YOU'RE AN ACE, ASUMI.
DUMMY!

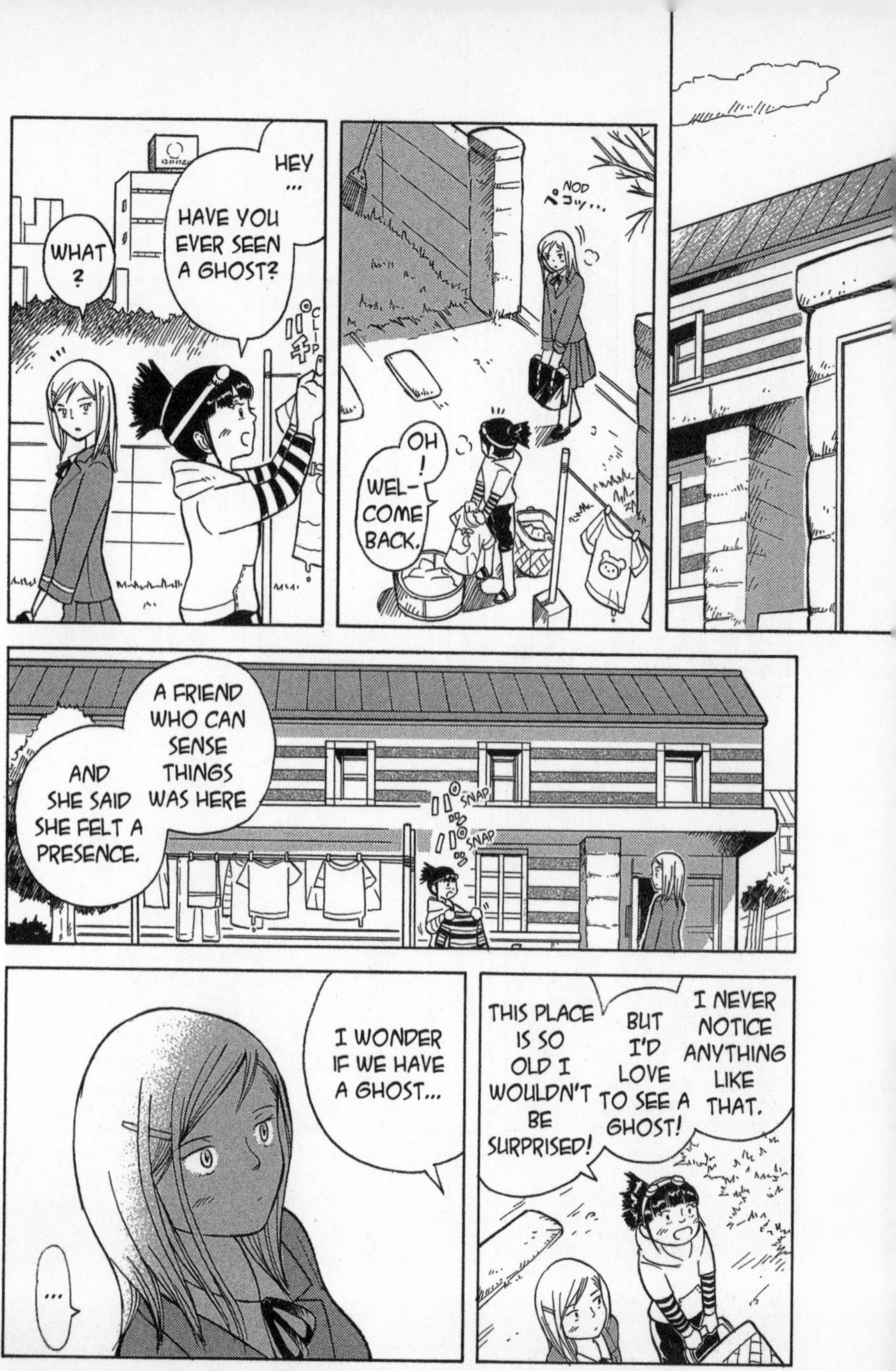
NOD
OH! WELCOME BACK.
HEY... HAVE YOU EVER SEEN A GHOST?
CLIP
WHAT?
A FRIEND WHO CAN SENSE THINGS WAS HERE
AND SHE SAID SHE FELT A PRESENCE.
SNAP
SNAP
I NEVER NOTICE ANYTHING LIKE THAT.
BUT I'D LOVE TO SEE A GHOST!
THIS PLACE IS SO OLD I WOULDN'T BE SURPRISED!
I WONDER IF WE HAVE A GHOST...
...

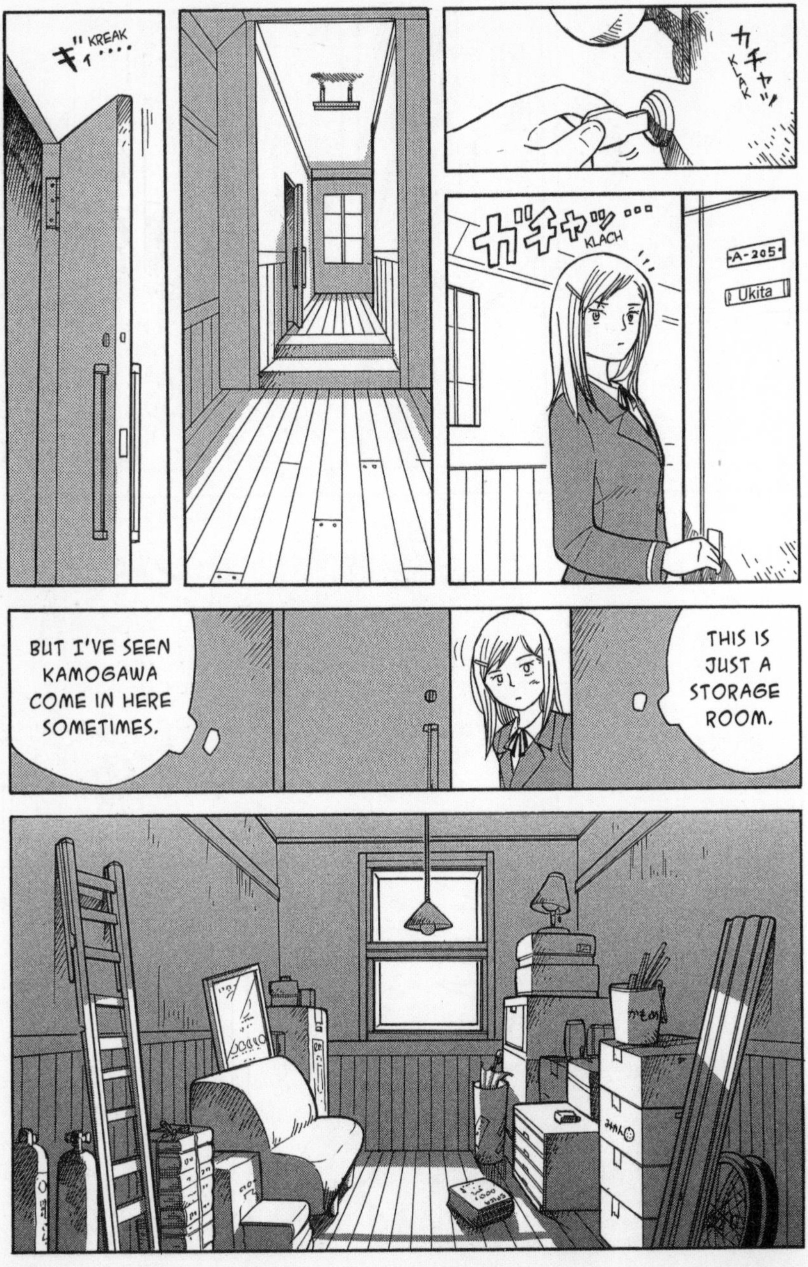
カチャッ
KLAK
ガチャッ...
KLACH
A-205
Ukita
ギィ....
KREAK
THIS IS JUST A STORAGE ROOM.
BUT I'VE SEEN KAMOGAWA COME IN HERE SOMETIMES.

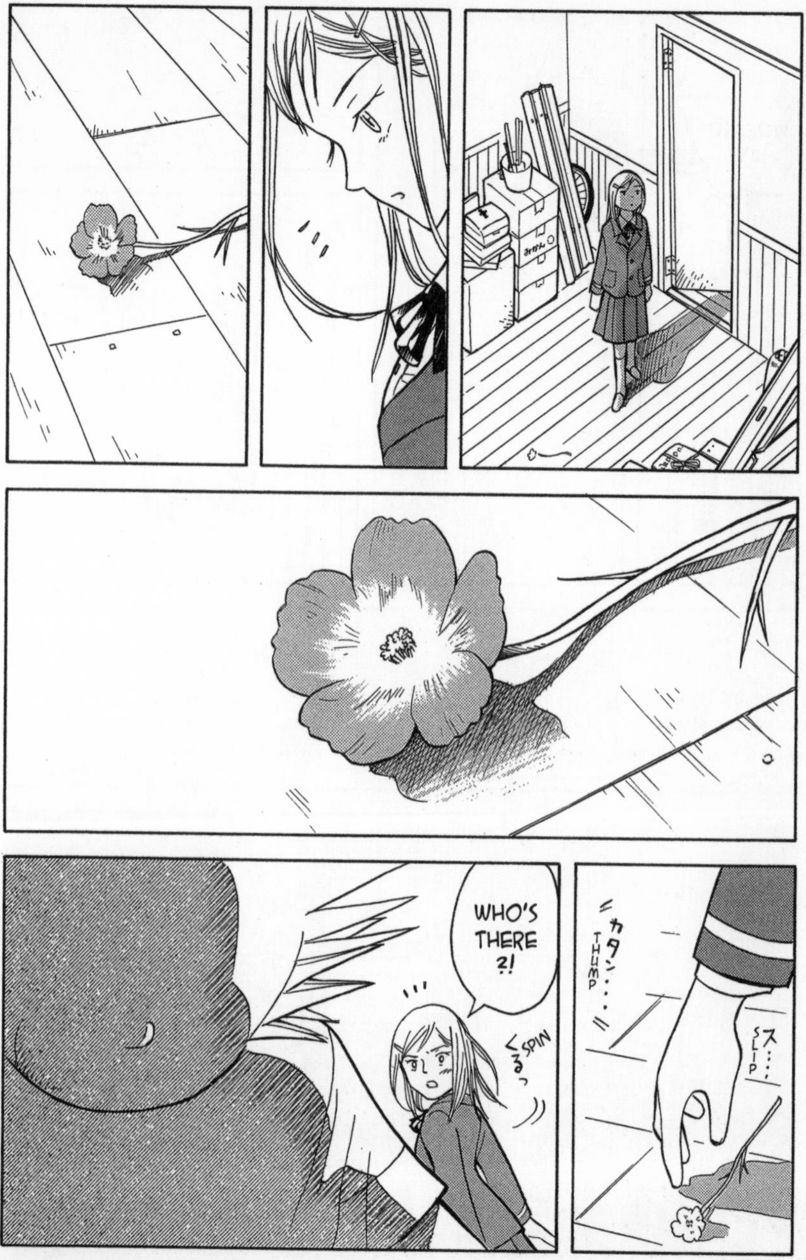
カタン・・・
THUMP
ス・・・
SLIP
WHO'S THERE ?!
くるっ
SPIN

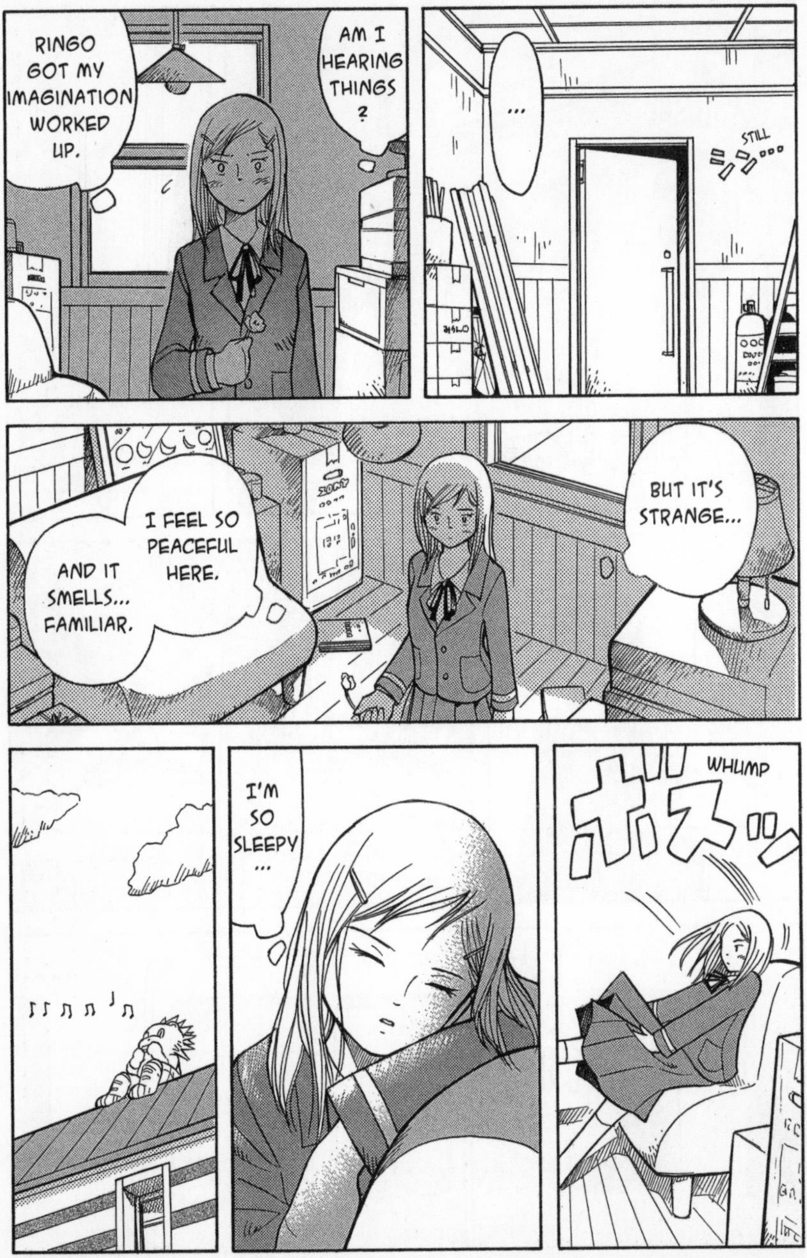
...
STILL
AM I HEARING THINGS?
RINGO GOT MY IMAGINATION WORKED UP.
BUT IT'S STRANGE...
I FEEL SO PEACEFUL HERE.
AND IT SMELLS... FAMILIAR.
WHUMP
I'M SO SLEEPY...

RI-RI-RING!

I CAME THIS WAY LAST NIGHT

BUT IT'S NOT HERE.

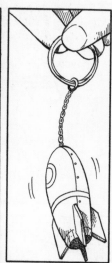

TRAIN DEPARTING ON PLATFORM 2...

STEP
STEP

RI-RI-RING!

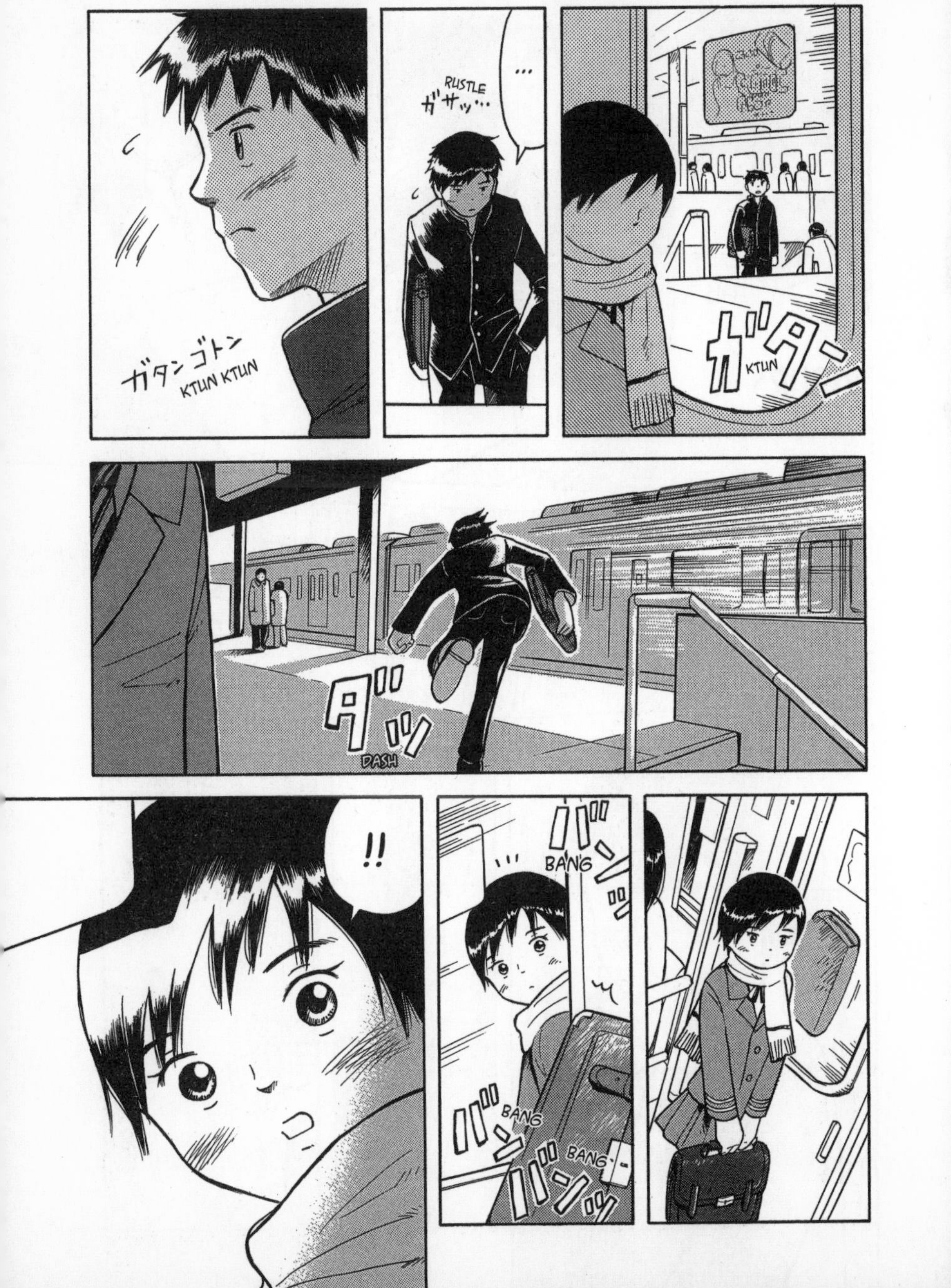

ガターン
KTUN
RUSTLE
ガサッ…
…
ガタンゴトン
KTUN KTUN
ダッ
DASH
バンッ
BANG
バン
BANG
バンッ
BANG
!!

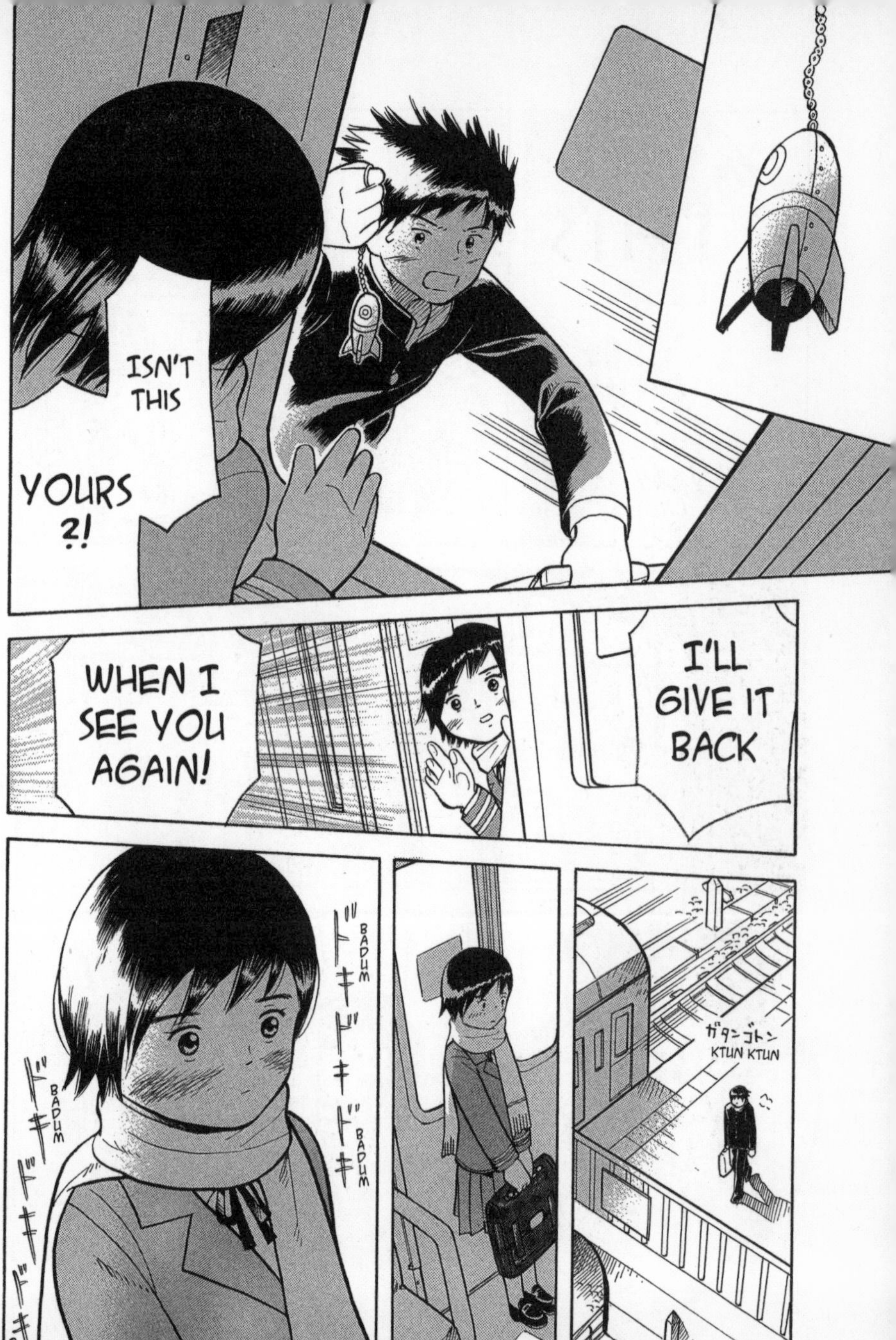
ISN'T THIS YOURS ?!
I'LL GIVE IT BACK
WHEN I SEE YOU AGAIN!
ガタンゴトン
KTUN KTUN
ドキドキ
BADUM
BADUM
ドキドキ
BADUM
BADUM
ドキドキ
BADUM
BADUM

CONTINUED IN TWIN SPICA VOL. 5

THIS STAR SPICA

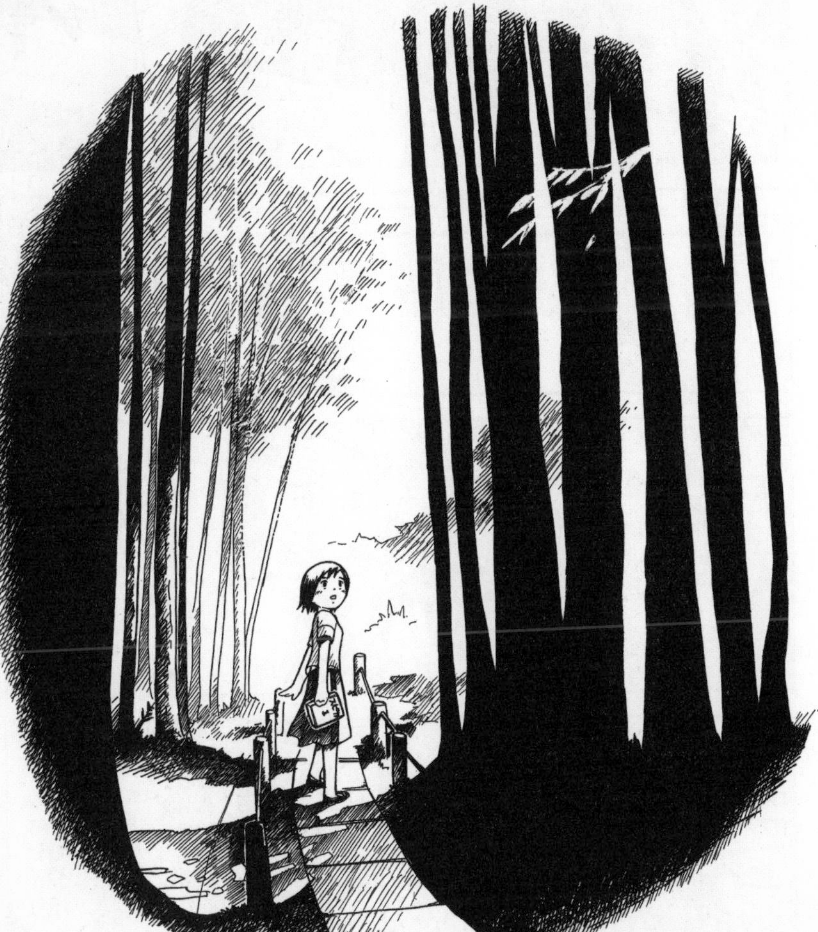

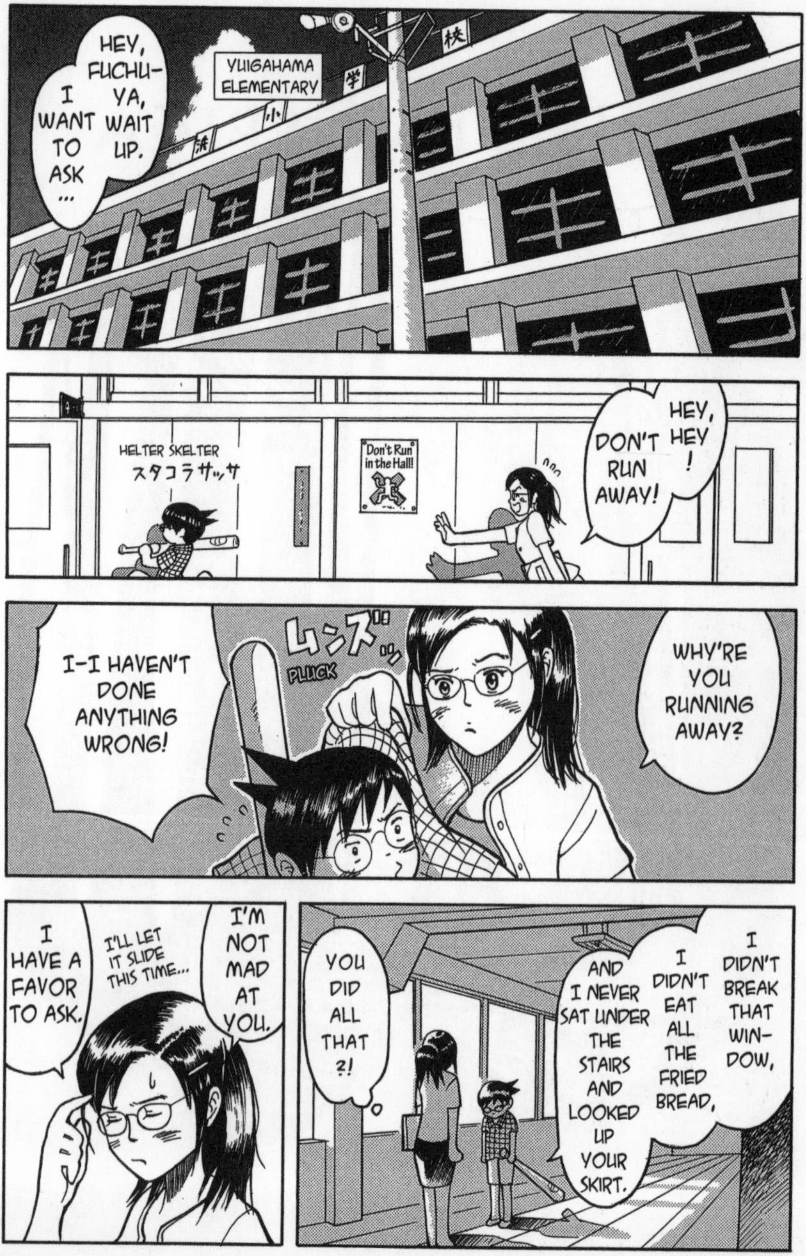
HEY, FUCHU-YA, WAIT UP.
I WANT TO ASK ...
YUIGAHAMA ELEMENTARY
HEY, HEY!
DON'T RUN AWAY!
Don't Run in the Hall!
HELTER SKELTER
スタコラサッサ
WHY'RE YOU RUNNING AWAY?
ムンズ
PLUCK
I-I HAVEN'T DONE ANYTHING WRONG!
I DIDN'T BREAK THAT WIN-DOW,
I DIDN'T EAT ALL THE FRIED BREAD,
AND I NEVER SAT UNDER THE STAIRS AND LOOKED UP YOUR SKIRT.
YOU DID ALL THAT?!
I'M NOT MAD AT YOU.
I'LL LET IT SLIDE THIS TIME...
I HAVE A FAVOR TO ASK.

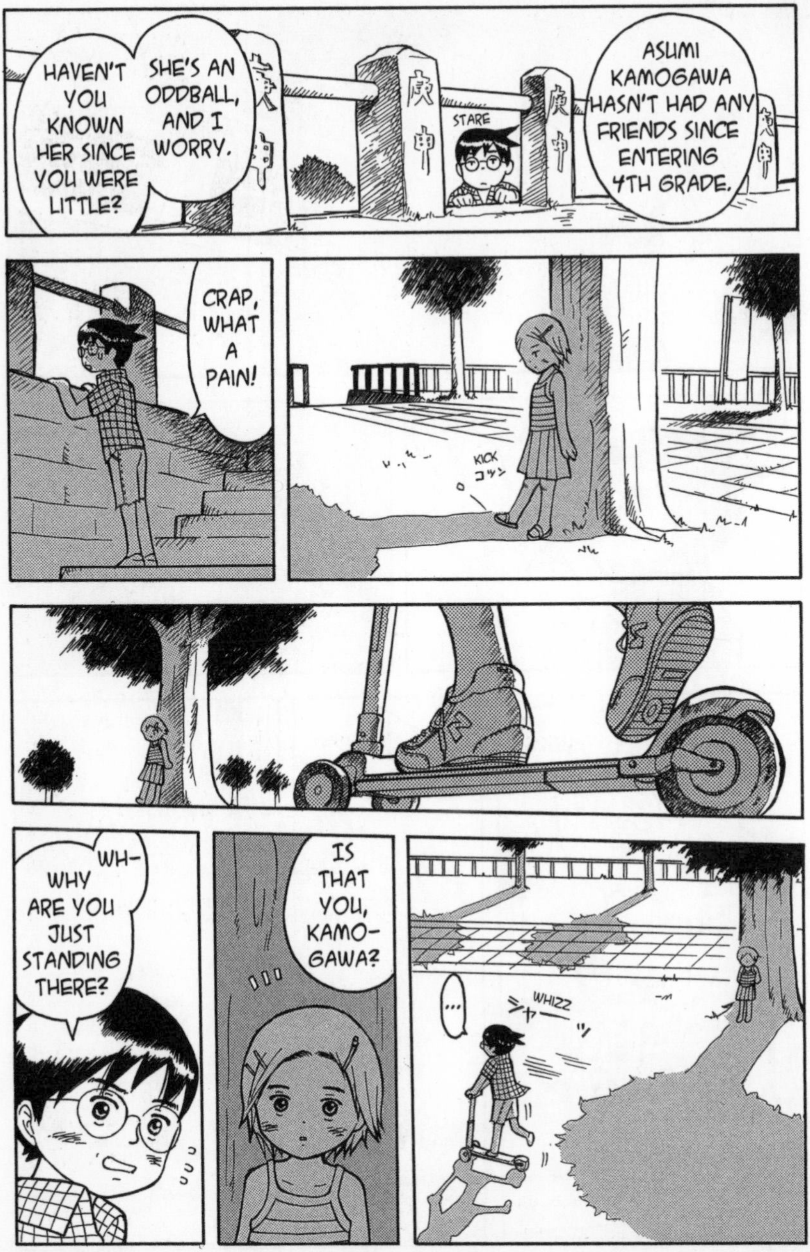
ASUMI KAMOGAWA HASN'T HAD ANY FRIENDS SINCE ENTERING 4TH GRADE.
STARE
SHE'S AN ODDBALL, AND I WORRY.
HAVEN'T YOU KNOWN HER SINCE YOU WERE LITTLE?
KICK
コツン
CRAP, WHAT A PAIN!
...
WHIZZ
シャーッ
IS THAT YOU, KAMOGAWA?
WH-WHY ARE YOU JUST STANDING THERE?

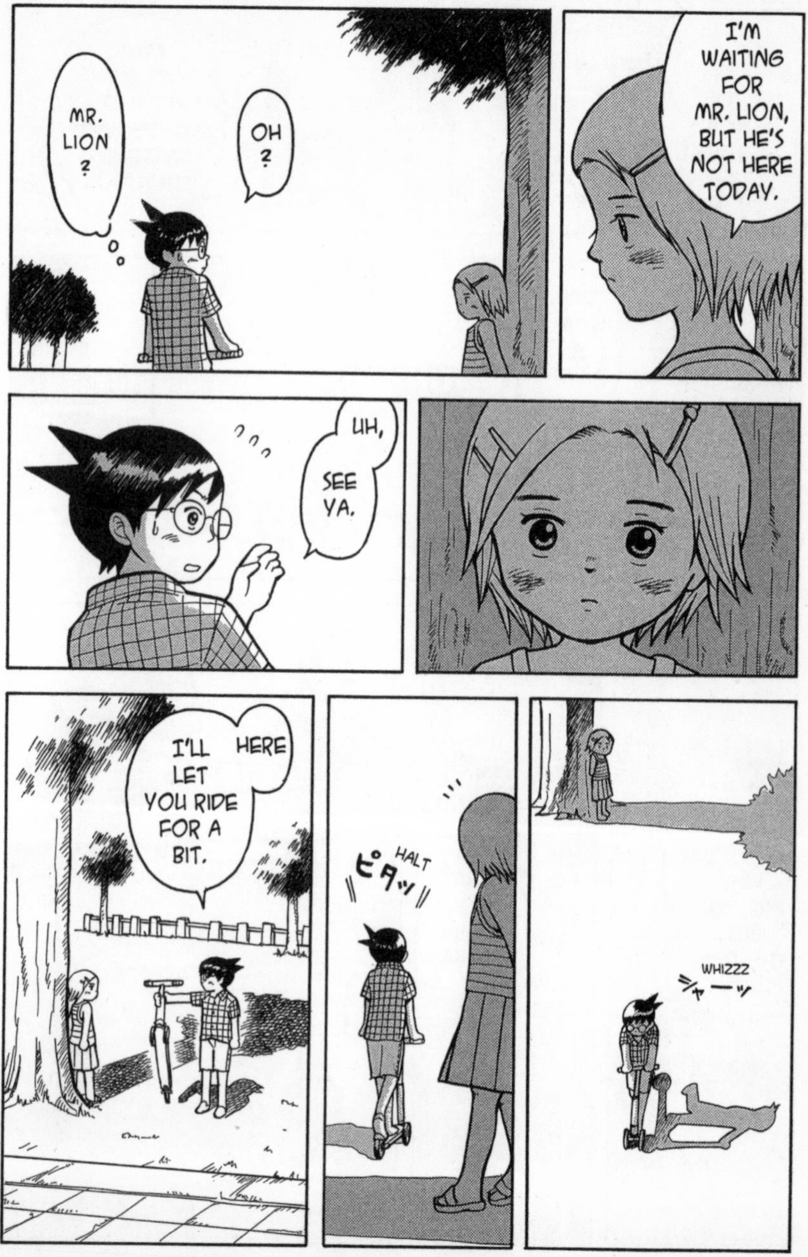
I'M WAITING FOR MR. LION, BUT HE'S NOT HERE TODAY.
OH?
MR. LION?
UH,
SEE YA.
WHIZZZ
シャーッ
HALT
ピタッ
HERE
I'LL LET YOU RIDE FOR A BIT.

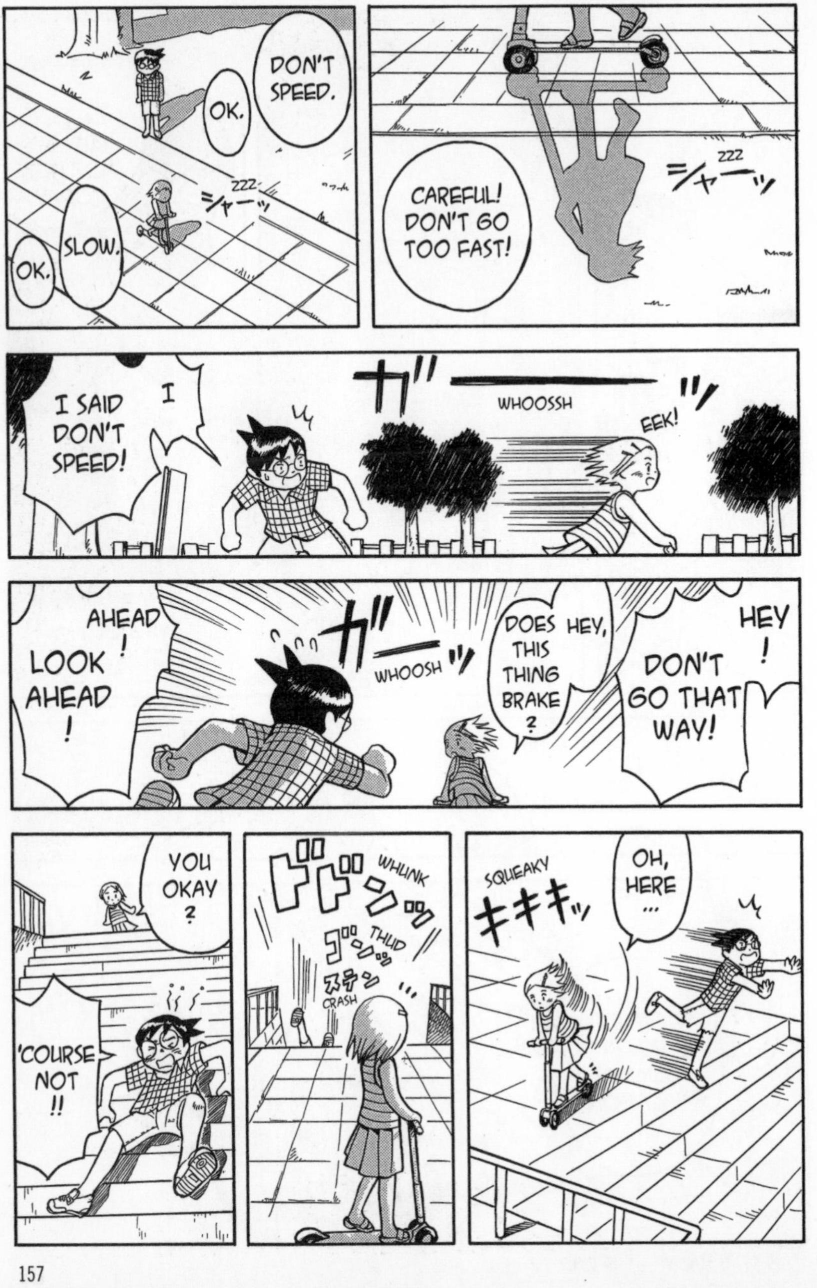
CAREFUL! DON'T GO TOO FAST!
ZZZ
シャーッ
DON'T SPEED.
OK.
ZZZ
シャーッ
SLOW.
OK.
EEK!
ガー
WHOOSSH
I
I SAID DON'T SPEED!
HEY!
DON'T GO THAT WAY!
HEY,
DOES THIS THING BRAKE?
ガー
WHOOSH
AHEAD!
LOOK AHEAD!
OH, HERE...
SQUEAKY
キキキッ
ドドンッ
WHUNK
ゴンッ
THUD
ステン
CRASH
YOU OKAY?
'COURSE NOT!!

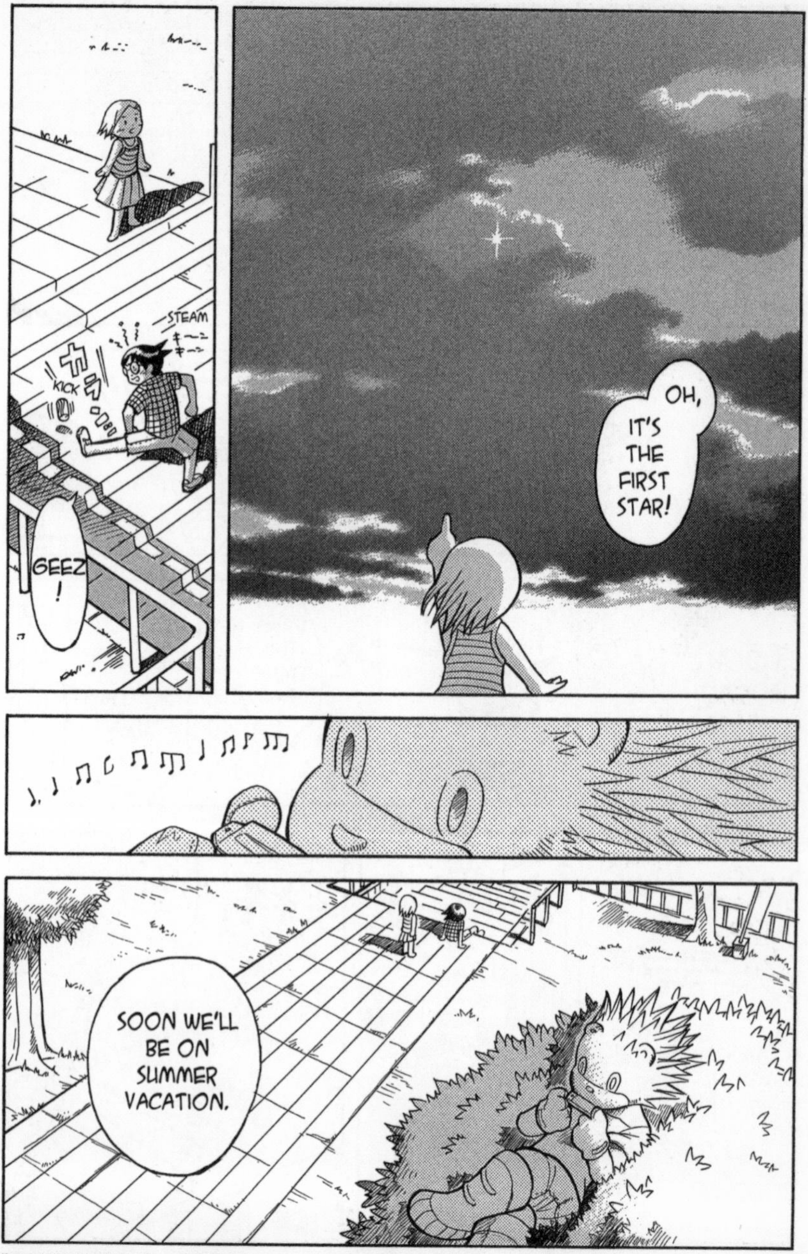
OH, IT'S THE FIRST STAR!
STEAM
KICK
GEEZ!
SOON WE'LL BE ON SUMMER VACATION.

"THIS STAR SPICA" —THE END

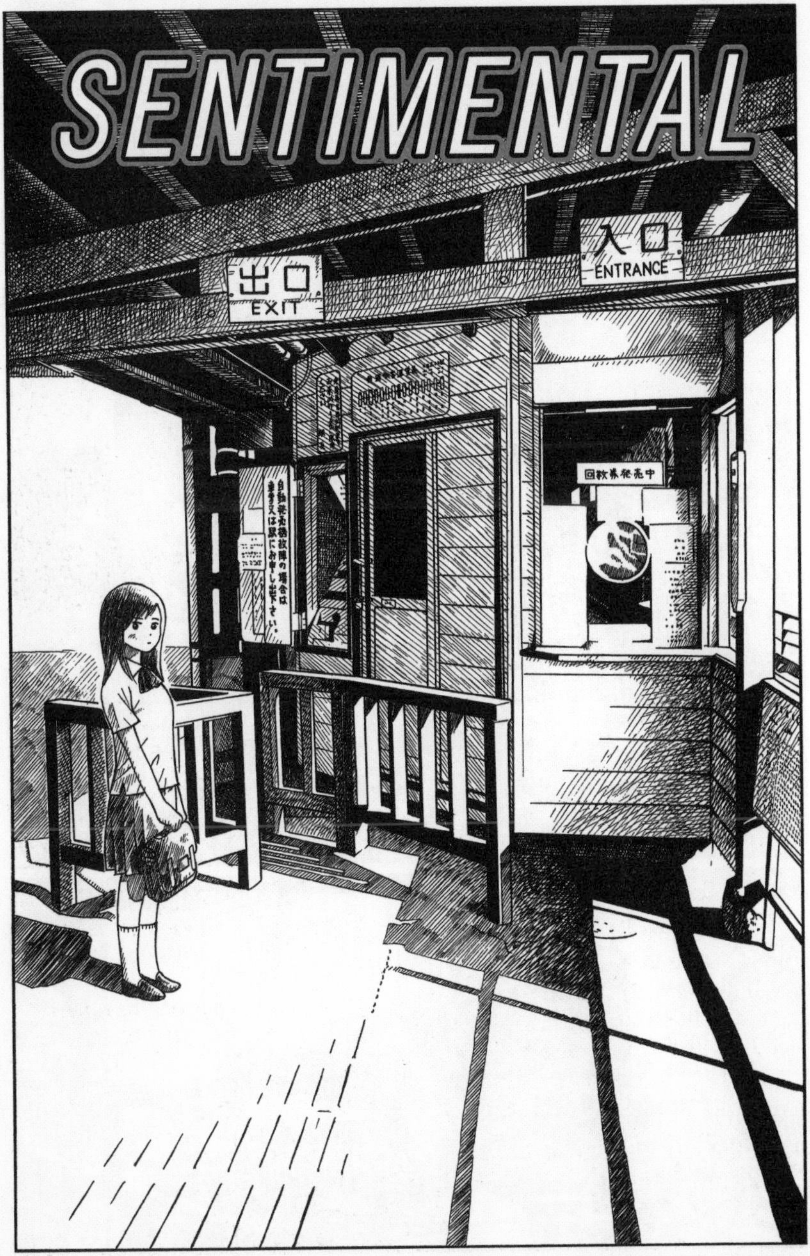
SENTIMENTAL
出口
EXIT
入口
ENTRANCE
回数券発売中
自動券売機故障の場合は
車掌又は駅にお申し出下さい。

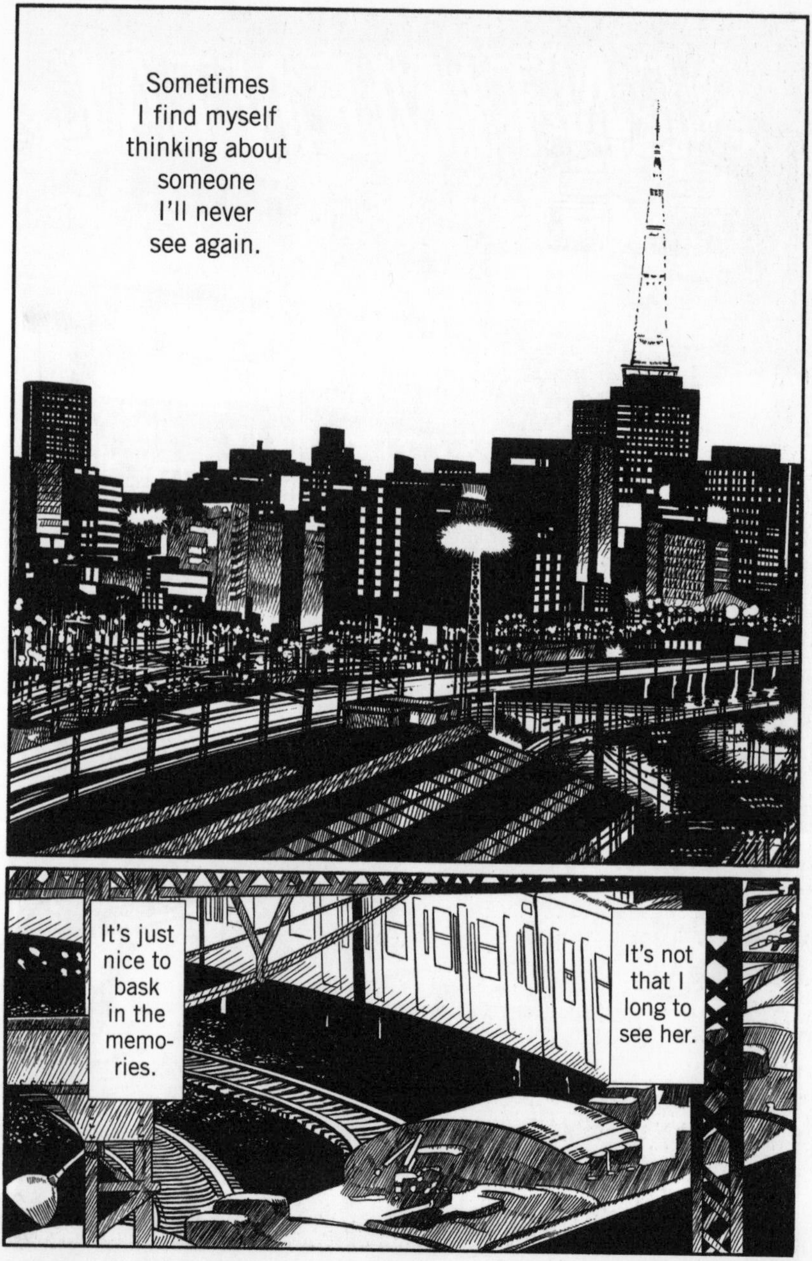
Sometimes I find myself thinking about someone I'll never see again.
It's not that I long to see her.
It's just nice to bask in the memo-ries.

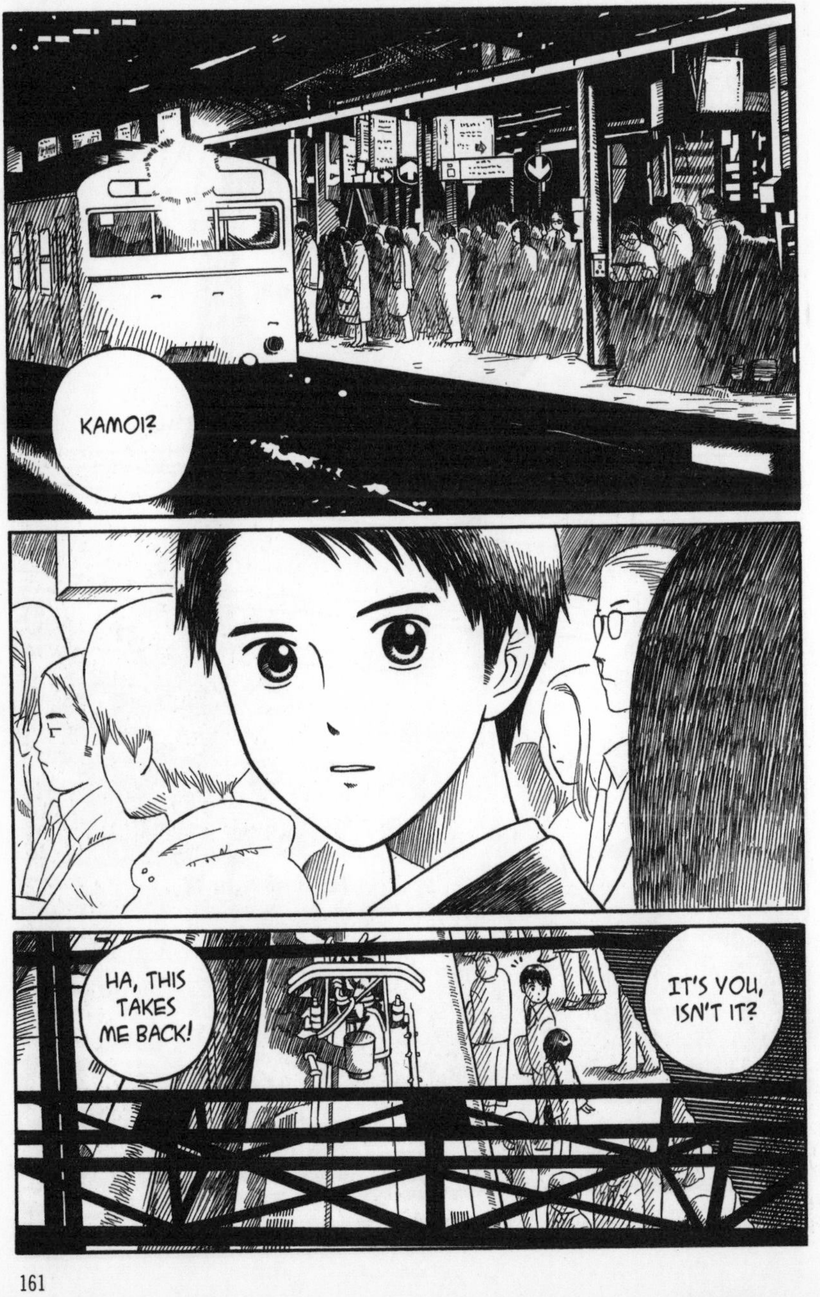
KAMOI?
IT'S YOU, ISN'T IT?
HA, THIS TAKES ME BACK!

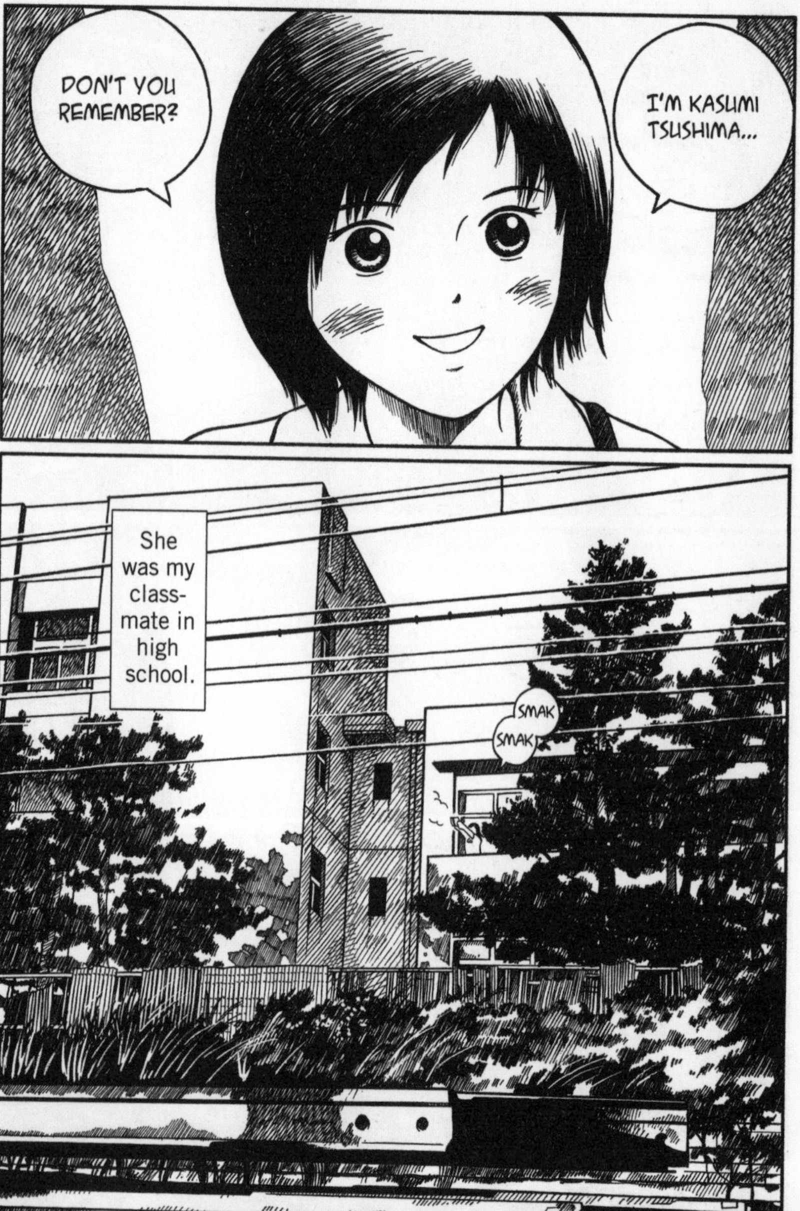
I'M KASUMI TSUSHIMA...
DON'T YOU REMEMBER?
She was my class-mate in high school.
SMAK
SMAK

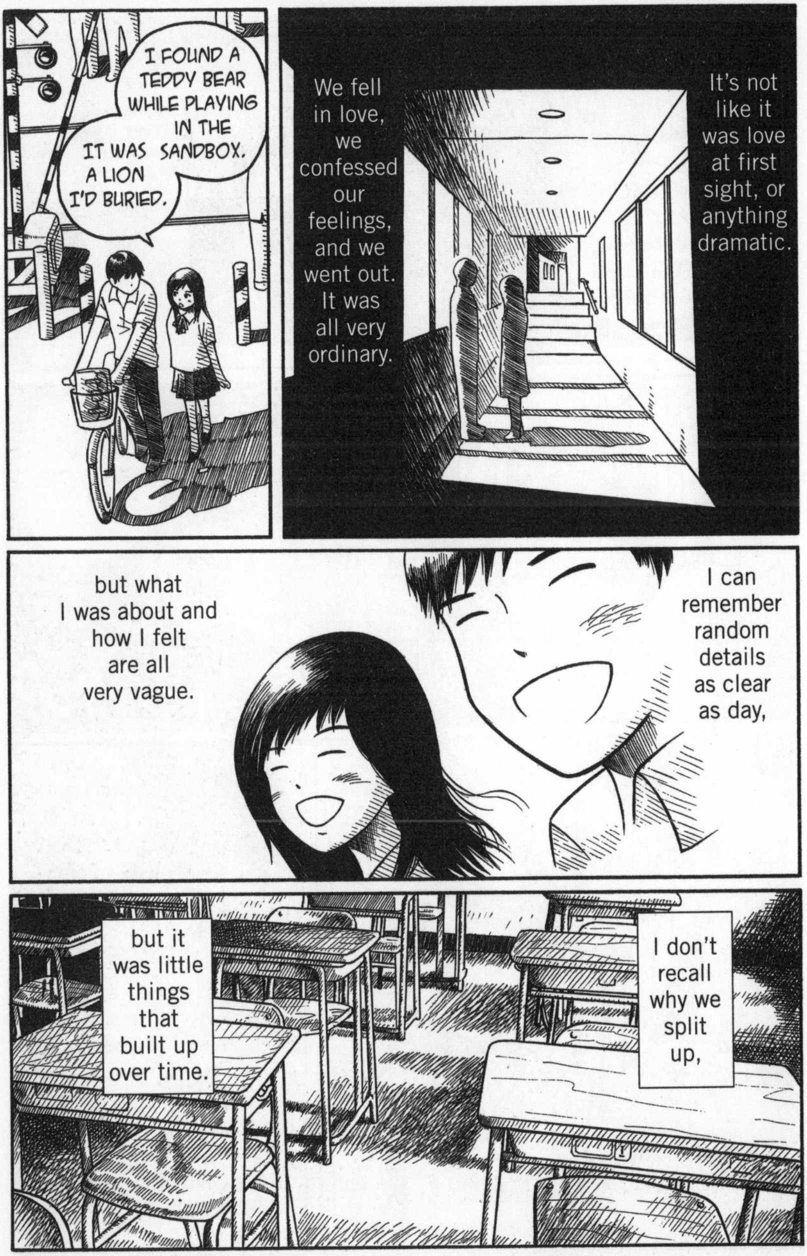
It's not like it was love at first sight, or anything dramatic.
We fell in love, we confessed our feelings, and we went out. It was all very ordinary.
I FOUND A TEDDY BEAR WHILE PLAYING IN THE SANDBOX.
IT WAS A LION I'D BURIED.
I can remember random details as clear as day,
but what I was about and how I felt are all very vague.
I don't recall why we split up,
but it was little things that built up over time.

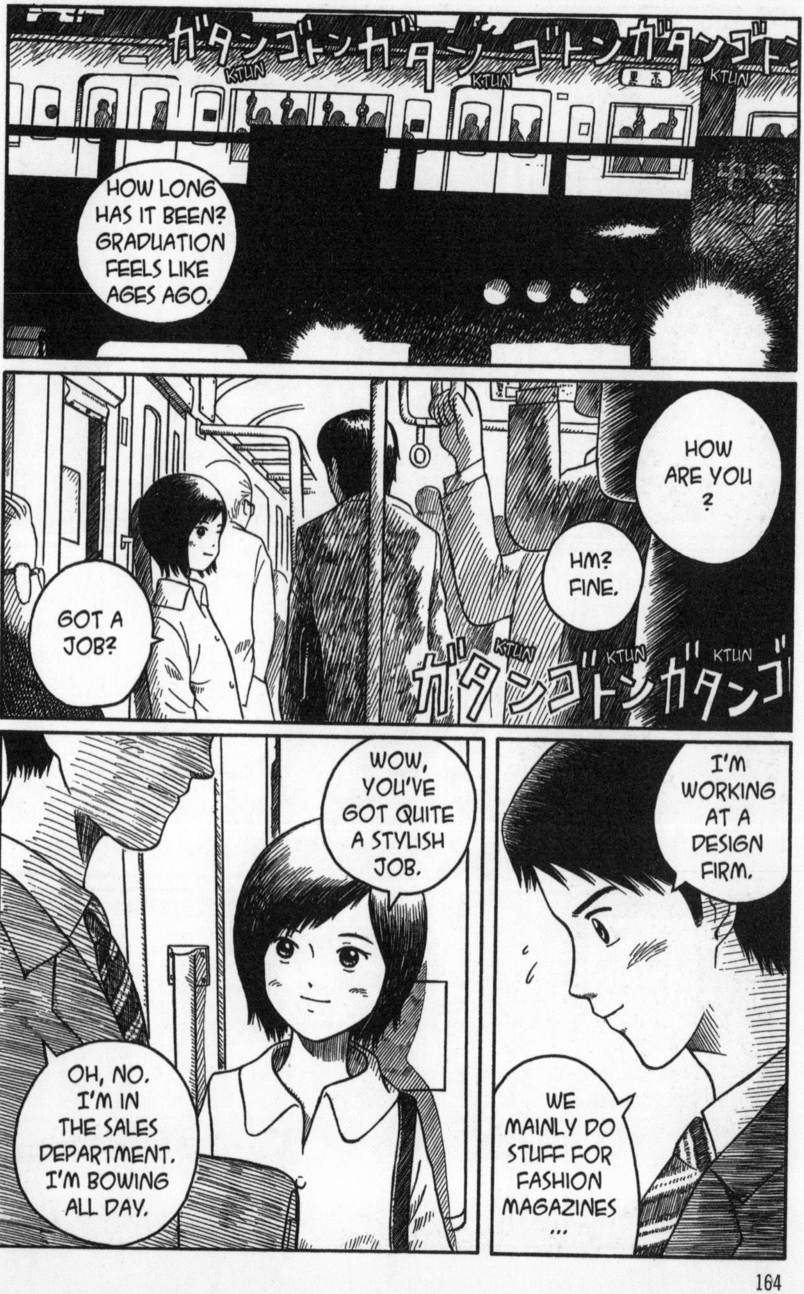
ガタンゴトンガターンゴトンガタンゴト
KTUN
KTUN
KTUN
HOW LONG HAS IT BEEN? GRADUATION FEELS LIKE AGES AGO.
HOW ARE YOU?
HM? FINE.
GOT A JOB?
ガタンゴトンガタンゴ
KTUN
KTUN
KTUN
I'M WORKING AT A DESIGN FIRM.
WE MAINLY DO STUFF FOR FASHION MAGAZINES ...
WOW, YOU'VE GOT QUITE A STYLISH JOB.
OH, NO. I'M IN THE SALES DEPARTMENT. I'M BOWING ALL DAY.

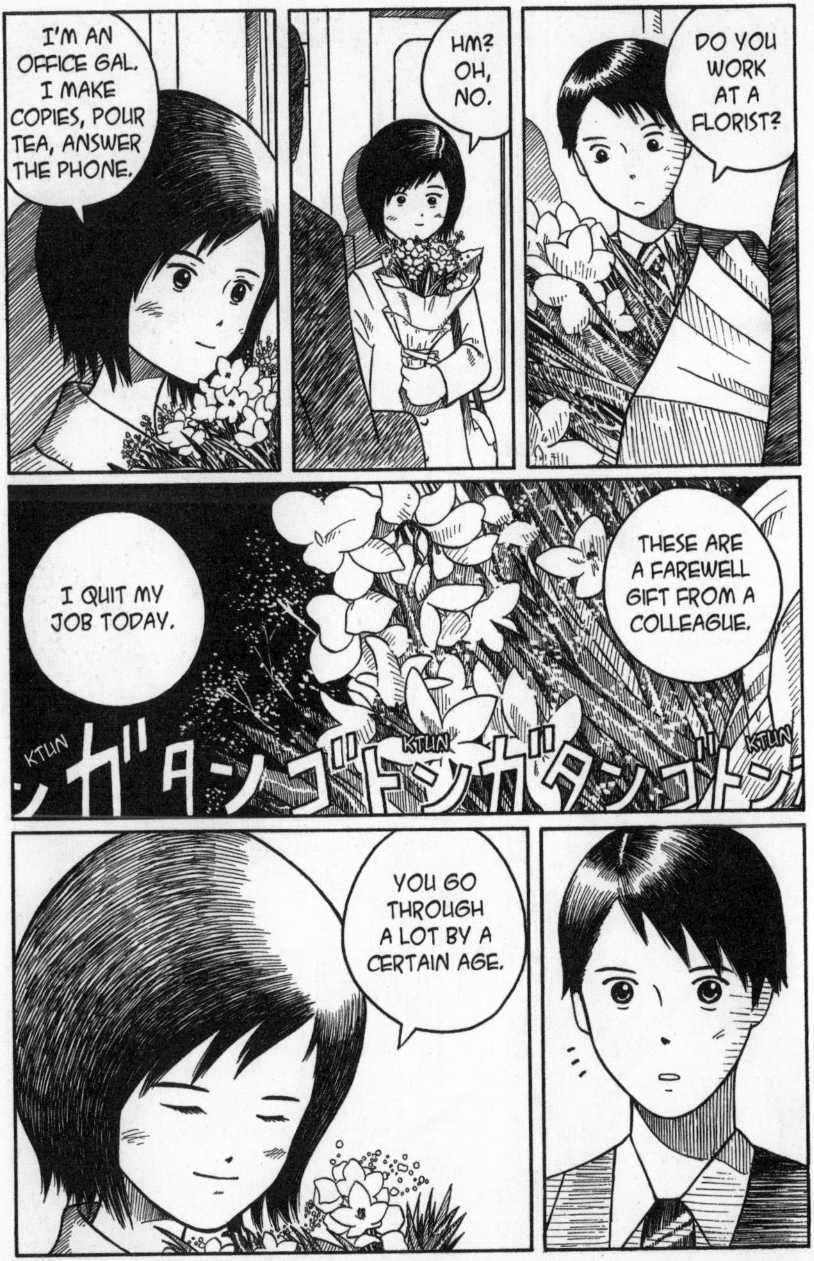
DO YOU WORK AT A FLORIST?
HM? OH, NO.
I'M AN OFFICE GAL. I MAKE COPIES, POUR TEA, ANSWER THE PHONE.
THESE ARE A FAREWELL GIFT FROM A COLLEAGUE.
I QUIT MY JOB TODAY.
KTUN
KTUN
KTUN
YOU GO THROUGH A LOT BY A CERTAIN AGE.

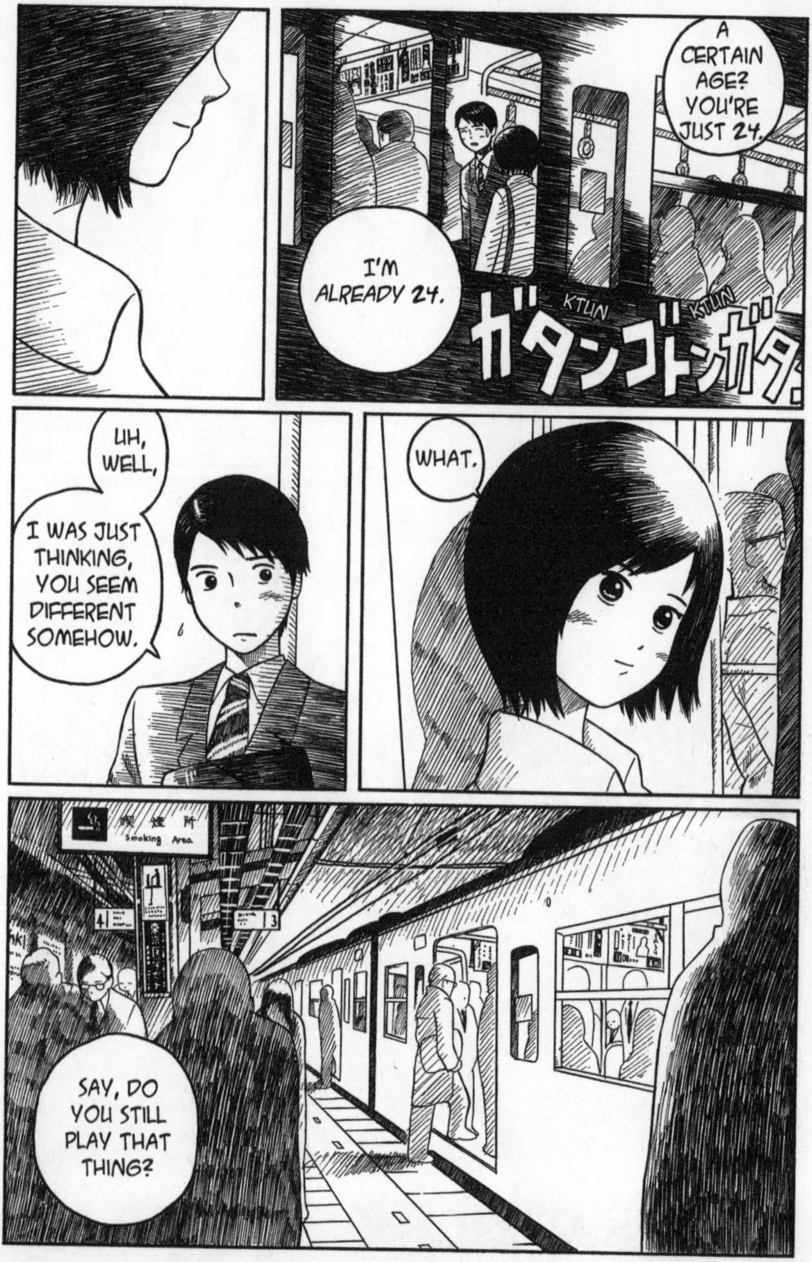
A CERTAIN AGE? YOU'RE JUST 24.
I'M ALREADY 24.
ガタンゴトンガタ
KTUN KTUN
WHAT.
UH, WELL,
I WAS JUST THINKING, YOU SEEM DIFFERENT SOMEHOW.
喫煙所
Smoking Area
SAY, DO YOU STILL PLAY THAT THING?

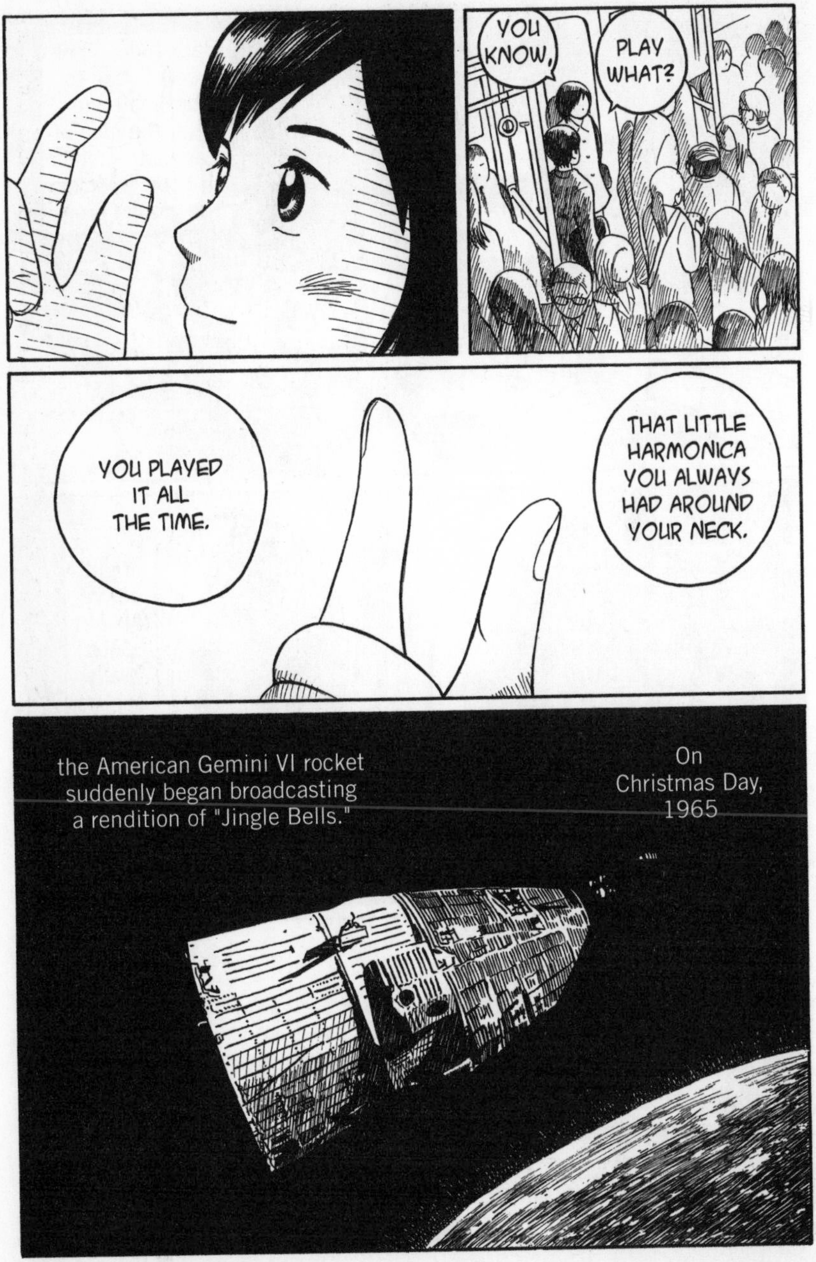
PLAY WHAT?
YOU KNOW,
THAT LITTLE HARMONICA YOU ALWAYS HAD AROUND YOUR NECK.
YOU PLAYED IT ALL THE TIME.
On Christmas Day, 1965
the American Gemini VI rocket suddenly began broadcasting a rendition of "Jingle Bells."

Back then, since rockets had to be small and light, the idea of an instrument on board shocked the ground crew.

Right before takeoff, pilot Wally Schirra

smuggled a 3cm-long harmonica around his neck onto the rocket.

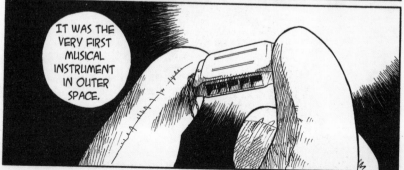

IT WAS THE VERY FIRST MUSICAL INSTRUMENT IN OUTER SPACE.

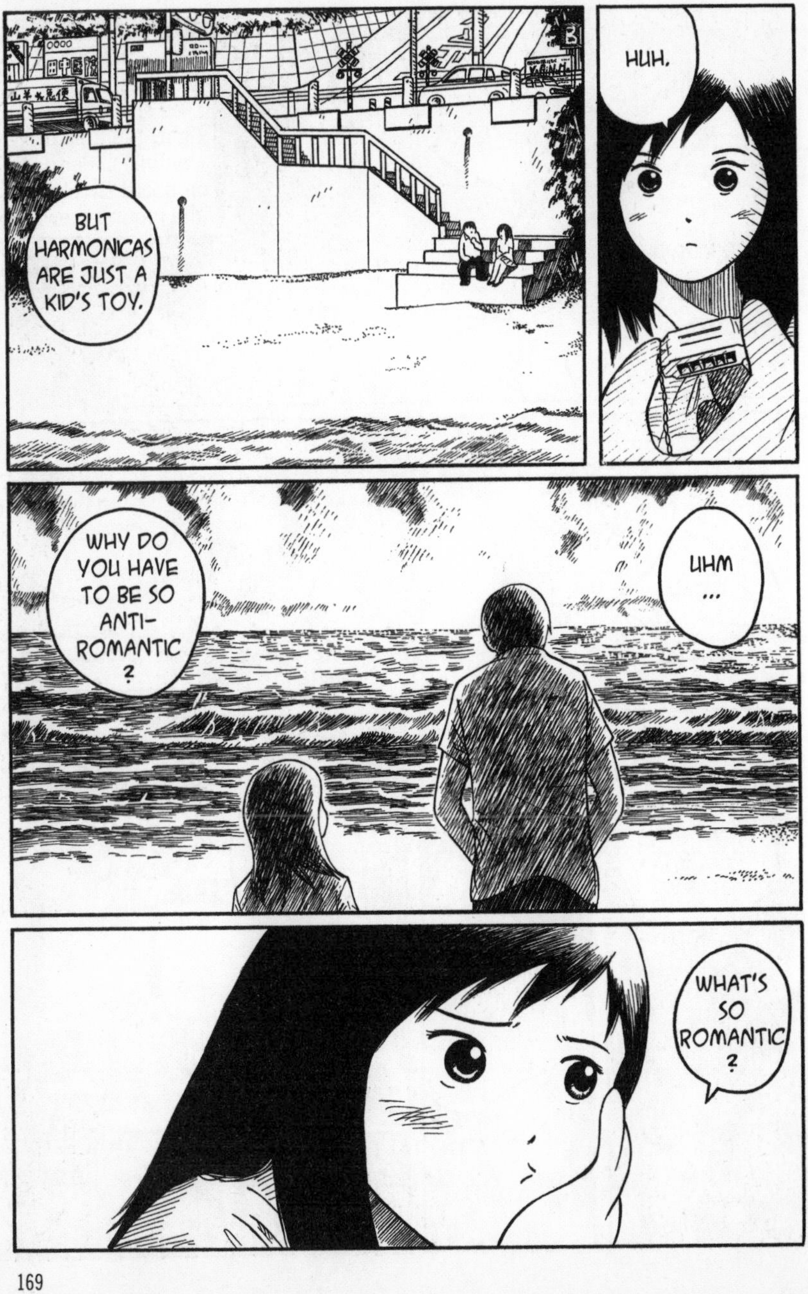
HUH.
BUT HARMONICAS ARE JUST A KID'S TOY.
UHM ...
WHY DO YOU HAVE TO BE SO ANTI-ROMANTIC?
WHAT'S SO ROMANTIC?

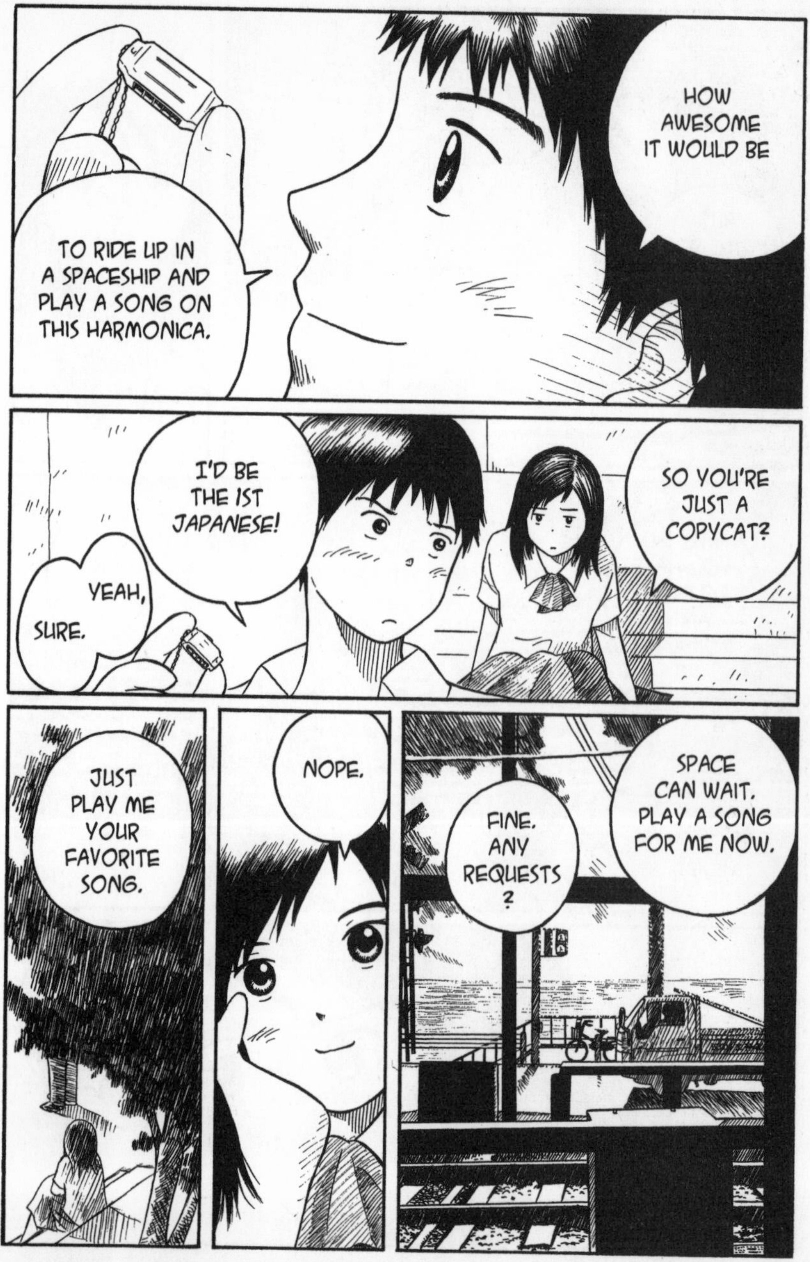
HOW AWESOME IT WOULD BE
TO RIDE UP IN A SPACESHIP AND PLAY A SONG ON THIS HARMONICA.
SO YOU'RE JUST A COPYCAT?
I'D BE THE 1ST JAPANESE!
YEAH, SURE.
SPACE CAN WAIT. PLAY A SONG FOR ME NOW.
FINE. ANY REQUESTS?
NOPE.
JUST PLAY ME YOUR FAVORITE SONG.

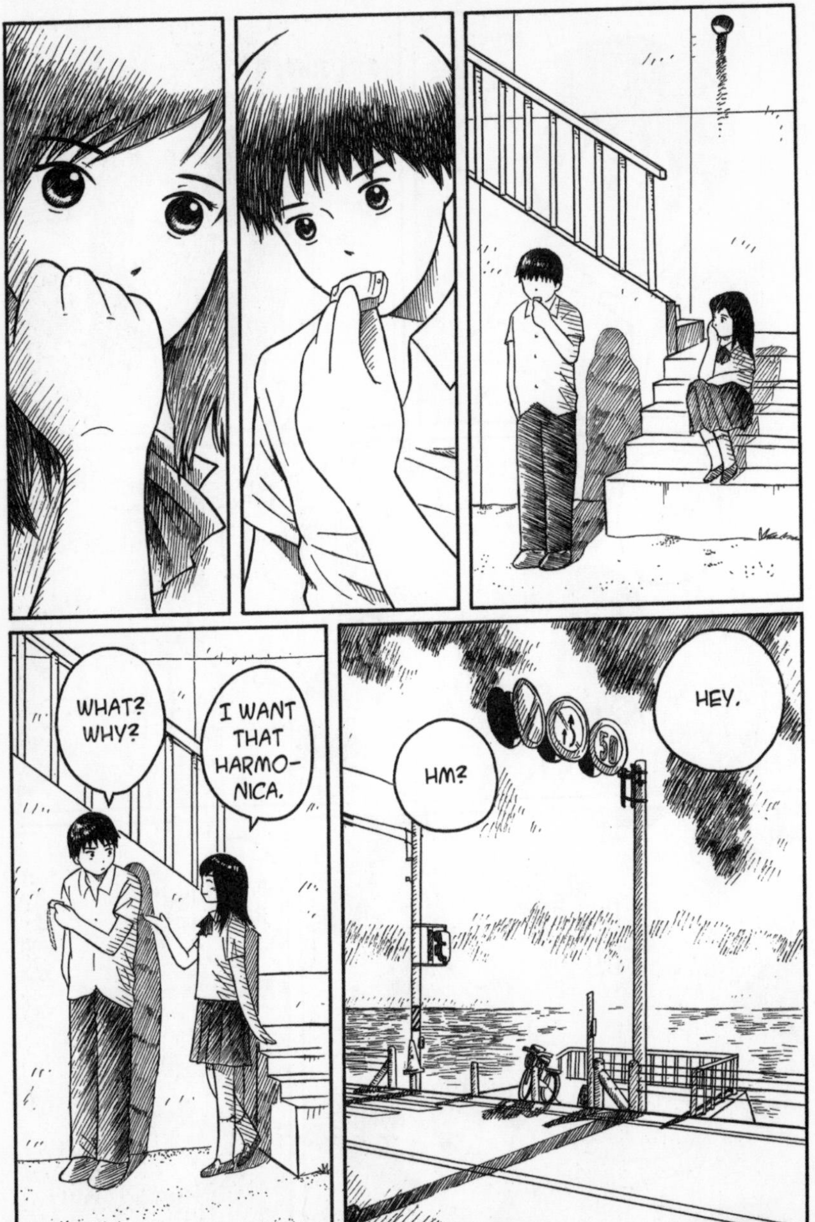
HEY.
HM?
I WANT THAT HARMONICA.
WHAT? WHY?

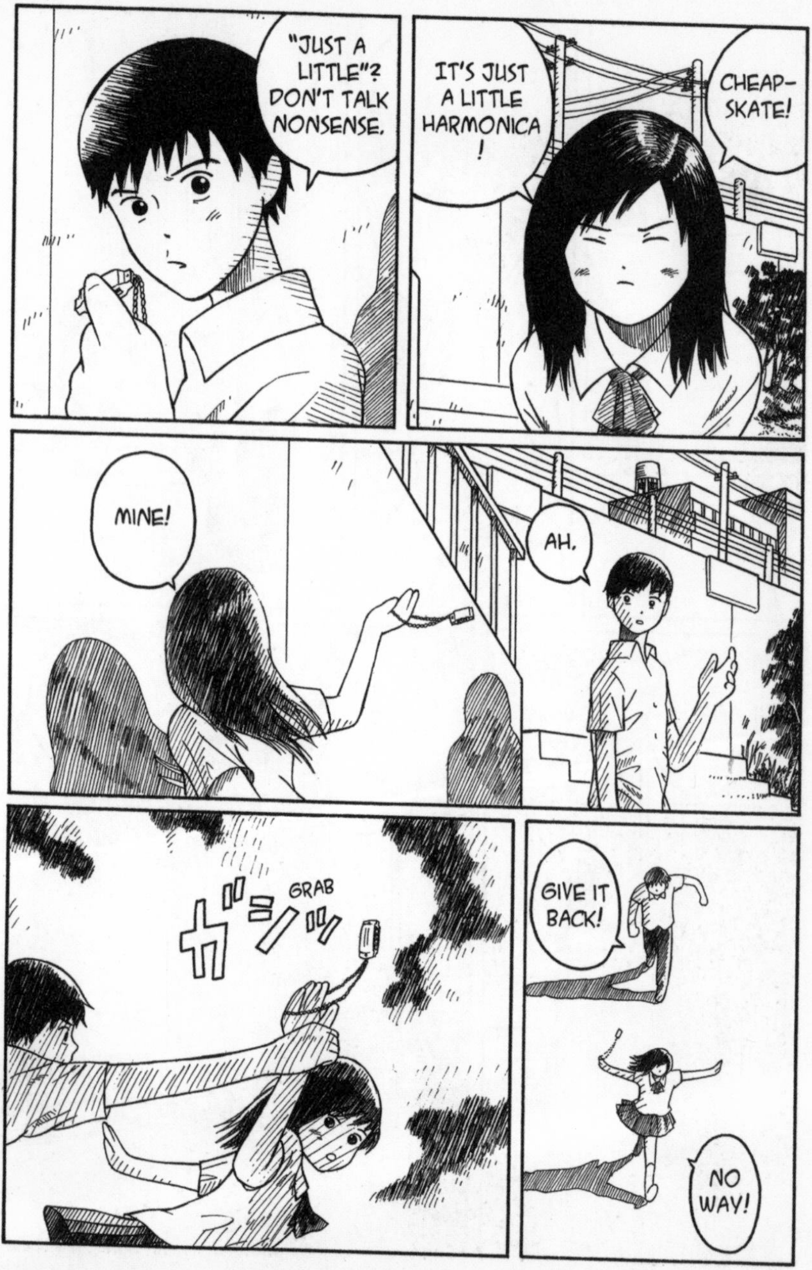
CHEAP-SKATE!
IT'S JUST A LITTLE HARMONICA!
"JUST A LITTLE"? DON'T TALK NONSENSE.
AH.
MINE!
GIVE IT BACK!
NO WAY!
GRAB

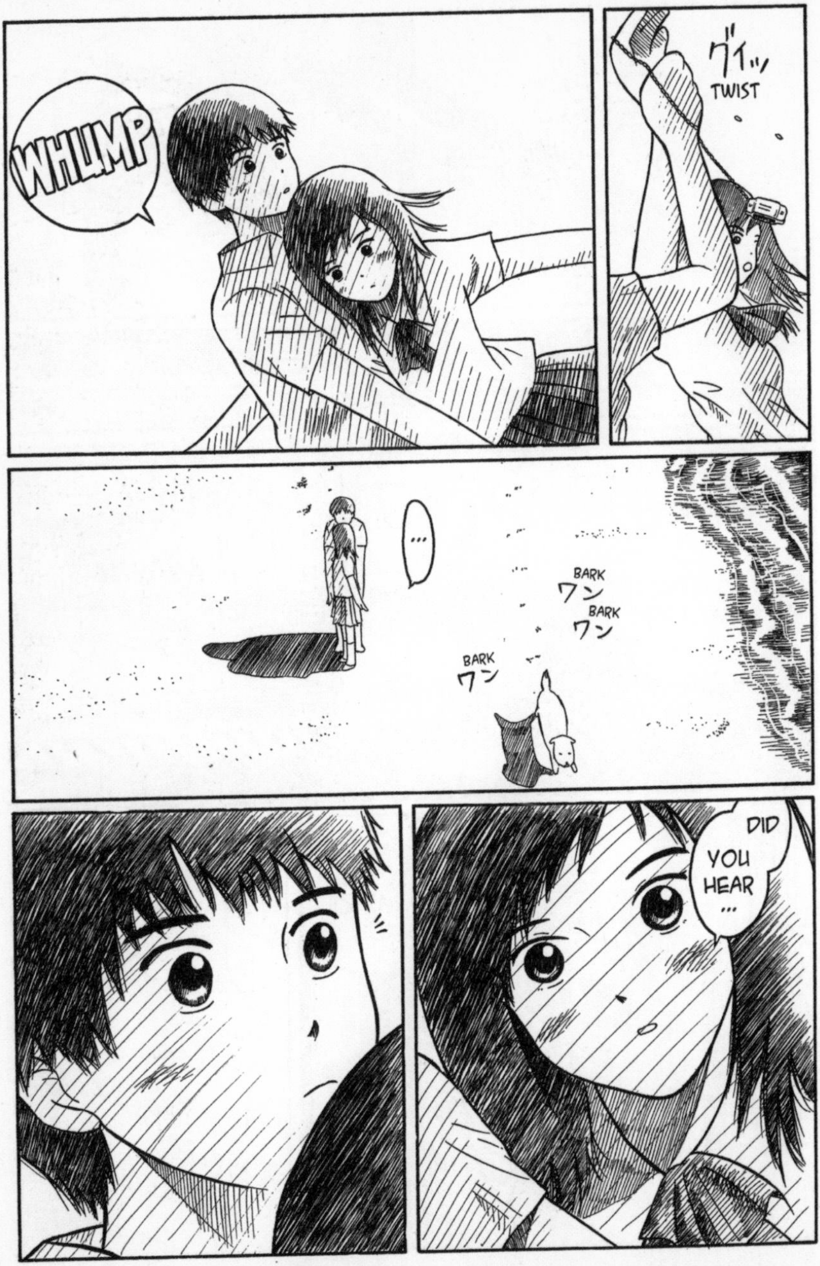
グイッ
TWIST
WHUMP
...
BARK
ワン
BARK
ワン
BARK
ワン
DID YOU HEAR ...

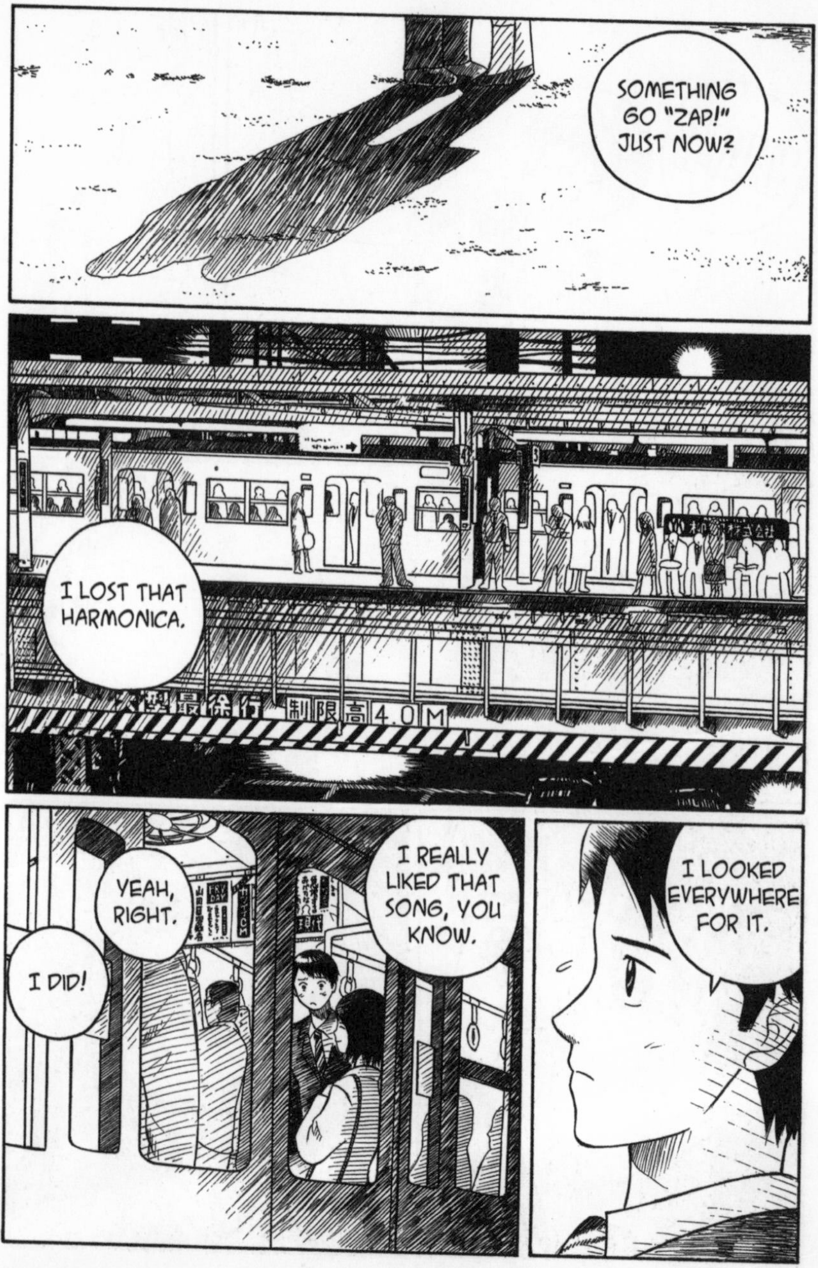

SOMETHING GO "ZAP!" JUST NOW?
I LOST THAT HARMONICA.
制限高4.0M
I LOOKED EVERYWHERE FOR IT.
I REALLY LIKED THAT SONG, YOU KNOW.
YEAH, RIGHT.
I DID!

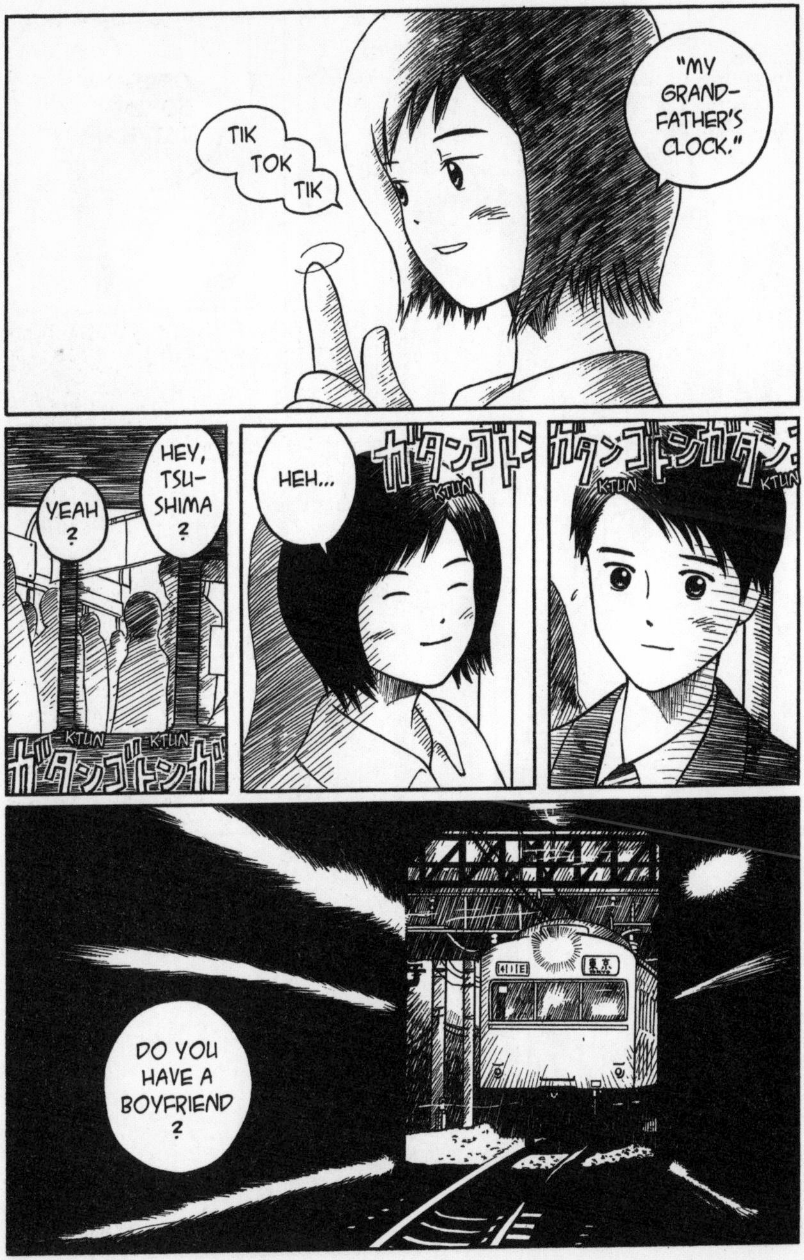
"MY GRAND-FATHER'S CLOCK."
TIK TOK TIK
ガタンゴトンガタン
KTUN KTUN
ガタンゴトン
KTUN
HEH...
HEY, TSU-SHIMA?
YEAH?
KTUN KTUN
ガタンゴトンガ
DO YOU HAVE A BOYFRIEND?

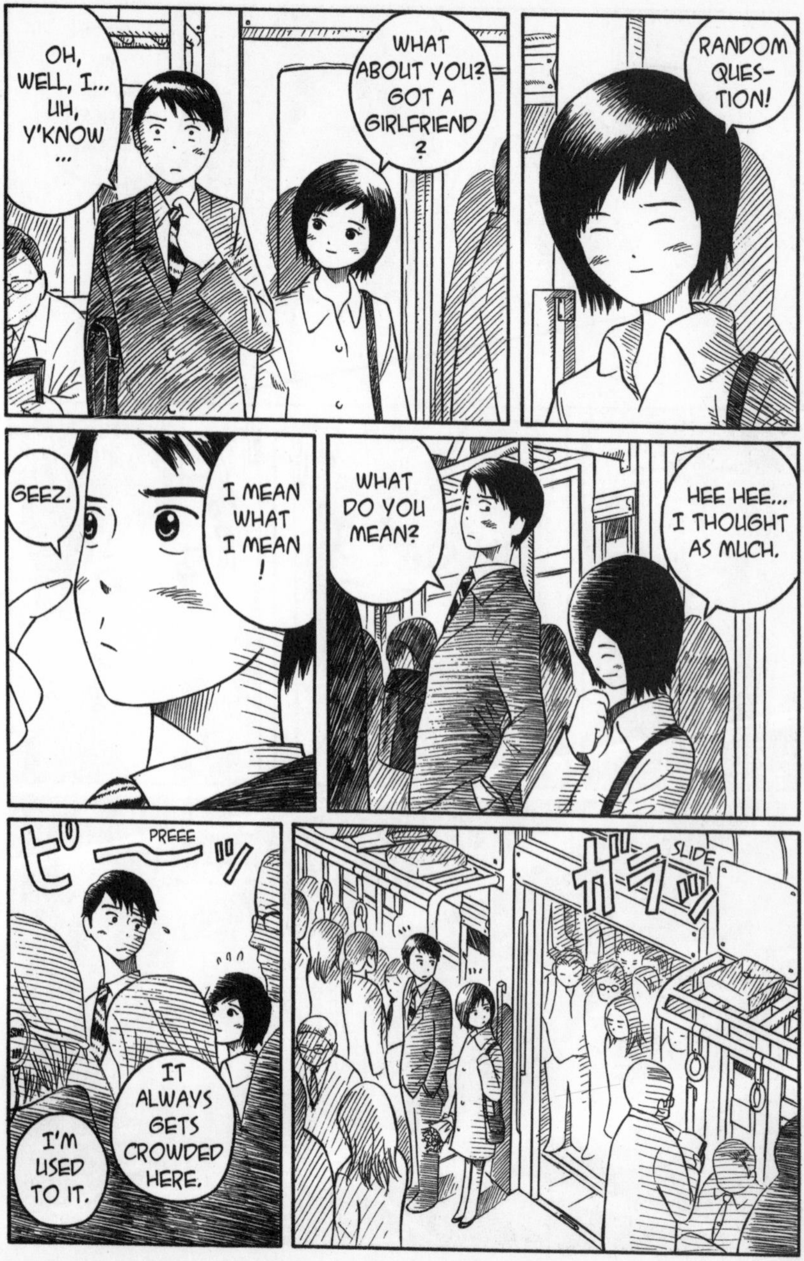
RANDOM QUES-TION!
WHAT ABOUT YOU? GOT A GIRLFRIEND?
OH, WELL, I... UH, Y'KNOW...
HEE HEE... I THOUGHT AS MUCH.
WHAT DO YOU MEAN?
I MEAN WHAT I MEAN!
GEEZ.
SLIDE
PREEE
IT ALWAYS GETS CROWDED HERE.
I'M USED TO IT.

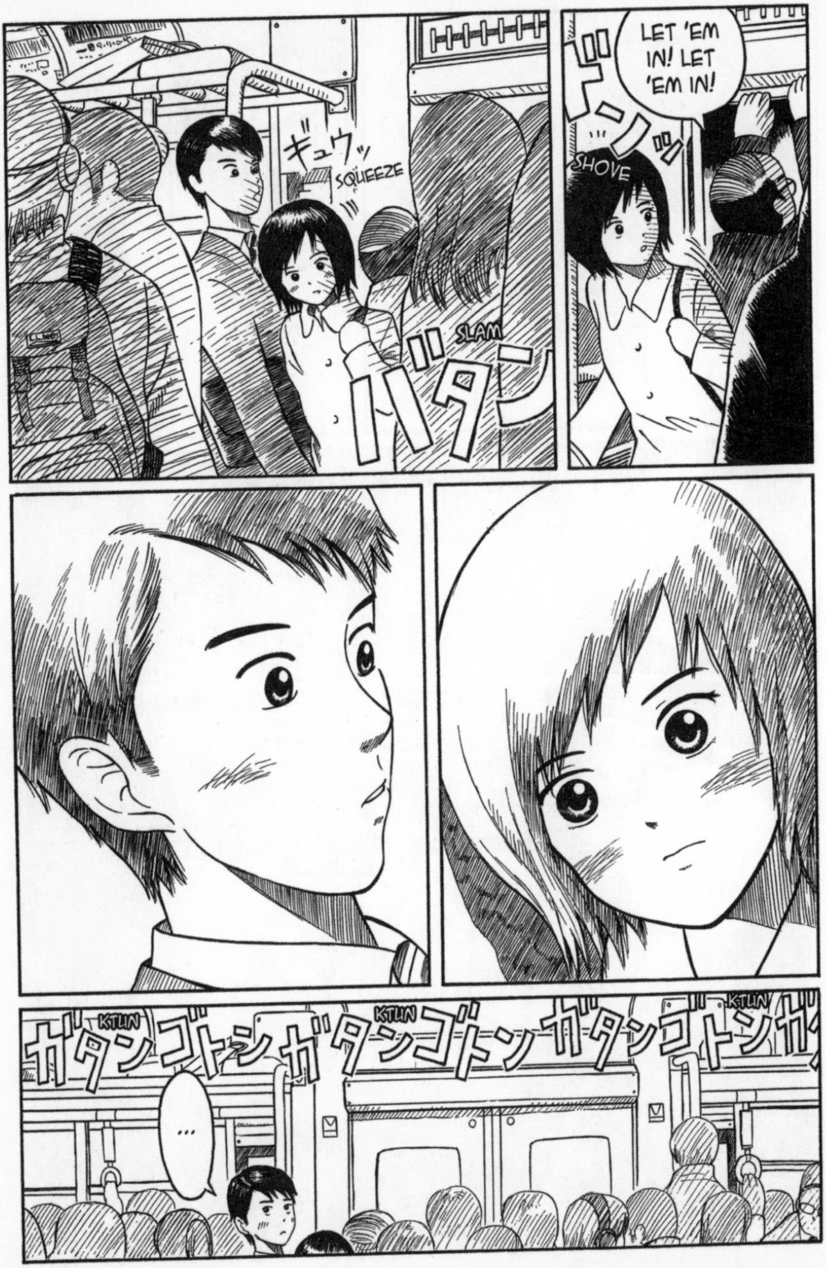
LET 'EM IN! LET 'EM IN!
ドンッ
SHOVE
ギュウッ
SQUEEZE
バタン
SLAM
ガタンゴトンガタンゴトンガタンゴトン
KTUN
KTUN
KTUN
...

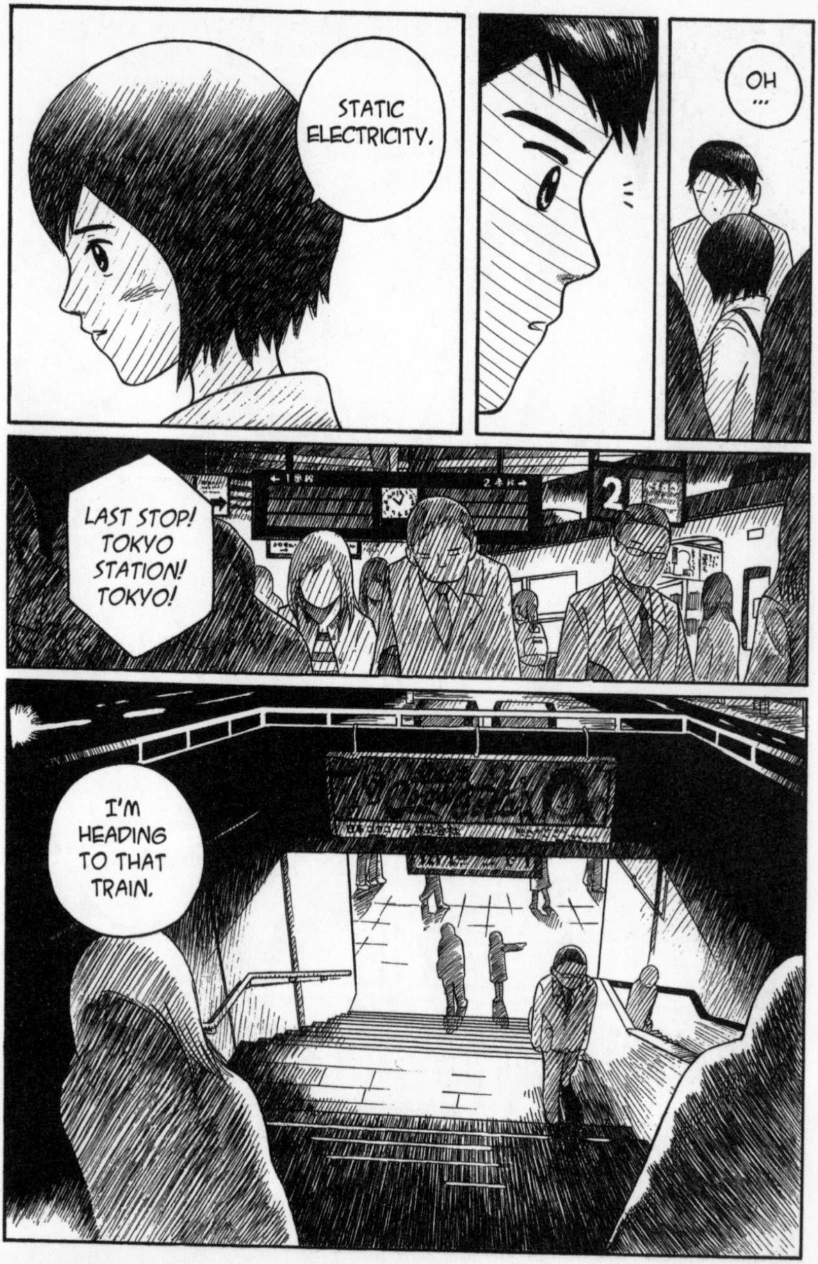
OH ...
STATIC ELECTRICITY.
LAST STOP! TOKYO STATION! TOKYO!
2
I'M HEADING TO THAT TRAIN.

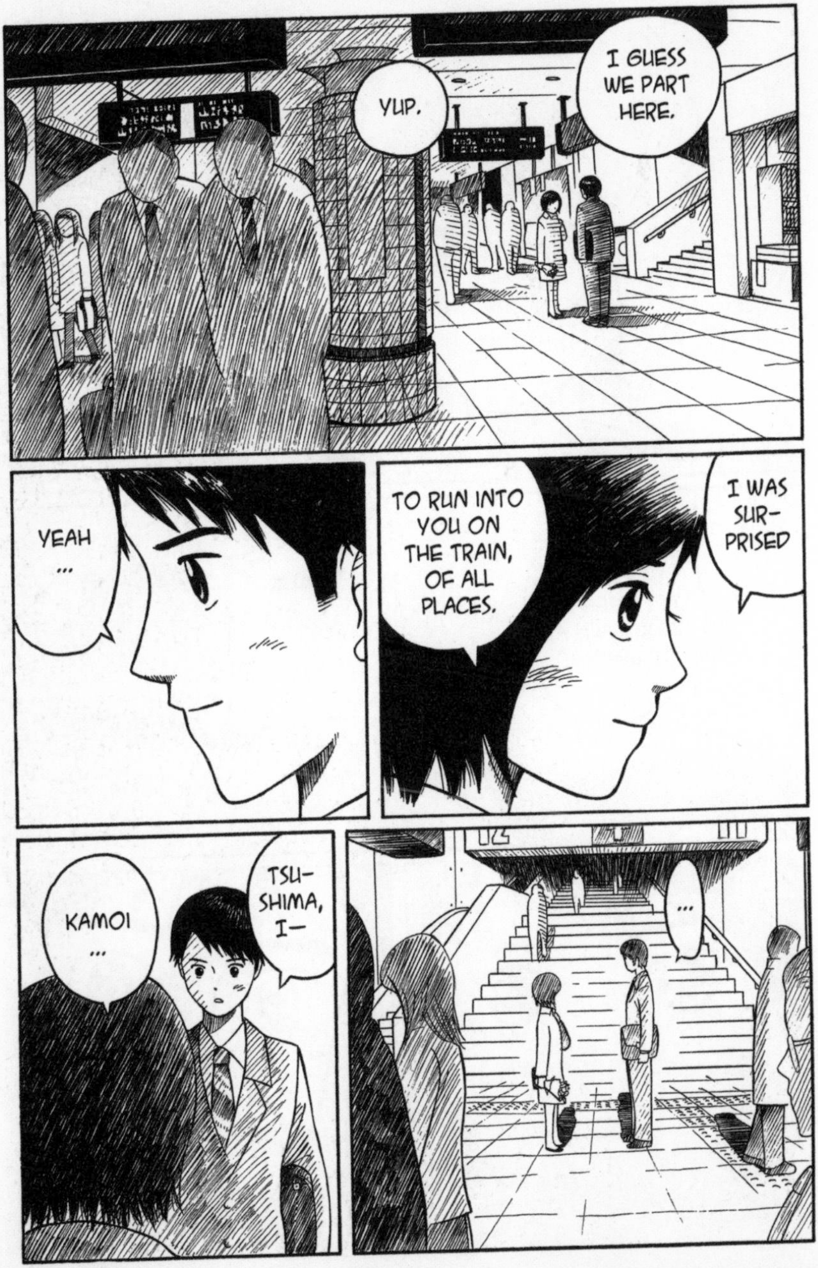
I GUESS WE PART HERE.
YUP.
I WAS SUR-PRISED
TO RUN INTO YOU ON THE TRAIN, OF ALL PLACES.
YEAH ...
...
TSU-SHIMA, I—
KAMOI ...

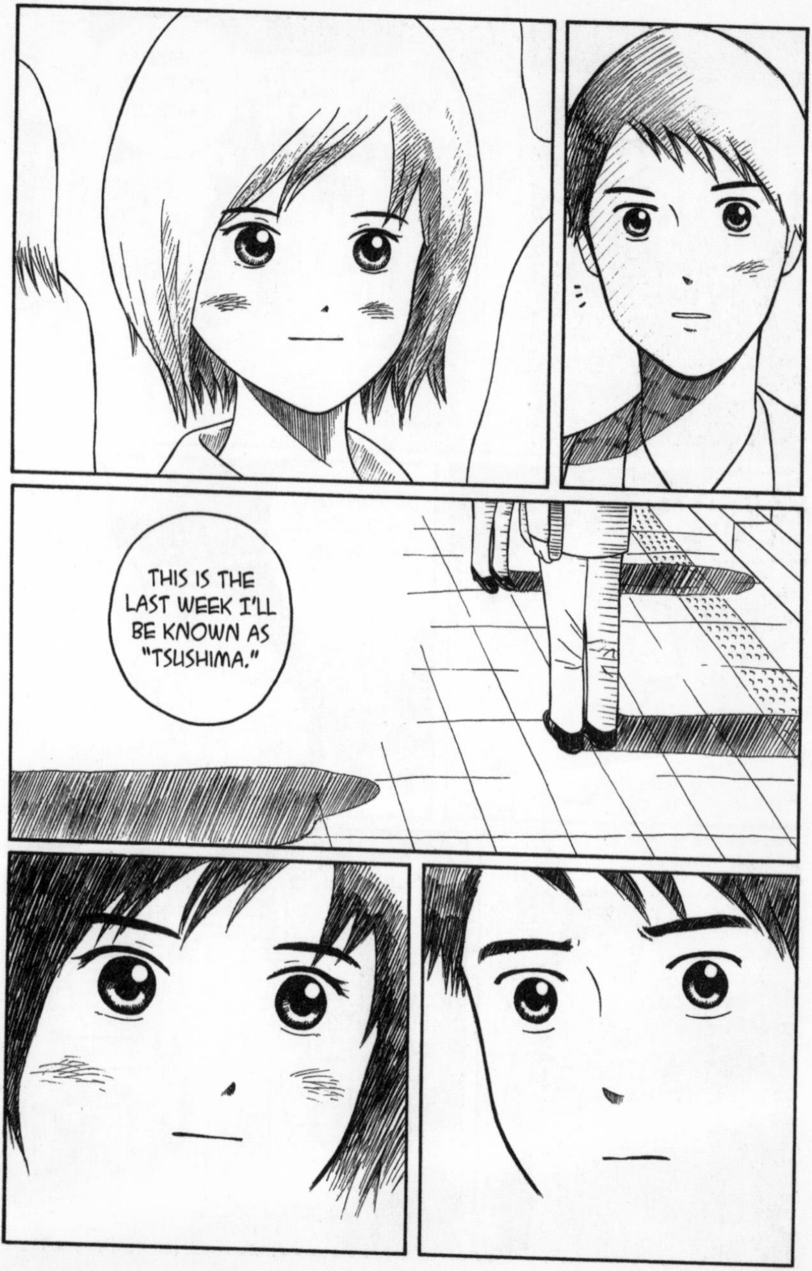
THIS IS THE LAST WEEK I'LL BE KNOWN AS "TSUSHIMA."

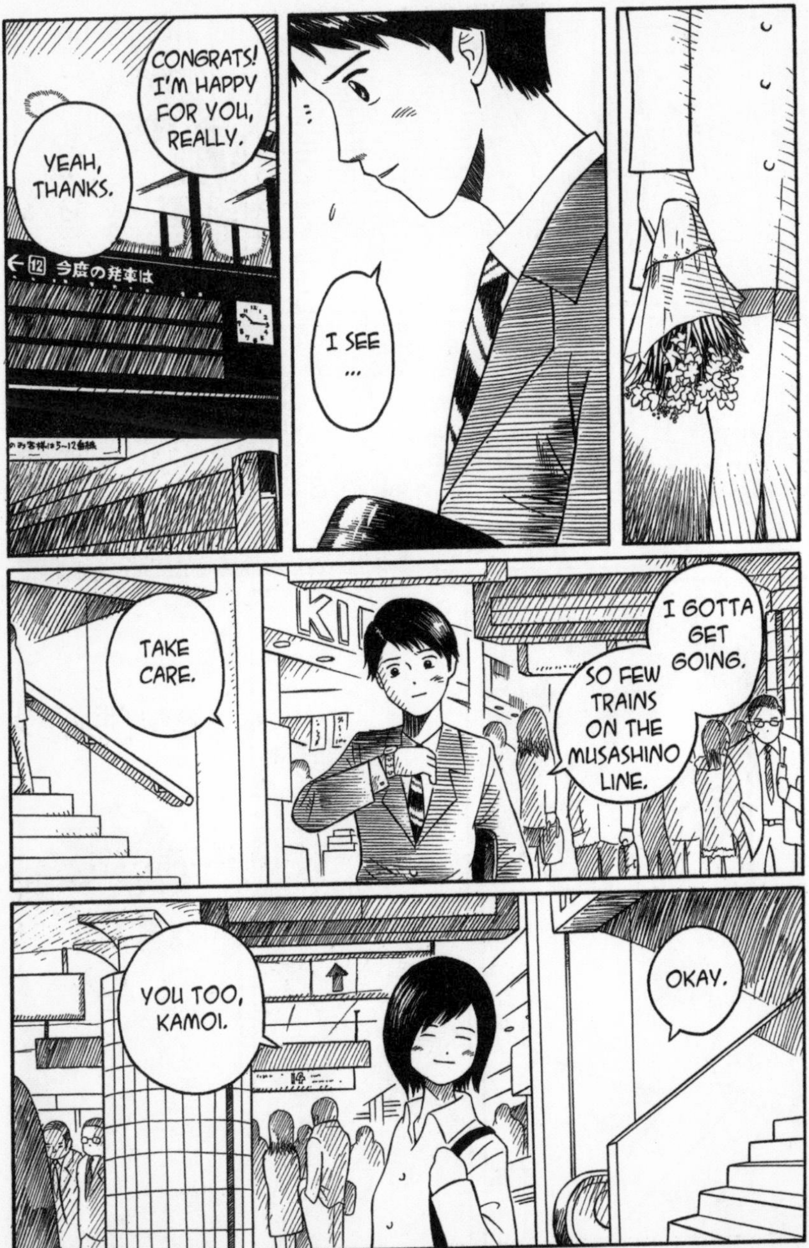
I SEE ...
CONGRATS! I'M HAPPY FOR YOU, REALLY.
YEAH, THANKS.
← 12 今度の発車は
I GOTTA GET GOING.
SO FEW TRAINS ON THE MUSASHINO LINE.
TAKE CARE.
OKAY.
YOU TOO, KAMOI.

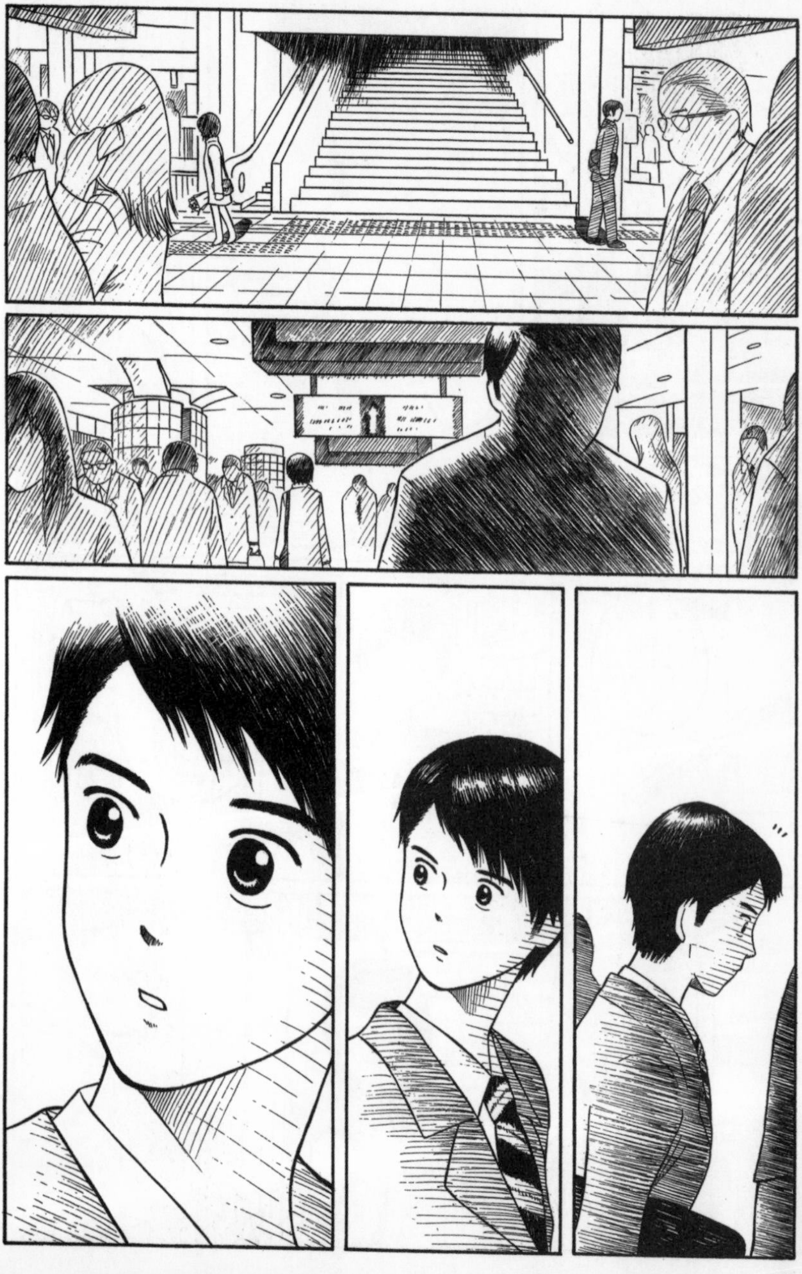

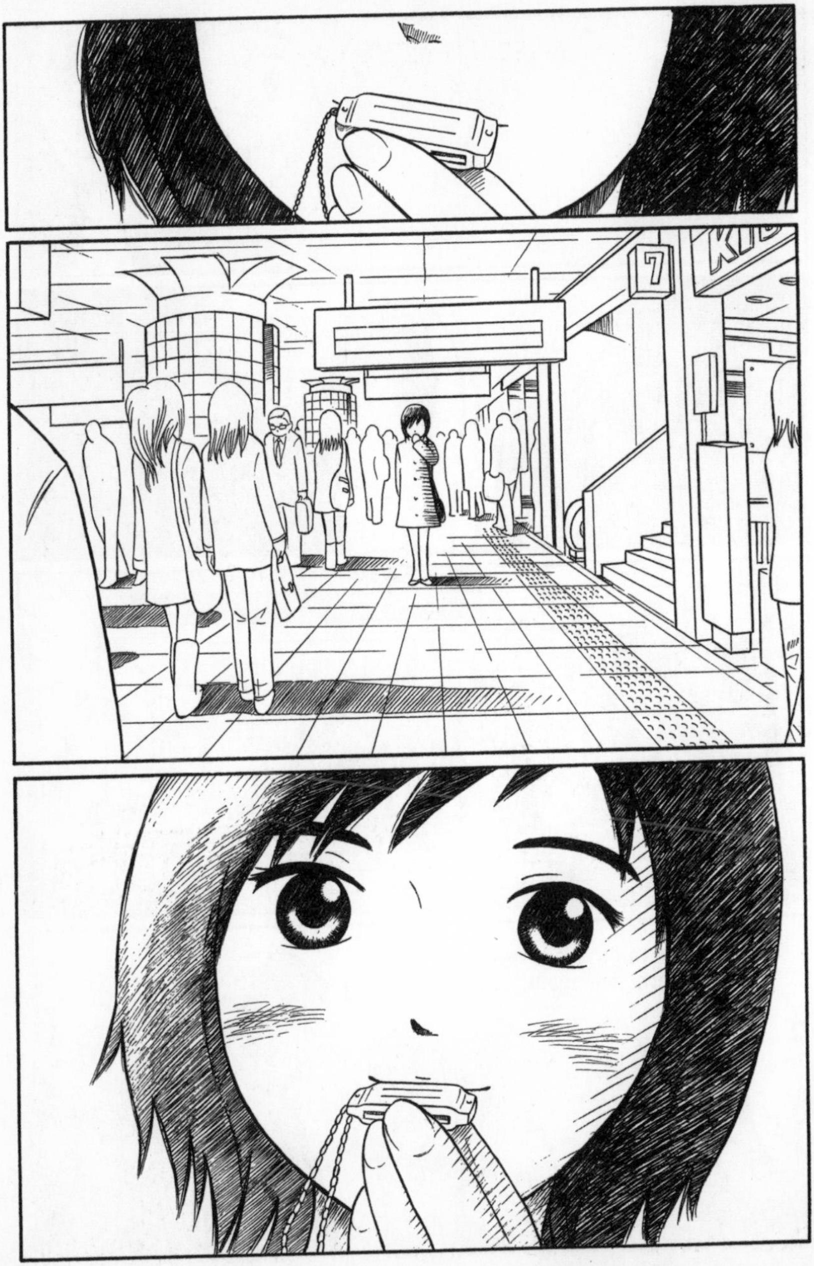
7

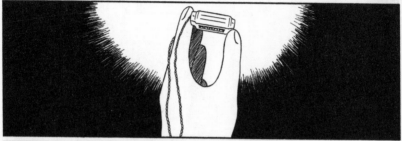

Sometimes I think about the girl
I'll never see again.

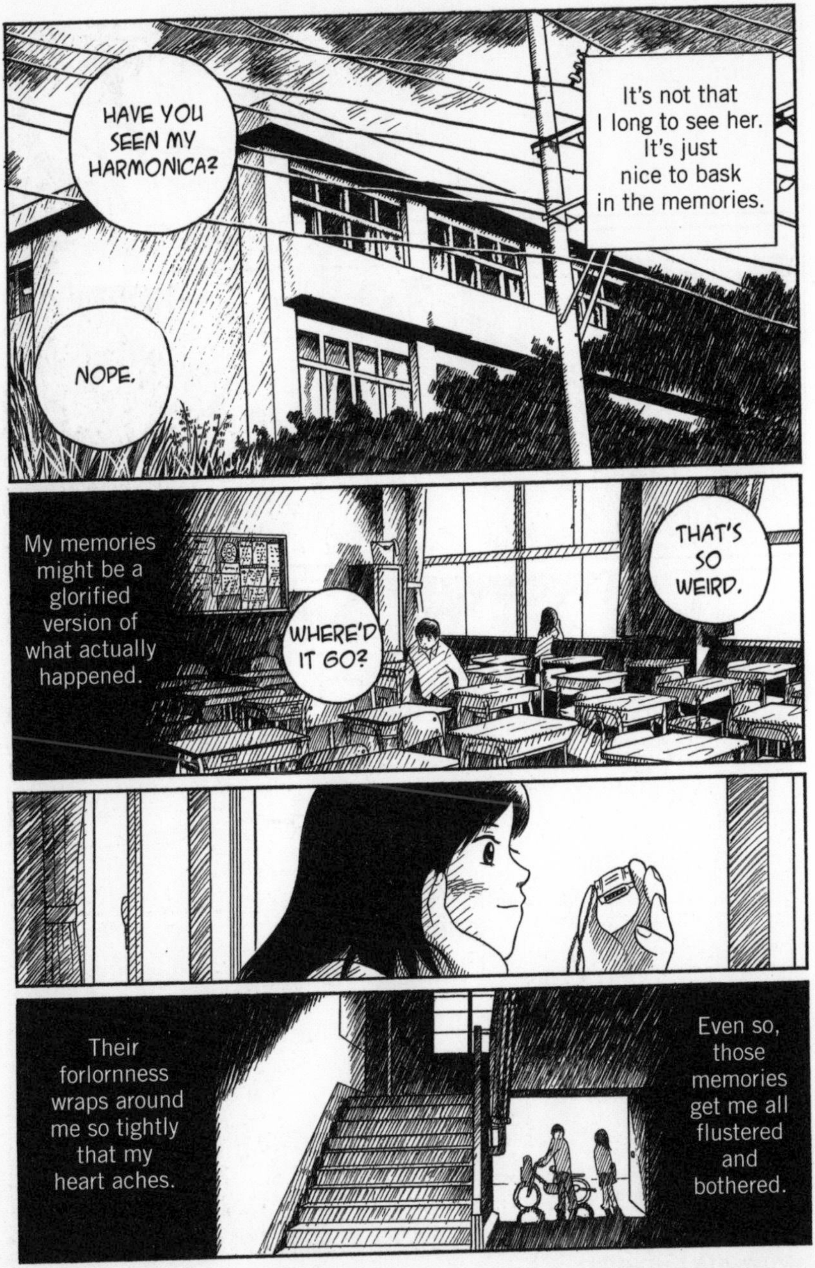

It's not that I long to see her. It's just nice to bask in the memories.
HAVE YOU SEEN MY HARMONICA?
NOPE.
THAT'S SO WEIRD.
WHERE'D IT GO?
My memories might be a glorified version of what actually happened.
Even so, those memories get me all flustered and bothered.
Their forlornness wraps around me so tightly that my heart aches.

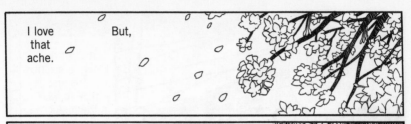

I love
that
ache.   But,

I love that
crushing, aching,
unbearable
forlornness.

I love that
ache that
comes when
I think of her.

"SENTIMENTAL" —THE END

ANOTHER SPICA

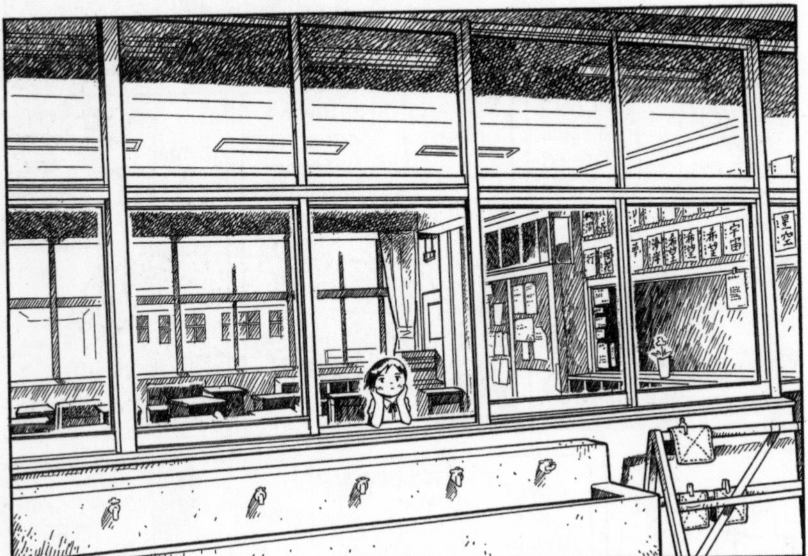
星空
宇宙
希望

KOU YAGINUMA

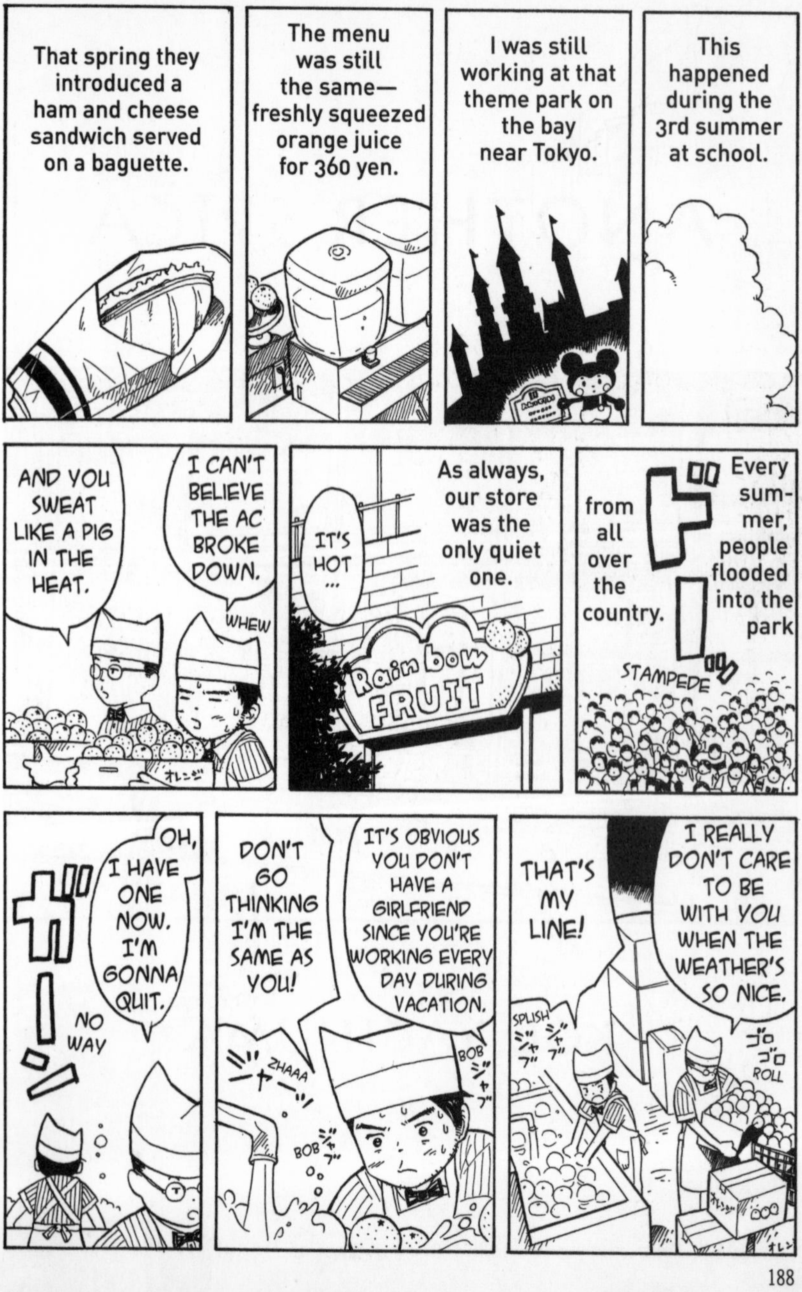
This happened during the 3rd summer at school.
I was still working at that theme park on the bay near Tokyo.
The menu was still the same—freshly squeezed orange juice for 360 yen.
That spring they introduced a ham and cheese sandwich served on a baguette.
Every summer, people flooded into the park
from all over the country.
STAMPEDE
As always, our store was the only quiet one.
IT'S HOT ...
Rainbow FRUIT
I CAN'T BELIEVE THE AC BROKE DOWN.
WHEW
AND YOU SWEAT LIKE A PIG IN THE HEAT.
I REALLY DON'T CARE TO BE WITH YOU WHEN THE WEATHER'S SO NICE.
ゴロ ゴロ ROLL
THAT'S MY LINE!
SPLISH ジャブ ジャブ
IT'S OBVIOUS YOU DON'T HAVE A GIRLFRIEND SINCE YOU'RE WORKING EVERY DAY DURING VACATION.
DON'T GO THINKING I'M THE SAME AS YOU!
BOB ジャブ
ZHAAA
BOB ジャブ
OH, I HAVE ONE NOW. I'M GONNA QUIT.
NO WAY

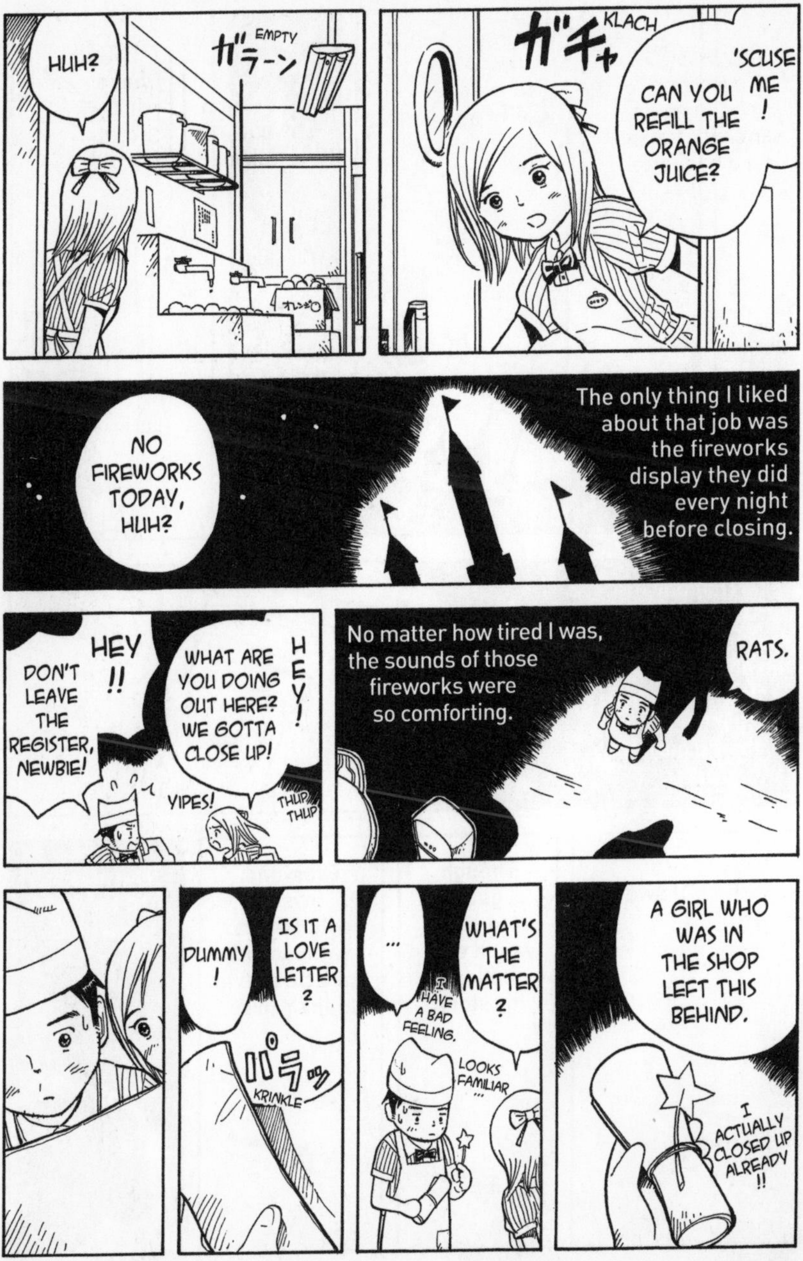

ガチャ KLACH
'SCUSE ME!
CAN YOU REFILL THE ORANGE JUICE?
ガラーン EMPTY
HUH?
The only thing I liked about that job was the fireworks display they did every night before closing.
NO FIREWORKS TODAY, HUH?
RATS.
No matter how tired I was, the sounds of those fireworks were so comforting.
HEY!
WHAT ARE YOU DOING OUT HERE? WE GOTTA CLOSE UP!
HEY!!
DON'T LEAVE THE REGISTER, NEWBIE!
YIPES!
THUP THUP
A GIRL WHO WAS IN THE SHOP LEFT THIS BEHIND.
I ACTUALLY CLOSED UP ALREADY!!
WHAT'S THE MATTER?
...
I HAVE A BAD FEELING.
LOOKS FAMILIAR...
IS IT A LOVE LETTER?
DUMMY!
パラッ KRINKLE

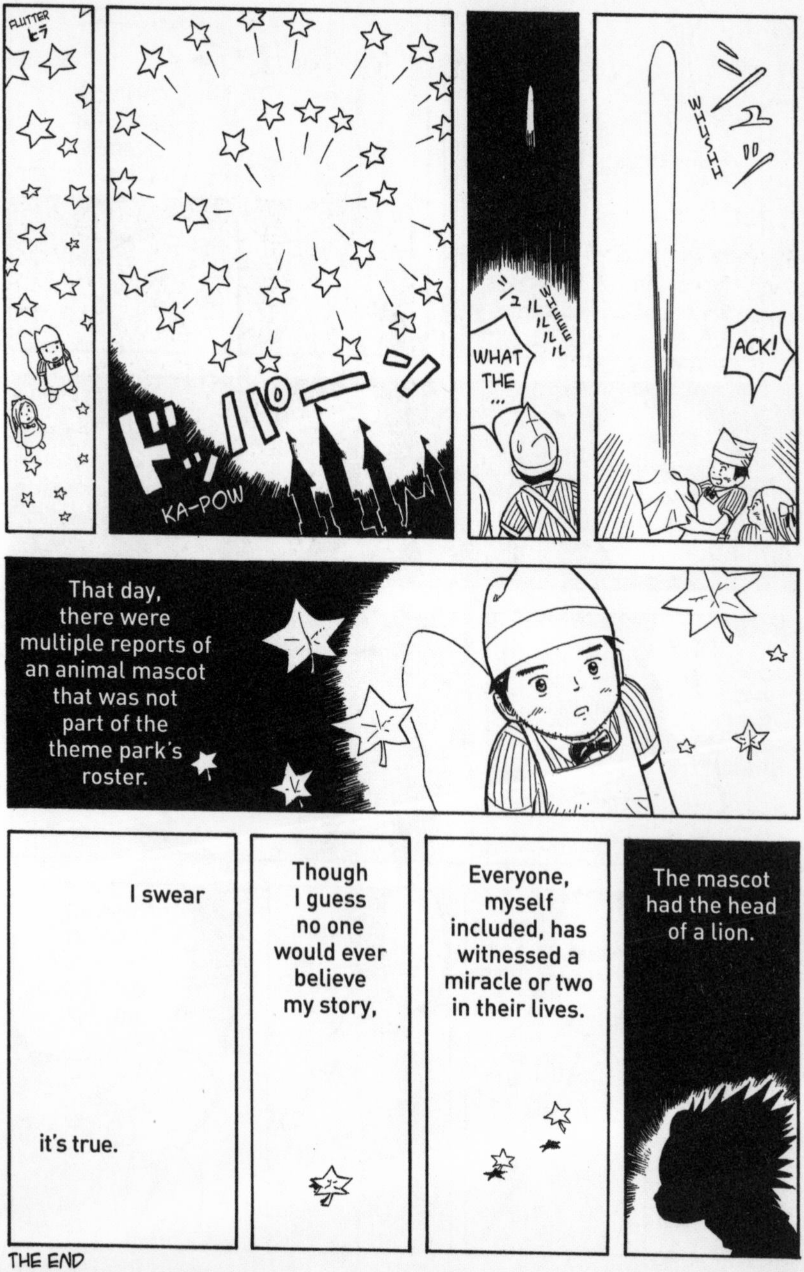
WHUSHH
ACK!
WHEEEE
WHAT THE ...
ドッパーン
KA-POW
FLUTTER
ヒラ
That day, there were multiple reports of an animal mascot that was not part of the theme park's roster.
The mascot had the head of a lion.
Everyone, myself included, has witnessed a miracle or two in their lives.
Though I guess no one would ever believe my story,
I swear
it's true.
THE END

Note on the Translation

P. 114

As readers may recall from the extra story "Asumi" in volume one, the Sanzu River is the Japanese equivalent of the River Styx. Beyond it lies the land of the dead.

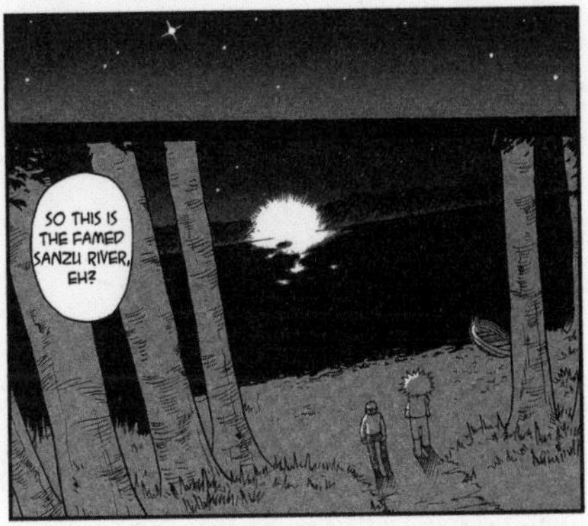
SO THIS IS THE FAMED SANZU RIVER, EH?

Production - Hiroko Mizuno
          Maya Rosewood
          Rina Nakayama

Copyright © 2010 Kou Yaginuma
First published in Japan in 2003 by MEDIA FACTORY, Inc.
English language version reserved by Vertical, Inc.
Under the license from MEDIA FACTORY, Inc.

Translation Copyright © 2010 Vertical, Inc.
Published by Vertical, Inc., New York

Originally published in Japanese as *Futatsu no Supika*
by MEDIA FACTORY, Inc., Tokyo 2003
Futatsu no Supika first serialized in Gekkan Comic Flapper,
MEDIA FACTORY, Inc., 2001-2009
"Kono Hoshi Supika" first published in Gekkan Comic Flapper,
MEDIA FACTORY, Inc., 2002

This is a work of fiction.

ISBN: 978-1-934287-93-4

Manufactured in Canada

First Edition

Vertical, Inc.
1185 Avenue of the Americas, 32nd Floor
New York, NY 10036
www.vertical-inc.com